X

8.00pm

# LORD LLOYD
### AND THE DECLINE OF THE
# BRITISH EMPIRE

ALSO BY JOHN CHARMLEY

*Duff Cooper: The Authorized Biography*

# LORD LLOYD

## AND THE DECLINE OF THE

# BRITISH EMPIRE

1879 – 1941

### John Charmley

WEIDENFELD AND NICOLSON · LONDON

To my mother

First published in Great Britain by
George Weidenfeld & Nicolson Limited
91 Clapham High Street, London SW4 7TA

ISBN 0 297 79205 9

Photoset by Deltatype Ltd, Ellesmere Port
Printed by Butler & Tanner Ltd
Frome and London

# CONTENTS

# ILLUSTRATIONS

Emilia Lloyd, George's mother
Sampson Samuel Lloyd, George's father
'Georgie', 1883
George and Sam Cockerell at Eton, c. 1891
The young attaché: Lloyd at Constantinople, 1905–6
Drawing of Blanche Lloyd, 1918
The perils of polo: Lloyd, with bandaged head, examining Percy
Loraine's wounded leg, Therapia 1906
The intelligence officer: Lloyd interrogating a Turkish prisoner in
Egypt, 1916
'Lloyd of Arabia', 1917
With T.E. Lawrence on a bombing mission, 1917
'Off duty': boating at Bombay, 1920
Inaugurating the Sukkur barrage, 24 October 1923
Staff group, Bombay, 1920
Mother and child: Blanche and David, 1922
The dapper man about town: George Lloyd, 1930s
The High Commissioner at the unveiling of the war memorial to the
Indian dead at Port Said, 1926
Blanche by Glyn Philpot, early 1930s
'Air Ace': George Lloyd winning his wings at the age of fifty-eight
Lloyd at Portman Square, 1935
Lloyd as Colonial Secretary, 23 July 1940, inspecting the Palestinian
Auxiliary Military Pioneer Corps
Lloyd greeting George VI at the Colonial Office, 1940

(All the photos belong to Lady Lloyd's collection and are reprinted
with her kind permission)

# Acknowledgements

Historians should proceed in a chronological manner. My first debts are to James Lees-Milne and Alastair Forbes who both, quite separately, suggested to David Lloyd that I should write this book. Since that first step both of them have provided invaluable help, with Jim Lees- Milne not only lending me Lloyd's letters to him, but also answering my questions about him. To both of them I am grateful.

David Lloyd decided to take their advice and to him I am indebted not only for the chance to write a book which has been of absorbing interest and great enjoyment, but also for a friendship which I came to value greatly. Long evenings spent discussing his father and every other topic under the moon were great fun, and the bravery with which he endured his last illness was heroic; that he did not live to see the book completed saddens me – but he knew what I was going to write and never, in any way, attempted to influence my interpretation. Peace be with his shade.

My debt to Jean, Lady Lloyd, is an immense one. She was always a firm supporter of the project from its beginning and it was only through her that David lived long enough to see it well on its way. Since his death in November 1985 she has helped me in so many ways that I can scarcely enumerate them. She has read every chapter from the draft stage, making no attempt to influence what I wrote, but making many helpful suggestions and providing invaluable encouragement and support. 'Official' or 'authorized' biographies are often, and rightly, suspect, the biographer paying the price of discretion and flattery in return for access to information; in this case, as in that of Duff Cooper, I have been remarkably fortunate: the information was provided and no price exacted.

George Lloyd's papers have been at Churchill College, Cambridge, since the 1960s and without the work of successive archivists at that hospitable and incomparable place this book would have taken much longer in the making. During the course of writing, many more volumes of Lloyd papers came to light; they all now repose with the earlier volumes. To Marion Stewart, the Archivist (and a veritable Queen of archivists at that), and her assistant Christine Conlon, I can only offer, again, my deepest thanks and affection; they have borne with my depredations upon their archives and my demands upon their time with saintly patience.

To the Keeper of the Archives, that sparkling historian and *boulevardier*, Correlli Barnett, I am grateful for all manner of good things, not the least of which is his splendid company. I would like to thank him and the Master and Fellows of Churchill College for electing me to an Archives Fellow-Commonership in the summer of 1986 which was not only of inestimable value in enabling me to complete this book, but also admitted me to the pleasure of their society. I am grateful to Professor Tony Low for discussing with me Lloyd's role in India in the 1920s and 1930s, and to Mr Andrew Worrall for bearing with my constant references to George Lloyd in the many conversations which I enjoyed with him during our stay in Cambridge.

For their help and for permission to quote from papers to which they hold the copyright I am grateful to: the Rt Hon. Julian Amery MP (Leo Amery Diaries); Dr B. Benediktz of Birmingham University Library (Austen and Neville Chamberlain Papers); Mr Charles Janson; the Keeper of Records at the India Office Library; the Librarian of Pembroke College, Cambridge; the Keeper of the Public Records at the Public Record Office: if there are others whose copyright I have inadvertently infringed I hope they will accept my apologies and advise me of the fact so that I can extend my acknowledgements to them in future.

The British Academy and the Supplementary Research Grants Committee of the School of English and American Studies at my own University of East Anglia provided the finance which started this project on its way and helped towards its completion. I am grateful to them both and would like also to thank my own university for helping to provide, in difficult times, conditions in which serious research can still be done.

I have learnt much about Lloyd's time at the British Council from the work of Miss Louise Ramsden-Atherton whose thesis will be an important contribution to our knowledge of pre-1939 British diplomacy.

I would like to thank my colleagues Professor James Jones and Dr

ACKNOWLEGEMENTS

Geoffrey Searle for, once more, taking time off their own work to
examine the results of mine; both myself and the manuscript are
much the better for their company.

My editors at Weidenfeld, John Curtis and Linda Osband, were, as
ever, towers of support, and I should like to thank them and my
agent, Felicity Bryan, for all their help. Only the families of historians
and writers can really appreciate the sufferings of my wife Thea and
my twin sons, Gervase and Gerard; only historians and writers can
appreciate how much I owe to their patience and forbearance.

But I hope that everyone here mentioned will pardon me if I say that
my greatest debt is to the dedicatee of this book.

John Charmley
Norwich, 1986–7

# PROLOGUE

Acorns do not grow in the shadow of a great oak and other trees nearby are put into the shade by a mighty neighbour; this last has been the fate of the first Lord Lloyd. The causes which he championed: the Empire, rearmament, opposition to the India Bill and to Hitler, were all taken up later by Winston Churchill and, because of this, Lloyd's fame has suffered. If he is remembered at all by historians it tends to be because he was associated with causes which were associated with Churchill; such are the ways of history and historians.

When I was asked by the late Lord Lloyd to write this biography I did so because of a long-standing interest in the imperialist wing of the Conservative Party. On the surface Lloyd would appear to be an almost perfect specimen of the type as imagined by left-wing polemicists. He was educated at Eton and Trinity College, Cambridge; his family were involved in banking; after several years of travelling in the Near and Middle East he entered Parliament as a Conservative. He married into the aristocracy and, after a 'good war' between 1914 and 1918, he went off to govern Bombay. There he locked up Gandhi and kept law and order. After a short sojourn in England between 1924 and 1925, he became a peer of the realm and was sent to govern Egypt. As High Commissioner between 1925 and 1929 he struggled to crush the Egyptian nationalist party (the Wafd), even employing gunboats for the purpose. In 1929, after quarrelling with a Labour Government, he resigned and returned home. During the next six years he opposed the attempt to give India greater self-government, fighting alongside Churchill in what historians have seen as one of his more unfortunate campaigns. On the plus side he was an anti-appeaser. He became Colonial Secretary under Churchill but was accorded little time to achieve anything. Thus the thumb-nail sketch.

Every item in that sketch is correct, but cumulatively, as I soon discovered, they amount to a most misleading picture. His family were upper-middle-class industrialists and his earliest job was in the family firm which made steel tubes. Lloyd entered politics because Joseph Chamberlain's tariff reform campaign expressed a view which he had already formed on his own: that is that only by attention to the economic foundations of her strength could Britain survive as a Great Power. This goal he pursued throughout his life. Travel in the East convinced him that Germany was undermining British power in the region and he fought, first as a politician and then as a soldier, to defeat this threat. As an imperial administrator he paid close attention to the economic needs of the peoples over whom he was set, and in India in particular he initiated mighty irrigation works which benefited the lives of millions. There, and in Egypt, he fought against the post-war mood of weariness which would cast away the Empire. In the 1930s he continued this struggle, foreseeing that, without her Empire, Britain must become an impoverished little island in the North Sea. The same foresight enabled him to see the Hitler menace and from Conservative platforms, the office of Chairman of the British Council, and then as Colonial Secretary, he opposed this new German threat. Thus Lloyd on a closer inspection.

But the very process of sifting through so many of his letters and other papers blurred the clear outlines of earlier thoughts. No man is merely a stereotype. The Oswald Birley portrait of him, resplendent in blue robe, sash, stars and decorations, is certainly the personification of the imperial proconsul; but what are we to make of him in Arab dress with Lawrence of Arabia or in Savile Row suit with Noël Coward? In business suit or in shirt-sleeves and shorts, some features do not change – the jet-black hair, the round head and, most of all, the piercing black eyes – with a look of uncertainty behind the eagle's gaze he habitually assumed?

Why was it that George Lloyd spent most of his life away from England, tramping the wide world? Was he afraid of something? Was he searching for something? If so, what? Why, with his intense ambition, did he never stoop to the sort of stratagems which such men habitually have resort to to obtain power? Why, above all perhaps, did this intense imperial patriot seem so un-English to so many people? Where was the impersonal, pompous proconsular figure of legend when the young men who had known him said how charming, how unaffected and how companionable he was? Could the Lloyd of rumour have written such tender and sweet letters to his son? In place of the earlier, bold outlines, a bundle of contradictions seemed to be left.

These contradictions are worked out and explored in the pages that follow where it will be seen that traces of the earlier pictures remain, like great stones after the tide has ebbed. Inevitably in the life of any political figure it is the deeds which attract the most attention; it is by the things he did that the politician most merits the attention of posterity; but not wholly; and not in this case.

Lloyd's personality is unusually enigmatic; perhaps that is always so with those for whom religious faith is the centre of their being. But some generalizations may be hazarded, if only to colour what follows. By long hereditary process Lloyd was a Quaker and a Welshman, even if he was born in England into the Anglican faith; there was in him both the quietness and the 'inner light' of the Quaker and also the mysticism of the Celt. One of those who knew him commented to me that he was 'the least vulgar man of his generation' and that he possessed 'moral purity'. How was such a man, equipped as he was with an intense ambition which had to be harnessed to a great cause, to make his way in the world of politics? Lloyd George provided an exemplar for what might be called the 'Taffy' Welshman, with his hymn-singing, his nonconformity, his eloquence and his wicked ways; that sort of alien was easily comprehensible to the English politician. But George Lloyd was not that sort of alien.

The pages that follow try to explore what sort of alien he was and attempt to answer some of the questions here posed.

# 1

# DOLOBRAN AND BIRMINGHAM

George Ambrose Lloyd was a man of paradoxes. Although he was the greatest of imperial patriots, he did not look English; his dark eyes, jet-black hair, round skull and dark complexion led at least one friend to think there was 'some Armenian, Greek or Turk somewhere'. Nor was his appearance the only thing about him that was alien; the same friend commented that 'there was always something a little un-English in his hard and fast view of things'.[1] Like two other great imperialists, Lord Milner and Rudyard Kipling, George Lloyd shared neither the looks nor the outlook of the English.

That he should have appeared un-English is hardly to be wondered at for, although he was born on 19 September 1879 at Alton Hall in Solihull in Warwickshire, the very heart of England, Lloyd was, as his name suggests, a Welshman; indeed, so Welsh was he that he was wont to say that there was no English blood in him. His complexion and features were those of the original inhabitants of these islands, those ancient Britons driven into the fastnesses of the mountainous west by the Romans.

It was to one Aleth, King of Dyfed in the eleventh century, that the Lloyds traced their origins, and to one of his descendants, Celwyn, that they owed their name; he it was who settled in Llywdiarth about the year 1300, and it was from Llywdiarth, 'valley of the Lloyds', that the family took their name in the sixteenth century when the Welsh adopted the English practice of taking surnames. Celwyn's great-grandson, David, was the first Lloyd to own property at Dolobran and it is a melancholy coincidence that the second and last Baron Lloyd of Dolobran should also have been named David.[2]

Until the 1660s the Lloyds dwelt at Dolobran Hall, prosperous country gentlemen, doing their duty as Justices of the Peace and local worthies, but Charles Lloyd, head of the family at that time, had in him that mystical strain which was to show itself time and again in the family, and he joined the Society of Friends. Becoming a Quaker in the 1660s was not something to be done lightly. Because of their inability to swear the Oaths of Allegiance and Supremacy, Quakers were barred from holding any public office; they were, moreover, liable to persecution.

Charles Lloyd suffered a decade in prison in Welshpool, 'a nasty dirty place', where he was joined by his wife Elizabeth and his brother Thomas. It was in these insalubrious surroundings that Charles's first son, another Charles, was born in 1662. By the time the family was released from gaol in 1672 their home was in ruins and much of their property had been stolen. But Charles Lloyd was of the stuff of which martyrs are made, and he stayed at Dolobran until his death in 1698. It was his second son, Sampson, who began the family connection with Birmingham. He moved there in the year of his father's death to join his wife's people. As a non-incorporated borough Birmingham was not subject to the Conventicle Act and dissenters could practise their religion there without fear of persecution.

His brother Charles, who remained at Dolobran following the death of their father, founded an iron-works there in 1719. South Wales was not, at this time, the obvious place to make iron, being far from the main centres of population and lacking easy and cheap means of communication with them, so it need not surprise us that the business failed to prosper. In 1742 it moved to Birmingham where things went better with the Lloyds and the family soon gave further signs of the commercial acumen which was to make the name of Lloyd famous.

It was Sampson's son, Sampson ii, who helped found in 1765 the bank which still bears the family name, and thenceforth banking and iron-working became the foundations of the prosperity of the Lloyds. They were in the right place, Birmingham, at the right time, the start of the industrial revolution. It also fell to Sampson ii to divide the family into two branches. By his first wife, Sarah Parkes who died in 1729, he had a son, Sampson iii (family pride leading to a certain lack of imagination in the question of Christian names); by his second, Rachel Campion, whom he married in 1731, he had six sons and five daughters.

The second boy of this second marriage, Charles, known as 'the Banker', together with Sampson iii, ran the bank after the death of their father in 1779 and the two branches of the family continued to reside in the Midlands co-operating in business for the next century. It is with the reunion of the family in the early nineteenth century that our story properly may be said to begin.

Sampson Samuel Lloyd, born in 1820, and the great-grandson of Sampson III, was the first of the Lloyds to forsake the family religion and also the first to enter political life. In both religious persuasion and political affiliation he resembled his grandson, George Ambrose. His spirit was quickened by the Tractarian movement and he joined the Anglican Church. In politics he was, as many High Churchmen were, a Liberal–Conservative. This last fact frustrated his desire to become MP for Birmingham, for local politics were dominated by the Quaker John Bright and (a little later) by the radical Unitarian, Joseph Chamberlain. He did, however, sit in the Commons, first as MP for Plymouth and later for Rugby. A director of Lloyds Bank (and chairman from 1869 until 1887), he took a keen interest in economics and was, for eighteen years after 1862, President of the Association of Chambers of Commerce of the United Kingdom. In this capacity he espoused the cause of protectionism or 'fair trade' long before it was taken up by Chamberlain and called tariff reform. It was his eldest son, Sampson Samuel II, who reunited the family in 1868 by marrying Emilia Lloyd, his third cousin once removed.

Emilia Lloyd's father, Thomas Lloyd of the Priory, Warwick, (1814–90) was a grandson of Charles Lloyd 'the Banker'. Thomas Lloyd had two things in common with his cousin Sampson Samuel II: he was a director of the family bank and he was an Anglican; however, in one thing the two men differed: politically Thomas was a Liberal. Known as an 'advanced Liberal', he was Lord Mayor of Birmingham in 1859–60 and played a large part in persuading John Bright to become MP for the city. None of this prevented his welcoming his daughter's marriage to Sampson Samuel II; indeed he and his son-in-law seem to have been on the best of terms, as he entrusted him with the management of his estate.

Sampson Samuel II and Emilia had six children: Charles Llewellyn, who was killed in a football accident at Eton in 1889; Thomas, who was to inherit the Priory and the bulk of the family money; Gwendoline (Gwen), Eva and Emilia (Milly); and finally, George Ambrose, the subject of this biography.[3]

Six months after young George was born the family moved to Budbrooke House, conveniently near the Priory. They were a happy and self-contained family. Sampson Samuel divided his time between farm management and a small iron-works which he helped to found. He was a gentle, genial man, content to dwell at peace within his habitation surrounded by his growing family and his wife. If portraits are anything to go by, Emilia Lloyd was a woman of remarkable beauty: with raven-black hair, high cheek-bones and a dark com-

6

plexion, she could have been taken for a Spaniard; she passed on these physical characteristics to her youngest son, along with her shyness and love of travel. In 1890, on the death of Thomas Lloyd, the family moved into the Priory where Sampson Samuel could devote himself to farming. But he did not neglect his business venture, and his steel tube-making firm, S. S. Lloyds, prospered.

Happy families have little history, and this was the case with the Lloyds of the Priory. There is little to be said of George's earliest years save that he grew up in a loving and close-knit family circle. He did not go to school until the age of twelve when (notwithstanding the fate of his eldest brother) he was sent to Eton. From thence he passed to Trinity College, Cambridge, in 1898.

Young George's tutors' reports indicated that he was an apt pupil, quick at his books, but even quicker to sample the delights of the river. In 1897 and 1898 he coxed the Eton rowing eight to victory, whilst in 1899 and 1900 he took the Cambridge eight to victory over Oxford in the boat race. Ostensibly reading history, his real interests lay elsewhere. But the smooth pattern of his life was shattered in 1899.

If, in later life, George Lloyd gave the impression to some that he was in perpetual pursuit of some unattainable end, a restless nomad, wandering the face of the globe with no place to call home; if he seemed a soul displaced from its proper habitation, then some of these things owed their origin to the events of 1899. Until then he had been the happy youngest child of a close family; suddenly, in the space of a month, he was an orphan with no home of his own. His mother died on 18 March of a neglected chill at the early age of fifty-one, to be followed by his father (who was fifty-three) on 15 April of pleurisy and blood poisoning. The Priory became the home of his eldest brother Tom, and he moved with Milly and Eva to Hill Wooton near Warwick, and later to 5 Hobart Place in London. The psychological effects of this trauma can only be guessed at, but it is not fanciful to see in this sudden termination of childhood, this tragic exile from Eden, the origin of his restlessness. He was never again to live in one place for as long as he had dwelt at the Priory.

This chronic restlessness manifested itself immediately. After coxing the eight to victory in the 1900 boat race, 'Skinny' Lloyd (as he was known to his contemporaries because he was the heaviest cox ever to take a crew to victory) went down from university without taking his degree. He then proceeded, not into the family business but to travel. His journeyings continued for the rest of his life.

# 2

# THE LURE OF THE EAST

Displaced from Eden, George Lloyd, like Kipling's Tramp-Royal, took refuge in the ' 'appy roads that take you o'er the world'; and, like that gentleman, he found ' 'E liked it all'. Thus another paradox was created as this un-English imperial patriot spent most of his life outside the British Isles; but he would have agreed with Kipling: 'what should they know of England who only England know?'

After going down from Cambridge he went off on a long tour of India during which he fell under the spell of the East. He made further journeys to Australia and America in 1903, and then chose to lay the foundations of his political career in the Near East. Only between 1910 and 1914 did he spend any substantial amount of time in England. He was in the Middle East for most of the Great War, and between 1917 and 1929 he was (for all but eighteen months) in proconsular appointments in India or Egypt. By the time he came back to England in 1929 he could have reflected that he had spent most of the century abroad.

Even before the deaths of his parents he seems to have exhibited a love of travel. A casual aside in a speech made towards the end of his life reveals that his 'first contact with Islam was when I stayed away too long from Eton at the age of fourteen and went to Tetuan on my own'.[1] Nothing more is known of this extraordinary episode, but the contact thus made was an enduring one – indeed it forms one of the central themes of his story, for he always loved the East and was always made restless by travel. As he once wrote to his son:

> I tremble to think how restless it [a journey to Kashmir] will make you – 'and the poplar breezes will blow in your head' as the dear old Turkish proverb says, for many a long year to come: and you will never forget the scent of the garlands, frangipan and jasamine [sic] and all and all. And you will see the flame of the forest in the jungles when the hot weather

comes on – Lord! how I have loved it all; *nearly thirty years of it* David, in different parts of God's wonderful Asia. It's often hot and dirty and beastly, but it gets you all the same.[2]

Lloyd belonged to that generation of children who grew up with the literature created by the existence of the Empire and designed to celebrate it; Rider Haggard, Henty and Kipling were the staples of his reading, and his imagination, always of a romantic turn, was fired by their vision of the British Empire as spreading civilization and Christianity to 'lesser breeds without the Law'. The Empire was responsible for the governance of millions of bodies and souls; to rule it properly demanded the very highest qualities of the best type of Englishman. When the novelist Compton Mackenzie met Lloyd in 1915 he 'began for the first time in my life to understand that Imperialism could touch a man's soul as deeply as Religion';[3] but his observation was only half right; for Lloyd, religion and Empire were inextricably tangled together.

In this we may find some explanation of the lure of the East and also of the lure of public life. The long exile from public life pronounced upon the Lloyds by their religion had been broken by both Lloyd's grandfathers, but politics for their own sake had no attraction for their grandson; they needed to be mixed with something that would give expression to his sense of mission. In him the mystic and the man of business were combined.

After returning from India in 1901 Lloyd joined the family firm of Stewart and Lloyds as their youngest director and settled himself, with his usual thoroughness, to master the details of the steel tube-making business. His brother Tom described the attitude of his fellow-directors to their eager young colleague thus: 'George was a clever boy but he wanted to be a colonel before he had been a lieutenant.'[4] Youth, enthusiasm and avidity for novelty have ever been at a discount in England. He found the reluctance of his fellow-directors to modernize their plant and their methods of production intensely irritating. They were content with their dividends and looked not to the future. They found it expedient to send their young dynamo abroad to investigate markets for their goods – but this only helped make things worse.

In early 1903 he went to Australia and later to America. In both places he saw future perils for the British steel industry. American plant was so much better, their organization and techniques well in advance of Britain's, which helped explain why Stewart and Lloyds were losing their Australian markets; he returned demanding changes.

What Lloyd was demanding in his parochial sphere another Birmingham businessman, Joseph Chamberlain, had begun to preach

on the national stage. On 4 November 1903 Lloyd went along to Birmingham Town Hall to hear Chamberlain speak. The great man had embarked upon his tariff reform campaign, declaring that England was subject to unfair competition and should impose tariffs on foreign goods, as well as developing her own industry and the economic resources of her Empire. His message was no dry economic one but rather an imperial and moral crusade: many young men flocked to his banner and his campaign made an obvious appeal to a patriotic young industrialist who had seen enough of the Empire to be captured by the romance of it and enough of industry to be appalled by the archaic British attitudes. This was the watershed of George Lloyd's life. Before this date there is no sign of any interest in politics; thenceforth tariff reform was to be his lodestar. As he wrote to Austen Chamberlain many years later: 'I should never have come into politics at all had it not been for Mr Chamberlain's personality and policy.'[5]

In his study of the tariff problem and his devotion to the Empire Lloyd had one constant guide and friend, Samuel Pepys Cockerell, whose influence it is impossible to overestimate. The two had been boys together at Eton, friends at Trinity and were, at this time, sharing digs in Pont Street. He encouraged Lloyd and shared with him his dreams. For both of them Chamberlain's message was not only an analysis of what they felt was wrong with Britain, but a remedy for it, and they quickly immersed themselves in the activities of the Tariff Reform League and the study of political economy. Evidence of their keenness can be gleaned from Lloyd's diary for 1904 which finds them attending classes in political economy – including lectures on the Poor Law by Sidney Webb. Lloyd began attending the House of Commons to listen to debates. The speaker who left the most mark seems to have been Bonar Law who made a 'good speech' on 9 February.

George Lloyd had now found a direction to his life and for the rest of his days he was to follow it with remarkable consistency. His own ambitions for himself could be subsumed and legitimized by service to this higher cause. With an independent income of £2,000 a year he could afford to devote himself to the tariff reform crusade. The evangelical zeal of the movement and its earnestness attracted both the Celtic and the Quaker elements in his nature. In his eyes politics were not the 'great game', but a means of saving and regenerating that great instrument of civilization, the British Empire; such a seriousness of approach would render him forever an oddity in British politics.

It was one thing to decide that politics would have to be endured, but quite another to settle on how they were to be entered. To go to the House as nothing more than a young industrialist with some experience of travel and the making of steel tubes was not, he and Sam decided, the right way forward; first he must acquirè *real* experience of the challenges to British power. That this could only be done through travel made the plan all the more attractive to Lloyd.

In January 1905 he refused the offer of a post from Stewart and Lloyds in London and on 18 March set off on the Orient Express for Constantinople. It seems to have been Sam who directed Lloyd's attention to the region as one where Germany was encroaching upon a traditional British sphere of interest with her building of the Berlin–Baghdad railway; he hoped to become a commercial attaché at Constantinople. Gertrude Bell, whom he met at this time, promised to do her best for him. Already a renowned traveller, she and Lloyd swapped travellers' tales, and we find him confessing to her in late April that he had made 'a great mistake in driving to Tarsus instead of riding, as I found the road quite exceptionally bad even for this country and the result was that the vehicle came to bits'.[6] Returning home in May, Lloyd did everything he could to secure a quick return to the Near East. Through Miss Bell's efforts and those of Sam (who was working for the commercial department of the Foreign Office) he achieved his wish and arrived in Constantinople as unpaid honorary attaché on 9 November 1905.

Evidence exists though to suggest that imperial patriotism was not the sole motivation for Lloyd's wanderings. At some time during this period he showed the first evidence of an interest in the opposite sex. He was never a ladies' man: this, and his partiality for male company, led some to suspect that he was homosexual in his inclinations; for this there is no proof. He was to fall violently and suddenly in love with an eminently suitable young lady in 1910, and he seems to have done so in 1904. The object of his love in 1904 was Lady Constance Knox, but her father, the fifth Earl of Ranfurly, did not regard the younger son of an industrialist as a suitable match for his nineteen-year-old daughter and forbade them to meet. More than a decade later Lloyd wrote to her when she had chided him with his restlessness, commenting that, 'the person that was so much responsible for many years of my wanderings ought not to complain'.[7] So it was not just ambition and duty which sent him eastwards. 'Puss' Knox married Major Evelyn Milnes Gaskell in 1905, but she was not lost to George Lloyd's life story, although it was to be many years before he felt able to write to her again.

'Old Stamboul' before the 1908 revolution was just the place to forget a lost love. The presiding genius in this, the decadence of the long rule of the House of Osman, was that aged intriguer and perennial survivor, Sultan Abdul Hamid II – Abdul 'the damned', who for over thirty years had been playing off the European powers against each other.

The chief British player in this game of international intrigue was not the Ambassador, Sir Nicholas O'Conor, able diplomat though he was, but the senior dragoman, G. H. Fitzmaurice. Described by T. E. Lawrence as possessing 'an eagle-mind and personality of iron vigour',[8] he had lived most of his life in the Ottoman Empire, knew everyone and everything worth knowing, and by his prestige, presence and sympathy acted as mentor to the group of talented young men whom Lloyd joined at Constantinople.

Lloyd found his companions a stimulating mixture of professional diplomats and amateurs. Among the former were two men who went on to make names for themselves in the service, Laurence Oliphant and Percy Loraine, the latter becoming a close friend for life; to these was joined, a little later, a youthful Alexander Cadogan who was, thirty years later, to preside over a Foreign Office which Lloyd had come to execrate.

The amateurs, as is the way with the breed, were more picturesque, the two most exotic being Mark Sykes and Aubrey Herbert. Sykes, heir to a Yorkshire baronetcy and considerable prospects of wealth, was a man of great charm, talent and consuming ambition; it was not surprising that he and George Lloyd failed to become bosom companions – each recognized in the other a rival. Lloyd later commented: 'Quelle type he is, but he is supposed to be good at his job – which is the main thing';[9] there would never be any love lost between the two men. But they both found common ground in liking the half-blind and wholly eccentric Aubrey Herbert, whose typewritten notes attested both to his poor sight (he could not see to write) and to his wit and political acumen. The model for John Buchan's *Greenmantle*, it was a wonder to everyone that he survived his adventures; but as Lloyd observed of him: 'Oh, well, I think most of us feel that there is a special little cherub up aloft who looks after dear Aubrey.'[10] The three young men recognized themselves as a 'triumvirate', but only Herbert had no ambitions to be Caesar.

Sam advised George to 'find time to sweat up what you've really gone for' and 'settle on some definite branch of the Eastern Question and really make a study of it'.[11] There was little need for such exhortations. Lloyd told Gertrude Bell on 17 November that: 'I am already convinced that I have done the right thing in coming here to work for a bit, as everything I think promises to be interesting in the extreme.' He had settled on Turkish finances and 'German schemes' as his two subjects to 'get up'.

Fears about German intentions was already a commonplace phenomenon among tariff reformers. Sam wrote on 3 December 1905 that:

The Germans in London and the Germanophils have started a society
for tightening the ever-loosening bonds between the two countries . . .
but that kind of thing isn't really much good and the very fact of its being
thought necessary by the Bishops etc. who play the leading part only
seems to emphasise the very hostile feeling which exists.[12]

Lloyd was only too conscious of the dangers to be apprehended from
Germany. In early January 1906 he wrote:

One only wishes that a little more interest was taken in England over the
Baghdad railway before it is too late – and before long it must I think be
too late unless something is done! It makes one inclined to scream but as
it is one can do nothing.

For the first, but not the last time, he despaired of Parliament,
telling Gertrude Bell that what Britain needed was 'an Imperial
Parliament qualified to take an intelligent and expert interest in outside
affairs – and most Labour members are limited in their interest purely,
or mainly, to social questions and insofar I dislike seeing a Labour
Party'.[13] His feelings were not to change – even when that Party
became the governing one.

His fears about 'German schemes' were confirmed by his own
explorations of the region in which the penultimate sections of the
Berlin–Baghdad railway were being constructed. He left Constantinople in April 1906 for Beirut, travelling through Smyrna and
Palestine. But it was not all hard work and noting the terrain, the
distance between stations and the progress of work: the presence of
Aubrey Herbert on the stretch between Smyrna and Jerusalem saw to
that.

At Gaza the travellers were informed by the consular agent that they
would not be able to travel through to the Egyptian frontier. Herbert
was unconvinced and decided to 'ride through the night and go over the
frontier with an Arab robber chieftain'. Lloyd, being less reckless,
departed by 'a different way', only to meet his former companion the
following day wandering between Gaza and Ashdod. They decided to
return to Gaza, but were told by the Turkish police that this was not
possible; so they pressed on for Cairo – the frontier now having
mysteriously become open again. They arrived there after a month's
journey on 23 April – 'Aubrey in great *dishabille*'. Lloyd was delighted
to meet Lord Cromer, the agent-general in Egypt, whose work he
admired. From there it was back to Constantinople to compile his
report on his trip, cheered on by Sam's comment in a letter written on 7
April that if he stuck to it:

Some of my sixteen kids may come across a portrait of yourself one day
with something of this kind: 'Perseverance guts and brains, wrecked the
German Baghdad trains – G. A. Lloyd and Great Britaine.'[14]

# 3

# EASTERN EXPERT

Lloyd's views on the political and diplomatic situation at this time can be gleaned from a letter which he wrote to Gertrude Bell in early 1906:

> The political horizon here bears still some very black clouds – especially around the Persian Gulf – and one hopes the Government will be ready to take a very strong line, at once if necessary, over any questions which may arise. I'm glad you think the Government are doing well – I'm not sufficient of a party politician – tho' I cordially loathe C[ampbell]-B[annerman] and all his works – to be glad to see the country harmed by any Government, but your attitude towards this Government is one that I never understand, because you have travelled so much and seen the value of Empire and yet you sympathize with a party who avowedly place England before the Empire and who are attempting to shirk the big German bogie by making friends with it, which to my mind is verily nourishing the viper that only wants to sting you till it is stronger. What does their Mediera [sic] policy, their Red Sea policy, their Persian Gulf policy, their Persia policy all mean, if it is not a carefully thought-out anti-British policy? There may be room for both of us in Europe but there is absolutely no room for two Western Moslem powers.[1]

These insights pointed him towards the political arena, but for the first of very many times he found himself trapped between ambition and wanderlust. He asked Sam whether it was time to return and hunt for a constituency and received the reply that: 'If G. A. Ll. is going to make a success he will make it whether he goes to the Persian Gulf or to the Constituency – provided he sticks to it'; but the burden of Sam's advice was that it would be best to return to London where he could 'decide to take up seriously the Persian problem . . . using your spare time in learning the political lie of the land'. He could, Sam thought, write a book – for which purpose it might be better not to have any official position: 'You might get a roving commission from *The Times* or *Morning Post* which would be far more useful to you in every way.'[2]

But Lloyd could not decide. It was characteristic of him to become so engrossed in local concerns – and their wider implications – that he could not quite bear to leave them, even for the best of reasons. By this time the German threat was becoming an obsession. As he told Miss Bell in July 1906:

> What is wanted both here and at home is that there should be more courage to grasp the nettle and to escape from the negative point of view to the positive. I'm *sure* Germany is working all over the world at lessening our influence, and where no positive result is obtained she keeps us busy while getting commercial advantages in return for her kindly advice at the Palace.[3]

His general views on foreign policy reflected this overriding concern. He did not, for example, agree with the 1902 Anglo–Japanese Alliance, despite the fact that it had been negotiated by a Conservative Government because it was a stumbling-block to better Anglo–Russian relations:

> I always felt, let Russia try and Russify the Manchus and Ching-Changs – let her try – it might take her a hundred years and keep the fire going between Russia and Japan – while we turned to deal with Germany. However, we could still deal effectively with Germany if only we had a little courage – but I have great hopes now that Hardinge is at the Foreign Office that things might go better.[4]

He was quite prepared to let Germany into Mesopotamia as this would lead to Russo–German conflict, 'for it must not be forgotten that Russia will be more powerful than ever before many years are out'.

These reflections informed his political thinking and his writing for the next decade, and by his energy and his capacity for sustained hard work, he was able to make some impression upon official circles. His first 'mention in despatches' by the Ambassador, Sir Nicholas O'Conor, came in July 1906 when he was commended to the Foreign Secretary, Sir Edward Grey, for his 'linguistic attainments'. O'Conor wrote that:

> In this and many other ways he has shown a most praiseworthy zeal and ability in the interests of the Public Service and has willingly placed at my disposal the information and experience acquired in several journeys which he has undertaken at his own expense in various parts of the Turkish Empire.[5]

Nor was it long before the results of his journeys began to bear fruit in the form of memoranda which greatly added to Foreign Office knowledge of the nature of 'German schemes' in the Persian Gulf.

On 24 July O'Conor transmitted to Grey Lloyd's report on the

Hedjaz railway.[6] An exhaustive tour of Arabia convinced him that reports of German influence in the region were exaggerated and that the railway to Mecca was a 'purely Turkish enterprise', designed to increase the Sultan's control over the Holy Place of Islam; it was 'fairly clear that German influence as exercised at present by means of the Railway amounted to little or nothing in a direct way'.

A further memorandum from him in November on this subject received the dignity of going into confidential print.[7] It gave an exhaustively detailed account of the construction of the railway, the problems of building and financing it as well as a description of all the stations between Damascus and Madawwere. As far as the military potential was concerned, Lloyd reckoned that it would allow twenty military trains to leave within the first twenty-four hours after mobilization. Some idea of the detail of the report can be gained from his observation that:

> The new locomotives on the Hedjaz Railway (forty-six tons weight) can all draw a weight of 168 tons at a speed of twenty-three kilometres per hour. Only on the gradient south of Amman must the speed be diminished to fifteen kilometres per hour.

These were useful things to know a decade later when he was helping Lawrence of Arabia to blow the lines up. But for the moment it was gratifying for him to learn from Sam that the Foreign Office view was that '[Lloyd] thoroughly understands all the Turkish Question' and that the Foreign Secretary, Sir Edward Grey, had minuted on his report on the Hedjaz railway: 'A v. interesting and thoughtful memorandum.'[8]

If it was an exaggeration to say that Lloyd had all the Eastern Question at his fingertips, it was only a little one. In addition to his reports on the railways, he also prepared papers on Turkish finance and irrigation schemes for the Foreign Office.[9] But these labours were no more than a rehearsal for the massive 249-page report on conditions for British trade in the Persian Gulf which was to establish beyond any doubt his reputation in official circles both as a 'coming man' and as an expert on the Near East.

In late 1906 he suggested to the Board of Trade that they should sponsor a tour of the Gulf which would allow him to investigate patterns of trade there and report on opportunities for British companies. After some hesitation and discussion the proposal was finally accepted, and on 5 January 1907 he was informed that he had been appointed as a special commissioner to investigate trading prospects in the area north of the head of the Persian Gulf.[10]

What Lloyd really needed was a rest. Dysentery and fever had weakened him and were to leave him with a legacy of ill-health. It was bitter experience which lay behind the advice he was to give his son many years later: 'the East is a little unforgiving if you take liberties with your health'.[11] Percy Loraine, who had just been posted to Teheran, tried to persuade him to go there for a rest and to lead

> a quiet sedate life. You needn't play polo or bridge: you can slack to your heart's content and when you are feeling energetic we will ride out to some Persian garden such as Hafizsang, and lie on the grass bathing in the sun and reviling O'Connor [sic]. *Si cela ne te tente pas tu es fou ou amoureux – sinon les deux* [if that doesn't tempt you you must be mad or in love, if not both].[12]

Maybe he was both. In any event, the offer was turned down and he embarked upon his task.

He started from Bombay, which might seem odd until it is noted that much of the Indian trade with the Gulf went through that port and that in the absence of any records of trade statistics in the Ottoman Empire, it was wise to start off with some imperial ones. From Bombay he proceeded to Basra in mid March to start his journey of over 2,500 miles.

Sam had been delighted at the news of George's mission and told him that whatever happened he would get 'an extraordinarily interesting journey at HMG's expense' and experience which would make his name.[13] As prophecies go this one went quite well. If he ended up £500 out of pocket that was entirely because he refused to accept the full remuneration offered; and Lloyd certainly could not complain about the journey itself. From Bandar Abbas on the Persian Gulf he wrote of his arrival at Muscat thus:

> An extraordinarily picturesque place lying at the head of a small cove, whose sides are formed by immense bare jagged rocks of granite which reflect the heat down and make it a real furnace. The winter heat there is never below eighty degrees – and being early spring we had about ninety degrees when I was there which is quite cold for Muscat.[14]

For once he actually found somewhere warm enough to suit his tastes. He enjoyed the journey and loved being 'out in these parts again . . . it is so interesting that I can only pity anyone in England in the cold'.

Thus it was that he spent the next three months wandering the Gulf region: cajoling information out of recalcitrant local officials, travelling with camel caravans, making notes, and generally sinking himself in the environment he had come to love so well. Nor did he allow his official duties to prevent him doing what he enjoyed most: riding off into the wilderness with a friend and trying to get to some inaccessible spot by the most difficult route.

In late April he left Baghdad accompanied by the British agent at Bushire, Pat Ramsay, bound for the holy city of Kurbela in Persia.[15] Because of floods they made slow progress and had to travel by an odd mixture of conveyances, including some rather unsteady flat-bottomed barges: 'dust, heat and flies, together with the roughest road on earth' often made him 'wish we had brought a caravan and gone in comfort' – but he revelled in it all. Nor, as he discovered at Kurbela, did journey's end necessarily bring relief. He and Ramsay slept out on the roof of the house of a British subject and 'for some five hours we suffered the tortures of the damned from fleas and the largest congregation of cats I have ever seen'; even their Arab guide found it too much and confessed to being unable to sleep, and 'strolled up and down the roof all night, calling upon Allah to witness to the uncleanliness of these Shiahs'.

Journeying thence to see the excavations at Babylon they encountered soldiers on the road who pointed rifles at them and tried to arrest them when their boat struck a mud-bank, and 'for a few moments it looked like serious trouble and bloodshed'; but a mixture of firmness and conciliation saw them out of danger. After Babylon it was back to Baghdad, encountering on the way a sandstorm

> which filled our eyes and throats to choking point, and Pat, who was unaccustomed to this form of travelling, was very miserable, and as he would swear all the time swallowed an unnecessary amount of sand.

Despite having fallen ill with dysentery, in May he left Baghdad for the Black Sea coast of Turkey – a journey lasting over a month, enlivened by the usual floods, bandits, sandstorms and other natural hazards.[16] On the road he noted some exotic phenomena including

> remarkable sulphur springs which are known locally as Ebed Atesh, or 'Place of Eternal Fire'. These lie in a hollow like a small crater, and in it thousands of jets of flame burn continuously. The area of the fire is some fifteen yards square. At night the sky is lit up with these for great distances round.

At the end of his mission in August, from the deck of the steam-tramp *Sappho* on the Black Sea, he wrote to his sister Gwen who was worrying about the prospect of going out to India:

> I have just spent six months of a furnace climate to which one could add no comforts such as are to be had in India – no punkahs or ice – no cool drinks, but life seemed a buzz of flies, sand and glare, of hot muddy drinks from wells which were better not to examine [*sic*].

He felt, he said, 'inclined to swear' at those 'super-fatted souls who stay at home and criticize the work we do abroad in circumstances of which they have no comprehension'. He wondered how such people would fare in the region of the Gulf known as the 'Marshes',

> where you have to dine in top boots and three pairs of trousers in spite of the heat to protect your legs being bitten by the millions of flies. How would they like to have a hot whisky and soda and to drink it in sudden gulps out of a tumbler which has a cover to it to keep the insects out, or to spend all day underground and go out for a ride in the evening and be cheered by seeing plenty of funeral processions, the result of that day's cholera.

That, he wrote, was Baghdad for you, and he was, to boot, 'nearly £500 out of pocket on the top of it'. Yet he was 'utterly willing to do it because I believe it is the good way to spend the money one has inherited'.[17]

This was all very noble, but Lloyd's already shaky health now threatened to give way entirely as he went down with fever. Loraine wrote hoping that it was 'no more than the old thing again', but advised him to 'take care of yourself for some little time and take a good spell of white man's country before you next go a-wandering'.[18] Similar warnings came from Sam Cockerell, who encouraged him to direct his attention to the end for which he had undertaken these hardships – his political career.[19]

At this time Lloyd was optimistic that either a general election or, even better, a by-election, would provide the occasion for his entry to the House of Commons, but as 1907 passed with nary a prospect of either, his natural boredom with domestic politics began to reassert itself and he grew doubtful, consulting his friends as to other avenues into public life. In continuously bad health, he spent the latter part of 1907 pondering his future, recuperating, and writing up his report for the Board of Trade.

It was not until the middle of 1908 that his health began to mend, but he had, in the meantime, received some gratifying signs of recognition from the official world. In March he was questioned by ministers at the Committee of Imperial Defence about the German threat in the Gulf; whilst in July he was asked by the Foreign Office to intervene to prevent the British shipping combine in the region allowing the German-controlled Hamburg–Amerika line to establish itself in the Persian Gulf trade.[20] He had also, by the middle of the year, been adopted as the prospective Unionist candidate for the seat of Wednesbury, near Birmingham. All in all, things seemed to be looking up; all that was needed was a general election – but the Liberals stubbornly refused to oblige and he was left to his own devices a while yet.

The 'Young Turk' revolution in Constantinople in 1908 brought a request from *The Times* for him to travel to Turkey as a special correspondent and the paper's chief diplomatic correspondent, Valentine Chirol, even suggested that he might like to make his connection a more permanent one.[21] Although tempted, George declined the offer. But he did visit Turkey and also produced some articles for the press, most notably a long piece on 'Some aspects of the Reform movement in Turkey' for Leo Maxse's *National Review*.[22]

It was disappointing to find, on his arrival back in England in October, that his report had not been published:

> Matters are going very well for us in Turkey, and if only the break-up of the Empire can now be checked we ought to have magnificent opportunities, political and commercial prospects in the country.[23]

But as Gertrude Bell commented:

> It's difficult enough to arrest the attention of ears that are accustomed to hear nothing but the echoes of victories and defeats in the House of Commons.[24]

It was, however, a fruitless labour preaching the strategic importance of the Turkish Empire to a British public weaned on Gladstonian rhetoric about the 'unspeakable Turk'. Lloyd's argument was that British diplomacy in the Balkans had to be based on the realities of power politics, not the vapourings of liberal sensibilities.[25] Turkey was, he asserted, of vital importance to the Empire both because of her geographical position in relation to the sea-routes to India, and on account of her role as the religious centre of the Moslem world. It was, he warned, not from Russia but from 'the wedges of German influence' being driven into the Balkans that the danger to Britain's interests came.

This was not a popular position to adopt: Percy Loraine disagreed with his '*morbus germanicus*',[26] arguing that the Germans were a useful counterpoise to Russian ambitions in the Gulf. But to Lloyd this was a short-sighted view. He made it plain in his report on trade in the Gulf, which was finally published for confidential circulation in late 1908, that the Germans were making steady inroads into British markets there which were now precariously based almost entirely on 'command of the cotton goods or "Manchester" trade'.[27] He saw here the same problems as beset Stewart and Lloyds – lack of initiative and enterprise – and he warned presciently that, 'Manchester manufactures may in the future find an increasing difficulty in maintaining their hold over Eastern markets against the products of cheap labour and the increasing up-to-date methods of Japan.' Only the equally cheap labour of India would allow the Empire to maintain any major trade with the region unless British traders 'take up new lines of business'. There was, he pointed out, a considerable demand for 'cheap goods' which was being met by the Germans; he was right – but no one listened.

# 4

# POLITICS AND LOVE

Lloyd had now established himself as an expert on the Near East, but he had moved no nearer to making his mind up about a parliamentary career. In December 1908 he withdrew from his candidature at Wednesbury, feeling that his own involvement with Stewart and Lloyds would detract from his advocacy of tariff reform by the 'imputation of personal motive' during an election campaign.[1] He toyed with the idea of trying to enter the diplomatic service or else going out to Constantinople to see what was left of the 'Old fraternity at Stamboul',[2] but, in the end, confined himself to visits there in 1909, finding a sad strangeness in revisiting the mysterious palace of Abdul Hamid now open to the public; he felt that 'Old Stamboul' was slipping away from him.[3] Like it or not, and he was not sure he did, politics seemed the only road open to him.

In 1909 he was adopted as the Liberal Unionist candidate for the marginal Liberal seat of West Staffordshire. It is interesting to note that he did not stand as a Conservative, preferring instead to wear his Chamberlainite colours on his sleeve. Indeed, during his speeches in the constituency, he nailed those colours high on the mast-head. All progress, he argued in one speech, was 'a sort of race and to say that it does not matter how fast we are being caught up by other countries just because we are ahead today is obviously foolish'.[4] He argued that only tariff reform could protect Britain's industries and provide the dynamo for imperial federation, and he berated the Liberals for their foolish complacency. As the Lloyd George budget raised the political temperature, George Lloyd denounced it in fine style, and in the election of January 1910 he defeated the sitting Liberal member by 5,892 votes to 5,327, a majority of 565;[5] Fitzmaurice commented: 'What's in a name? The salvation of the Empire. I prefer George Lloyd to Lloyd George.'[6]

Lloyd's main interventions in the House were on matters concerning the Near East. He eagerly interrogated government ministers on matters such as the Baghdad Railway and conditions for trade in the Gulf.[7] But there was a limit to how far he was prepared to embarrass what was, after all, the Imperial Government, just for the sake of making political points. As he told Leo Maxse in June 1910, much as he hated the 'Grey atmosphere at the FO', and much as he could have 'torn the FO to pieces' on their policy in the recent crisis over Crete, he had to 'spare our general interests'.[8] This, of course, spiked his political guns just at the point where they carried most fire-power, but there was no remedy for it; he would not play politics with imperial interests. As ever, his own intense personal ambition had to submit itself to the wider ends for which he had entered politics; he was, in truth, an odd politician.

In September Lloyd visited Canada, travelling as far west as Vancouver, spreading the gospel of imperial federation and tariff reform. But soon after his return to England he was plunged into a fresh election by the Liberal desire to curb the powers of the House of Lords. In the second election of the year his majority went down to 475, but he still won comfortably. However, for his party as a whole the results were frustrating. Their recovery from the débâcle of 1906 was confirmed, but the Liberals, now dependent on the support of Labour and the Irish, would be able to push ahead with their plans to emasculate the powers of the Lords; then they would have to do something about Home Rule for Ireland: the political horizon was black with storm clouds.

The Unionist Party, in a disaffected mood, vented its wrath on the party leader, Arthur Balfour. A sceptic by nature, and not least on the tariff question, 'A.J.B.'s' detached style of leadership seemed to many unsuited to the storms ahead, and Maxse's *National Review* carried the less than enigmatic inscription 'B.M.G.' – 'Balfour must go'. Lloyd, who shared this view, objected to his decision to submit the question of tariff reform to a referendum should the party win the next election. Walter Long, one of the leading contenders for Balfour's place, wrote to Lloyd on 20 December arguing that 'we must be united' and that,

> although it is obviously impossible for every able and competent man to agree with every detail of the policy of his Party it is surely possible for us to subordinate individual feelings and unite in defence of the common policy of the Party.[9]

But these, the arguments of the party man down the ages, failed to convince him; he would rather break before the storm than compromise his principles.

It is, therefore, no surprise to find Lloyd on the die-hard or 'ditcher' wing of the party in 1911 over the question of the reform of the House of Lords. His spiritual home was in the 'last ditch', and he deplored any attempt to allow the Liberals to reduce the powers of the Lords. But if this was no surprise, the same could not be said of the news in July of his engagement to be married.

On holiday at the Herbert villa at Portofino in May 1911 he wrote to Sam in melancholy vein:

> I don't know why but I don't want a bit to go on travelling around – and I suppose that after this place one can't find anything so good. I think I'm an unsatisfactory person mentally and get more restless instead of the reverse. I love it all yet I can't stay still – I wish it were not so.[10]

The reason for this outburst was to be found among the particularly 'charming' company at the Castello, to be precise, in the tall and statuesque form of Miss Blanche Lascelles, Maid of Honour to Queen Alexandra. For the first time since the disappointment of 1904–5, George Ambrose Lloyd had fallen in love.

There had been no woman in his life since 'Puss' Knox, but now he was, once again, smitten.[11] The romance developed as a very one-sided affair. Miss Lascelles, who had evidently enjoyed his company, wrote to him on 11 May regretting that her duties at Court had obliged her to return to London so soon.[12] On 19 May she accepted an invitation from him to go to a dinner party he was giving at the Commons and wrote to ask if there was not a 'female of your acquaintance' with whom she could come: 'For it alarms me so appearing at the gates of your august habitation, all by myself with the chances of being taken for a suffragette!'

George's first letter to Blanche is undated. Its contents and tone are characteristic of the writer:

> We had a splendid meeting at the Albert Hall last night, quite like one of the earlier Chamberlain meetings – it will do so much good just before the meeting of the Imperial Conference – I forget if you agree about Preference? I think it matters much more than it appears to – which is untrue of most political movements.

But if this contained little romance, George soon overcame his reticence and pressed his suit in typically whirlwind fashion. He proposed to her and was accepted on 16 or 17 June;[13] within twenty-four hours she had changed her mind. In an undated letter from this period he wrote telling her that:

> I only want you to understand that the only thing I care about in the wide world is that you should be happy. I'm so utterly sure and I want

you to be sure too. You see I've known days and weeks ago, and given you already all there is of me – mind, heart, reason, everything – I couldn't go to bed without trying to explain to you. I want you so to understand.

She wrote on 18 June blaming herself 'so dreadfully' for having 'thought I was sure when I wasn't':

But you know I didn't mean not to be true. There aren't any short cuts to happiness are there? One has got to walk every step of the way and not be afraid of anything. That's why I mean to go on letting you see me if you can bear it. It may be cruel – I don't know, that's one of the risks. Anyway I believe it's true what you said yesterday that you know me a great deal better than I know you.

She had been rushed by George into accepting his proposal, and now needed time to think; but he continued to press his point. His impetuosity almost brought this second suit the way of his first one. The Lascelles family were even more aristocratic than the Knoxes and held neither politicians nor industrialists in high esteem. Blanche, more- over, was high-mettled and easily frightened and was, for a time, worried by stories that, given his dark complexion, George was of Jewish descent.

He took a long walk in Richmond Park – 'I always have to go under open skies and to open spaces to see clearly' – and then wrote to say that he now saw he had asked 'too much too quickly'. In another letter on 19 June, however, he began to push again, reassuring her that he knew she cared for him, even if she did not know her own mind as well as he knew it:

You cared enough to say yes only two days ago and it was only afterwards when you realized that you had taken a step that you began to doubt – please believe me it is only the fear that comes and must always come to everyone when they have taken a big step in life that has made you feel not sure.

He was, he added,

more certain than life itself that I can and shall make you happy completely and it simply isn't possible that you will throw away all that makes up my life and all that I have given you – and can never now take back – just because you are afraid. If it is a plunge it is only into something that will I know make us both happier than before – only believe this, for I think a man knows these things more surely than you can at first.

Such intense urgency hardly helped his case – or Miss Lascelles.

Fortunately George was not entirely without feminine advice on how to conduct himself. When she replied to his outpourings by inviting him to a dinner party, he responded that 'it's all got to be as you want it to be':

You see in future I'm going to eclipse Patience itself for Lady C[arnarvon] tells me that I'm always in such a hurry over anything I want badly. I'm *so* sorry if I've been unfair and impatient and worried you terribly, I can't tell you how sorry, but you must just try and understand what it feels like to be built like I am. I've never known how to go round a curve when there was a shorter road, however rough. But I'm learning.

This, as it turned out, was a much better way to calm her fears, and on 11 July their engagement was announced.

What manner of woman was this who had achieved the unlikely feat of distracting George Lloyd's attention away from the peers' crisis and the Eastern Question? Tall and slender with dark hair, she was the archetypal statuesque aristocratic beauty. Born in 1880, she was the second daughter of Commander the Hon. Frederick Lascelles RN (rtd), brother of the Earl of Harewood. He was, as his obituary was to put it,

> the essence of the old time tory squire: a true patriot, a grand sportsman, a stoic, a reactionary, ever suspicious of change and of governments; an Englishman ever bitter against the foreigner, a man of genial humanity, who hid his tender feelings under the cloak of ferocity.

Passionately devoted to hunting, he would spend four days a week in the field as often as possible – and woe betide the guest who turned up at Sutton Waldron House on one of those days for, as the second hunter was used to pull the dog cart, it meant a long walk from the station. A vivid picture of 'the Hon. Frederick' is given in an undated letter to Blanche from her brother Alan (who was always known as Tommy); commenting upon their father's ceaseless reiteration of certain themes, he thought that the only way to satisfy him was to 'draw up and print XXXIX articles, on lines like this':

> a. That the House of Lords is a pack of old women.
> b. That if we mark the words of the Hon. F. Lascelles, Old William will be in Buckingham Palace before five years.
> c. That the said old William knows very well what he is about.
> d. That the Hon. F. Lascelles is not influenced by any 2½d scare in the Press, but he's said exactly the same thing for years. (Nem. con.)
> e. That the Penny Post and the House of Commons are the curse of the country.
> f. That there's not the smallest hope, not the *smallest* hope – no hope at all until we listen to [Admiral] Charley Beresford.
> g. That *there's* a man who *does* know what he's about (cf. old William) not one of your silly mandarins . . .
> h. That it's not the slightest use the Hon. F. Lascelles talking, but that when said old William does come, it will unquestionably be 'who'd ha' thought it'.

It was only to be expected that he would greet his daughter's suitor with ambivalent feelings; the man was, after all, a politician. As he told Tommy on 6 July:

> From what you say it might be worse. I have heard of the man and politics is a dirty business – and a poor one – at least on our side. According to Blanche, from whom I only heard this morning, he is sufficiently well off, but she does not say whether he has a father or any other relations.[14]

But he quickly came to like his prospective son-in-law who held such sound views on 'old William', the shortcomings of politicians, and the need for a strong navy.

Why had Blanche decided to accept her ardent suitor? The two years preceding his proposal had been, from the point of view of romance, frustrating ones for her. Although she enjoyed her position at Court, she felt that her chances of a suitable marriage were passing by. She was thirty in 1909, a year which saw some of her remaining unmarried friends reach the altar, and she felt Time's wingèd chariot at her back. It is not surprising that her first reaction was to accept George Lloyd, nor that having done so she should have hesitated. Having finally accepted him she immersed herself in planning for the wedding which took place in November. Even in that short time it had become apparent to them both that they had much in common.

Blanche had taken a keen interest in the first 1910 election, during which she had canvassed energetically for a young Conservative candidate, Edward Wood, who had married her friend Dorothy Onslow in September 1909. She was an ardent Conservative and followed with interest, if not always with approval, her fiancé's account of the development of the constitutional crisis over the powers of the House of Lords.

Following their narrow victory in the 1910 elections the Liberals proposed to amend the powers of the House of Lords; unsurprisingly Lloyd ranged himself firmly alongside those Tories who resolved to resist this to 'the last ditch'. It was, however, typical of him to fret on discovering that Blanche did not share his views in every respect. He told her in August that, 'I feel more and more sure of my view, but I can't deny that I felt worried at your feeling strongly the other way.' As so often during their short courtship, Blanche tried to inject a note of common sense into his anxieties. On this occasion she wrote to him on 2 August to say:

> Dearest, you mustn't worry even a little about my disagreeing now over the Peers. It isn't possible that anyone as old as I am, who has thought *al*

*all* about anything shouldn't have some kind of views is it? And it would be a perfect miracle if they entirely coincided with yours in every detail: it might even be a bad thing, because we are probably meant to modify each other aren't we?

And, in a prophetic vein, she continued:

Of course you'll change me more than I shall change you because you're the stronger of us two – that's just as it ought to be – and we shall each do our share.

Even as she said, so it came to pass.

But did he make her as 'completely happy' as he had promised in the first exuberance of their love? The human condition seems to rule out the attainment of such a blessèd state, but within the limitations implied by this rather broad caveat, theirs was a happy union. A common interest in politics and his career provided the most enduring bond, and the birth of their son David in 1912 brought them both such joy that it almost made up for the sorrow that she could have no more children. He undoubtedly bullied her, but she was not unwilling to be bullied – provided she was also loved. Love, unlike beauty, is in the eye of the receiver and who shall attempt to comment upon the secrets of the human heart?

He was undoubtedly faithful to her as she was to him. Lloyd was not a man who found feminine company congenial and there were times when her nervous temperament was too much for him to bear; at such moments he would take to the open road. A fastidious man about his appearance, he found her total lack of interest in clothes difficult to fathom and would sometimes go to the length of getting her to try on hats in her nightdress in order to get her to buy a new one. Blanche was a country girl who loved her home, but she did her best to put up with his wanderlust.

For the first two and a half decades of their marriage, while George held public positions which gave her a role, Blanche was happy and so was their marriage. Not least amongst the results of the great tragedy of his career in 1929 was that this state of affairs was to change. But in 1911 'there seem[ed] to be absolutely infinite possibilities of being happy . . . and all because you and I have found each other'.

# 5

# TOWARDS THE STORM

George and Blanche were married at St Margaret's Westminster at 2.15 p.m. on 13 November 1911. They spent their honeymoon in Turkey, where Blanche was introduced to his many Turkish friends and got her first taste of the East and of his love of travel. On their return they settled down at 99 Eaton Place, where they were to live until 1914. Had it not been for the expense and trouble of West Staffordshire, they would have been very comfortably off. His gross income for the year 1910–11 amounted to £3,787, over half of which came from shares in Lloyds Bank and Stewart and Lloyds. He owned two properties in Birmingham, which brought in £184 a year, and the rest of his income came from various investments. In July 1913 he secured a directorship at Lloyds Bank which gave him an extra £600, and Blanche's marriage settlement brought in another £350 a year. The financial problems caused by the expense of a political career became only one of the reasons which led Lloyd to question whether he should continue with it.

Before their marriage he had tried to convey to Blanche the reasons why he was in politics; writing in August 1911 he wondered if he could make her 'understand how much I want in my small way to play the biggest game, even if in so doing one fails and never is able to do all one would like'. He need not have worried, she understood. But the problem facing Lloyd was how to 'play the biggest game'. His views on the role of an MP were very firm. He opposed strenuously the Liberal proposal to pay MPs, telling Blanche on 8 August that this 'struck at the old principle of British politics that it was our duty and pride to give gratuitous service to this country whenever it was in the power of a man – even at a sacrifice – to do so'. He was quite disgusted when, as he wrote on 9 August, 'literally two minutes after the Veto Bill was passed, the Commons voted themselves £400 p.a. – a pretty object lesson to the country!' Not only was this 'horribly dangerous', but it would, he thought, 'just about finish clean politics in this country within ten years'.

This was not hypocrisy. Although he was very far from being a poor man, he had to make considerable financial sacrifices in order to remain an MP. West Staffordshire was an expensive seat to contest and cost him at least £300 a year in subscriptions to the local association; in addition to being a marginal seat and far from London, it was also a very large constituency and needed plenty of 'nursing'. As early as September 1911 he was looking for a new seat but decided not to take the offer of Woolwich from Central Office. Nevertheless the continuing expense of West Staffordshire could not be borne indefinitely and, despite offers of increased subscriptions from the local association, Lloyd continued to hunt for a new seat.

In an undated letter probably written in 1912, he confessed to Blanche that he was

> passing through a horrid torment of the mind on the subject of politics and my future in them. It is a thing I alone can decide. . . . But I get more and more unhappy about it. . . . I find myself utterly out of touch with my Party and cannot get back into touch.

He found his colleagues 'hopeless on defence', shifty on protection and hysterical on Ireland, but he could not 'become a Radical' and was 'not a Socialist'. Blanche wrote in October 1912 of her growing conviction that 'Parliament is not the right road, for the next few years at any rate', especially when it meant perpetually living beyond their income. But she was equally sure that they ought not to waste all the effort he had already put in 'unless you were very sure that you were embarking on something in every way more satisfactory'. On the other hand, though, came warnings from the doctors that 'to go on in politics would mean perpetual breakdowns'.

Lloyd knew of only one method of coping with great fatigue – travel. In September 1912 he took himself off across the Channel, despite the fact that Blanche was heavily pregnant. He confessed to her in a letter written from France that:

> I have got the wander-fever attack on me badly again. I suppose it's looking at the sea and the ships and the wind in the trees and the smell of the open, open air.
>
> Please God, you and I will take such a pilgrimage one of these days as will cure us both of it all forever: but it will have to be a long one I fear to cure me.
>
> I want to take you to Erzerum over the shale mountains of Kurdistan through the Desira to Lake Van, and smell every night the wood fires in camp, and hear the mule bells astride the tent door. I want to ride the

same pony every day for weeks and weeks and all day, to shoe him myself again, and swim him across the river and only wash when God gives me a stream to wash in, and forget that the Speaker ever lived or that so vile a thing as Parliamentary misrule existed – the soldiers in England don't stand to attention over thousands of miles every sunset to salute Parliament. But from Buda Pest to Baghdad they turn towards their throne every night and salute the Sultan. *That's* ruling and not the pettifogging direction that we call Government.

There were, he told her, so many parts of the globe he had not yet visited, particularly Africa and South America: 'fancy living and dying without knowing all those new smells and missing the million brain photos that one could collect'. One lifetime was infinitely too short to cram it all in. Still, he reflected, if they could do so then,

when we were quite, quite old we could sit and travel it all again – one couldn't then be afraid of the longest journey of all, it would only be adding a splendid one to the series.

Britain seemed to him so small and tame and he lamented that 'the real sixteenth-century roving spirit is dying out'. It was, he concluded, only half humorously, 'due to having had Cecils to rule over us for so long. I should like to make A. J. B[alfour] Governor of Uganda and then frame him when he came back.'

He returned from his wanderings for the great event, which Blanche recorded in her diary thus: 'My son was born at 5.30 on the morning of Monday, September 30th. He weighed 8lbs 4oz and was the fattest thing of his size you ever saw.' Her pregnancy and the delivery were quite easy, but on 4 October she became seriously ill with a kidney infection and was, for a time, near death. Lloyd stayed with her, sleeping on the floor to be close to her if she needed him. But she survived and with the birth of Alexander (after his godmother, Queen Alexandra) Frederick David (who was always known by his third Christian name), a new joy was added to their lives.

George continued to be restless, confessing to Sam in November: 'I hate the House of Commons so badly that I despise myself for not having the initiative to abandon it, but perhaps that is indolence and lack of desire.' But it was not easy to decide on an alternative career. He thought of trying to become private secretary to the King, but correctly supposed that having been a 'party politician makes that impossible'. He could not, as he had written to Blanche in mid 1912, 'bear to be a failure, for my sake and still more for yours'; nor did he see any reason why 'I should – and I won't'. So it was that they decided to give politics a chance – until the next election.

One reason for this increasing distaste for politics lay in the growing realization that much of the Unionist support for tariff reform was nothing more than rhetoric; a more cynical or less romantic man than George Lloyd would have known this all along, or else would have realized it sooner. In early 1913 the party leader, Bonar Law, was faced with a rebellion against 'food taxes' from his own back-benches. He tried to quell this with a nicely ambiguous speech and, when that failed, he threatened to resign. To avert this a 'memorial' was drawn up for Conservative MPs to sign; it asked him not to go, but also to abandon 'food taxes' until after the election. Most MPs signed it, but when Lloyd went into the committee room where it was kept he decided that he 'could not sign away for tactical reasons a policy I had preached and believe in and which was no minor policy but the first plank'.

It was both a sign of his growing political stature as well as of the habitual pusillanimity of Conservative MPs that he should have been strongly pressed to fall into line. He wrote to Joe Chamberlain's son and standard-bearer, Austen, explaining his position, but was advised, albeit 'sorrowfully', to sign.[1] But he continued to refuse and was, with another ardent tariff reformer, Leo Amery, one of only five MPs who did not sign the memorial.

It was with a sense of great relief that he and Blanche left England at the end of January 1913 bound for British East Africa. To his disgust he had to travel on a German liner, but there were consolations; finding that 'the boat is slow, food bad, and the band devilish', he took some pleasure in anticipating that he would be able to 'run down' German liners to intending passengers!

One object of their trip was to allow Blanche to recover her health and to give George a much-needed rest, but it was also in their minds that East Africa might provide that alternative career. He was exhilarated by what he found there. Writing to Sam on 16 March he called it 'a most inspiring place' where 'everything is just beginning and there are countless openings for anyone who chooses to keep his eyes open'. It made him

> want to give up Parliament and come out here and do all the things! I only wish I had come out with you seven years ago. We should both have been rich men by now, for people are making money hand over fist.

On the advice of Ewart Grogan, a friend who had settled there, Lloyd bought two plots of land in East Africa. He and Blanche spent a happy month sightseeing and investigating the beauties of this new and untamed land and Lloyd prepared a report for the Colonial Office detailing the advantages that would accrue from building a rail link to the coast.

The long voyage back gave them another chance to visit Lloyd's old haunts at Constantinople, where he eagerly gathered details of the Balkan wars; the next time he saw the Dardanelles it would not be as a tourist.

When they returned to England Lloyd was ardent in his pursuit of the interests of the colonists, pressing the Government to build a railway to the coast and writing articles extolling the potential of East Africa. He had had a glimpse of life as it might be led – which merely made him more dissatisfied with the one he was leading.

In July 1913, having been offered a safer and cheaper seat at Shrewsbury, he finally gave up West Staffordshire – much to the regret of the local party officials. But he was, in fact, thinking of giving up politics altogether. Writing to Blanche on 10 October, he told her that he was 'looking for a City job and would chuck Parliament for it'; he had, he said, begun to 'feel that it is really not worth it as nowadays one seems absolutely impotent to do good inside'. But as no suitable job turned up he remained at Westminster.

Given his interest in the Balkans he watched earnestly the crisis which resulted from the assassination of Archduke Franz Ferdinand in June 1914. His main fear as the crisis reached its peak was that the Government would not 'stand firm', in which case 'our influence and perhaps more will be shattered'. As it happened, 'Fate decreed that [he] should play a not entirely unimportant part in the opening of the drama'.[2]

· The first sign for Lloyd that all might not be well was hearing a *sotto voce* aside from Asquith to the Speaker on 31 July: 'But Sir, this is no concern of ours.' He talked this over with Blanche at dinner and she persuaded him to go to the French Embassy and find out the latest news. What he found there shook him. His old friend the Ambassador, Paul Cambon, was in a terrible state, greeting him with: '*Monsieur Georges, il vous reste de l'honneur dans votre pays* [Monsieur Georges, the honour of your country depends upon you].' Despite their friendship Lloyd was not going to take that sort of remark from any foreigner; he pulled him up short and asked him what the devil he meant. Cambon replied:

'I have just been to see Sir Edward Grey and he says that under no conditions will you fight.' Cambon's voice almost trembled as he went on to say: 'That is what he said. He seems to forget that it was on your advice and under your guarantee that we moved all our ships to the south and our ammunition to Toulon. *Si vous restez inertes, nos côtes sont livrés aux Allemands* [If you do nothing, our coasts will be handed over to the Germans].

Despite Lloyd's angry denials, Cambon persisted with his story that

Grey had said he could do nothing because the Conservatives would not support them; clearly this *canard* had to be laid to rest.

On his way back to Wilton Crescent Lloyd stopped off to talk to the Director of Military Operations, General Sir Henry Wilson. An intensely 'political' soldier, Wilson kept in close touch with Conservative leaders and, as a confidant of the Liberal Government, was well placed to give advice. He confirmed Cambon's story.[3] Lloyd decided that it was time to put pressure on his own leaders to make the Liberals do their duty: at last there was some point in having remained in politics.

From Wilton Crescent he wrote to Austen Chamberlain expressing his fears that 'the Government are going to back down and fail in their adherence to the Triple Entente'; commenting that it would be 'superfluous' to say how 'ruinous and suicidal' such hesitations would be, he asked if there 'was nothing you could do to get our leaders to do their share in stiffening the Government's spine?'[4] Having posted this he telephoned his colleague Leo Amery and the journalist Leo Maxse and enlisted their help in his campaign.

Saturday 1 August was a day of strenuous activity. Lloyd telegraphed Lord Lansdowne, the Conservative leader in the Lords, asking him to come up to town immediately. He then telephoned Admiral Charles Beresford who was a friend of the Russian Ambassador, Count Benckendorff, and asked him to find out the latest news on that front. Having done this he then managed to prevent Arthur Balfour leaving for Hatfield House. In the afternoon, whilst Amery set off for Westgate to get Chamberlain, he and Beresford went to Wargrave where Bonar Law and F. E. Smith were spending the week-end. Perhaps Lloyd had been wrong to suppose that all traces of the Elizabethan spirit were gone from English life for, upon arrival, they found Law and F. E. playing tennis and had to sit 'on a bank patiently until they had finished'. Law was 'merely querulous', clearly thought Lloyd was interfering in matters which did not concern him, said that he had told Asquith all that he could, and refused to go to London. Beresford, whose temper was a good deal hotter than Lloyd's, managed to change Law's mind.[5]

Amery had an easier task with Chamberlain but, thanks to engine failure, the two men did not arrive back in London until the early hours of Sunday morning. They were met at Charing Cross by Lloyd who reported on events so far.[6]

He had, he told them, been summoned to a meeting of Conservative leaders at Lansdowne House at midnight. Feeling the difficulty of trying to persuade his leaders on his word alone, he had managed to enlist the help of Henry Wilson. Years later he described the scene thus:

> I can see the picture now as we were shown in, HW following me in a black inverness cape and an opera hat, looking for all the world like a gaunt conspirator. As we were announced Lansdowne was sitting primly at his table in the middle of the room facing us. The Duke of Devonshire was half asleep on a sofa. Bonar was prattling in a corner by the fire.

At Lansdowne's invitation Lloyd explained why he had acted as he had, and then Wilson gave his story 'from the inside'. After they had spoken Lansdowne showed 'great decision and clarity'. Turning to Law he said: 'Bonar, we must get hold of the Prime Minister tonight.' But a telephone call to Downing Street elicited only the news that Asquith was asleep and must not be disturbed. It was thus decided to draft an ultimatum to the Government, impressing upon it the vital importance of standing by British commitments to France and Russia.[7]

Although the Lansdowne House meeting did not break up until 3 o'clock in the morning, its participants met again soon after 9 o'clock. Chamberlain, prompted by Lloyd and Amery, took the lead in drafting the final note that was sent to Asquith.[8] Historians have usually been dismissive when discussing the influence of this ultimatum on the Government, but the most recent and most convincing study of the period, by Dr Keith Wilson, demonstrates that it did, as Lloyd always believed, play an important part in pushing Asquith towards taking the steps which led to war.[9] The ultimatum put an end to the excuse proffered to Cambon that the Opposition could not be depended upon, and it strengthened the position of Sir Edward Grey. Lloyd's role had been a small but vital one in the final decision.

It was with relief that he listened to Grey's declaration of war on 4 August. Already Lloyd was preparing to join the Warwickshire Yeomanry in camp, but one last 'pogrom and mobilization of the Unionist leaders' came first. The news that the supposedly pro-German Haldane was likely to be appointed to the War Office enraged all good Unionists, especially since it was accompanied by stories that the British Expeditionary Force had not been despatched to France; Lloyd helped in bringing pressure to bear, especially on the King, to oppose the appointment, and he took great pleasure in the selection of Kitchener for the post. Thus, having played his part, he turned with relief from the mundanities of politics to what he hoped would be the glorious simplicities of war.

# 6

# WAR

In one sense George Lloyd was superbly suited to the war which had just broken out. He had long warned against the German menace and, in the years immediately preceding 1914, he had supported Lord Roberts' campaign for the introduction of conscription; in March 1914 he had taken a yeomanry officer's training course at Woolwich, following this up with attendance at the Warwickshire Yeomanry's annual camp in May. Psychologically and materially, he was ready for the conflict. Yet, from the very start, he was unhappy and, as the war went on, this state did not change. Initially he was unhappy because he feared that the war would be over before he could get to France. He envied Sam for his flying skills because they would bring him 'brilliant and wonderful tasks',[1] and he fretted as he trained in camp and rounded up horses for the regiment. He took refuge in the thought that:

> Only good can come from any form of sacrifice, be it of leisure, comfort or peace of mind, and all that is good in this country has been bred of great sacrifice and we have no right to shirk our share whatever it may be.

But he begrudged the sacrifice of mere leisure and comfort, things he had little use for anyway, and he longed to be at the front. But he also wanted to be of *real* use and worried lest he should be doing something more than preparing to die for his country. All these moods he passed through during the course of August 1914; for the rest of the war he went through the whole gamut of them again and again.

The break with his previous life was almost total. Save for letters to Sam and Blanche, Lloyd was plunged into the military world, far away from politics – at least that was what he hoped; and he was correspondingly disappointed to discover that army life had its politics too. His zest for the coming conflict was not the product of a lack of imagination and he realized that death was his lot; the prospect brought him the perspective on life which he so often lacked and with it came the opportunity to let Blanche know that she was the most important thing in that life:

> I just can't tell you what your love is to me, it is everything in the wide world, everything sinks into nothing besides it in my life and I only hope that slowly He may make me more worthy of it and of you.

Like those Ottoman troops whom he admired for their devotion to the Sultan, Lloyd was fighting for the Empire, not for Liberal England. For Asquith and company he had but scorn. As he told Sam on 22 August, those who were sending territorial regiments like the Warwickshires to France bore 'a heavy responsibility. Two weeks' training a year in a standing camp is terribly little experience to be equipped with to meet trained German soldiers. In addition we are terribly short of equipment.' It was not until the end of August that they all received swords! Nor were his harsh words reserved exclusively for the Liberals. Writing to Blanche on 25 August he remarked contemptuously that:

> Sixty years of Cecils in a cosmopolitan system have killed much patriotism and national feeling: please God it is not yet dead and that it may revive – but it is a big risk.

He was fighting for national honour and for patriotism and took a quiet but intense pride in the behaviour of women like Blanche whose reaction to the crisis was described thus by Sam:

> She is indeed splendid: there is no doubt that to play that part well women require colossal heroism, and every bit of it – cold, calculated bravery and absolute self-sacrifice which really makes one take one's hat off in reverence.[2]

Newbury Camp and the breaking-in of horses was no substitute for the grand sacrifice which Lloyd wanted to make and so he pulled what strings he could to make something happen. On 24 September he was offered two jobs as interpreter, one in Serbia[3] and the other in Constantinople.[4] As Turkey was still neutral he plumped for the Serbian post, but then discovered that the Yeomanry would soon be sent to France. He felt that he 'would rather go to France as a subaltern than Serbia as a general' and caused acute annoyance at the War Office by declining Serbia. The result of this was that he found himself 'wanted nowhere'.

To outsiders Lloyd gave an impression of almost ruthless self-confidence, but the truth was far from that. He was morbidly afraid of being thought to be acting in his own self-interest and at moments when he was vulnerable to such a charge he was afflicted by what he called 'my storms'. Such a nerve-storm overcame him now and he wrote to Blanche on 4 October pouring out his fears and saying of his 'storms': 'They are my failing I know and I do want to cure them so badly. If one is not master of one's own self one can be master of nothing else, that is certain.' But this was not quite accurate. It was because of this difficulty that he tried so hard to master his environment and the externals of life, hoping thus to cure the uncertainty he felt at the core of his being. His 'storms' were the inevitable price he paid for his ambition and the immense effort of will-power by which it was supported. It was Blanche's greatest service to him for the first two decades of their marriage that she could provide a sympathetic audience for his woes; it was only when her own nerve-storms became pronounced in the 1930s that the roles were, to an extent, reversed.

Lloyd's chagrin knew no bounds when, after turning down the Serbian job, he discovered that the battalion was not bound for France. He grew more and more depressed, not least because of his own inability to influence the course even of his own career, never mind the events of the great world. But the intervention of the Ottoman Empire in the war in November finally enabled him to get into action. As a fluent speaker of Turkish and Arabic he quickly found himself seconded to intelligence work in Cairo.

With the prospect of action his mood became heightened, almost fey. To Sam he wrote:

> What a curious and complete ending this is to all we had foreseen and all the spade-work we had done. When I look back now I remember that it was you who first awoke my sleeping mind to the realization of the whole German aim and it has been with me ever since that day when in Pall Mall we looked at a map of Asia Minor in the windows of Hugh Rea's shop. There is always this that whatever the issues, national or personal, may be, I think you and I can feel free from responsibility in the sure knowledge that the little we have been able to do has been done towards a now provedly correct goal. One realizes now, with all the grimness and greatness of the daily war, why we had a panic at the end of the first black week before the declaration of war as to the contribution I had made towards the decision of going into the war. Anyway, I shall never regret that, for the alternative would have been ruin to all we had ever worked or cared for.[5]

The news that he was off to Egypt came on 12 November,[6] the day after his wedding anniversary. The day before he had written to Blanche:

> Heavens, how miserable I was this day three years ago, and how little I knew what a good piece of luck I was in for. It has been a good three years with plenty of incident and motion: not quite enough travel and a bit too

much anxiety, but in the next three years we will cut down the latter and increase the former.

He was almost right.

Lloyd was so constituted that he immediately felt doubts as to whether he had done the right thing. He hoped to spend enough time in Egypt to discover if there would be any fighting and then, having seen action, to return to France. He had, he told Blanche on 7 December, 'done my simple best to be in the most active place at all times'; but 'if I were to miss a show in Egypt and then miss it in France as well, it would break my heart'.

He arrived in Cairo on 18 December and was assigned to the Intelligence Department, dealing with matters east of the Canal. It was not long before Lloyd was again lamenting his inaction, telling Sam (who was stationed near by in Ismailia) that, 'there isn't much scope at present. I don't seem to be able to hit a winner in this war and whatever I do seems to go wrong'.[7] Sam came over to cheer him up and found him at Shepheard's Hotel:

He and Aubrey [Herbert] are both in the Intelligence Department of the War Office. There are in the Department two Palestine archaeologists, [Leonard, later Sir Leonard] Woolley and [T. E.] Lawrence, both intelligent fellows. The Department, mainly under the driving force of George, has done invaluable work already, collecting and tabulating information and initiating ideas.[8]

Sam hoped that Lloyd would 'take his proper place as a man of broad views based on sound knowledge and backed by character and drive'. The problem was that:

He has lost all sense of proportion in his burning desire to get somewhere where he can expose himself to physical danger. At the moment he would rather be a Tommy in the trenches than Generalissimo in Cairo. He wants to be shot at. *A pity he hadn't been shot before involving G.Britain in the war!*

Sam's exasperated solution to this was to tell his friend that 'he should return to England and take digs at Scarborough' which had been shelled by German ships.[9]

When Lloyd finally achieved his ambition during the Turkish attack on the Canal in February 1915 he found it an almost mystical experience. Sitting in a bastion with a young Sikh officer as the Turks advanced, he 'enjoyed it immensely': 'it gave me for the first time in this War that incomparable feeling of peace that at last I had got into action, if only a minor one'.[10] Indeed, as it became clear that the British were going to launch a major operation in the Dardanelles, Lloyd began to feel positively optimistic, writing to Blanche on 19 March that the Yeomanry were bound for the same place as himself: 'It really is planning out wonderfully well isn't it, after all our anxieties and worries?'

Lloyd was appointed to the staff of General Birdwood and, as Sam commented:

> You might think that George, with his knowledge of the East and a career based upon it, might consider that to be upon Birdwood's staff at the taking of Constantinople would be the very acme of what he could desire, but it is just not so . . . were it not that Birdwood has told him that the restricted area of the Gallipoli peninsula would make it difficult for him to keep out of the firing line, he would be sorely tempted to chuck it and go to the Yeomanry.[11]

Lloyd's part in the operations was brought to a temporary halt at 10.30 p.m. on 20 March by the arrival of a telegram, 'telling me the news of Sam's death from small-pox'.[12] It was only four days earlier that they had dined together – and now he was dead.

For Lloyd it was a sickening blow. His friendship with Sam had been the centre of his life from his Eton days until his marriage, indeed not even the latter had put an end to their friendship and, as Sam had written to him in September 1911, 'It seems as though in some miraculous way your friendship were reflected in her and doubled and I suddenly find myself with two best friends and yet one friendship.'[13] Lloyd had tried to describe something of what that friendship meant in a letter to Blanche on 5 September that same year:

> You see, we have lived and done everything together since we were quite children, and even when we were both abroad kept extraordinarily in touch so that when we came back we just started up together just as if we had never been separated – I just tell you this because it may make you understand how big is the feeling that has come into one's life that can make one break into that sort of friendship. Men rarely, I think, have very great friends, their lives are too busy and various, but when they do they are just the deepest friendship possible – a friendship which only the love of a woman that comes once in a man's lifetime can supersede.

He could indeed have said with King David: 'very pleasant hast thou been unto me: thy love to me was wonderful, passing the love of women'. With Sam's passing went a great part of his past.

Lloyd went straight to Ismailia to oversee Sam's funeral:

> We took him in an ammunition carriage through the camp and I walked by Sam through the little town to the cemetery. He is buried on the edge of the cemetery close to the desert.[14]

He paid a local man to tend the grave. Visiting it nearly a year later he was glad to see that it 'was the only grave . . . that has any look of care or love bestowed on it':

> I liked as I looked at it just to feel that it was not being left lonely, but I could not feel that the place contained Sam at all, so alive is he to me somewhere.

Blanche came out from England as soon as she could and shared with him his grief.

It was the end of an important chapter of his life.

# 7

# GALLIPOLI

The Allied landings at Gallipoli in late April 1915 finally gave Lloyd the chance to spend a prolonged period under fire. He set out from Lemnos on 25 April and landed at Kaba Tempe with the ANZACS, right in the thickest of the fighting: 'for three days', he told Blanche, 'the battle never let up at all, the din incessant – no words can describe'. Thenceforth and until September his time was divided between serving on Birdwood's staff with the ANZACS, where his heart told him to be, and his work as intelligence officer at GHQ Cairo, which was where his head said he was needed most.

For her part Blanche thrilled at the exploits of the ANZACS, but could not hide her fears for her husband who, in 'the midst of that grim and desperate fighting', was holding his 'life in [his] hand pretty nearly the whole time'. She always tried to spare him the anguish which she felt, not wanting to add to his burdens; as 'your wife and David's mother' she thought it was her task to bear the trial without flinching. She had her relief work in Battersea and 'Mr D' to keep her busy, but ever her mind wandered towards George. Her nerve-storms, which she hid from him, were often severe, but she kept going, borne up always by the thought that she must do her duty and be worthy of him and of Sam. Nor was she totally without support, for his letters were a constant staff, as she told him on 4 May:

> My stars were quite hidden – and now you have shown them to me again and given me a fresh supply of faith and courage to carry me along. Oh my dear, how can I thank God ever for giving you to me with all the wonderful happiness and peace that the very thought of you brings. I really don't think I could bear life at all as it is at present without the constant thought of you, of all your wonderful love and the splendid work you are doing.

It was the same spirit, manifested in a million other places, which carried the Empire through the Valley of the Shadow of Death. Lloyd witnessed other demonstrations of it amongst the 'gallant Tommies' at the front who went laughing to their deaths. He had always told Blanche that '*le peuple est si bon*', and what he now saw on the beaches of Gallipoli confirmed him in this belief. Not that he had any illusions about the soldiers; they were

> just the same men who have all the irritating domestic qualities of the British working man – who strike unceasingly – who seem hopeless to deal with and dead to patriotism – but in them is some island stuff, some peculiar inbred qualities of self-reliance and buoyancy, which it would seem is impossible to bring into being except just now and then in a great emergency.

The only thing which could defeat such a spirit was, he thought, the incompetence of the 'old gang' at the top.

Compton Mackenzie the novelist, who worked with Lloyd at GHQ, asked him at this time how he 'with his faith in the divine right of the British Empire . . . could excuse the stupidity of those in charge of its fortunes'; he received the reply: 'Ah, but they're not necessary. We must get rid of them. They're in the way! They're in the way!'[1] Lloyd had never liked the idea of forcing the Straits and would have preferred, like so many in Intelligence HQ Cairo, to have landed at Alexandretta which could, for a fraction of the cost in men and gold, have resulted in the Ottoman Empire being bisected. But as he complained to Blanche on 9 May: 'There was no plan: that I know for sure, for they had neither maps ready nor plans nor any vestige of intelligence prepared, we had to do it all in a hurry from Cairo.' He was not convinced by the story that Churchill had 'jumped' the Cabinet into undertaking the operation in the first place – and even if it was so, what a comment that was on the Cabinet. Lloyd had warned that the Turks were no push-over and had been ignored; now, when he reported that they were reinforcing the Peninsula in depth, the red-tape wallahs in Whitehall merely said he must be wrong. To top it all there was the spectacle of Asquith telling everyone that there was no shortage of ammunition, when every soldier could tell him different.

Reports from London did nothing to cheer Lloyd up. Leo Amery, who had visited the Peninsula in the summer, did his best to push Lloyd's views when he got home, but to no avail:

> They were interested, mildly concerned, but in the end the answer always was: 'We have given our General all the troops he asked for and more, we can't interfere in his strategy, and we must wait and see what happens.'

The problem was that there 'wasn't and is not now any real idea of what they are after with this Dardanelles business'. The lack of organization was woeful: Kitchener was a one-man band with no strategic gift; and the Prime Minister, 'Squiff, the arch-enemy of England', drifted along 'drowsily', waking up occasionally only 'to prevent the Cabinet either coming to a decision or dissolving in a tumult'. Amery thought that the latter was the 'only solution. We must have another Government, different not only in detail but in its whole spirit and system', and he encouraged Lloyd to come back for the session: 'We members who have seen something of the show with our own eyes can, I believe, be of use at home more than anywhere else.'

The entry of the Conservatives into a coalition with 'Squiff and co.' hardly seemed to help matters when Austen Chamberlain could write: 'So far we are working well together here and no personal difficulties have interfered in our co-operation. I hope that we shall justify our existence.'

Lloyd complained to Blanche that:

> When I look round the one thing that hits one in the face is the very small number of men who are efficient. What is the cause of it? Is it the system of education, is it something in the character we are breeding?[2]

It was frustrating to find that the 'regular' soldiers would not act on his advice because they distrusted him as a 'politician'; but then, as one of his colleagues in Military Intelligence (another 'civilian') put it, 'we think the staff above the rank of captain are shits'.[3] That officer, who also complained of being 'so BORED', was soon to liven things up for both himself and for Lloyd – his name was T. E. Lawrence.

Lloyd's insistence on 'efficiency' could, as Mackenzie recorded, be a little wearing to those lacking his ascetic devotion to duty. His immediate superior, Colonel Ward, found him particularly tiring:

> The sight of Colonel Ward sitting hunched and sullen at his desk under the flow of his rhetoric fanned the glowing embers of his missionary ardour to a fierce flame. I have often thought that on such occasions his own chief must have presented himself to Lloyd as a refractory native chief who was standing in the way of imperial development.
> 'I wish you'd go away, Lloyd, and let me get on with what I'm doing,' Colonel Ward would mutter sulkily.
> 'Then no action is to be taken?' Lloyd would rasp out, his voice acquiring a kind of harshness and a higher pitch, and even becoming slightly nasal in his indignation at such supine obstructiveness.[4]

Tact was not his strong point.

Ever since May Lloyd had been pressing his superiors to ask the Government to take effective measures to weaken the economy of the

Ottoman Empire by disrupting the transport of coal from Zungulduk in the north-eastern Bosphorus as it went through the Black Sea. This was done in a small way in June and was quite effective, but lack of co-ordination between the Russians and the British soon resulted in the abandonment of the enterprise. Irritated by Ward's refusal to heed his information that coal supplies were again moving freely, Lloyd wrote to Austen Chamberlain and others. The pressure paid off. Sir Ian Hamilton transmitted a long report on the question written by Lloyd to the War Office on 29 September, including the recommendation that 'an officer should be sent to Sebastopol to confer with the Russian authorities there' about improving communications between the two allies. To no one's surprise Lloyd found himself selected for the job.[5]

On 29 September he was ordered to go to Russia and impress upon the Russian Government 'the great importance' of the matter and its bearing on the Gallipoli campaign. The most welcome aspect of the mission was that before going to Petrograd he had first to travel to London to receive fuller instructions from the War Office. He left the Dardanelles on 1 October and, travelling by way of Naples and Paris, reached home on 9 October. After hasty briefings at Horse Guards Parade, he took ship for Archangel on 11 October.

Although Lloyd's visit to London was so short, it did at least allow him to see young David for the first time in more than a year. Every one of Blanche's letters had reassured him that 'dear Mr D certainly doesn't forget you', but it was nice to see for himself. Neither then, nor later, was Lloyd anything of the heavy father and he loved the descriptions of domestic life provided by Blanche, particularly those which showed that David had a mind of his own. In June 1915 she had regaled him with the tale of how she had tried to wean David away from sleeping with his nanny. He had not been at all pleased with the news that, henceforth, he was to sleep with Mummy and had rejected the proposal with all the force that a two-and-a-half-year-old boy could muster. Blanche had pretended to go along with his wishes but as soon as he was asleep nanny left the room and she moved in. But at one o'clock in the morning David woke and

> set to work to howl steadily for Nanny. His will is the strongest thing I've ever known in relation to so small a body, he wasn't frightened or unhappy, but just outraged, furious, and determined to win.

And he did win – that night.

He eventually settled with Blanche and she was able to report that he talked 'incessantly of you', quoting one charming incident as an example. Waking up rather early one morning, David was told to lie still and wait until Mummy was ready to rise, but instead of going to sleep he 'lay talking to himself quite happily – and presently I heard him say: "Daddy *would* say 'what a good boy David is', wouldn't he?" '. Evidently father had no need to fear that he would be forgotten. But she 'took care to keep from him any bad news and, when David was taken ill in early July and the specialists were unable to diagnose what was wrong, she did not tell Lloyd until everything was better – even though it was hard at moments like the time when David clutched her hand and said, 'in a little husky voice, "Don't go Mummy. I want you stay with me Mummy and take care of David."'

If it was nice to see David then it was even better to see Blanche again. Her letters had always tried to maintain a cheerful tone, even when things were not going well, but, insensitive though he could occasionally be, Lloyd was well aware that she found things difficult and that, as she once confessed:

> I feel sometimes the hopelessness of trying to tell you in a letter how I think of you and love you and long for you . . . I would give everything in the world to have your arms round me for five minutes and hear your belovèd voice.

Even if the mission to Russia gave him nothing else, it gave him a chance to do that. Lloyd was not a great romantic and sometimes seemed to take her for granted, but during the trials of the Great War their love sustained them and even so brief a reunion fitted them both to bear whatever problems lay ahead.

At the War Office Lloyd had been told that the only way to expedite his mission was by personal contact with the Tsar; this he soon found to be true. The Russian Minister of Marine, Admiral Gregorovich, confessed to ignorance of the whole question of Turkish coal and had no idea about how its transport was to be disrupted. On 27 October Lloyd travelled to Mogilev for an interview with Tsar Nicholas II. He was keen to help, telling him that: 'You may inform Lord Kitchener from me that I will follow the matter up personally and that everything possible shall be done.'

Lloyd was impressed by what he saw in Russia; he told Blanche on 27 October: 'It is all so tremendous in its possibilities, so gigantic in its follies and so splendid in its spirit that one is amazed at it.' He had no great hopes of their proving efficient, but the award of the order of St Anne at the Tsar's hand brought the mission to one sort of satisfactory end.

Lloyd arrived back in England in late November, when he was able to snatch a few more days at home while preparing a report on his mission for the War Office and awaiting an interview with the King on 27 November. Lloyd's mood was optimistic as he headed back to Cairo in early December: the mission had gone well; he would be returning, with any luck, to Birdwood's staff; and, best of all, the plans they had been making since August for Blanche to come out to Cairo and join him were reaching fruition and she was due to come out in late December; it is to be hoped that he enjoyed his period of optimism – it was the last one for a long time.

The first sign of the blows which Fate was about to deliver came in the form of a letter from General Callwell of the War Office; dated 15 December it informed Lloyd that because of the threat from German submarines and the possibility of a fresh campaign in the Middle East, ladies would not be allowed to proceed to Cairo: so much for Blanche's visit. Then he received a letter from Blanche, written at the end of December: 'I am sorry to say that my hope of a new David has not come off for the moment.' This murrain fate was compounded by a farcical rigmarole over his posting which aroused all the frustrations he had felt earlier over the way some regular soldiers discriminated against 'politicians'. He poured out the story in a long letter to Blanche on 8 January 1916:

> On arrival at GHQ Mudros everyone seemed very pleased to have me back and all went well except that I learnt indirectly that the CGS (Lynden Bell) had had a letter from General Callwell saying that I should be needed in Egypt as soon as the Dardanelles operations were over and that the CGS took exception [to this]. . . . All the same it appears that they sent a telegram to General Maxwell asking if he wanted me. The day after the telegram was sent I . . . was told that I was going to be sent as staff officer to General Byng commanding the 9th Corps.

This dismayed him because the Corps was doing nothing except sitting in Egypt. He told Bell that he would prefer to join his own regiment, the Warwickshire Yeomanry, but was informed he must obey orders. Resigning himself to his fate, he then discovered that Byng had found someone else and that Clayton had now agreed that he could rejoin his regiment.[6]

When he got there he found that Maxwell wanted him at Military Intelligence and had telegraphed the news to Bell, who had not waited for a reply. It was with relief that he joined Maxwell and was set to work rounding up those in Egypt who were trading with the enemy. A thorough survey soon revealed that German firms were trading in Egypt with impunity because the Government had never prohibited them from operating – this evidence of fresh inefficiency appalled Lloyd.[7] But, even as he was beginning to tackle this serious and important problem, the old prejudice against 'politicians', which had so soured things at Gallipoli, raised its head again. As he told Blanche on 8 January:

> A few days later I met the CGS who asked me what I was doing in Cairo. I replied, 'Serving under General Maxwell', he replied, 'I sent you to your regiment.' I said I went there and found orders from Maxwell (under whom my regiment was) to join his staff. I had no option or desire to do anything but obey. He seemed very annoyed at the unanswerability of this and said, 'Anyway, I shall tell Maxwell I want you to be sent to your regiment at once.' I said that any orders I received I should instantly obey . . . [but] Maxwell said . . . he needed me for special work. . . . The CGS was refused therefore and is very annoyed.

It was unfortunate in view of this that a few days later, when the reorganization of GHQ MEDFORCE was complete, Lloyd once more came under Bell's direct command. Despite the importance of the work he was doing, Bell ordered him to rejoin the Warwickshires, turning down a request from General Birdwood for Lloyd to join his staff. From Salhie where the Yeomanry were stationed he wrote to Blanche on 27 January (before Birdwood's request had been finally refused):

> There is a determination apparently that few yeomanry officers and no politicians should be on the staffs under Medforce control. As I combine both in an acute degree in their minds I imagine that I shall be kept here. . . . It is all a very odd way of treating war, but there it is.

And there he did remain. He told Blanche that:

> There is absolutely nothing to do and the monotony is extreme. There are only three officers in the regiment that were here when I left it, and almost all the men are changed. Indeed, since Suvla one may call it a new regiment. So I feel rather a fish out of water. In addition to this they have without me a great superfluity of officers and they are rather embarrassed by my return.

Blanche's prediction that 'you may find time hanging rather heavy on your hands in the Regiment' was quite correct. But there was something to be said for a spell of regimental soldiering. The Gallipoli campaign had been an arduous one for Lloyd and he had twice succumbed to attacks of dysentery and had felt 'rather seedy' for some time; now he had a respite.

> I have a small tent to myself here and have bought some straw matting for a few piastres in the bazaar so that I am very comfortable, almost too much so I feel. Although my colleagues are very dull they are nicer fellows than Medforce. They have a gramophone which is rather a bore, and they sit round it like hypnotised fox-terriers every evening for hours together while I sit in my tent and read or write.

He found an outlet for his energies in learning Italian and devising ways to keep the troops amused. The latter found camp rather dull with nothing to do, so Lloyd would take some of them out hacking. He described one such expedition thus:

> We rode out through the palm groves to a bazaar on the edge of the desert near a mud village. They jumped everything *en route* until the obstacle (usually a mud wall) had been reduced to the level of the desert, fell into ditches, and on arrival at the bazaar, chaffed the local faquirs and ate halva and oranges until any but a Yeoman would have been sick. I told them who the different peoples were, showed them how to differentiate between Bedawin and non-nomad Arabs, and they were interested like children; altogether it was an afternoon that in a simple way was quite repaying.

He reassured Blanche on 13 February that he was

> quite happy with the regiment. It is a great rest cure and the healthy life is doing me no end of good, and the energy I shall be able to store up will enable me to do more again directly the opportunity arises.

# 8

# AMBITION AND FRUSTRATION

Despite what he said to Blanche, Lloyd chafed at his enforced idleness; others too felt that he was literally wasting his talents on the desert air. Blanche started the campaign to persuade him to return in early February by suggesting that he should come home to chivvy the Government. A few days later Puss Gaskell wrote in like vein:

> You ought to be in England! . . . the greatest need now is for some [of the younger men] . . . to come and fight here in England against the spirit of incompetence (if not worse) which haunts the Government. You have strength, knowledge, and that personal magnetism which gives the power of leadership.[1]

Leo Amery put the case even more strongly in a letter on 26 February saying that he was 'not sure one ought not to chuck the soldiering altogether'. The situation in the country was, he thought, 'very curious':

> Not only the country, but even the House of Commons are very sick of the Government – and old Squiff in particular. But they are still obsessed, especially in the House of Commons, by two pre-war notions: one, that nobody but a mandarin can govern; and second, that a change of Government must mean a replacement of the whole outfit from PM down to junior Whips by another lot. So they look round and say 'who is there?' 'Milner – impractical' i.e. never thoroughly interested in the old party game. 'Carson – impractical' i.e. more interested in winning the war than in Cabinet handling. 'There is no one else' – i.e. no front benchers, and *ex hypothesi* no one now in the 'Government' would join the 'Opposition'. What we have got to make them grasp is that we don't want another lot of twenty-three instead of the present lot, but that we want in place of Squiff, AJB, McKenna, Bonar and whoever else from the vaguely-defined inner circle of power, a really effective Cabinet of four or five – let us say Milner, Carson, Ll. G. and Austen – who see eye

to eye and will be responsible (Heaven alone can decide which of them would be the actual PM) for the war.

But to get to that blessed state required first 'a break-up of the present crowd', which was where Amery, Lloyd and Co. came in:

> Our materials are (a) the Unionist Party – a flabby, jelly-like material containing a number of nodules of solider substance. Given time and effort fully three-quarters of these could be stiffened into a solid fighting crowd; (b) the Liberals – a flabbier jelly of which about a quarter could eventually be stiffened up; (c) Labour and Irish – delicate and mildly explosive substances requiring firm but capable handling.

Amery urged that there was, at home, 'real room for your abilities'. If, by the end of the letter, Lloyd suspected that this sudden rush of advice was not coincidental, he was right; Amery concluded his exhortations by saying that he had asked Blanche to repeat them.[2] The problem was that this advice promised to advance Lloyd's career and so he hesitated whether to accept it or no; the horror of seeming to be a place-seeker ran deep.

But it proved impossible to ignore politics. In late February 1916 Lloyd's designated successor at West Staffordshire, Philip Ashworth, wrote to ask if he would consider resigning the seat as he was tired of waiting;[3] this would have suited him well enough, but the sitting MP at Shrewsbury, Butler Lloyd, showed no sign of vacating *his* seat for George. Corresponding with the Mayor of Shrewsbury about the matter, Lloyd learned that 'the Coalition Government is in bad odour throughout the whole country'.[4] His own pre-war prejudices against 'politicians' had been modified by what he had experienced at the hands of regular soldiers; he wrote to Blanche on 6 February about Leo Maxse:

> I confess to becoming annoyed with him about his facile abuse of all politicians and all except soldiers. This is a very easy line of criticism and it is popular today – it is more than that, it is three-quarters of the truth. But he is very wrong if he thinks that he can safely leave the settlement of all post-war problems to soldiers. My experience of both tells me that soldiers are, I fear, no more honest or wide-minded than the average politician – and their knowledge of foreign affairs is pitiable.

He was, however, by no means convinced that he wanted to come home and join in the politicking. He told Blanche on 20 February:

> I am more and more sure as time goes on that I want to be on administrative as against parliamentary work. This is rather a good moment to adjudge one's real feelings on the question, because when one is in the middle of the Parliamentary surge one may always feel the sea to

be rougher than it really is. Here, from the dry shore of boredom, one can measure things better. I still am sure that I am best at running people and things than in arguing and plotting in the House.

There can be no doubt that he was correct in his self-analysis. He had, he told her, thought of writing to Chamberlain asking if he could 'fit me into some post before the war is ended':

> If he did this it would give me a good start, because one would be out of all the struggles of new parties and groups which must take place after the war, and one could later on, when they had settled down, see which one to join.

His main problem was to know whether Austen and company would think 'the demand quite absurd' or 'natural and suitable':

> I am sure this is a good moment to break away into a small Governorship of some kind if it could be done and one is just about the right age to begin. Early enough to stand the racket of being out of a job a little later on for four or five years while a hostile Govt were in power and yet able and eligible to go on again with higher posts before one were too old.

His future career was already taking firm shape in his mind. Blanche played a vital role in helping him decide, acting as his (discreet) sounding-board in London and passing on her own views on the question. After some epistolary explorations of the theme, it was decided that he would try to look for an opening in imperial administration.

For the moment, however, he was stuck with the boredom of the routine of 'a second in command of a squadron of cavalry';[5] but the siren voices urging him to London sounded louder. Aubrey Herbert, who arrived in Cairo in late March on Admiral Wemyss's staff, wrote on 22 March that:

> Your saying you are very happy with your yeomanry isn't the point. The point is to get you where you are most useful. It seems to me pretty clear that the place indicated is Mesopotamia.[6]

But it was difficult to see how to get Lloyd there. Herbert said that T. E. Lawrence, who was leaving Cairo for Arabia, hoped to have a word with Percy Cox, the British agent at Basra whom Lloyd had met on his tour of the region in 1907; Herbert himself, in his usual flamboyant way, stirred things up in a way Lloyd never could:

> HASTE. Yesterday I went to the H[igh] C[ommissioner] and said you had been Special Commissioner in the P[ersian] G[ulf] on which you had written the only referential standard work. It was a bloody mis-application of material to make you look at fetlocks. He agreed and said

that you would be properly employed within ten days. I hope it is the PG and also that I did right.[7]

Whether it was this unconventional approach, or Lawrence's intervention with Cox, Lloyd found himself charged, at the start of April, with a mission to Basra. But the result of this was that he missed returning to France with the regiment: as he complained to his immediate superior, Colonel Chamberlayne, on 7 April: 'I am still feeling pretty miserable at having missed that show. I don't seem to be able to strike any luck in this war any way, and I hate going off to Basra more than ever.'[8]

T. E. Lawrence described Basra at this time thus:

Our headquarters are on the bank, and there are usually dozens of row-boats and launches along the shore . . . no wharfs, no piers, no signs of a port, no roads; no one would ever dream that we had been in occupation of the place for months and months.[9]

That Lloyd should end up there was hardly surprising, as most of his old friends and colleagues had also fetched up at Basra.

There was Sir Percy Cox himself, supervising the British occupation of Basra and the impending revolt in the Hedjaz; T. E. Lawrence, whose fame was to be made in such a strange way by that revolt, but who was at that time helping Aubrey Herbert to try to bribe the Turks into letting General Townshend and his men leave Kut; and finally, Gertrude Bell, who wrote to her father on 14 May:

George Lloyd has just come out to work with Sir Percy. It will make a great difference to me to have him. I hope he will find time to ride with me sometimes in the morning, when we can talk things over and help each other.[10]

She reported back to Blanche that he was 'looking really well' and 'younger than ever', contriving 'to look smart and spruce, in some mysterious fashion of his own, when everyone else was melted and dishevelled'. This 'faculty . . . for extreme personal neatness in circumstances which cause almost everyone to slouch' conjured him up better than almost anything else for Blanche and she could

so picture you going into some Indian store or dago shop of strange appearance, and demanding hair-wash, and coming away triumphant with an immense bottle of peculiarly vicious arsenic-green brilliantine, with which to keep your hair to the required standard of polished smoothness . . . it is all so *you* and so very dear! A combination of an immense capacity for work and adventure with a certain amount of dandyism is to me fascinating; it was what made the Scarlet Pimpernel so attractive, that he always wore the most priceless lace ruffles, and had his nails manicured, except on the occasions when circumstances forced him to be disguised as a coal-heaver.

Lloyd had not looked forward to renewing his acquaintance with the heat of Basra; at 95°F without much shade, even he felt a little 'limp'. Travelling via Bombay (whence he was to return sooner than he imagined), he arrived at Basra in early May, only to find that Lawrence, with whom he was supposed to be working, was no longer there.

Lloyd's main task was to bring up to date his own report of 1907 on trade in the Gulf; in a letter which he wrote to Sir Valentine Chirol on 28 June 1916 on the conclusion of his labours, he summed it up as

> a most depressing task. I go so far as to say that if it had not been for the respite from German competition which the war has given us, the position had gone beyond recall. The merchants who nine years ago were full of an unjustified but easy confidence as to the impregnability of their position in Persian, Turkish and Gulf markets are now the first to admit that they were, at the beginning of the war, a beaten body.

Even now the merchants could do nothing but carp about how 'unfair' it was of the 'Huns' to subsidize their trade to the region, even though so many of them had proved only too willing 'to go in with the Germans for the sake of being able to continue a little longer' – thus participating in 'their own funeral'.[11] Lloyd's report made sorry reading, especially when read in conjunction with his earlier one; all the things he had prophesied there had come to pass.[12] He had little hope that the British traders would band together or that they would show sufficient energy to try to retrieve the position.

Having completed this task the question of what to do next arose. Lloyd watched with interest the initial stages of the revolt in the Hedjaz of the Sherif of Mecca backed by the British, but there seemed no chance of his staying there to watch it develop. Blanche continued to urge him to return home and take up some political or administrative position and he confessed to Amery: 'I keep on feeling that one could be of far more use at home, and wish I could come and help you and all that you are doing.'[13]

But against the lure of London was set the magnet of the East. Lloyd's joy at being back there transmitted itself even on paper and even when he was merely describing his daily routine:

> Now that it is so much hotter [he wrote to Blanche on 22 June] I no longer take exercise in the morning, but begin work in the office about 6.30 a.m. and work till 8.30 and then breakfast. After that pretty busy till three when one has a meal which cannot be described as lunch or tea, but

consists generally of rivers of lime juice and toast and butter. After that, work again until 5.30 and then I go out for a ride, always by myself. I ride out through the date gardens on a very nice mare . . . and by then Arabs are coming back from work and I sometimes talk to them as I ride to practise my Arabic and get used to the patois talked here. Then one gets out into the desert just about when the sun is setting, when one gets the double pleasure of the relief from the sun and the unwearying beauty of the slanting lights and the thousand colours. I think that some forebear of mine must have been a gipsy, for my delight in wide spaces and in Nature's daily rehearsal of sunrise and sunset is unquenchable and I never get used to it.

Alone, in the vast clean emptiness of the desert as the sun set, his restless soul found peace.

But away from that great solitude lurked the fears and furies of ambition. One reason for wanting to get home, and it was not one which he ever admitted to anyone save Blanche, was the fear that he was being left behind in the struggle for political preferment. Service in the Dardanelles and the Middle East was all very well, but it took him away from London and the notice of those who decided on the apportionment of offices; contemporaries like Sir Mark Sykes, who remained in London working for the War Office and the Foreign Office, seemed to be overtaking him. There was between Lloyd and Sykes the unspoken but clear enmity of two very different kinds of men pursuing the same goal.

Sykes, a wealthy baronet with any amount of charm and a self-confidence which some called arrogance, had established for himself a name as an expert on the East and had found a niche in those spheres where military and diplomatic problems overlapped. He had little liking for the seemingly colder and more reserved Lloyd. In his correspondence with Aubrey Herbert where he was (of course) 'Caesar' and Aubrey 'Pompey', Lloyd was 'Crassus', the third and least regarded of the triumvirs. Lloyd, for his part, found Sykes slovenly, self-serving and *louche*; the sort of man who, after being received by Queen Alexandra when he returned from a mission to Russia, put an announcement to that effect in *The Times*. He was irritated to find at Basra that:

> The whole situation here has been prejudiced as far as this office is concerned by Mark Sykes's attitude here. His bitter and outspoken anti-Indian attitude was much resented and this was thought to be the point of view which we held in Egypt.[14]

And he was to approve neither the fact nor the contents of Sykes's celebrated agreement with Georges Picot dealing with the post-war settlement in the Near East.

Blanche, who was increasingly acting not only as confidante and adviser, but also as George's eyes and ears in London, counselled him wisely, writing on 26 July:

> Men like you are so scarce: if one goes through all the younger members with as open a mind as you like, it is impossible to pick out half a dozen who have made any real mark of any kind . . . it seems to me that there is no need to regard even Mark Sykes, who is a competitor in your particular line, in a spirit of rivalry, as far as practical things are concerned. Even if his abilities are not over-rated (as I always suspect they are) . . . there is room to spare for him as well as you.

It was good advice – but it did not quite soothe his anxieties.

In late August 1917, having finally completed his work at Basra, he was able, for the first time in two years, to return to England on leave. Once in London in early September he looked round for openings in Whitehall. At dinner with Austen Chamberlain on 9 September he asked bluntly what his political position was. Perhaps Chamberlain, like Amery on another occasion, was 'amused by the naiveté of his interest in himself', for his reply was a perspicacious one which could be applied to Lloyd's whole political career. Drawing an analogy with the selection of pictures at the Royal Academy, he said:

> He should not place him among the pictures which have *got* to be hung, but in class B – which consists of two sections – those who ought to be and will be hung if room can be found for them – and those who will eventually get hung if they persevere, but about whom there is no particular hurry. He put G[eorge] in the first of these sections.[15]

Ever since the formation of the Coalition in May 1915 Lloyd had kept Chamberlain informed of events in the Middle East, and some extracts from his letters had been circulated in the Cabinet. He learned now from Austen that his report on trade conditions in the Gulf was also to be printed for the Cabinet; this seemed a good omen for the future.[16]

Another figure with whom he discussed his future was, like Chamberlain, to play a malign part in his career a decade later: this was Sir William Tyrrell of the Foreign Office. Lloyd had known him for years. Tyrrell had, as Blanche recorded, 'the reputation of being an inveterate and merciless intriguer'; but she was sure that he 'would not deliberately go out of his way to do George a bad turn'. Hindsight invests this comment, as it does so many other things, with an almost unbearable irony. But on this occasion the advice was harmless. Lloyd's eye had alighted on the post of Financial Adviser to the High Commissioner in Egypt and Tyrrell said there would be no harm in sounding out Chamberlain about the possibilities of such an appointment. Even at this early date Blanche noted of Tyrrell that:

His is a curious and interesting personality – something that repels combined with something that attracts; astonishingly able, vitriolic in his criticisms, pathetic in the great handicap which spoils his career and his life.[17]

The handicap was his addiction to alcohol which had already resulted in a period of prolonged 'leave' from the Foreign Office and a warning about his future conduct; but as the Lloyds were to discover a decade later, his habits did not change.

From General Birdwood, now in France, came a request for Lloyd to join his staff, but once again, to everyone's frustration, Lynden Bell said he 'could not be spared'. Writing sadly to Birdwood, Lloyd commented that if, when he returned to Cairo, he found himself stuck once more with the regiment, 'I shall no longer feel tied by any wish to play the game by him and I shall take whatever steps appear convenient to serve outside his command.'[18] Before leaving Egypt there had been a *rapprochement* with Bell and Lloyd hoped that this fresh setback did not portend its dissolution. He even went so far as to write to Bell to assure him that he had not prompted Birdwood's request.[19]

It was with mixed feelings that Lloyd left for Egypt on 18 October. Arrival in Cairo confirmed his worst fears: there was no special job for him, and Bell, whilst expressing no animus, could only offer him work with Clayton at Military Intelligence. Lloyd wrote to his sister Milly on 17 November:

Shakespeare was never less truthful than when he remarked that 'journeys end in lovers' meetings'; on the contrary, journeys end in hot weather, sandflies and disordered livers.[20]

But even as he wrote this, he was on the move again.

# 9

# LAWRENCE AND THE ARAB BUREAU

Lloyd was, in fact, on his way to Mecca: his mission was to meet with Sherif Hussein and discuss the progress of what has become known as 'the revolt in the desert'. In doing so he was following the same road as his former colleague at Cairo, T. E. Lawrence. Lawrence's exploits in the desert were to gain him lasting fame as 'Lawrence of Arabia', but when Lloyd set off for Mecca, accompanied by Colonel Brémond of the French army and an Italian, Colonel Barnabi, these things lay hidden in the future.

The origins of the revolt lay back in the tangled web of correspondence between the British High Commissioner in Egypt, Sir Henry McMahon and Sherif Hussein in 1914 and 1915. Professor Elie Kedourie, whose book on the subject, aptly titled *In the Anglo–Arab Labyrinth*,[1] dispels the many myths which have grown up around it, has pointed out that McMahon's letters, which the Arabs later claimed promised them an independent state, were so vague and in such poor Arabic that they could mean almost anything anyone wanted them to mean. One of Lloyd's new-found friends in Cairo, Ronald Storrs, the Oriental Secretary at the Residency, was, in addition to being a great Arabophile, not quite the Arabist he thought himself, and the combination of his romantic dreaming and poor Arabic were to prove fatal, especially when Lawrence's self-dramatizing histrionics were added to the brew.[2]

Sherif Hussein, who had kept up the correspondence hoping to get arms and promises of support from the British, was finally driven to take up the standard of revolt in mid 1916 when it seemed that the Turks were about to take reprisals against him for his neutrality. With help from the Royal Navy and the fact that Ottoman forces were too widely dispersed, the Sherifian forces captured the ports of Yambo and Rabegh in July and threw the Turks out of Mecca. But the future of the revolt was by no means certain. As Lloyd told Puss Gaskell in mid December 1916 after talking with the Sherif:

> From a Moslem point of view it is, of course, very interesting, but it is a very complex and difficult job. While we are supporting the revolt, we can do very little to interfere with the course of the campaign, which owing to Arab military incompetence is in a constant state of jeopardy. Almost laughably so, for the whole situation is Gilbertian, were it not that rather important issues are involved! It is one of those side-shows, which may so be termed so long as things go well, but once things go ill, may have effects out of all proportion to the size of the campaign.[3]

Much controversy has surrounded Lawrence's part in these events; Lloyd, who had known him since 1914 and who was an expert on the region, was in a good position to see for himself what his old colleague had been doing.

Lloyd shared Lawrence's partiality for the Arabs and his hostility towards the French. The Sirdar (Commander-in-Chief of the Egyptian Army), Sir Reginald Wingate, told him that the French, who had secured their interests in Syria and the Lebanon by the secret Sykes–Picot agreement, were chary of making the Sherif King of the Arabs;[4] they were also, without telling their allies, trying to get the Francophile Ottoman Bank established at Jeddah. Lloyd, with his knowledge of banking, advised the Sirdar not to allow this – advice which he took.[5] Wingate asked him to go to Jeddah and Rabegh and report on his impressions of the situation there.[6]

Lloyd arrived at Jeddah on 22 November and soon found fresh evidence that Brémond, the French attaché, was 'working rather more on a line of his own than in great concert with our general aims'.[7] He took the opportunity to 'soften down the rather prickly relations between Wilson and Lawrence'.[8] But the great question to be decided was what sort of help the British should give the Sherif. Brémond wanted them to press Hussein to ask for the despatch of British troops to the region, but Lloyd did not agree as he told General Bell in a letter from Yambo on 2 December:

> Anyone who advises sending white troops to Rabegh or any other spot fails, in my judgement, to appreciate the nature of the movement, for such a step would go far to break down the personal force of the tribal movement. Those tribes who trust us would think it unnecessary to go on fighting, so great do they believe the power of England to be, and those who distrusted us would probably throw in their hand, believing that they were only assisting in putting their country under the ultimate yoke of the British.[9]

Lloyd wanted the British presence there to 'be as small as possible' – a few trained Arabists at most.

On 10 December Lloyd and Colonel Wilson went to Mecca to discuss the matter with the Sherif himself. According to Storrs the 'dominating characteristic of the Grand Sharif is a captivating sincerity of utterance, enhanced by a benignant and noble simplicity of demeanour'.[10] Lloyd concurred. A meeting between the two British soldiers, Brémond and the Sherif on 11 December seemed to produce a result favourable to the Frenchman, but by the following day he had decided that he could not be seen to be dependent upon Christian troops to hold Islam's holiest places.[11] But Brémond almost prevailed by playing on Wingate's fears that, without Allied troops, the Turks would crush the revolt; only a hurried visit from Lloyd dissuaded Wingate from this view.[12] London approved this line and no commitment of British troops was made; had this not been so then there would have been no role for Lawrence 'of Arabia'.

The visit to the Sherif had been interesting and not without its amusing side. Lloyd told Puss Gaskell on 18 December that:

> The Grand Shereef of Mecca paid a visit to us the other day – unique and picturesque – he said his midday prayer in my room, a thing which I may safely claim has never previously occurred to any other Christian![13]

He told Austen Chamberlain that they were 'very lucky to be dealing with a man who has such unusual qualities of head and heart'.[14] Like Lawrence and others in the Arab Bureau, he saw that they were playing for 'great stakes':

> Our relations with the Shereef are intimate and cordial, and we have laid the basis of a deep friendship between him and Great Britain. Should things go well, his influence in the Moslem world will be immense and an intimacy with him would give us an assistance in dealing with Moslem affairs that we have not had before.

So cut off from civilization was Lloyd that he only heard 'the welcome news of the fall of the Cabinet at home'[15] when he was on his way back to Cairo. Birdwood wrote to him from France saying that he expected 'to hear that you've been recalled to England to take over as Under-Secretary at the Foreign Office'.[16] Lloyd had expected no such thing, but the fall of the detested Liberal Government and the rise of Lloyd George supported by a Conservative-dominated coalition could not but improve his prospects of employment.

Leo Amery, who became one of the military secretaries to the expanded War Council, urged Blanche to encourage Lloyd to come back to London and try to get a similar post, but whilst he was tempted, Lloyd was not sure he wanted to leave what had become a very interesting job.[17] He was, by early 1917, feeling somewhat better about the course of his war: the Hedjaz revolt was the sort of adventure which he loved; he had just been awarded the DSO for his work in *WHAT WORK* Mesopotamia; and, at the beginning of February, he found himself sent back to England on a special mission to brief the War Office and the Foreign Office about the situation in the Hedjaz. He arrived in London in late February and spent several relatively relaxed weeks discussing the revolt with the authorities there.[18] When he left London on 12 May it was in company with Mark Sykes and Georges Picot on a 'semi-political, semi-military mission to deal with questions arising among the Arab population during our coming campaign in Palestine'.[19]

The journey back to Cairo was made unduly hazardous by the French navy, who placed their distinguished passengers on a slow boat, carrying cordite, which developed engine trouble; it was a wonder the ship was not torpedoed.

Back in Cairo Lloyd was plunged into planning for the future of the Middle East after the collapse of the Ottoman Empire (which was now taken for granted). He worked on plans for helping the successor states[20] and prepared papers on the Sykes–Picot agreement. Lloyd wanted to establish a British sphere of influence in the Red Sea and warned that he did not

> consider that French recognition of our 'predominant commercial and financial position in the Hedjaz' is sufficient to safeguard the position which we are bound to secure in that area. . . . Should we permit the influence of any other foreign power in the . . . area, we shall risk creating a Baghdad Railway question in the Red Sea, which, gradually developing, may impair our relations with France and Italy in the future.

At last it seemed as if some of Lloyd's dreams were coming true. Not only was Britain establishing a Middle Eastern Empire for herself, but imperial unity, the cause for which he had always fought, seemed to be coming nearer. When he had been in London he had urged Lloyd George to adopt a policy of Imperial Preference, which the Government now seemed to be doing; and more than these mechanical things, when he looked around him he saw

> Wellingtons and Worcesters, Sydney or Brisbane and Scotsman all talking and fighting, swearing and smiling together in this amazing old desert – 'I have gathered my peoples from the East and the West . . . and they shall be one people.'

He was not anxious to leave such scenes for Whitehall.

Then there was the fact that Lloyd enjoyed being back in the desert, even if it meant the 'same old jumble of camels, horses and men and guns, the same old food and the same old impenetrable cloud of dust'; it allowed him to be 'in the heat and the happenings again and to live in the open'. 'The older I get', he told Puss Gaskell on 6 May, 'the more do towns stifle me and the open sky gives me peace and content.'[21] The award of the Cross of the Order of India (CIE) in June was the seal to this feeling of well-being.

But, as ever, ambition was the serpent in this Eden. Arrayed against the wanderlust and the desire to travel 'God's good earth' with the wind blowing on his face, were the forces of worldliness. Twinned with his own desire to 'get on' was the patriotic instinct that

> there is only one utterly intolerable thing to me any time and especially intolerable in this war, and that is not to be full of work – not to be able to fill the unforgiving minute with sixty seconds worth of distance run. If I may not do it here I *must* find somewhere where I can.[22]

By the time he penned those words in early September, he was feeling increasingly superfluous in Cairo.

As early as February Blanche had been urging him to follow Amery's advice and come home to wait for a job in the War Cabinet Office, but Lloyd insisted that he would only come if there was a job waiting for him.[23] When he was in London in March Chamberlain had offered him a post as his Parliamentary Private Secretary, but had not been surprised when the job was refused:

> I cannot but feel that any promising young MP, and above all a man of the ability and experience of George Lloyd, would be throwing himself away by accepting such a position.[24]

In June 1917 Puss Gaskell and Blanche urged him 'strongly' to return; Chamberlain, who in September said that he could wait another month or two, was by October singing the same tune; the voices of Amery and Herbert joined in the song.[25] In September there arrived a letter from an old friend, Henry Page Croft, who had just formed a breakaway group calling itself the National Party, asking if Lloyd would join it,

> and become one of the leaders of the new Movement in the House of Commons. If it is not impertinent of an old friend to say so, I have always regarded you as one of the few men at Westminster who can really help to make the new England in the hard days that are to come, and I feel that if you can possibly see your course open, that your destiny is at Westminster.[26]

But Lloyd refused to be drawn. Such restraint was all the more creditable given the growing temptation to come home and intervene in politics which news from London prompted.

The 'spinelessness of the F[oreign] O[ffice]' over opposing French ambitions in the Hedjaz made his blood boil, as did a speech by Lord Robert Cecil in the House in May declaring that Britain's war aims were 'only peace and international amity'; writing to Puss Gaskell on 31 May he exploded:

> Was there no one in the House to challenge so infamous a retreat from Asquith's original and continued statement on that point? . . . Bob Cecil seems to have neither sanity nor imagination and the result is dead metal.[27]

The problem with the letters from Amery and company was that none of them contained the offer of a definite job; as he told Puss in late July:

> I don't know about coming home. I really don't. . . . I'm not following a 'whim' in staying here. It isn't my wanderlust as you think. I don't think you realise always that we too may get pretty war-weary sometimes. Dull company, monotony of work and to me worst of all lack of independence. But no one at home seems to want me very particularly. Milner, who before taking office used to profess that I was the one person he would need at his elbow when he took office, shows no anxiety – and with Bonar – the ineffable – I have no part or lot. Austen has resigned. It is certain that were I to come home I could in three or four months make myself useful somewhere, but is it right for us MPs to show the example of rushing home just at a time when we are recruiting once more to the ranks even those who have served their time and been passed out as unfit? Can't we do better things and show a better example by sticking it out and serving alongside the people we are supposed to lead, and of whom we shall have to be real leaders before long?

In a rare and revealing passage of self-examination he went on:

> There was a great friend of mine once who taught me all that was ever worth knowing in life – now buried not so far from here – and from him I learnt that you could only hope to lead men if you shared their worries and played the fitful game of life alongside them. In old campaign days of Tariff when we were trying to change the stubborn mentality of a people who had thought one way for eighty years, what success we had was solely due to getting right down among the people and I learnt more of England in the Tyneside slums and in such places than I ever thought possible or would have been possible from the ordinary platform.[28]

Page Croft's idea posed a dilemma, but he told Puss:

> You see, they lack brains. Their aim and honesty is fine but you must be able to state your case to the world in terms which will not only convince the public of your honesty but also of your capacity to give effect to your aims . . . if one joined them one could only do so if one could bring with

one a few people possessing brains as well as courage. Duncannon is *pour rire* – Page Croft a good fellow but a little too much of the platform hack to give dignity and weight to the movement. And yet it has very great possibilities which must not be disregarded.

For the moment he stayed out in Palestine:

> Here at any events virtue is its own reward for as far as the public are concerned no one has ever heard of the existence of this show. But we get a lot of prisoners and kill a lot of Turks and pull our little weight to the full I hope. And one can't hope to do anything more. One would have liked to do something outstanding in this war to show one was worth something but somehow I don't seem to have been able to have done it, which is a bore, but can't be helped.[29]

But there were many compensations. During July and August he found himself in charge of intelligence operations in the region and was able to go down to Akaba which Lawrence and the Arabs had just captured. He told Wingate on 17 August that:

> Lawrence . . . has done wonderfully good work and will some day be able to write a unique book. Generally the kind of man capable of these adventures lacks the pen and wit to record them adequately. Luckily Lawrence is specially gifted with both.[30]

Indeed he was. At Akaba Lloyd dined with Feisal and Zeid, the Sherif's sons, 'picturesque enough with all the slaves and the dim candle light on the floor of the mud hut. But I would just as soon dine at the Carlton myself.'[31]

The arrival of a new Commander-in-Chief, General Allenby, put an end to this fulfilling role and Lloyd's hopes that it would become permanent, and it was therefore with eagerness that he responded to Chamberlain's letter of 1 August when it reached him in mid September. He did not want to return immediately for reasons which will become apparent but, on hearing from Austen that a delay of a month or two would not matter, he finally resolved that he would quit the Middle East before the year's end.[32]

The reason why Lloyd did not want to go home at once lay in his plans for the immediate future which he outlined to General Clayton on 30 September. He had, he wrote, been puzzling over where he could be of most use and had decided that rather than go forward with a cavalry division,

> I could be still more useful in a personal way to Lawrence. He is overworked and he must be overstrained. If he is to remain in the field at his most responsible job I do think he must have the companionship and relief of some other white man congenial to him. I could never in any way

attempt to take the lead in that job. I am not even remotely qualified. But in his curious way he has rather an addiction to me and if he liked to have me with him to accompany him on his 'stunts' I believe my presence might help to keep him going over this show.[33]

Lloyd lacked the sense of self-dramatization and the urge to martyrdom which propelled Lawrence into his self-imposed mission, but he sympathized with his objectives and was attracted by the means he employed. There have been those who have written Lawrence off as a charlatan, but Lloyd, who was on the spot at the time, never took this view; he saw his old colleague as an adventurer out of Rider Haggard.

From Akaba he reported that:

Lawrence is quite fit but much oppressed by the risk and the magnitude of the job before him. He opened his heart to me last night and told me that he felt there was so much for him still to do in the world, places to dig, peoples to help, that it seemed horrible to have it all cut off as he feels it will be – for he feels that while he may do the job he sees little or no chance of getting away himself.

Lawrence, who spent so much of his life covering his traces and making a mystery out of himself, was also, on occasions, given to bursts of self-revelation, and Lloyd was glad to be the confidant of his fears. He thought him

a very remarkable fellow – not the least fearless like some who do brave things, but as he told me last night, each time he starts out on these stunts he simply hates it for two or three days before, until movement, action and the glory of scenery and nature catch hold of him and make him well again.[34]

Lawrence was setting off to destroy the main bridge on the railway line from Mecca which was bound to be heavily guarded – hence his fears. They set off from Akaba on 24 October in the company of a Royal Engineer officer, Captain Wood, 'a couple of slaves and one Syrian servant of Lawrence's'. The journey passed quickly and they had much to talk about:

The necessity of tying down the Arab movement to the military purpose, its original aim and objective, and to risk no breach of faith with the Arabs by raising hopes beyond it – the possibility of my being able to raise Kerah on my own if his northern venture succeeded – what was to be done vis-à-vis the French in certain northern contingencies.

Lawrence's navigating skills left much to be desired; searching for the railway line, he first led them within a few yards of a station where the alarm might easily have been raised, and then,

[we carried on] for some reason or other being convinced that if we marched faithfully with our eyes fixed on Orion we should find the railway again. An hour's pursuit of Orion shook Lawrence's faith and I insisted on a compass.

Lloyd's attempts to cut the telegraph wires were no more successful – he managed to shin up the pole but 'fell from the top'.

Despite these antics they reached El Jaffer (which was not where the map said it was) safely on the morning of 28 October. There they discussed the question of whether Lloyd should go on with them, but although he wanted to,

> Lawrence said definitely that he thought it was useless and that although he did not pretend he would not like me to come he felt that any additional individual who was not an expert at the actual demolition only added to his own risk. He would like me best to go home to England for he felt that there was a risk that all his work would be ruined politically in Whitehall and he thought I could save this; failing this he would like me to rejoin him either in the north or in Kerah as soon as the bridge job was over, but he wanted me to tell Clayton that he did not want anyone else with him. *AND WANTED TO SEE THE BACK OF LLOYD*

George left for Akaba the following afternoon.[35]

He made notes of Lawrence's plans if he succeeded in raising all the tribes he wanted:

> Situation resultant:- Sherif's flag flies along coast from Acre northwards: French protests? Our attitude? Feisal's attitude will be non negotiatory – 'What I have taken I keep.' – L. not working for H[is] M[ajesty's] G[overnment] but for Sherif. Had no instructions except to hamper communications.

According to this note Lawrence was encouraging Feisal (Hussein's second son and the leading Arab figure in the revolt) to ignore the Sykes–Picot agreement which was, at best, one 'between France and England for partition of a country in armed occupation of forces of Sherif of Mecca'.[36] Clearly Lawrence was going to need supporters in Whitehall; this finally made Lloyd decide to return home.

# 10

# THE ROAD TO INDIA

The choice between war and politics had now been made, even though Lloyd was unwilling to admit it; but the political scene to which he was returning was changing in ways which he found most uncongenial. The Lloyd George coalition proposed to extend the franchise to all adult males and women over the age of thirty – which would bring Britain near to being a complete democracy and increase the number of electors from seven to twenty-one million. Blanche, knowing well her husband's views on votes for women, wrote sympathetically in July 1917:

> I know how the suffrage nightmare must be poisoning your hours of solitude – and it really is rather hard on you that such an infamy should have been forced upon you when you were almost looking the other way.[1]

Blanche was right as regards votes for women; that he could not stomach, but he could not agree with those who, like Puss Gaskell, confessed to 'hating' democracy. The letter which he wrote to her on 4 October 1917 in reply comes as near as anything he ever wrote to expressing his political creed. It was, he commented, 'a pity' that she hated democracy:

> You might hate it in Italy or Greece but our people are so fine taken all in all. I think what you hate and I hate is the Radical method of giving expression to Democracy – e.g. Whiggery trying to keep up with the times – fraudulent, feeble and as dangerous as it is futile. But democracy was great in Elizabethan days. Trades Unions were powerful and patriotic, Elizabeth chose her men from the ranks often as not, and there was just that impishness of policy and method that made the 'late and glorious' Edward popular in the crowd or that really sustains Winston through his many adventures. *Good economics* (a) Empire vis-à-vis the rest of the world and (b) vis our own people – i.e. distribution of profits in

67

high wages; *Impregnable Defence* and *Constitutional Tranquillity*, these three are really our only Trinity of political need. All else follows.

Lloyd remained an unrepentant and unreconstructed Unionist, distrusting Socialists and Radicals equally:

What's the use of talking about detailed social reform? When the people have high wages and can pay for good housing they will see that they get it and if landlords stand in the way they will have to quit. But they won't – the higher building value an owner can get on his property the better he is pleased. Good and high wages we must have. Prices won't follow up in the same rate as regards elementary foodstuffs because these are practically raw materials, and if we organise our Empire on a Preferential system we are going to get these cheaper than anyone else. You can get the Elizabethan system back if you try, and with it Elizabethan good cheer and reasoned piety of nationhood. Don't you think so? And would you hate democracy then? Is it a proof that Monarchy is bad because Philip of Spain was cruel or Philippe Egalité an ass? In the same way is it a proof that democracy is bad because Asquith was crooked and taught the people evil of their destiny? . . . better the folly of the many than the corruption of the few. . . . Anyone can make a state efficient for a while by means of an autocracy, it's statecraft sublime to keep four nations and four continents close welded in aim yet world free in method. We've done it all but a bit and it's a bigger game than autocracy.

These were the ideas which underlay his involvement in politics; many of them were to be expressed to a wider public in a book called *The Great Opportunity* which he wrote with Edward Wood during the course of the year and which was published in late 1918. Along with the ideas went a sense of frustration; as he told Puss:

It's easy enough to talk any way, but the fact remains that I'm thirty-eight, just, and not done a hand's turn yet towards the things I care about. It's damnable, but there it is. I don't quite know why I've covered five pages of random talk about nothing – Please forgive. The only thing that may upset the coach is this women's suffrage business – It's all wrong. Government is going to be difficult with it, and as for electioneering! my word!! Can't you see it next time. Men will make any kind of fool of themselves for a pretty woman and will do to the end of time – thank heaven – and why wouldn't they? But it's another matter if women are really going to vote for the *beaux yeux* of the candidates. I believe they will. It's human nature any way. It will simplify the choice of candidates won't it? I must stop writing rubbish![2]

Perhaps he realized that he had revealed more of his inner mind than he normally did.

Far from being a die-hard cynical old Conservative, he was a romantic Tory democrat who was constantly being let down by 'the people' who refused to prove themselves worthy of his vision of England. When his constituency agent, Mr Buck, told him in 1916 that 'the people' were growing tired of the war, his comment to Blanche was that Buck was talking of the 'shopkeeper class of people . . . my hated middle man':

> It is meet and right that this class should feel for once how great is the burden of Empire which the other two classes of the Empire have borne always but which they never up till now felt the weight of . . . [they] may value the Empire more now that they have paid something for it.[3]

But alas for these brave hopes, born of a projection of his own romantic spirit, neither his own class, nor any other, wanted to pay the price of Empire. After four years of war they all felt they had borne enough and longed for an easier life, thus falling for the illusions peddled by liberal dreamers with their League of Nations and their covenants without swords: in this lay the tragedy of George Lloyd's career and it was his fate to struggle unavailingly against the spirit of the age.

However, before he could do anything about his own dreams two things were necessary: the return of peace and a prominent place in Parliament; December brought conflicting omens. The Shrewsbury Unionists announced that in the event of a snap election they would keep Butler Lloyd as their candidate,[4] which was inconvenient, but as this eventuality was unlikely to materialize, hardly tragic; just as Lloyd decided to stay in Palestine there came the offer of a job. On 20 December he received a telegram from Blanche: 'Austen has asked War Office for you as Secretary British Delegation Inter-Allied War Financial Council combined special personal work for him. Hope agreeable.'[5] Far from being 'agreeable', he tried to get Clayton to ask the War Office to let him stay in Palestine, but it was to no avail.[6] So, somewhat cross with both Chamberlain and Blanche, Lloyd returned to England in early January 1918.

Once again Lloyd's characteristic impatience had led him into difficulties which he could never admit were entirely of his own making. He had complained, often bitterly, about the prejudice shown to territorial officers and MPs in the army, he had often said he would like a job at home, and it was these things which poor Blanche relied upon for guidance when, on the evening of 18 December, Chamberlain suddenly sprang his offer upon her asking for an immediate decision. But even as she accepted the job she had an inkling that her husband would not approve.[7] Despite the fact that he had just been laid low with another (and serious) attack of dysentery, he did not, as he told Puss on 5

January, 'want to come home just now or to leave the desert work which is not only unique in character but is one which so few people are either able or asking to do'. He also gave her an insight into the real reason for his reluctance to return:

> If I sat long in the Commons and had to look at Bonar's face I should put up the white flag at once. I couldn't do it. I feel more and more like Kipling's soldier after the South African war:
> > ' 'ow can I ever take on with awful old England again / 'and 'ouses both sides of the street' etc. etc.
>
> I suppose it's fine to be a great man, but I'm not sure you are not a better one under God's good sky in the wind and the sun. I think I said the same thing to you one of the very first times we ever met – and it's a long time ago – and I daresay you have forgotten it by now.[8]

This mood continued to possess Lloyd when he was back in England. He could not settle to his new job, telling Chamberlain that 'it should be understood that when I am required for military service I am free to go'.[9] This meant that he was not offered the Secretaryship of the Committee, which, in turn, deprived him of a real job of work. Although he did testify before the Middle East Committee of the Cabinet on the economic situation in the Gulf and prepared papers for Balfour on Egyptian finance, none of these things really fulfilled him.[10] Even before Lloyd finally took Chamberlain's offer of a post as his assistant at the Inter-Allied Conference, he was writing to Puss, who had accused him of 'preferring dollars to dreams':

> Your taunt . . . went home, though it was unjust. The fact is that I'm utterly and completely restless and find no place in the streets of England – it's stupid – but there it is.

He revealed something about the reasons which had first set him tramping the world all those years ago when he commented to her that: 'in any case the person that was so much responsible for many years of my wanderings ought not to complain!'[11]

This restlessness was not helped by the many problems thrown at him. With Shrewsbury and West Staffordshire affected by the re-drawing of constituency boundaries, Lloyd was no longer certain of a seat in the Commons; he was also now fairly certain he did not want one. In late February he gathered from the India Office that there was a chance that he might be appointed Governor of Bombay or Madras but, even as he was trying to restrain his impatience, the Colonial Office asked him to become Governor of British East Africa.[12]

There was a certain irony in this, for, at the end of 1917, he had sold the two plots of land which he had bought there during his visit of 1913.

The offer, from the Colonial Secretary, Walter Long, came at the end of February, and Lloyd asked for time to think about it.[13] Blanche's diary captures their anguish:

> He would very much rather have an Indian Governorship, as leading to much greater things in the end. He does not want to go out of politics for five years, which may easily mean for life, without being assured that he is not entering a *cul de sac* and that the public work he is taking up instead is a worthy and satisfying alternative.[14]

Things hung on agonizingly until April when, just as the Colonial Office chose someone else, Lloyd received the news that both Bombay and Madras had, in fact, been allotted elsewhere months before. Blanche recorded their despair:

> Time alone will prove whether we were right or wrong in holding upon the chance of an Indian post which is what we *really* want: but we feel now that this offered a great chance of happiness with congenial life and work, and that it was flying in the face of providence not to seize it.[15]

For the next three months they were to persist in the gloom induced by such reflections, this despite assurances from Willy Tyrrell that East Africa was too small a job for George. Indeed, as the months passed without his being offered any alterantive work, their pessimism deepened.[16] He did, in late May, take on a post with Lord Robert Cecil who was in charge of the blockade of Germany, but he found few outlets for his restlessness – and those were not in office work.

Lloyd began to attend the House again, speaking in April in favour of the Montagu–Chelmsford proposals for India which allowed power to be devolved from the centre to the provinces; this intervention was to prove more significant than he imagined; or was his speech a deliberate attempt to bring himself to Montagu's attention? He had certainly met Chamberlain's successor at the India Office and had been told by him, in September 1917, that had it not been for other things, he would have taken Lloyd with him on a tour of India; so he knew that such a speech could do him nothing but good.[17] He also attended meetings of a Conservative grouping under the aegis of the Marquess of Salisbury which was to lead, indirectly, to his first book.

Lloyd had decided against having anything to do with Page Croft's National Party, feeling, correctly, that its members carried too little political weight to be of any use and that they had made a false move in breaking away from the Unionist Party. Ironically the same charges were to be levelled against the India Defence League in the early 1930s – when Page Croft was to be one of Lloyd's strongest allies. These things could not have been said of the grouping within the Party

71

presided over by Lord Salisbury, although its 'weight' consisted more in the character of its members than in anything it did.

Salisbury, its chief ornament and titular head, was widely respected as the standard-bearer of the Cecil tradition and spoke with particular and peculiar weight to what might be called the old Conservative tradition in the party, appealing back beyond the rough Unionism of Joe Chamberlain to the days when the party had been led by aristocrats and gentlemen such as his father, the great third Marquess. Lord Robert Cecil, Salisbury's brother, also attended meetings of the group, although he was taking his angular figure off after the Holy Grail of the League of Nations and was soon traversing rarefied regions unknown to sensible Conservatives. Salisbury's nephew, Lord Wolmer, son of the High Tory churchman, Lord Selborne, and a future supporter of Lloyd's on India in the 1930s, made up the third of the Cecilan trio. The two non-Cecil members were Lloyd himself and his friend Edward Wood (later Lord Irwin and Viceroy and, still later, Viscount Halifax and Foreign Secretary, before concluding his career as Earl of Halifax and Ambassador to Washington in the Second World War).

The group, which became the germ of a wider grouping after the 1918 election whose aim was to preach morality at the increasingly Mephistophelian figure of Lloyd George, was united by a common devotion to High Churchmanship; but in some ways Lloyd sat uneasily in its midst. Blanche recorded in her diary that meetings of the coterie would be useful in defining

> how far the Cecil attitude can adapt itself and become allied with the more progressive and practical spirits like George's, and how far the latter can rightly be restrained by the old traditional point of view.[18]

Lloyd, as we have seen, had often been impatient with the 'Cecil' point of view, regarding it as effete after the achievements of the great Marquess. But the Salisbury connection, with its emphasis upon duty, religion and honesty, was nevertheless, temperamentally, very appealing to Lloyd, whose closest friend there was Edward Wood.

Blanche was a long-standing friend of Dorothy Wood, Edward's wife, and it seems to have been through her that Lloyd came to know them well. He and Wood entered Parliament in the same year, with Lloyd helping his new friend prepare his maiden speech in 1910.[19] Wood was the youngest son of Lord Halifax, the leading Anglo-Catholic layman; he and Lloyd had obvious common interests in their religious views, and their friendship grew from this.

Lloyd admired the fact that, despite his withered left arm, Wood had served at the front, and he would have agreed with the comment that he was 'the highest kind of Englishman now in politics'.[20] Through the deaths of his elder brothers, Wood had become the heir to his father's title and, by 1918, was beginning to tread the path which was to lead him, seemingly without effort, to viceregal splendour, the Foreign Office and the Washington Embassy. He and Lloyd were, in time, to drift apart politically, but at this time they were close enough to begin work on a pamphlet on the challenge facing contemporary Conservatism.

Lord Birkenhead, Halifax's biographer, has observed of their friendship that:

> There was something in it of the attraction of opposites, Lloyd full of movement and vitality, of instant decisions and sudden passions, his striking face burned deep by eastern suns, his nature impatient and autocratic, his true bent administrative and the exercise of power; and Edward, reflective and sober, a stranger to impulse, preferring a reconnaissance in force of each problem, and slow to kindle at his friend's flame. They were as fire and water, a strange alignment of authorship.

These pertinent and perceptive observations make it strange indeed that Lord Birkenhead should have supposed that Lloyd 'had, in fact, little to do with the writing of the pamphlet'. He comments that in the book's 'consciousness of class structure . . . interest in agriculture, and most strongly in the insistence on the Christian society' the 'hand of Edward Wood' was 'heavy and unmistakable';[21] which may be so but Lloyd was as interested in these things as Wood. It seems, in fact, to have genuinely been a work of joint authorship – with Lloyd providing the driving force.

*The Great Opportunity* owed its genesis to a visit by the Lloyds to Garrowby, Wood's home in Yorkshire, on 28 June. Lloyd went there to speak to Wood's constituents on the campaign in the Middle East, but stayed to discuss with him the writing of a pamphlet provisionally entitled 'St George for England'.[22] Blanche described its purpose thus:

> To set forth their views of the creed which ought to be preached by a regenerated Unionist party. Of course Edward is temperamentally and by education, much more, I should say, a true Conservative than George is; but I think he is genuinely stirred by the vast and crying needs of the time, and anxious to evolve something practical and progressive that is not destructive to satisfy them. If George is not too impatient and Edward not too unenterprising, I think they might make a very useful combination.[23]

In this, Blanche was correct. The book, which came out in late 1918, enjoyed a great *succès d'estime* and became, for a time, the bible of progressive youthful Conservatism.[24] Edward Wood was destined to benefit more from this than was George Lloyd, but that was mainly due to the fact that, by the time it was published, Lloyd was more interested in the reconstruction of post-war India than he was in post-war England.

*The Great Opportunity* served two purposes for Lloyd: firstly, it gave him something to do during June and July when it seemed that no further military work was going to come his way; and secondly, with its emphasis upon what needed to be done in the way of devolving power from Westminster and reviving industry and agriculture, it would re-establish his political position for the coming election which it looked increasingly likely he would take part in. No further offers of administrative posts had come after the East African fiasco in April, and the new seat of Stafford, carved out of part of his old seat, asked him to stand as its candidate in the election.

But Lloyd had not been forgotten. He spoke in the Commons in favour of the Montagu–Chelmsford reforms on 6 August, and on the following day the first of the eponymous reformers wrote to the other that:

> I have had some difficulty about finding a Governor for Bombay. Both G. Lloyd MP and Elphinstone were considered by everybody I enquired from really good men. I have decided on Elphinstone, a mundane, conventional type of Governor because the PM came to the conclusion that he might want Lloyd in this country.[25]

Something of this was evidently conveyed to Lloyd, for it came as a 'complete surprise' when, on the morning of 21 August, Montagu asked him to become Governor of Bombay. Lloyd accepted at once, later writing to thank Montagu for 'the confidence which the offer implies' and the 'friendship' it showed.[26]

He immediately telegraphed to Blanche and his utter delight shines through the letter he sent giving her the details:

> I have always hoped that perhaps someday I should achieve just sufficient to make the people who thought you a fool for marrying me think again. I haven't yet done so, but perhaps I may yet do so. That is a foolish little sentiment but I do hate snobs so![27]

As they would pass through Egypt on their way to India he could, he reflected, look forward to seeing General Bell who had done so much to block his military career.

There was, of course, a last-minute hitch or two. Lynden Bell struck again, asking for Lloyd to be sent out to Egypt, this before the news of the Governorship was announced; and the approval of the Conservative leader, Bonar Law, had to be obtained. Bell was put off with the excuse that Robert Cecil needed Lloyd at the Foreign Office and, when Law remained silent, Montagu and Lloyd George appointed Lloyd all the same.

The news was published on 1 October, a few weeks after Lloyd's thirty-ninth birthday, along with the announcement that the new Governor was to be made a Knight Commander of the Indian Empire and go to Bombay as Sir George Lloyd. Letters of congratulation flooded in from all quarters: Paul Cambon, recollecting George's great role in 1914; Lord Wolmer, commenting upon the 'singular distinction and opportunity that you should have such an immense task thrown at you when comparatively young'; and perhaps most satisfyingly of all, from his father-in-law, that gruff old sailor who was delighted for two characteristic reasons: 'Bombay is a first-class appointment and may lead to anything. And it will take you out of the H[ouse] of C[ommons], which is no place for a gentleman now-a-days'.[28]

Austen Chamberlain, who had advised Montagu to appoint Lloyd, wrote a generous letter of congratulation which may be taken to mark the apogee of their relationship.[29] A contingent of prominent pressmen – Garvin of the *Observer*, Dawson of *The Times*, and Lord Beaverbrook – all wrote in lyric vein, whilst from his brother Tom, reclusively holed up in the Priory where, having disapproved of the war and refused to take any part in it, he was now excoriating Lloyd George, came a letter of deep pleasure and the evocation of

> Budbrooke, our parents, our first journey together to Eton and many other memories. The amphitheatre, the great cloud of witnesses and those whom we have known who now look down upon our arena.[30]

But conscious as he was himself of his duty to the dead, especially to Sam and all those pre-war hopes, Sir George Lloyd's eyes were now fixed very firmly on the future: all his life he had been conscious of great powers within himself and the craving for responsibility to match and test those powers; now he had his great opportunity. It remained to be seen what he would make of it.

# 11

# THE GREAT OPPORTUNITY

Writing to the Viceroy on 5 September, Edwin Montagu expressed the hope that he would

> like George Lloyd whom we are sending to Bombay. It is a new experiment which Chamberlain backs enthusiastically. He has parliamentary experience, is rather of the Ronaldshay type but cleverer, has a delightful wife, and is very keen and earnest. He is very grateful for the opportunity and can be regarded as a working Governor. It is not by any means a conventional appointment, and if I do not look upon it with confidence, I at any rate look upon it with hope.[1]

Lloyd was conscious that this was his own 'great opportunity' but, as he told Blanche on 22 August:

> I am not frightened by the immense difficulty of taking on the job at so exceptionally difficult a moment. It gives me a wonderful chance to make good doesn't it? Success under such circumstances would be a remarkable success.

Blanche was equally conscious of the challenge awaiting them, but less confident about what the future held, even if comforted by the reflection that, as she recorded in her diary on 16 November (the day before leaving London): 'even if we fail, owing to the *great* difficulties of the present state of things in India it won't be the sort of failure that matters'.

They had less than two months to prepare themselves for Bombay, which made it difficult to collect all the staff and clothing which they would need. But the delay did mean that they were in England to witness the Armistice and the end of the war with Germany. But, whilst thankful for the end of that awful struggle, their minds were bent on what now lay before them. On 7 November Montagu wrote that, 'after interminable negotiations with the Admiralty, the P. & O. and the

Council, embracing all subjects from submarines to cows to provide milk for his baby', Lloyd was about to sail.[2] They left London on 17 November.

The further eastward they moved the more they became disturbed by the behaviour of their predecessors in Bombay, the Willingdons. Lord Willingdon, a mild-mannered, pleasant little man, was held by observers to be much under the thumb of his large, comely and dominating wife – something confirmed for Blanche by the discovery that whilst her rooms at Government House were very grand, George's were not; a state of affairs which did not prevail for long. Willingdon had been reluctant to leave for Madras and it had been his insistence that Lloyd's appointment must not be announced until October, which had caused problems over getting ADCs and planning for the future. At Cairo, where they stopped on the journey, Blanche discovered that this was not the only disservice which they could expect from the Willingdons. Lloyd reported that an old friend had told her that:

> Lady Willingdon has been carrying on a campaign of deprecation against me with everyone, officials and residents alike, that she has succeeded in creating an atmosphere of great hostility to both my wife and myself.[3]

Blanche recorded in her diary that the formidable Lady had been telling all and sundry how sorry she was that Bombay was being landed with 'a mere unknown local politician . . . simply because for party reasons it was desirable to give him something'. Although she tried to laugh it off, Blanche was naturally disturbed by the idea that they were going to arrive in Bombay preceded by such a 'character'.[4] On top of this the Willingdons then announced that they were going to leave Bombay the same day the Lloyds arrived, which would mean they would not give the traditional dinner for their successors by which outgoing governors usually introduced the newcomers to local society.[5] But they did not let this spoil their arrival at Apollo Bundar on 16 December.

Indeed, in the three days preceding their arrival, Blanche had been far more worried by the swollen face which an abscess of the tooth had given her than by the odd behaviour of 'Lady W.'. But when she rose early on the morning of 16 December her face was back to its natural size and, tall and elegant in a white georgette frock and a big white straw hat trimmed with white lace, she looked every bit the governor's lady (even if she did not feel it) as she stepped into the launch which took them to the quayside:

> Sir George stepped out of the launch wearing a white topee, grey frock-

coat and trousers with the GCIE insignia breasted upon the coat. Although known to be young, he looked younger than what many people expected. He has not lost his military appearance, and he wears a small moustache.[6]

Blanche's thoughts as they ascended the red carpet which covered the half-dozen steps from the quay to where the Willingdons stood centred on David and fears that he might cry out at the seventeen-gun salute which greeted them; but he did not. Then it was into the job.

After shaking hands with dozens of people, hearing the first of what was to be many municipal addresses, and after Lloyd had inspected the guard of honour (the South Staffordshires, by a curious coincidence), they went in the state barouche to Government House on Malabar Hill where, watched by the Willingdons who had, rather rudely, already breakfasted, they ate their breakfast. Blanche noticed that her ungracious but domineering hostess's method of keeping up the dignity of the King's representative 'consists largely in never saying please or thank you and in perpetually intimating to all who approach that she is there to give orders and that they are there to obey them'.[7] Luncheon was an equally strained occasion and Blanche was relieved when the Willingdons departed at 4.30 p.m. But this sense of relief lasted only until the evening when they had their first state banquet. Their first day set the pace for the rest of their stay.

Montagu had forecast a 'quiet life' for the Lloyds during their first months at Malabar Point and there were many reasons why it would have been more convenient if things had turned out this way. In the first place there was Lloyd's fatigue. He had driven himself hard before the war and during it he had worked even harder, often in tiring desert conditions racked by ill-health; now he was plunged as a tyro into India's largest state at a particularly delicate moment. He was the first governor to be appointed since the announcement of the Montagu–Chelmsford reforms and, even as he arrived, the Viceroy and the other governors were about to enter conclave on the matter.

The main feature of the reforms was the introduction of 'diarchy', which meant transferring some powers from the centre to the governors and their councils upon which Indian representatives sat. Blanche's account of the matter to her sister Helen (or 'Whelk' as she was called) shows where her sympathies lay:

> The whole problem . . . is how to give a measure of self-Government to a nation which is quite obviously not ready for it, but which can only become necessary for it, ever, by practising. The only way of solving it is to evolve the kind of scheme which seems to me the only kind for any really successful Government – i.e. a working plan that is just as illogical as human beings themselves but which does somehow work.[8]

Lloyd, whilst doubtful of 'success', nevertheless thought it 'right – and inevitable' that steps towards Home Rule for India should be taken.[9] He did not share the views of some of his colleagues that, because it was cumbersome and illogical, diarchy was unworkable; as he told Montagu on 26 December:

> The risks of an imperfect scheme are infinitely smaller than the risks of doing nothing at all. In constitution-making or mongering you'll never get agreement on the perfect scheme.[10]

For those who, a decade and a half later, were inclined to dismiss Lloyd as a hopeless 'diehard', such views would have come as a surprise, but, as we shall see, his Indian policy, unlike Churchill's, was founded upon actual experience of Indian conditions.

He certainly had a rough introduction to those conditions, despite his own hopes and those of Montagu. Lloyd found the 'whole place seething with excitement and unrest' as a prominent agitator, Horniman, was busy organizing disorder in mills and the railways.[11] Within a fortnight eighty out of the eighty-five cotton mills in Bombay were out on strike, leaving 150,000 men idle and ready to riot.[12] It took active intervention by Lloyd to bring the strikes to an end and his verdict was that even if it was

> rather a beastly situation to have to taste before I had got to know even my officials, yet I think in a way it has helped in so far as people have got confidence in me earlier than I could have hoped.[13]

His vigour and resolution certainly impressed itself upon his Council and, as Blanche wrote: 'they know now that he's a *man* and a force to be reckoned with'; here again, first impressions acted as harbinger for the rest of his time in Bombay.[14]

Some idea of Lloyd's reactions to the first taste of his new post can be gleaned from a letter written to Montagu on 12 February:

> You ask me how I like my life here. First of all it is the most strenuous life I have ever lived. I have always worked fairly hard but I have never had work to compare with this. I suppose one will be able to last it out but if I am to spend five years at the rate at which I have been compelled to live my first eight weeks I shall be fully ready for a little holiday at the end of it! One's every hour is planned months ahead and one is at work from early morning till dinner and then when that is done there are crowds of people to entertain.

But, if he hated the 'social side', he loved the work,

> which I find deeply interesting and the problems vast. I do not forget the proportions which they bear to the world outside, but India itself is such

a huge charge and there are so few to discharge it that it is a fine work worthy of any man to do: I felt that before I came, I feel it even more now. You remember that I said to you that even if this work led to nothing it was in my judgement a far finer piece of work than an Under-Secretaryship for a man with energy to undertake in his best years. I am sure that is true.[15]

The exhaustion was inseparable from the vast challenge. Although he was careful never to disparage his civil servants, there is no doubt that Lloyd found the administrative 'machine' at his disposal lamentably inadequate for his purposes. Blanche recorded in early January 1919 that:

The whole system of Indian administration is antiquated and cumbersome to an almost incredible degree. The principle throughout seems to be that you are obliged to have five incompetent, inefficient, ill-paid people to do the work that one good, well-paid worker could do better in less time.

In his Secretariat there was 'no such thing as a type-writer' and 'no one ever appears to take a copy of a letter' (a state of affairs apparent from the Lloyd papers). When, a few weeks after arriving, Lloyd had wanted to increase the pay of the police, he had ordered a telegram to this effect to be sent to Simla.

The whole Secretariat nearly fainted at the idea – it seemed as if such a bold step had never been taken before. The telegram was reluctantly sent, and evidently the other end was just as much galvanized by this unprecedented behaviour as this one – for they immediately replied, sanctioning the increase, and the new scale of pay was able to be included in the Budget. But this kind of machinery is not well-suited to George's temperament.[16]

Nor was it suited to the tasks which he saw before him.

The aftermath of war brought with it economic and social dislocation which carried the seeds of civil unrest even without the activities of Gandhi and the Home Rulers. The best answer to the latter was not just a 'firm hand', but also good government in the interests of the people. What Bombay – and by implication and extension India as a whole – needed was a dose of Tory democracy in action: given strong and capable government there was no need to fear the antics of Gandhi, Horniman or any of the other voices clamouring for independence.

The biggest problem facing Lloyd was the acute shortage of housing on the island of Bombay itself. Despite what had been said in the welcoming address by the Municipality of Bombay about its enlightened policy on such matters:

They are responsible and unashamed for a system of housing and sanitation which would have caused the worst of Abdul Hamid's Valis to blush crimson. Bombay, '*urbs prima India*', is a disgrace, its Municipality a conspiracy of landowners.

His predecessors had drawn up schemes to reclaim land in the Back Bay and North Island, but:

> Everybody before me has been broken in his attempts by the power of the landlord class and the apathy of the great mass of the people. If it is to be done it must be a surgical operation, otherwise things will drift on again as they have done for twenty-five years. I expect I shall very likely fail, but it is worth trying.[17]

But, as Lloyd told Montagu on 26 February, it would require money and help from London, because successive viceroys had said it was too expensive to be contemplated.

If Bombay was the happiest and most satisfying period of Lloyd's career it is because it presented him with challenges like the Back Bay scheme and the Sukkur barrage – administrative and economic problems which his talents were superbly adapted to solving. By September 1919 he and his Council (and the hand of the former is more discernible than the hands of the latter) drew up a report on the housing situation and a programme of action which included the creation of a development authority for 'Greater Bombay'. By December he was able to put a complete plan before Montagu. The formidable problem of finance was overcome by an expedient which was damned by all the 'experts', the flotation of a loan on the Indian money market backed by the security of the Bombay Government. It was spectacularly successful, not least because of the Governor's energetic fund-raising. He had to push the scheme through his Executive and Legislative Councils and chivvy all concerned. But by dint of unremitting energy and sheer force of personality, the Back Bay scheme was implemented and, by the time Lloyd left Bombay, the land was being reclaimed and there was money to build houses on it.[18]

The same was true of the other great constructive work he began, the mighty dam at Sukkur, or, as it was known after 1935 when it was opened, the Lloyd barrage. Here again were problems of finance, civil engineering and administrative sluggishness, but the objective was one which drew forth all Lloyd's energies. It was in 1855 that Lieutenant J. G. Fife of the Royal Engineers had first suggested the creation of an irrigation scheme to utilize the waters of the Indus over six million acres of rich alluvial land in Sind, but seventy years later nothing had been done. As Colin Forbes Adam observed:

> The long story of frustration itself would almost have dared him to try his
> hand, had the immense and romantic qualities of material betterment,
> and the sound business qualities of the scheme not at once captivated
> alike his idealism and his practical shrewdness.[19]

This challenge, once taken up in 1920, was never laid down until the
end of his period of office, and one of his last acts was to lay the
foundation stone of the Lloyd barrage. These two great projects were
all that Lloyd wanted in the way of memorials to his work, but neither
of them did anything to help solve one of the most pestilential problems
facing him – the activities of agitators like Gandhi.

As an imperialist and a believer in the civilizing mission of the Raj,
Lloyd was by temperament as ill-fitted to understand Gandhi as he was
well-suited to deal with the Back Bay scheme. Seen through the
distorting lenses of post-imperial guilt and the cinema screen, Gandhi
has attained the status of secular saint; and this despite the writings of
that other hero of the left, George Orwell, who thought there was a good
deal of the charlatan about him. A study of Sir George Lloyd's career in
Bombay throws no light upon the character of the Mahatma which
may be safely left for discussion amongst his admirers and those of
George Orwell; Lloyd would have rested content with Chelmsford's
verdict: 'Dear me what a d----d nuisance these saintly fanatics are!'[20]

Discussion of the Montagu proposals for reform may have taken up a
good deal of time during Lloyd's first months as governor, but they did
nothing to help quell the problems of the unrest engendered by famine,
cholera, and the aftermath of war, and made acute by that other
scourge clad in dhoti and wire-framed spectacles.

Between January and April Lloyd was busy touring his presidency
and acquainting himself with its problems. Normally April brought
relief. As the temperature in Bombay rose and the damp heat became
unbearable, it was usual for the Governor and his entourage to retreat
to his residence at Mahbleshwar, high in the Western Ghats where the
fresh, cool mountain air brought welcome deliverance; but not this
year. On 9 April Chelmsford wrote home that:

> Gandhi has given notice to Lloyd that he proposes to publish an
> unregistered paper contrary to the law. I think Gandhi has come up
> against the wrong man for I have no doubt that Lloyd will handle the
> question wisely and forcibly. I am sure that we were right to put Lloyd in
> *vice* Willingdon. Throughout he has shown himself ready to act when he
> was sure of his ground.[21]

Chelmsford had good reason to be relieved.

He had recently had news from the Punjab of unrest caused by
protests against the Rowlatt Act which was designed to allow the

authorities to intern without trial suspected agitators.[22] A few days after his letter to Montagu came the Amritsar 'massacre' when 379 Indians were shot during a riot. This increased tension and, for a time, 'it seemed as if it might so easily turn into the Mutiny again'.[23] Bombay was in the eye of the storm as the home base of Gandhi and once more Lloyd found himself facing a major crisis before he had settled into the saddle.

Blanche's letters to her sister convey the atmosphere at Government House:

> It is extremely difficult for George to decide exactly what is the best way to take the necessary action against the worst stirrers up of all the mischief. . . . My poor George is working literally sixteen hours a day and is fearfully tired – but I feel pretty sure he will manage to come out on top. He has had very little respite from anxiety and crises of all sorts ever since we arrived.[24]

Having obtained Chelmsford's consent, Lloyd decided to deport Horniman, who promptly declared that he was too sick to be moved. Lloyd waited a fortnight and then, at the end of April, enforced the deportation order. Gandhi declared a day of fasting and prayer for Horniman but unhappily fixed upon the day of one of the great Deccani marriage-feasts and, as Blanche recorded:

> Very few people prayed – so that if the reinstatement of Horniman is to depend upon the yielding of the Almighty to the importunities of faithful friends in Bombay, I fear he stands very little chance of a return passage. He will have to fall back on the Labour Party in England and the faddists in the House of Commons.[25]

Although Lloyd was not able to get a prolonged stay at Mahbleshwar, he had broken the impetus of the agitators.

His achievement did not go unnoticed or unappreciated. Chelmsford wrote to Montagu on 30 April:

> Lloyd had the most difficult task of all . . . because Gandhi was strongest in Bombay . . . as he has a clever scheming lot against him. He certainly couldn't have used O'Dyer's methods. They would signally have failed.[26]

Montagu sympathized with Lloyd in his next letter on 1 May:

> Poor man! What a disturbed time you have had since you accepted your great responsibility! You went to Bombay filled, I know, with an enthusiasm for the progressive development of your Presidency. . . . Beginning with strikes and going through to rebellion has, I fear, sorely dislocated your programme and seriously deflected your activities. Never mind! You've established a reputation in India and in England for

patient though firm, wise though vigorous handling of your difficulties.[27]

Such praise was manna in the wilderness and Lloyd replied that:

> I promised you I would do my level best to justify your confidence and to
> have succeeded so far gives me great heart for the future. But at present it
> is all tight-rope walking and I am bound to make some mistakes. I shall
> try to make as few as possible.

He was, he said, determined not to arrest Gandhi – a determination
increased by the fact that at their first interview that 'misguided saint'
(as Chelmsford called him) had said: 'I wish to goodness Sir George
you would arrest me.' Instead he would arrest all his associates, thus
leaving the Mahatma isolated: 'I am afraid he is really pretty wicked, as
cunning as a fox and at heart bitterly anti-British.'[28] But, for the
moment, Lloyd's sensitive and skilful handling of the situation had
saved Bombay from serious unrest and confirmed his reputation as a
firm but fair governor. If the first six months had been hectic they had
also allowed him to show his mettle.

# 12

# BOMBAY LIFE

Of all the letters of congratulation which Lloyd received, one written by Austen Chamberlain on 18 June 1919 gave the most pleasure. It reported Edwin Montagu as saying: 'Well, he [Lloyd] has done extraordinarily well and I owe you a great debt of gratitude for recommending him to me.'[1] But there was no question of being able to rest upon these laurels – even had Lloyd been so inclined. The continuing problems of nationalist unrest, cholera, famine, constitutional reform and the planning of the Back Bay and Sukkur barrage schemes, all gave even his tireless energy enough to do. But there were other problems which seemed more amenable to swift resolution.

The first of these was financial. The war had provided Blanche with a not unwelcome opportunity to economize. Lloyd, who valued money only as a means to an end, was always open-handed, but Blanche had a Yorkshirewoman's sense of its value. During the war she had proved an 'Iron Chancellor' and had actually managed to reduce their overdraft from £12,000 to nearly £4,000. Although Lloyd was pleased with this, he suspected that such economy was being purchased at the price of comfort, but could never get her to admit as much. His appointment as governor necessitated large expenditure and he felt not only that 'it was worth cutting a dash', but that doing so was 'part of the job'. They spent £4,000 of their own money on equipping themselves for Bombay.

As a result of the appointment Lloyd lost £1,000 a year in income (£400 from the Commons and £600 in director's fees from Lloyds Bank), but he expected his official salary of £13,000 a year and allowances of £2,000 to cover most of his costs; it proved to be quite otherwise. Within a few weeks of arrival, he was telling Montagu that 'the cash question is acute. . . . Prices have doubled and trebled – they have also now put on a super-tax which further decreases the salary.'[2] It soon became apparent that he was going to have to spend at least £2,000 a year out of his own income (which was about £5,000). As he told Montagu on 31 May:

> I am having to spend £5,000 a year of my own to make both ends meet and even so Government House is in rags. . . . I don't think I ought to have to spend all my private income trying to pay my way.[3]

Montagu did manage to secure an increase in the sumptuary allowance, but it was clear that whatever Bombay promised for the future, it did not include financial ease.

Another problem which seemed susceptible of immediate solution concerned that future. When Lloyd had left the Commons it had been 'without one single regret of any kind or shape',[4] and Montagu's reports of the new House did nothing to change this view: 'It looks in part like a TUC and in other parts like a meeting of a Provincial Chamber of Commerce.'[5] He had no desire to return there when he had finished in Bombay: 'I shall never again have the energy to fight elections, for this work will take most of the energy out of me before I have done.'

On 18 July 1919 Lloyd put a proposal to Montagu:

> It is simply this, that I think on the whole it would be a considerable help to me to have a peerage both as regards my work here and as regards the future, and therefore if you'll give it me I should like to have it.[6]

The ingenuous way in which this proposal was put forward amused Montagu, who, nevertheless, promised to 'consider' the proposal.[7] The tone of this reply agitated Lloyd who reacted in a characteristic manner:

> It is so hateful and intolerable to me that you should think I am just an ordinary title-hunter here for what I can get rather than what I can do that I think I must restate my reasons for writing the letter I did. . . . I have not been accused ever of being a politician 'on the make' and I would clear out of politics at once if I really thought people thought that of me and I was betrayed into writing you that letter simply because somehow or other I thought that you would in your mind never put me in that *galère*. . . . Please don't think me unduly sensitive: it isn't that, but these things become in public life almost ones of personal honour and not ones in which one can risk the slightest misunderstanding.[8]

There matters rested – for the moment.

But the affair affected his relations with Montagu. It has been observed before that Lloyd's intense personal ambition was subsumed in his imperial patriotism, and he shared the common High Tory view that there was something discreditably self-serving about a career in politics, but unlike friends such as Billy Ormsby-Gore and Edward

Wood,[9] he stood in no line of succession to a peerage. He wanted a 'public platform' for the things he believed in and therefore wanted a peerage; Montagu, despite the sympathetic tone of their correspondence, had not understood; henceforth Lloyd was a little wary of him. Unfortunately, there was not much solace to be found in the Viceroy, Lord Chelmsford.

During the crisis with Gandhi from April to June Lloyd found Chelmsford 'first-rate to work with, prompt, sympathetic and courageous – I could wish for no better'.[10] But on the personal level he was not attracted by his 'cold manner and lack of any evident human sympathy'.[11] Blanche described him to her 'beloved Whelk' as 'a stickler for etiquette' and it was, perhaps, unfortunate that at their first meeting with him she should have forgotten to curtsy whilst George managed to wear his GCIE the wrong way round.[12] But Lloyd's success in dealing with Gandhi and his support for diarchy soon established a good working relationship between the two men. In late 1919 he could tell Montagu that, 'I get on well with him [but] he just fails in the human touch somewhere, I think.'[13]

Montagu's feline temperament craved details of Lloyd's difficulties with his chief at Simla, nor was he disappointed. In early 1920 Lloyd complained that:

> I feel as if I were talking to a block of marble, and I am afraid he looks upon my enthusiasm and desires as a tiresome form of strident lunacy. Perhaps it is my fault, but there it is. It discourages me to work with someone who never shows one gleam of sympathy or understanding.[14]

Although Lloyd warned that such outbursts were not to be taken entirely tragically, they were frequent enough to warrant another conclusion. But the marriage of Chelmsford's daughter Joan to Blanche's brother Tommy in 1921 created a fresh link between Simla and Malabar Hill and eased social relations. However, it was not until the reign of the next viceroy that Lloyd was to miss Chelmsford's qualities.

Montagu and Chelmsford were the only two superiors whose activities impinged upon the Governor of Bombay, but that did not mean that he was supreme autocrat in his vast domain which ran from Karachi in the north several hundred miles south to Kanara. He had to work closely with his Council which consisted of two Europeans and an Indian. The Europeans, Mr Curtis and Mr Carmichael, differed in quality and usefulness. Blanche's first impression of Curtis was that he was 'a dour sort of man with a rather exhuberant wife',[15] but she soon found him 'hasty, irritable . . . easily flustered' and inclined to breakdowns, the first of which came in December 1919.[16] Carmichael, who was the more helpful of the two, a 'steady, reliable, level-headed man', lacked initiative and, under the strain of Lloyd's first year, collapsed with influenza towards the end of 1919. The Indian member, Sir Ibrahim Rahimtoola, was 'very intelligent, progressive and . . . has more imagination than the other two', but he too lacked forcefulness, thus leaving much of the burden to fall back on the Governor.[17] In addition to these, but on a different plane, were the numerous Indian princes with whom Lloyd had to deal, all of whom needed careful handling. Even without the stresses and strains already delineated, the job was a demanding one.

Lloyd spent more time than most governors at Malabar Point. He found it 'amazingly attractive', planted as it was on top of a hill with the sea on three sides. The governor's residence was a 'big low bungalow house' and there were 'guest houses separate in various parts of the compound'.[18] Forbes Adam recalled that what was beautiful by day assumed, in the 'hot dark-blue nights . . . a magical quality':

> From the veranda of the State rooms the reflection of the rising moon laid a heavy silver carpet over the waters below, at the further end of which was spread 'the Queen's necklace', the great semi-circle of bright far-off lights, which the town threw round the bay.[19]

There were two other official residences, one at Mahbleshwar, the other at Ganeshkind, near Poona, Blanche described the latter as

> an imposing edifice of stone, much more like a (rather inferior) English country house than most in India. It has some five rooms, but between you and me and this sheet of paper it struck me as rather pretentious and I infinitely prefer the bungalow kind of house which one gets here and at Mahbleshwar – it is so much more right for the country.[20]

Mahbleshwar was a big 'two-storied bungalow built of red stone', surrounded by a terraced garden with big beds of flowers and shady trees which gave on to views of the jungle and the mountains beyond, 'brown and bare against the bright red soil of the roads'.[21] When she and Lloyd first went there in December 1918 they immediately 'fell tremendously in love with it at first sight – it struck us as a Portofino place, full of peace and calm beauty, and a wonderful kind of other world romance'.[22] The Government moved there from April to the end of May (when the rains came) and Blanche held it to be not the least of Gandhi's sins that his activities in April and May deprived George of a much-needed sojourn there.

In each place Lloyd's permanent staff provided a changing backcloth to life. He brought out with him two ADCs: Con Benson, who had just married Blanche's old friend, Lady Violet Elcho (sister of Lady Diana Cooper); and Collie Knox, later to become a well-known popular journalist but at this time 'the youngest thing [Blanche had] ever seen' equipped with 'a bad stammer' which he had acquired by falling out of an aeroplane.[23] Both were charming, but Con Benson also managed to be efficient. In addition to these were Major Greig, the Military Secretary, and one ADC left behind by Willingdon, Captain MacEwan. Knox left in mid 1919 to be succeeded, to Blanche's delight, by her brother Tommy. The addition to this circle of Colin Forbes Adam, who was to marry Blanche's cousin Irene Lawley, transformed it into a circle of men who provided Lloyd with congenial company in which to relax.

Only these intimates saw the man beneath the proconsular mask. Benson described him thus:

> George's life was never made the happier by regal display, but he believed completely in its importance, because as the appointed representative of his King, it would have been *lèse-majesté* to do less. I know this because I have seen him, five minutes after the red carpets have been rolled up, in shorts and a shirt, blissfully sailing a small boat around Back Bay, and revelling in the glory of an Indian sunset, or sitting informally at a piano surrounded by his Staff strumming delightfully, and rather indifferently, topical tunes, his tongue clenched between his teeth and slightly protruding, shouting with laughter over the lyrics of some new song of the moment, and next abstractly wandering off into melodies which stirred and touched his heart, such as *Men of Harlech* or the School choruses of his youth.[24]

Sir George Lloyd GCIE, CIE, DSO, Governor of Bombay, was the King's representative, but he had not entirely ousted the George Lloyd of yore. In this small group he could relax, 'rag' and be 'ragged', and seek solace from the ever-present troubles of his presidency.

The heavy burdens of his first year as governor gave Lloyd few opportunities for such pleasures and Blanche worried constantly about his health, particularly as the approach of his fortieth birthday reminded her of the advent of middle age. She reported to her sister Helen that he was rather 'sad' at the approach of such a milestone:

> He minds it quite as much as you and I can do: in fact I think he minds it *more*! But as long as he remains as young and as vigorous in mind and body – and *looks* about thirty-two – I don't think he need really be very unhappy.[25]

September was a month to bring on reflections of mortality as it also saw David's birthday. Blanche was sad to leave him behind when they set off in October for their much-needed holiday in Kashmir and she recorded in her diary that he

> looked rather wistful with his big brown eyes under his big topee – and flung himself with both arms round my neck to say goodbye. Bless his darling heart. I do wish he needn't grow up quite so fast.[26]

But she put any sad thoughts behind her as they departed for the hill-country and holidays.

Lloyd had told Montagu in August that he was looking forward to 'some fishing and duck-shooting' and a rest which would set him up 'for a hard winter's work again in Bombay';[27] and things came to pass as he had written. Kashmir was

> a real paradise for sport – a different kind of shooting and fishing every day [Blanche wrote] – so you can imagine how George, Tommy, Con and the rest enjoyed themselves. It is like a glorified Scotland on a much larger scale – with the marvellous climate thrown in – no rain or mist or wind – still, perfect, gloriously sunny days – with air like the bubble of soda-water that has been first iced and then electrified. It is wonderful – and doing us all heaps of good.[28]

As ever, in such surroundings, Lloyd recovered both health and spirits – which was just as well for the return to Bombay at the end of October was to see him resume fresh burdens.

One of the problems with having acquired such a reputation for efficiency in a system renowned for the opposite was that everyone who had something which needed to be done dumped it on 'His Excellency'. Everything had 'to be put through ultimately by his personal driving power. . . . And if you are acting as a dynamo for a whole large Presidency, all day and every day, it is unquestionably killing work.'

With the Back Bay scheme, the constitutional question, the persistent rumblings of nationalist unrest all heaped on top of his normal duties, it is no wonder that, by the end of 1919, Lloyd was showing signs of great strain, being troubled in particular by neuritis in his right arm which made him very 'seedy'.[29] Fortunately Blanche was on the spot and able to persuade him to get away to Sind for a brief holiday at the year's turning. But even so, it was a badly over-tired Governor who returned to Bombay in January to face the problems of 1920.

# 13

# TAKING THE STRAIN

When the Lloyds returned to Bombay on 13 January 1920, it was with a sense of *déjà vu*; once more they were greeted by a strike of mill-workers and dockers and by the inevitable calls for the Governor to intervene. For the rest of the month Blanche saw so little of her husband that when he came into her room on 30 January whilst she was writing to her sister, she broke off with the comment: 'I had meant to manage a good letter to you, but George came in and wanted to talk, and his moments are so rare that I must take advantage of them.'[1] Developments elsewhere provided consolation for his immersion in work.

In early January Blanche's Aunt Constance, Lady Wenlock, came to stay, accompanied by her daughter Lady Irene Lawley. Lady Wenlock provided Blanche with congenial company, but it was Lady Irene who provided the main talking-point as she quickly cut a swathe through the ranks of the young male staff. Lloyd's new assistant private secretary, Colin Forbes Adam, lost his heart to her but, to Blanche's annoyance, she did not reciprocate. In fact, Irene's gay progress aroused mixed feelings of envy and admiration among the female inhabitants of Government House, but she showed no signs of choosing a husband, causing Blanche to comment:

> How I wish 'getting married' didn't matter so desperately to us women –
> and yet of the ones who don't, so few make a success of life. . . . It is only
> sometimes that the ceaseless business of attracting and cajoling,
> annexing and dangling – and all the heartburnings, jealousies, dis-
> appointments and false positions inevitably attached, make one feel so
> tired of sex![2]

Forbes Adam, known at Malabar Point as 'Pop Eye', was a persistent wooer; refusing to be deterred, he followed her back to Yorkshire in October and they were married in November. His quiet charm and good humour had already won him a place in the Governor's inner circle of friends. This alliance by marriage cemented the connection and Colin and Irene Forbes Adam were among the closest friends of the Lloyd family; and it was to Colin that Blanche and David were to turn when the question of writing Lloyd's official biography arose in 1945.

But whilst Irene was still causing havoc with the hearts of the ADCs in Bombay, there had come a piece of news which delighted Blanche and took even Lloyd's mind off some of his problems. On 31 January her brother Tommy, who was serving temporarily as an ADC, wrote to tell her that he had proposed to the Viceroy's daughter, Joan Thesiger. Lord Chelmsford gave his blessing and Tommy's uncle, Lord Harewood, gave them £30,000, and so it was that the couple were able to get married in March. Preparations for this event occupied much time, but, alas, the alliance did nothing to ease the growing tension between Malabar Point and Simla caused by Lloyd's sensitiveness to suggestions that Chelmsford was trespassing on his preserves.

Lloyd's proposal to finance the Back Bay scheme by floating a loan on the Indian money market had aroused the Viceroy's suspicions, whilst Chelmsford's suggestion that the Native States – within the presidency there were over three hundred of varying size and importance – should, henceforth, fall under his control, had provoked the Governor of Bombay to angry protests. Arrangements for the marriage forced both men into closer proximity than either wished, but a visit from the viceregal pair to Bombay only a few weeks after the wedding turned out to be the proverbial straw on the back of an already weary camel.[3] Montagu, who rather enjoyed hearing of the problems which both Lloyd and Willingdon had with Chelmsford, wrote that he was glad to see that his relationship with the Viceroy was not based on the

> dulling of your temper or the restraint of your energies. When a knife is brought into contact with a stone, handled well, the knife returns to the conflict sharp. I foresee from your letters that your character and temperament are being handled by you well, and the whetting that they receive in Viceregal conflicts will add to your success.[4]

But he did his best to smoothe over their relations, writing to Chelmsford that men of Lloyd's

> indefatigable energy and self-confidence naturally have strong points of view, but he is a man who, so far as my experience goes, shows an equal reaction to appreciation and sympathy.[5]

There was, however, no improvement in relations; it was quite otherwise with the Willingdons.

After the circumstances surrounding Lloyd's arrival, there had been little contact between him and Willingdon; but the tragic fate of one of Blanche Lloyd's dogs altered that. In early June it was discovered that her cairn terrier had rabies, which meant that the whole family had to go to Ootacamund in the Madras Presidency for the Pasteur treatment. For Lloyd, who had been ill with sore throats, influenza and the general effects of overwork, it provided an unexpected and welcome break – at least once it was decided that none of them had rabies. But Madras meant the Willingdons and that could have made their stay both awkward and unrewarding; but it proved otherwise.

Blanche found Lord Willingdon 'very much *le mari de Madame*' and concluded that 'his success – which is great – is due to her push and go and his own personal magnetism and social irresistibleness'.[6] She watched with some amusement the contest for domination between George and the formidable Lady Willingdon:

> I think George has almost made a conquest of her mainly because he will stand no sort of nonsense from her and gives as good as he gets all the time. She respects and understands this and has told him frankly that she began by hating him but now likes him a great deal.[7]

Lloyd reciprocated her respect.

This improvement in relations with the Willingdons came just as those with the British community in Bombay underwent a sharp deterioration caused by Lloyd's attitude to the Amritsar massacre and its aftermath.

Those in the 1930s who stigmatized Lloyd as a 'die-hard' imperialist would have been surprised to have discovered that over Amritsar he took an eminently liberal line. This did not go down well with the English community in Bombay, as Blanche recorded in her diary at the end of July:

> The Europeans are as bitterly pro-Dyer as the Indians are against him; and they both condemn the Government – for diametrically opposite reasons. George, I fear, is incurring a measure of unpopularity among the Englishmen in Bombay for being known to consider Dyer's action ill-judged and indefensible directly one is asked to identify it with the policy of the British Government.[8]

Lloyd told Austen Chamberlain that he did not think that

> anyone can justify Dyer's action at Jallianwallah Bagh: it was quite indefensible – the misfortune was that it should have fallen to, perhaps an honest, but thoroughly stupid soldier to deal with the situation.[9]

Lloyd was no unthinking 'die-hard'. If he defended the Empire it was because he believed in its civilizing mission, and actions like Dyer's had

93

no part in his vision. He saw that the post-war world posed many challenges to the Empire, but was far from thinking that repression was the way to meet them. In March 1920 he wrote to Montagu that he had told a right-wing Conservative MP, William Joynson-Hicks ('Jix'), that although things were bad and 'often depressing',

> they would have been far worse except for the Reform scheme [in India]. . . . We have got to pilot this country through a dyspeptic, disaffected and irritable stage by courage and confidence, and it is not the slightest use to wag our heads and talk gloomily about revolution.[10]

This attitude was based upon confidence in the future and in the genius for ruling shown by the British. Lloyd told Montagu in April that he did not believe that

> we are going to be driven from India either now or for decades to come, if ever; in any case I refuse to work on that assumption. I believe we are going, almost entirely owing to your reforms and our national character, to complete our task to guide India to full self-government under the Crown. But we are in an extremely difficult and dangerous stage, where we can neither afford to be illiberal and unsympathetic, nor can we afford to be weak. The guiding 'tag' or formula is this: 'to pay out rope and hit the agitator hard'.[11]

Lloyd put this 'formula' into practice in Bombay. At the same time as providing law and order he also offered housing and irrigation schemes. This would make British rule both secure and popular, as well as depriving Gandhi of grievances to exploit. It would then be seen that his 'quaint, tortuous mind' and talk of 'soul-force' were irrelevant to the real needs of the people.[12] As he told Montagu in August, there were no panaceas, only hard work and 'negative remedies [such as] the future avoidance of the series of blunders steadily committed during the last fifteen months': that is the Rowlatt Acts, Amritsar, the failure to impose tariffs and, most of all, the failures of the Government of India:

> If you ask me specifically what are the remedies for the situation today I can only repeat to have someone of vision and courage at Simla. These people are children and must be treated as such . . . [they need] unwearied courtesy and patience, coupled with absolute and un-flinching firmness.[13]

It needed no deep thought to divine who Lloyd had in mind for this taxing job.

On 20 August he wrote to Blanche's friend Sibell Long (whose father-in-law, Walter Long, was a member of the Government) confessing that, although he had told her once that he did not want to go to Simla, he had 'changed [his] mind simply because I should like to handle the job and believe that I could do it'. He realized that he had little chance of being made Viceroy, but found it 'maddening' to 'feel and see the weakness of it all when . . . the whole country is only longing for a definite lead'.[14] He told Montagu in October that he would 'love to be given the opportunity' but realized that this was unlikely.[15] Hearing from home that his name had been mentioned, he asked Austen Chamberlain to give what support he could.[16] His name had indeed been mentioned, but Field Marshal Sir Henry Wilson summed up the prevailing view when he wrote: 'George Lloyd . . . is a very good young fellow but he is 10 to 15 years too young for Viceroy.'[17] But it was not until the end of the year that Lloyd was put out of his misery when the appointment of Lord Reading was announced.

Lloyd never was to get the post he wanted above all others, and his hopes for the Empire were to suffer a like fate. He had, it soon became clear, overestimated the willingness of both politicians and the British people to make the sacrifices necessary to maintain the Empire. The first sign that this might be so came in August 1920 with the announcement that the Government had accepted Lord Milner's recommendations for an agreement with the Egyptian nationalist leader, Saad Zaghloul, which would give Egypt independence under certain conditions.

For Lloyd the news came 'like a bombshell'. He told Montagu that it would 'depreciate very heavily the effect of the reforms here' as the Indian nationalists would say, 'Egypt has won her independence and India has not.'[18] To Lawrence Lloyd wrote:

> I don't know what to think about Egypt – perhaps it's right perhaps it's wrong – we all know what happens to Empires when they begin to withdraw their legions; but what I do know is that in India we can't stand this fast bowling from Whitehall. What we have done in Egypt is going to obliterate the reforms here completely. . . .[19]

He had said the same thing to Willingdon the previous day:

> The real truth is that we can't withdraw the legions: every schoolboy knows what happened to Rome as the legions began to do so. Besides, I could never have fought in the war if I had not been sincere in my belief that we had a real responsibility towards these people. Does it not seem as if through fear of difficulties we were being faithless to those responsibilities?[20]

It was as he became convinced that successive governments were, in fact, trying to prove 'faithless', that Lloyd found himself forced into what was to become a 'die-hard' position.

As predicted, the Egyptian announcement gave a stimulus to

Gandhi and other agitators such as Shurkat Ali. Lloyd wanted Montagu and Chelmsford to make up their minds what policy to adopt towards this fresh unrest – suppression or *laissez faire*:

> I have always told the Viceroy that I would agree to either policy on condition that if he chose the former he should guarantee that both he and [Montagu] . . . should go through with it at all costs. It would involve some serious disturbances all over India at first, possibly some bloodshed; I am not willing to embark upon this line of policy if we are to be asked from any quarter to let the agitators out once we have gone for them. To take all the odium of 'repression', all the bitterness caused by riot and bloodshed, and then before the full fruits of firmness have ripened to give way to clamour would be the height of folly and would yield disaster.[21]

Had he known that it was precisely this policy which British governments would soon choose to follow, he would have despaired.

In November Lloyd told Montagu that, 'If you asked the honest views of ninety-nine percent of the sensible people in India today as to whether they would welcome Home Rule in a shorter time, I feel confident that they would say no.' He thought that it was important that the British should be seen to be moving towards self-government for India, even if that could not finally be achieved until 'the Indians are in character, education, and standard of life, really equal with a white man'. For Lloyd the root of the difficulties was the problem of race: 'the Indian peoples feel that their self-respect as a people has been insulted by events [such as] . . . the Punjab'. It would also help on this score if Britain stopped affronting Moslem opinion in India by her policy towards Turkey and the division of the Ottoman Empire among the gentiles.[22] After the Indian elections in January 1921 it would, he thought, be necessary to cross the Rubicon: 'We cannot go on drifting vaguely, I think that is clear; we must either attempt to make terms with Gandhi or we must put down the Movement.'[23] The imminence of a visit from the Duke of Connaught and of Chelmsford's departure had created a dangerous atmosphere where everyone wanted to avoid unrest at any cost; Lloyd wanted to put an end to this situation.

Whether there would be a show-down with Gandhi in 1921 remained to be seen, but three things were bound to happen: the Montagu–Chelmsford reforms would come into operation; Chelmsford would depart; and so, alas for Lloyd, would Blanche, who had to accompany David to school in England in May. The Lloyds did wonder whether Lord Reading, a Jew, a Liberal, and a man whose reputation had been tarnished by the Marconi scandal of 1912, was really the right choice as Viceroy;[24] but his affability and good humour made such a pleasant change from Chelmsford's coldness that they were prepared to welcome him. If Lloyd felt any disappointment (and it is hard to believe that he did not) he kept it to himself, telling Montagu on 15 January 1921 that: 'I am quite content to be here and to hold this fort so long as I am doing it to your satisfaction and that of the Government and so long as my health holds out.'[25] Montagu's warning to 'be careful of yourself' because 'we cannot afford to lose our best men through allowing them to work themselves to death', was much to the point, but not easy to heed.[26]

The long struggle to raise the money for the Back Bay scheme, combined with his other worries and responsibilities, had left Lloyd tired and out of sorts. The elections at the end of the year, followed by the Duke's visit and a prolonged struggle with his Council over the budget in early 1921, hardly made for a quiet mind and good health. He confessed in early March that,

> I am feeling rather played out and cannot get fit again, but if only I could get away for two or three weeks somewhere I think I should mend – but there is no possible chance of that I'm afraid.[27]

Blanche's departure put an additional strain upon him, as Colin Forbes Adam recognized:

> Instead of facing difficulties with exuberant energy and resource as he had done in the past, he now had to draw upon his reserves. The fire and the determination and the resource would be there at need, but the summoning of them was heavily to tax his will-power and endurance.[28]

# 14

# DEALING WITH GANDHI

With the departure of Lord Chelmsford in April 1921 Lloyd's career in Bombay entered a new phase. He had come to India in the middle of the Viceroy's term and had been very much the 'new boy'; now he was firmly in his stride, but the success of his labours would depend upon the new man from England, Lord Reading. Given Reading's political antecedents it was not to be expected that he and Lloyd would get on well together, but first impressions on both sides were surprisingly good for two men of such fundamentally different character.

That one was a Conservative whilst the other was a Liberal was as nothing compared with the fact that Reading might have been designed as Lloyd's antithesis. A Jew, as a young man Rufus Isaacs had been 'hammered' on the Stock Exchange before making himself a second, highly successful, career as a lawyer. A suave and plausible man, his advocacy relied for its success upon these personal qualities. His career as a Liberal politician had almost crashed to ruins in 1912 over the Marconi scandal, and to Lloyd and other Conservatives he remained Kipling's 'Gehazi' – 'a leper white as snow'. But if it was to prove, in the long term, impossible to conquer such rooted mistrust, it was to be equally difficult not to succumb, at least initially, to the Viceroy's undoubted charm.

Reading landed at Bombay on 2 April. Lloyd found him both 'winning' and 'sympathetic' – if 'unwilling to commit himself to any definite statement of opinion on policy':[1] the charm and the irresolution thus noted were permanent features of the new viceroyalty. Reading's own impressions of Lloyd are apparent from a letter which he wrote to Montagu on 13 April:

> Lady Reading and I liked both Sir George Lloyd and Lady Lloyd very much. I was struck by their capacity and he is full of drive and energy; she is attractive and has dignity, presence and manner.[2]

And when Reading had his first talks with Gandhi in May Lloyd told Montagu:

> I think he is on the right track and unless I am very much mistaken Gandhi is going to meet his match. Even Reading, however, admits the unusual difficulties of dealing with a man of Gandhi's mentality, and it is too early yet to be optimistic as regards results.[3]

But this honeymoon phase proved, as such phenomena have a habit of doing, somewhat illusory.

The first rift in the lute came not over Gandhi but rather over what proved to be the long-running saga of the transfer of the Native States from the jurisdiction of Bombay to that of Delhi.

Lloyd was always very sensitive, sometimes too much so, over matters which he thought concerned his own prestige as Governor of the Bombay Presidency, and his constant ill-health accentuated this tendency. Since the abolition of the rule of the East India Company the Native States had dealt with the Raj through Bombay; as part of the greater centralization introduced by the Montagu–Chelmsford reforms, this function would pass to Simla. Lloyd had opposed this and thought he had obtained a promise from Chelmsford that it would not go ahead until Reading had consulted him. When he discovered in July that the transfer had been approved, he wrote long and extremely indignant letters to Montagu and Reading going into, in excessive detail, the history of the Native States and of his dealings with Chelmsford over them. It was, he told Montagu, 'a very severe blow' and would 'render my position an extremely difficult one'.[4]

Reading was puzzled, telling Montagu with some bewilderment that Lloyd 'seems to feel very acutely' about the subject.[5] Montagu, who saw that exhaustion lay behind Lloyd's outburst, asked him to talk the matter over calmly with Reading, and added: 'it is out of the question for anything to happen to shake my confidence in you and my admiration for your work'.[6] Again Montagu had shown how well he understood the character of the man he was dealing with; once assured of sympathy and understanding, Lloyd calmed down and reopened the question with Reading. There the matter stayed, a subject of detailed discussion, until 1923 when, much to Lloyd's chagrin, the decision went against him.

The episode proved an unfortunate irritant in relations with Simla at a particularly bad time. Lloyd's doubts about Reading's ability to be firm with unrest had been quickened by the course of events. He had approved of attempts in May to drive a wedge into the coalition which had made Gandhi such a power and which was showing signs of strain by early 1921. The Rowlatt Acts had enabled the Khalifat Movement, Congress and the Muslim League to co-operate, but the Ali brothers, Shurkat and Mohammed, leaders of the Khalifat Movement, were beginning to find Gandhi's passive resistance and 'soul-force' increasingly futile. They openly incited the army to mutiny and advocated violence as a way of achieving independence. Reading asked Gandhi to urge non-violence onto them; in return he promised that they would not be prosecuted. But the manoeuvre did not put an end to violence and Lloyd thought it inadvisable, in these conditions, to allow a visit planned by the Prince of Wales at the end of 1921 to go ahead; but Reading decided that it should.

Henceforth the Viceroy appeared to be dominated by an anxiety to do nothing which might provoke violence; this seemed to include being firm on the law and order issue. It was only after prolonged vacillation that he let Lloyd arrest the Alis in July. Lloyd thought this a very ill-advised attitude to take:

> The agitators are trading on the impending visit, and are confident that we shall not dare to take any action against them for that reason and so feel they can do anything they choose.
> I have believed that in dealing with a post-war situation a patient policy within limits was wise, but once open incitement to violence or seduction of the army and police begins, all political considerations must in my judgement go by the board.

But he feared that it was 'highly probable that if riots result the authorities will go back on me and I shall probably get abused by everyone'.[7]

In this atmosphere the question of what to do about Gandhi became problematic. Lloyd told Montagu on 23 September:

> I do not desire to have to take Gandhi if it can possibly be helped: I have always been of the same opinion ... that we must work so as to demonstrate his failure *coram populo*. I still hope that we might succeed in doing this. But of course he may at any time force our hands and compel us to take action against him. I shall be much more pleased if public opinion drives him out of the field as a leader, and I am not at all sure that this may not yet occur.[8]

He reported that after the arrest of the Alis,

> the Moslems are very bitter against Gandhi for remaining free whilst their leaders are in gaol. Gandhi replies in effect that he has done all that anyone can do to get into gaol without success. The Moslems merely retort that they have been let in!

He was, he told Montagu, 'sadly afraid that there is a good deal of mutual recrimination going on in the Hindu–Muslim brotherhood!'[9] In fact, Hindu–Moslem co-operation was almost over.

As the time for the Prince's visit grew closer, Lloyd 'spared no energy' to make it a success; as he told Reading on 26 October 1921:

> I doubt if you can at all appreciate the difficulties of preparing and organizing a visit of this kind in a place like Bombay in the present state of political feeling. It is one of the main centres of agitation and Gandhi is almost always with us to fan the flames of agitation.[10]

Despite his best efforts there were riots and it soon seemed to Lloyd that the time had come to take action against Gandhi.

But, on 19 December, just before the Prince was due to arrive in Calcutta, Lloyd received a long telegram from Reading which seemed to him to show that the Viceroy was 'little short of panic-striken by the agitators in Calcutta'. He later characterized it thus to Austen Chamberlain:

> I am afraid it was a contemptible telegram. It asked me and my Government to concur in the following proposal, namely that if Gandhi would bargain to give the Prince a quiet passage . . . the Viceroy . . . proposed to agree to having a Round Table conference with Gandhi, withdraw all the arrests and let all the arrested out of gaol![11]

Lloyd responded by asking Reading for assurances that he would not open negotiations with Gandhi behind his back; Governor and Viceroy were moving towards a confrontation.

Reading told Montagu on 5 January 1922 that he did not agree with Lloyd that, 'under the guise of preaching non-violence Gandhi is really preparing eventually for a revolution by violence'; he refused to give assurances that if Gandhi was arrested there might not follow negotiations which would lead to his release.[12] This prompted Lloyd to write to Montagu telling him that his Council unanimously agreed that 'Gandhi must be prosecuted promptly';[13] he criticized Reading's pusillanimity bitterly.[14]

Finally, on 8 February, Reading agreed that Gandhi should be arrested on St Valentine's day; but when the day dawned and all the arrangements had been made, he changed his mind. Lloyd protested furiously, telling Montagu on 17 February that Reading's action had 'not only gone far to wreck my personal position in my own Cabinet, but has made a fool out of me and my Government in the face of both the Indian and British publics'; news of the impending arrest had leaked out, and now the extremists were 'laughing up their sleeves' and talking openly of having frightened Reading. Lloyd asked whether Montagu intended sitting 'with folded hands whilst revolution is prepared', declaring that he was not willing to do so: 'I am speaking very frankly to you. I don't apologize for it: there are times when loyal service demands plain speaking.'[15]

Reading, for his part, was cross that Lloyd had written to Montagu behind his back. Montagu, who was in a difficult position, with most of the Cabinet wanting firm action, sympathized with his Viceroy and thought that both Lloyd and Willingdon were 'provincial in their outlook'.[16]

Lloyd demanded from Reading written assurances about future policy as well as a free hand with regard to Gandhi, threatening resignation if he did not get them.[17] Willingdon agreed to support him and they went to see the Viceroy at the end of the month, determined to get their way or resign. Reading 'had little to say', claiming that he had 'been stampeded by the threats of one of his Indian colleagues'. This explanation thoroughly disgusted Lloyd, but, as he got his assurances, he did not resign.[18] Willingdon was satisfied; not so Lloyd who was 'still badly worried' and left 'sick at heart and with my confidence in Reading much impaired'.[19] On 10 March Gandhi was arrested. After a trial he was sentenced to six years' imprisonment; there was little unrest and the bubble was, for the moment, pricked.

The strain of the episode further worsened Lloyd's health, but an even more shattering blow was in store when, on 10 March 1922, Montagu resigned. During 1921 Lloyd had continued to emphasize to him the important role which British policy towards Turkey played in stirring up the Khalifat Movement; it was convincing Indian Moslems that

> England, once the friend of Islam, is now its most bitter opponent. With all respect, I do insist that the Cabinet at home must make up their minds whether they want an anti-Islamic policy or India – and they cannot have both. They will surely lose India if the Moslems really believe that England is hostile to Islam.[20]

He also pressed the same point of view on Reading: 'our present path, if pursued, must I think mean the loss of India to the Empire'.[21] Montagu, who was trying to persuade his colleagues of the correctness of this view, used Lloyd's letter in Cabinet,[22] and when Reading sent him a despatch on 1 March 1922 which incorporated the official view of the Government of India that the treaty of Sèvres needed to be modified, he was able to use that as a final lever. The telegram was circulated to his colleagues on 3 March and, without consulting them, Montagu authorized its publication before they had had a chance to discuss it. It had been clear to Lloyd George for some time that Edwin Montagu had become a liability to his Government and he took the opportunity thus proffered to force his resignation.[23]

This news 'came like a thunderbolt' to Lloyd, who promised to urge the same policy on his successor. He had, he wrote, 'lost a real friend' whose 'constant sympathy and support'[24] he would miss. This was so. Despite a few difficult moments, the relationship between the two men had become as close as letters would allow. Montagu had shown great understanding of Lloyd's character, made allowances for his ill-health and the great strain he was under, whilst always admiring the energy and great qualities which he brought to the job. His replacement, Lord Peel, was not of the same stamp.

The son of a former Speaker of the House, Willie Peel was the third Conservative peer to be offered the India Office and received it only because Lords Derby and Devonshire had refused the post. A taciturn and reserved figure, he was not the man to continue Montagu's policy of writing warm personal letters. By August 1920 Lloyd was writing to Austen Chamberlain asking him 'in confidence'

> one question . . . about which I am becoming rather concerned. Ever since Willie Peel has been in office I have felt an atmosphere of hostility towards me from the India Office. He has seemed to deprecate any direct communication between me and himself such as was always the practice of his predecessor.[25]

He feared that this was the result of his contretemps with Reading, but it seems more likely that such hypersensitivity was the consequence of overtiredness.[26] Certainly Reading bore him no ill-will and recognized that he was ill and over-strained. In fact, even before the *dénouement* of the crisis Blanche had thought him 'within measurable distance of a really bad breakdown', and he had had pains around the heart which had led to his being ordered by the doctor to take more rest.[27]

In April he finally got away to Kashmir with Blanche for a rest which, as Reading told Peel, was more than needed:

> He certainly was in a very queer condition when he came to see me; indeed he was in such an excitable state that I was quite alarmed; but he is very much better. He has been working very hard and has a highly-strung, nervous temperament.[28]

The holiday came just in time to prevent that 'really bad breakdown' and a few weeks of hunting, fishing and riding helped set him on his feet again. But he did not heed the warning and, once back in Bombay in June, set to work again as hard as ever.

Fortunately for his health there was now less to do and less pressure from outside. With Gandhi spinning wool in his cell, the Ali brothers fulminating in theirs and the Khalifat Movement suffering from

Ataturk's abolition of the Sultanate in Turkey, Indian politics began to move into more constitutional channels, looking forward to the provincial elections in 1923. On other fronts too the hard work was bearing fruit. The housing schemes were progressing well and the immense engineering obstacles in the way of the Back Bay scheme were being surmounted; the Sukkur barrage project had received the approval of the Indian Government and, in early 1923, the British Government added its own imprimatur. All this amounted to a formidable corpus of achievement and, back at his desk in Government House, Lloyd could write to Austen Chamberlain:

> There is very little news to give you from here: things have never been so quiet or so orderly since I have been here. I see no reason why this quiet and this order should not last so long as the Government keeps steady and makes no further concessions to the agitators.[29]

# 15

# ENDINGS AND BEGINNINGS

The relative calm of the period after Gandhi's arrest gave Lloyd leisure to indulge his wanderlust and to meditate upon the future; the first of these things was exceedingly good for him.

Rumours about his future were abundant. Blanche, who had returned to Bombay in November 1921 and had supported him through the crisis, returned to England in July 1922 to look after David. From there she reported that he was being spoken of as a possible successor to Allenby as High Commissioner in Egypt;[1] the Embassy in Turkey and the High Commissioner's Residence in Canada were also mentioned in connection with his name. Such rumours were cheering reminders that he had not been forgotten, especially welcome to one who was still bothered by what he saw as Reading's hostility; he told Blanche on 22 September 1922 that the speculation was pleasing 'not so much for the sake of this job or that but as an indication rather of where one stands in public estimation'. Of one thing he remained certain: 'If I had stayed in the Commons these years I should not only have been broke in pocket, but broke in heart.'

Although he had no desire to return to domestic politics, he watched the developing criticism of Lloyd George and the coalition with the interest natural to a man whose future depended upon its fate. Despite his previous political career, Lloyd was not amongst those Conservatives who wanted to get rid of Lloyd George. In 1921 he had favoured a continuation of the coalition because he feared that any return to the old party system 'must mean the splitting of the anti-revolutionary forces'. He told Puss Gaskell that it was all very well vilifying Lloyd George for his past, but what mattered was that he was now fighting on their side: 'I don't see anyone who can put up a better fight for us than L-G at the moment and until I do I'm on his side';[2] this remained his view. From Edward Wood and others Lloyd was aware of the growing hostility felt by many Conservative MPs towards the Prime Minister, but he did not share their feelings. Unlike many Tories, who considered the Irish settlement of 1922 a 'sell out', Lloyd agreed with the Prime Minister; of Ireland he wrote to Puss Gaskell: 'I always feel I want to drown the whole place.'[3] The overthrow of Lloyd George in October 1922 and the resignation of Austen Chamberlain from the leadership of the Conservative Party dismayed Lloyd.

With Chamberlain as leader there would have been hope of political preferment; none could be expected from Law. The old struggle between ambition and instinct, dulled for a season by the chains of office, was resurrected by the prospect of freedom. Lloyd told Puss Gaskell in March that he found it 'hard to believe that I am due home in December. I am almost afraid of settling down at home for I think I am a hopeless tramp.'[4] Ambition dictated Egypt or the Commons but as he wrote in July: 'I am afraid . . . the wanderlust is seizing me terribly. It never leaves me and is becoming a fever after being cooped up here so long.' He wanted to have 'a good look round Rhodesia', a 'rapid but exhaustive tour of Eastern Europe' and, most of all, he wanted to visit America. He knew that respectable folk like Puss would say that he 'must bide at home and get into the collar again', but 'all the same that is what I am feeling'.[5] He wanted 'a *long* wander and not a short one!' There was so much of the world he had not seen. But Lloyd did not think he would return to India, at least not for some time,

> because in this kind of a position one is terribly a prisoner and I have felt the isolation and restraint of it all very much. I don't think I'm built quite tame enough for this kind of job! Anyway I've borne my heel-ropes with great and exemplary fortitude but I'm not going to wear any more of the same kind until I've had a good chukker round in freedom![6]

The sudden illness of Bonar Law in May and his replacement by the relatively unknown Stanley Baldwin was a good thing from Lloyd's point of view, as he told Blanche: 'He is an extremely ordinary person but steady, honest and sound . . . not . . . in any way hostile to me I fancy.'[7] Puss wrote in July that there was a good chance of his getting a safe Conservative seat if he wanted one, but he thought that he was too out of touch with British politics to plunge straight back in and did not want to become either a backbencher or an Under-Secretary; and he assumed there was no prospect of being offered a Cabinet post:

> This being so and short of a conviction that it was a real public duty to re-enter the field of home politics I am disposed to think that I had better continue in the field of eastern administration if I am given the opportunity – a métier of which I do know something – or if I am not,

keep a free pen and a free voice to use as and when the occasion demands.[8]

In June when it was announced that Sir Leslie Wilson, a Conservative Whip, was to succeed him, Lloyd felt that his stewardship was drawing to its close.

But before it did there was one place he wished to visit again: Kashmir. He went to the mountains and snows there in October, this despite the fact that he had, a few months earlier, damaged his eye in a golfing accident. The reason for his persistence was that he wanted to go up to Peshawar to see the frontier and the Khyber Pass which he had never seen before:

> To see the Buddhist remains up the Khyber and to reflect that in Asoka's day *his* imperial care too was to guard that door; to remember Alexander's march down – and Bobs' march up – aren't they a series of Imperial reflections which must move even a Jewish ruler of this country![9]

Whatever they did for Reading, these sights and reflections had a profound effect on Lloyd. He enjoyed his time on the frontier enormously, perhaps because it was 'so little Indian' and so like his beloved Turkey; he waxed lyrical to Blanche:

> Oh my dear you don't know how this part, my old part, of the East eats into my heart and how I love it. I don't feel I *could* leave it all for Whitehall permanently. It is the thing that is most in me. . . . I am glad I came here, it is a wonderful parting recollection.[10]

It was a sign of how much the wanderlust was on him that when the departure came he did not accompany her straight back to England but returned instead by way of Egypt, Constantinople and Eastern Europe.

As the time for leaving drew near the press was filled with rumours of his next appointment. The Bombay papers tipped him for the viceregal throne after Reading, whilst some others thought that he might go to Turkey as ambassador. He would have liked either, but no offer came.[11] Lloyd's own verdict on his period as governor was expressed in a letter to his successor on 29 June 1923:

> I have had rather a rough time during my five years: I found the Presidency in the most complete state of lawlessness, agitation and disorder both politically and economically, but we've killed the agitation and you couldn't wish for a more orderly and peaceful charge than is this Presidency now.
>
> Its finances too will be handed over to you in considerably better shape than those of any other Government in India. The big irrigation and development schemes which I have inaugurated are all in full swing

and their finance provided for right up to the date of their completion, so
that I think you should have no trouble in regard to them.[12]

Nor would Reading have disagreed. He wrote to Peel in August:

> [He has] undoubtedly been a very successful Governor and has done
> really valuable service to Bombay ... especially in regard to the
> irrigation schemes in Bombay City. He has shown great driving power in
> following up and carrying out large schemes, notably that of the Sukkur
> Barrage, and has a special understanding of the complexities of financial
> arrangements. . . . My own impression at the moment is that he should
> be made a peer as a fitting recognition of his services as Governor.[13]

Peel replied that 'the tendency is at present rather to restrict the
bestowal of honours'[14] and Baldwin ruled against it, feeling that it
would set a bad precedent,[15] but Reading protested that:

> Lloyd is a very different case. He is a man of exceptional energy and
> capacity and has undertaken great projects in Bombay – larger than
> have ever been undertaken before; and he has also had a very difficult
> time during his Governorship. In my opinion his case should be treated
> as an extraordinary one on account of his exceptional achievements.[16]

But it was to no avail and it was perhaps with some irony that Peel
wrote back to a man who had received spectacular promotion in the
peerage from Lloyd George that, 'the prevailing view is that honours
have been cheapened by too lavish a distribution in the past'.[17]

Lloyd was awarded the Knight Grand Cross of the Star of India
(KGCSI) and made a Privy Councillor in the New Year's honours list,
but he was, he wrote to Blanche, 'so frightfully disappointed' at not
getting a peerage: 'I did want it so and I don't want to go back into the
House of Commons.'[18]

In November, just before Lloyd's departure, Baldwin surprised
everyone (including many of his colleagues) by calling a snap election
on the issue of tariff reform. Lloyd, whose loyalty to tariff reform had
never faltered, admired his courage:

> I can't tell you how proud and glad I am you should have done this –
> whether you fail or whether you win. ... To have become Prime
> Minister and to be willing to risk it all in favour of a great policy is fine.[19]

But the timing of the gesture caused him immense anguish as he
confessed to Puss:

> I don't think I have ever badly wanted to be home before, but since I
> heard this I have been feeling miserable at being out of it all and longing
> to be home to take a hand. It is really rather bad luck that I should be just
> six weeks, and only six weeks too late after five years' absence![20]

While the future of the country was decided, Lloyd found himself making farewell speeches 'night after night and day after day and not doing, I fear, much good to anyone'.[21] He and Blanche left Bombay on 8 December 1923, but for Lloyd the sense of ending was overriden by anxiety about what the future held. At Aden on the voyage home came the grim news that the Conservatives had lost over a hundred seats and that there was a real possibility of a Labour Government.[22]

Lloyd found some refuge from such a prospect in revisiting Egypt and Constantinople, but the results of the election pointed to just the sort of national crisis which he had said was the only thing that would draw him back to the Commons. As he wrote to Puss: 'It seems to me that we may have to recast our minds now and that everyone who wants to keep socialism out may have to combine quite apart from any party labels or doctrines.' He had, he wrote, promised himself six months' holiday before trying to do anything else, 'but I am going to find it very difficult to stick to. There is such a lot to do isn't there and life is short.'[23]

In Egypt he saw the tomb of Tutankhamun and took stock of the political situation there against the possibility that he might be appointed High Commissioner in succession to Allenby. From thence he revisited Constantinople, staying with an old Eton friend, Nevile Henderson, at the Embassy which held such memories for him. Stopping off in Switzerland before returning to London in early February 1924 he paid the price for looking at the tomb – breaking his collar-bone in a skiing accident. Thus, at last, in February 1924 he returned to London.

With 'Othello's occupation' well and truly gone he faced a dilemma. He wanted to pursue his public career, but the prospect of a return to the Commons and 'beginning all over again' was supremely un-appealing;[24] a peerage would have solved that problem, but with Labour in power there was little prospect of that.

But public life, as Bombay had shown, was expensive, and Lloyd was not a rich man; indeed the scale of expenditure he had felt obliged to maintain as governor dictated that some way of replenishing the family fortunes should be found. In these circumstances he could have been pardoned for putting the interests of his family first and capitalizing on the many business opportunities which came his way. He was at the peak of his earnings potential and could, had he so wished, have made himself a rich man; but ambition would not let him rest.

Soon after his arrival in England Lloyd had several long talks with Baldwin about his political future. At their first meeting Baldwin congratulated me upon the success of my administration in India and said that, as perhaps I already knew, he had definitely intended to send me to Egypt soon after my return and as soon as I had had a little holiday, but the results of the election had unfortunately deprived him of the power for the time being of doing what he wished, but he hoped the opportunity would not be very long deferred as he did not anticipate the Labour Government could remain for any length of time in power.

When, at a later meeting, Lloyd asked if 'there was any platform or other work I could do for the Party', Baldwin enquired if he still wanted to 'go abroad again' or whether he would prefer to serve at home. When Lloyd said that he would not be interested in a junior appointment Baldwin made it clear that, 'what he had in mind was a post in the Cabinet'. Lloyd said he would prefer 'to continue with a career in Eastern administration' and Baldwin reiterated his hope that he would be able to send him to Egypt: 'I said I hoped he would also consider me for India and he replied that the matter would have to be considered but that in any case going to Egypt need be no obstacle or bar to that end.' In response to Lloyd asking whether he should stand for the Commons, Baldwin said it would be better to wait until the election came; if it then seemed that the fight would be close he should stand.[25]

This was all highly satisfactory, the more so in that he had been disappointed at the lack of interest shown by old friends like Austen Chamberlain[26] and had sought the advice of Leo Amery on what to do. Amery's advice had been characteristically (alas) bad: to make a position for himself as 'leader of the fiscal movement outside of Parliament' until the Conservatives returned to power 'and then take his peerage and either join the next Cabinet or go out to India [as Viceroy] straight away'.[27] Most Indian governors had difficulty in readjusting to ordinary life and Lloyd was no exception; Beaverbrook's comment about Curzon is almost equally applicable to him:

> For the rest of his life . . . [he] was influenced by his sudden journey to heaven at the age of thirty-nine, and then by his return seven years later to earth, for the remainder of his mortal existence.[28]

At least, with Baldwin's promise, there was the prospect of a re-ascent into another heaven.

# 16

# EASTBOURNE, AMBITION AND INTRIGUE

It was, therefore, with a certain abstraction of mind that Lloyd turned to the task of recouping his fortunes. He resumed his place on the board of Lloyds Bank and acquired a directorship at the Shell Oil company; these, and his underwritership at Lloyd's, enabled him to reduce his overdraft. A spell at Bagnoles in the summer of 1924 helped to deal with another legacy from his Indian years – ill-health.[1]

Baldwin had been correct about the life-span of the Labour Government: in October Ramsay MacDonald resigned and called a general election. Lloyd, having 'pretty well decided not to stand',[2] spent a weekend at Hatfield House where he encountered Baldwin who encouraged him in this resolve; but two weeks before polling day Rupert Gwynne, MP for the safe Conservative seat of Eastbourne, died and the Chief Agent of the party urged him to step in 'and explicitly told me I was destined to be sent abroad soon after the election but that the possession of a seat would not be allowed to stand in the way'. So it was that, 'not without a good deal of reluctance to stand for Parliament and not be included in the Government (as I knew from my understanding with Baldwin I should not be)', Lloyd was, on 14 October, formally adopted as the Unionist candidate for Eastbourne.[3]

Blanche, who had spent much of her time since returning getting their house in Charles Street in order, found the campaign (her first since she had helped Edward Wood back in 1910) 'very interesting' – which was more than her husband did; he found the business of campaigning 'badly distasteful'. But it was a pleasant change from the old days in West Staffordshire. Eastbourne was a Tory stronghold, and he was campaigning in the most favourable possible atmosphere, but even so, the size of his majority astonished him. Gwynne had held the seat against a Liberal in 1923 with a majority of 1,880, winning 13,276 votes (some 53.8 per cent of the total). Lloyd, fighting both Labour and Liberals, collected 17,533 votes, 67.9 per cent of the total, and had a majority of 13,366 over his nearest rival – a Liberal with a mere 4,167 votes. It was a crushing victory, greeted with great euphoria in the Lloyd camp; Blanche recorded there was

> great enthusiasm at the result – and directly it was announced the whole crowd broke off their cheering and sang God save the King – which was rather an interesting manifestation of the way their minds worked – for they had realised the truth of the situation – that it is actually a fight between the British Empire, and all the constitutional foundation of it – and the theories of the Labour Party inspired by Bolshevist extremists.[4]

Their new MP told the waiting crowd that his record majority was a 'wonderful answer to the Bolsheviks and everything that was anti-British'.[5]

Lloyd told Puss Gaskell on 9 November that he did not 'like being back in the House', finding difficulty in 'stepping down from high office to the back-benches', but he was a 'fatalist' about the future: 'so long as one follows the thread of life wherever it leads, as long as one never shirks the fight, one can be content':

> Baldwin knows that I am not 'on the make' and I think knows that I am not one of those who would intrigue against him on the score of any disappointment and therefore it was safe enough to leave me on one side. I am really not in public life for what little, if anything, that I can get out of it, but for what I can give to it. I know that is an old-fashioned doctrine, but you see I am a Tory and was brought up like that – so you must not blame me. I did not stand for Parliament in order to get Office but because, believing it was going to be a very narrow issue all over the country, I felt it was the duty of everyone who could enter the fighting line if the occasion arose. The occasion was not sought by me, but when it presented itself, I felt I had no right to refuse.[6]

He did not tell her of Baldwin's promise of Egypt, but that news would, he thought, come soon enough.

But time passed and no call came. In January 1925 Blanche recorded in her diary their frustration over the 'present uncertainty' and the hope that 'it cannot last much longer';[7] it did not. In February Lloyd received a telegram from the leaders of the White settlers in Kenya urging him to apply for the post of governor of the colony.[8] As he had turned this job down in 1918 he was not inclined to take it now, despite the urgings of the new Colonial Secretary, Leo Amery.[9] It was, therefore, with a deep sense of shock that he received a letter from Amery on 12 March offering him the Governorship of Kenya, accompanied by a strong hint that he should take it because it would be all he would get.[10] As Lloyd explained in an emotional letter to Austen Chamberlain on 16 March:

Amery had gathered that any hopes I might have had about India were not likely to materialize at any very early date. He then added to my amazement that he thought I ought to know as regards Egypt, that whilst it had been intended until quite recently to offer me that post, you [Chamberlain] had recently decided upon another candidate.[11]

This was devastating news for, as Blanche recorded in her diary, 'the only question in our mind has been whether he might not possibly be considered a suitable candidate for India instead'.[12] Now it seemed to be Kenya or nothing.

Lloyd tackled Baldwin on 14 March and he 'made no attempt of any kind to dissent in the smallest particular from my account of what had passed between us'; Edward Wood confirmed that he had indeed been earmarked for Egypt but neither held out any hope that he would get it.[13] It seemed to Lloyd that all his years of work in the East had been 'rendered purposeless' and that his career was 'shattered'. He poured out the story of Baldwin's promises along with his own bitterness in a long and anguished letter to Chamberlain on 16 March. What had happened?

Amery's warnings to Lloyd had followed some remarks which Baldwin had made to him on 28 February; he had said that:

He and Austen had suddenly thought of Ronaldshay as better suited for Egypt than Lloyd, apparently in conjunction with the idea of prolonging Reading and then judging how R[onaldshay] might do for India. R[onaldshay] had already been offered Egypt so it was no use saying much, tho' I expressed the view that Lloyd was really the better man.[14]

The Lloyds learnt more of the story on 14 March from H. A. ('Taffy') Gwynne, the editor of the *Morning Post* (and brother of the late Member for Eastbourne). He said that the problem had arisen because the Secretary of State for India, Lord Birkenhead, wanted (mainly for financial reasons) to be Viceroy. He was said to be planning to keep his old friend Reading in Simla for another year or so until he was ready to leave the India Office. The competition, Ronaldshay and Lloyd, would be bought off; the former, as the more senior figure, was to be offered the substantial compensation of Egypt whilst Lloyd was to be given Kenya.[15] There is no independent confirmation of this but it certainly fits the facts as noted by Amery's diary. Birkenhead certainly considered the idea of becoming Viceroy – much to the dismay of Baldwin, who eventually vetoed the idea on grounds of health.[16] For the Lloyds the question now became one bigger even than the 'mere sacrifice of George's career': 'It is no less an issue than whether the brilliant crooks of the Cabinet are to continue to dupe the Prime Minister into disregarding the claims of loyal service in order to arrange appointments to suit their own convenience.'[17] They determined 'to fight to the limit of our power'.[18]

Lloyd had hoped that his letter to Chamberlain would help but, to his dismay, it merely brought forth what Blanche described as a 'real schoolmaster's letter . . . implying that G. had been unreasonable and warning him rather pompously against further "solicitations" or indeed action of any kind'; this, from a man whom he considered to be an old friend, was both 'irritating as well as wounding'.[19] The letter, written on 19 March, promised to reveal everything when they met; Chamberlain thought that Lloyd's hopes of getting Egypt were good – 'unless by undue insistence or too active a solicitation you yourself destroy them':

> Do not for a moment allow yourself to think that malevolent influences have been at work or that there has been a conspiracy against you. That would be to argue yourself unfit and to make your best friends doubt your judgement, but in any case do not allow yourself to become soured.[20]

But the day after he received this unpromising letter, George had a telephone call from Baldwin telling him that 'it is all right'.[21] The following day he received a formal letter offering him the post of High Commissioner of Egypt.[22]

The history of British involvement in Egypt since 1918 suggested that the post of High Commissioner was something of a 'poisoned chalice',[23] and the circumstances in which it had been offered him combined to make Lloyd tread warily before accepting it.

Lloyd saw Austen Chamberlain on 30 March, and this first formal interview provided plenty of warning that the road ahead would not be an easy one. Chamberlain, at his most stiff and formal, ticked Lloyd off for 'pressing his claims in the way he did', telling him that it had 'done him harm both with himself and with the Prime Minister'. Regarding this as tantamount to asking him to 'go out with a kind of slur upon him which he should not be called upon to take', Lloyd told Austen that he wanted some time to think over the offer.[24]

Although a meeting with Baldwin in early April seemed to clear the air, a further talk with Chamberlain on 6 April seemed to set things very much back where they had been[25] and it took a third meeting on 12 May to clarify matters; and even then, it remained apparent that there would be difficulties ahead.

Whatever his relations with the Government were to be, study of the Egyptian problem had already convinced Lloyd that his job was next door to impossible. The British had been in Egypt since 1882 but their position had never been defined. In 1914 when Turkey entered the war, a protectorate had been declared over Egypt, but the chance thus to regularize their position had been lost in 1919.

In December 1918 the British High Commissioner in Cairo, Sir Reginald Wingate, had refused to allow an Egyptian delegation headed by Saad Zaghloul Pasha to proceed to the Versailles conference and argue the case for Egyptian independence. Early 1919 witnessed outbursts of rioting in Egypt stimulated and directed by Zaghloul and his nationalist movement, the Wafd. The British response set a pattern that was to become depressingly familiar. A mission under the Colonial Secretary, Lord Milner, visited Egypt to investigate the disturbances. Impressed by what he took to be the strength of the Wafd, Milner declared, without consulting the Cabinet, that his aim was 'to reconcile the aspirations of the Egyptian people with the special interests which Great Britain has in Egypt'; for the next three decades Anglo–Egyptian relations revolved around this declaration.

Milner had been supported by Wingate's successor, Lord Allenby, who followed this up by releasing Saad Zaghloul from detention in Malta in early 1920, thus enabling him to enter into negotiations with Milner. In August 1920 the two men reached an agreement by which, in return for a British recognition of Egyptian independence, Egypt would confer on Britain 'such rights as are necessary to safeguard her special interests'.

Lloyd's reactions to the Milner–Zaghloul agreement have already been recorded; he saw it as the first sign of the recall of the legions to Rome. Milner's agreement stipulated that four points should be 'reserved' to Britain: control over the Suez Canal; the defence of Egypt; the protection of foreign interests; and the status of the Sudan, over which the Egyptian nationalists claimed sovereignty. Zaghloul refused to accept these conditions.

Zaghloul and King Fuad sought to use the British influence at the Residency in their struggle for supreme power, whilst Allenby and the Foreign Office (under whose aegis Egypt came) continued to hope that they could come up with some form of treaty which would embody the four reserved points and be acceptable to Zaghloul. This last was the diplomatic equivalent of Mr Dick's King Charles's head, but it allowed Zaghloul plenty of leeway in his battle with Fuad. However, the events of 1924–5 seemed to have tipped the scales towards the King.

When the British Sirdar (Commander-in-Chief) of the Egyptian army, Sir Lee Stack, was murdered in 1924, Lord Allenby blamed the Wafd, dismissed Zaghloul from the premiership and imposed a fine on Egypt. When the elections of March 1925 produced a Wafdist majority in the Chamber, Allenby demanded that it should be prorogued. Fuad

had been only too happy to comply and had suspended the constitution, ruling through a creature of his own, Ziwar Pasha, although the
real power behind the throne, one Nashaat Pasha, was not even an
elected deputy. Allenby and the Foreign Office were by no means in
agreement on the next step: the Office thought him too hard; he
thought the diplomats too weak. The result had been that Allenby had
quarrelled with the diplomats and had been removed. The omens were
not good for any successor who was not a member of the Foreign Office.

At his meeting with Chamberlain on 12 May Lloyd put forward his
view of the Egyptian situation; because the great tragedy of Lloyd's
career was bound up with accusations that he followed his own policy
in Egypt, it is worth noting what was said on the subject of Britain's
future policy on this occasion. Lloyd's view was that 'as things were at
present, the alternative to the present régime in Egypt was not, in my
opinion, "Cromerism" but annexation'; he did not, in other words,
foresee a return to the ambiguous situation of 1882 to 1914. In view of
the criticism which was to be directed at Lloyd by the Foreign Office for
taking this black-and-white view of things it is perhaps surprising to
note that Chamberlain did not challenge this statement. Lloyd secured
agreement that he should go to Cairo with 'exactly the same powers as
my predecessor had'. In view of the fact that he would be the first High
Commissioner to be appointed since the 1922 declaration, this was a
matter of some significance, implying that the position of the Residency
remained an important one. It was also agreed that Fuad would be
supported 'so long as he worked loyally with us in every manner'.[26]

On 20 May, the day his appointment was to be announced in the
House, Lloyd wrote to Chamberlain to say 'how grateful I am for the
confidence you have given me' and promised to 'give all my loyalty and
energy in order to try and make a success of the work entrusted to me'.[27]
Blanche noted in her diary that her husband had the advantage not
only of Chamberlain's friendship but also that of the Permanent Under-
Secretary at the Foreign Office, Willy Tyrrell, and that he had
'practically the whole of the FO behind him';[28] exactly what this meant
the next four years were to show. The only sadness in 1925, however,
was that the appointment meant an end to her hopes that Lloyd might
become Foreign Secretary or even Prime Minister; it was, she noted,
'definitely good-bye to home politics as far as one can foresee'.

# 17

# FIRST ROUND WITH ZAGHLOUL

Lloyd spent the summer of 1925 immersed in study of the Egyptian question. He read every important telegram which had passed between the Foreign Office and the Residency in Cairo since 1918 and he kept up a detailed correspondence with the acting High Commissioner, his old school-friend, Nevile Henderson. By October he had reached a number of sombre conclusions.

The 1922 declaration abolishing the Protectorate subject to a treaty covering the four 'reserved' points (the security of imperial communications; the defence of Egypt; the protection of foreign interests and the Sudan), far from leading to a settlement of the Egyptian problem, had rendered it more acute. Sultan Fuad, who had thus acquired the title of king, was pleased, and his Prime Minister, Sarwat Pasha, shared in some measure the hopes nursed in Britain; but the main beneficiary had turned out to be Saad Zaghloul Pasha. Sarwat, like other Egyptian 'liberals', found himself trapped between Fuad, who intrigued against the idea of a constitution which would restrict his powers, and Zaghloul, who condemned any government which paid heed to the four reserved points; his administration was of short duration.

It had been followed by a period of confusion which resulted in Zaghloul's arrival in power in January 1924. Attempts by Mac-Donald's Labour Government to obtain a treaty from him had proved fruitless and Zaghloul's intransigence won him plaudits in Cairo and strengthened his hand in his power struggle against Fuad. Only the murder of Sir Lee Stack in November 1924 had saved the King. Allenby's stern response had led to Saad's resignation and Fuad had later suspended the constitution, appointing as his Prime Minister the immensely fat and complaisant Ziwar Pasha.

Any opportunity which existed in early 1925 for the British to steer a middle course between Zaghloul, the Wafd and Fuad was lost during the course of the year as the King's evident desire for autocracy alienated men like Sarwat and the other leading 'liberal' Sidky Pasha. Henderson told Lloyd on 25 September that 'the present cardinal point in British policy must be to see Saadism smashed';[1] as he put it in a letter on 19 June:

> Saad stands for a state of mind in this country which is incompatible with any maintenance of the British position here. If ever we are to negotiate with the Egyptians about the reserved points or to make a treaty with them, that state of mind must have disappeared and something else must have taken its place.[2]

Aware of the danger that supporting Fuad would merely replace one absolutism with another, Henderson preferred 'a despot' to 'a demagogue'.

Henderson still believed that a middle course could be charted between the Scylla of absolutism and the Charybdis of demagoguery. During the summer he unfolded to Lloyd his hopes that Ziwar and the Liberal leader, Sidky, would co-operate on the basis of British backing and the restoration of the constitution.[3] But this was wishful thinking of a high order. Sidky may have hated Zaghloul, but he was not going to lose his own supporters by co-operating with Fuad nor was Fuad going to try to win his support by restoring the constitution. In fact, in September 1925, before Lloyd arrived in Egypt, Fuad drove out of Ziwar's administration the few remaining Liberals.[4]

The new High Commissioner would play a crucial role. The Wafd propagated the view that he was coming with full powers to negotiate a settlement with Zaghloul; but both they and Fuad also feared that the 'Indian tiger' was coming out to reintroduce 'Cromerism'.[5] From Teheran, Percy Loraine wrote to Lloyd:

> I haven't got much sympathy for the Egyptians, but I wonder if the wretched brutes realize what is in pickle for them! However, they want a Pharaoh, and unquestionably they are going to get one! Well, that's their worry.[6]

The months preceding Lloyd's departure in October 1925 seemed scarcely enough to deal with all the arrangements necessitated by his appointment; one matter proved particularly troublesome – the question of a peerage. His disappointment at not being made a peer after Bombay has already been noted; he was determined not to go out to Cairo without a title – 'for all orientals think extra highly of a Lord'. Somewhat against the wishes of the King (who would have preferred him to win his spurs first),[7] he was offered a barony in October 1925.

This raised the question of what title he should take. He would have liked to take the name of the family property at Dolobran, but when this was vetoed by his brother Tom, he settled on becoming 'Lord Llydiarth' after the 'valley of the Lloyds'; but here too he met with a check when the owner of the valley refused his permission. Feeling that he could 'not descend to a made-up name like Beaverbrook and Northcliffe', he decided to be gazetted as Lord Lloyd of Dolobran. This had the twin virtues of being 'unpretentious' and practical (mono-grammed linen would not need changing), but Lloyd feared that it lacked euphony. Certainly his fellow peers were to find it a tongue-twister, with 'Lord Lord', 'Lloyd Lord' and 'Lloyd Lloyd' all being tried as variants on a theme.[8]

Lord Lloyd of Dolobran in the county of Montgomeryshire (the final version was not decided until late October) arrived in Egypt in mid October 1925. Blanche registered three impressions: that it was hotter than she had expected; that the ceremonial welcome was badly managed (Bombay would have done it better); and that the Residency was 'about as bad as can be'.[9] The rooms were shabby, the furniture either cheap and nasty or old and worn out, and the 'garden' was a desolation; the Residency gave no impression of permanency to the British presence in Egypt.

Whilst Blanche despaired her husband despatched a ten-page letter to the Office of Works on 25 October; it detailed everything that was wrong with the house and demanded immediate action.[10] It took, however, some time to create comfort and 'an appearance of dignity' where none had existed before.

The political situation gave rise to feelings similar to those evoked by the state of the Residency. Writing to Austen Chamberlain on 25 October, Lloyd commented:

> I feel as if I had walked into a political bedlam where everything is strident and nothing is real – the most complete tangle I think I ever saw. I much fear that circumstances are not going to allow me as long a period for consideration as I should like.[11]

He thought that Henderson had made a great mistake by allowing Britain to become identified with the King's absolutism, but his problem was how to rectify this without giving the impression that he was favouring Zaghloul and the Wafd.

Lloyd determined to get rid of Fuad's éminence grise, Nashaat Pasha,[12] but was constrained by two considerations: the negotiations in train between Ziwar's Government and the Italians concerning the Libyan–Egyptian frontier; and the knowledge that Zaghloul would claim the credit for Nashaat's dismissal. It was thus necessary to wait until the negotiations were concluded, but the delay gave Lloyd time to make his attitude to Saad Pasha perfectly plain. It was the custom for all former Prime Ministers to leave their calling-cards at the Residency when a new High Commissioner arrived. To avoid any public insult to Zaghloul Lloyd refrained from returning any cards; but he took care to have private conversations with all the other ex-premiers, thus making it plain that Saad Zaghloul was *persona non grata*.

In the meantime political unrest grew. On 21 November 1925, in a united show of strength, all the opposition parties met at the Continental Hotel and declared themselves a legally constituted parliament. Fuad's suspension of the constitution was denounced, a call for fresh elections was made, Zaghloul was elected as President of the Chamber and a Liberal leader, Mahmoud Mahmoud, was made one of the vice-presidents along with a member of the radical Witantist party: this coalescence of Wafdists, Liberals and radicals boded ill for the British if they wanted to use the Liberals as a *via media* between the King and Zaghloul. The meeting also posed a fresh problem: it was clearly desirable to have elections, but if they were held in the current climate of opinion, the Wafd would win and Zaghloul would become Prime Minister; to allow this was to lose face, to veto him was to run the risk of unrest: it was a considerable dilemma.

Thus, even when Nashaat was forced out after the conclusion of an agreement with Italy on 6 December (he went to Spain as ambassador),[13] the High Commissioner had only cleared the ground to deal with a more formidable problem, Saad Zaghloul himself.

Lloyd's feelings after this first triumph were expressed, oddly enough, to the Labour leader on 29 December 1925:

> The removal of Nashaat Pasha has done great good as showing that we do not mean to allow unfettered Palace despotism. . . . It has done our position a great deal of good and I must confess that on the whole the King has accepted it well.[14]

Conscious that the Opposition could do much to encourage the Wafd by criticism of British policy, Lloyd was anxious to keep MacDonald informed of the progress made against autocracy. The Foreign Office was equally pleased. Tyrrell wrote to congratulate Lloyd on 6 January, urging him to try to sponsor a Liberal–Ittehadist (monarchist) government and recalling the 'two cardinal points' to be borne in mind if he ever did have to intervene publicly in Egyptian politics: 'One is that British intervention is requested by the natives; and the other is that a clear case for intervention must be made in the Commons here.'[15]

Efforts to secure support for Ziwar from the Liberals were undermined by his new electoral law introduced on 8 December which disenfranchised all those under the age of twenty-five. On 21 January 1926 the Opposition parties again united, denouncing the restrictive new franchise and summoning a 'national congress' of senators and former deputies; strikes and further unrest were promised. Ziwar was running out of friends and time.[16] To a man who had governed Bombay, the prospect of rioting was nothing: 'if they wish to make trouble they will get plenty of it'.[17] Refusing to encourage the malcontents by changing his plans he set off for a tour of the Sudan in mid January – to the dismay of the faint-hearts in the Residency. When he returned in early February, Ziwar, fearing unrest, had decided to take his advice to drop the new electoral law; this meant elections could be held in May.

The prospect of Zaghloul as Premier darkened counsel. Lloyd's view, expressed to Chamberlain on 14 February, was that although there were 'strong arguments in favour of a show of strength' he had not yet made up his mind whether to accept him or not.[18] The diplomats did not like the sound of this. Henderson wanted to cultivate Zaghloul before the election,[19] whilst the Foreign Office urged Lloyd to 'go as slow as possible in your kingdom'. Willy Tyrrell warned in early March that with trouble in Turkey and China and the prospect of a general strike at home, the Government could not afford the 'luxury' of allowing him to 'embark upon a big statesmanlike policy in Egypt'; instead a 'hand to mouth' policy was called for. He was urged 'to copy faithfully the attitude of your neighbour, the great sphinx'.[20] The diplomats still hankered after their treaty and were bent on keeping Egypt quiet; they feared that Lloyd might spoil the chances of both by taking 'firm' action. He did not agree; Lloyd's experience of the East suggested that only a firm policy would induce the respect which must precede real negotiations. The divide between these two positions was destined to grow.

Behind this divide lay not only two quite dissimilar habits of mind – although clearly Lloyd's love of firm and decisive action was anathema to diplomats reared on the belief that words were a substitute for deeds – but there was something more fundamental at issue. Lloyd had feared that the Zaghloul–Milner agreement signified the recall of the legions, but the return of a Conservative Government suggested to many that such a policy would be halted, if not reversed. Writing to Lord Reading in June 1925, Birkenhead tried to convey the new tone of imperial policy:

What is most important for you to understand is the general atmosphere of this Cabinet. It is one of reaction against weakness and surrender. I think that the influence of Austen, Winston and myself is very great. You will not fail to meet with full support in any matter which, paying regard to your own innate prudence, you become satisfied that strong action is necessary.[21]

The selection of a staunch imperialist like Lloyd for Egypt was a sign of this 'reaction against weakness and surrender'.

Birkenhead was, at this stage, wont to exaggerate the importance of his fellow former coalitionists and he was, it soon transpired, wrong about Austen Chamberlain. But if Austen soon took on the colour of his surroundings, there remained within the Cabinet a considerable group of ministers who supported Birkenhead's views: the Chancellor, Winston Churchill, and the Secretary of State for War, Worthington-Evans, were two of the most prominent, and they were joined by Leo Amery, Joynson-Hicks (the Home Secretary), Lord Salisbury, Douglas Hogg and Neville Chamberlain. But they did not have a free run in Cabinet.

The crisis over the appointment of Zaghloul revealed a fault-line in the Baldwin Cabinet on imperial affairs and the major voice on the other side of the argument was Austen Chamberlain's. Behind him was the Foreign Office with its desire for a liberal solution of the Egyptian problem and there were those in the Cabinet susceptible to this siren song: Lord Robert Cecil at the Foreign Office and the new Viceroy, Lord Irwin (formerly Edward Wood), were among their number, as was Baldwin. The charge that Lloyd went against the Egyptian policy of the Foreign Office raises the question of whether that policy was quite in line with government policy. The crisis over Zaghloul was only the first of many crises which suggest that Conservative policy and the desires of the Foreign Office were not always identical.

Lloyd rehearsed the arguments for and against accepting Zaghloul in two detailed letters to Chamberlain on 23 April and 2 May, as well as in a very long telegram on 20 May. He acknowledged that it would look odd in the eyes of public opinion to refuse office to a democratically elected Prime Minister, and whether in or out of office Zaghloul would be a power in the land; it might be politic to make him exercise that power openly as a responsible minister; and yet, despite this, Lloyd thought it would be fatal to British prestige to allow such an avowed enemy to hold office again and his vote was cast accordingly.[22]

Chamberlain responded on 20 May with a strong telegram urging acceptance of Zaghloul;[23] this brought a swift response from Lloyd's supporters. Churchill wrote on 21 May to express surprise that the matter had not been brought before the Cabinet,[24] and Amery, who thought that 'Lloyd is right', commented that:

> The Parliamentary business is, after all, a farce, and a universally recognized farce in Egypt, and to follow out its conventions as observed in England, regardless of the effect of doing so upon Egypt, seems to me very dangerous. The House of Commons here knows quite well that Egypt isn't England and that if the Egyptians want self-government it must be on terms of co-operation with us.[25]

Chamberlain retreated a little, covering himself with the excuses that no decision had yet been reached and that his telegram had been designed to elicit further arguments that could be put before the Cabinet.[26]

Wafdist success in the elections on 20 May brought on the crisis. Lloyd had kept up a steady stream of telegrams to London in favour of his policy and had taken care to see that the King and the leading Liberals would create no problems. So when, on 28 May, news came that Zaghloul was going to put himself forward, he telegraphed to London:

> I propose to talk to Zaghloul in a friendly but perfectly frank strain. I shall explain to him the natural anxiety felt by His Majesty's Government regarding his intentions in the light of his record. . . . I shall then endeavour to dissuade him from taking office at his juncture.[27]

Even as he was composing his telegram, news came from London that his arguments had been accepted.[28] What finally decided Chamberlain in Lloyd's favour was the account he received of his meeting with Zaghloul on 30 May 1926.

The most recent historian to have looked at this subject suggests that Lloyd tried to browbeat Zaghloul, but as she appears to base her account on a report by Reuter's correspondent, Gerald Delaney, who was not there, it has little to recommend it.[29] Lloyd, aware both of the arguments against his policy and of Chamberlain's attitude, did not want to give Zaghloul any excuse for criticizing him by being rude to him; instead he tried to make him see that it was not in his interests to take office at that moment, even hinting that this might be possible later; but 'Saad reciprocated neither my conciliation nor my frankness. He was evasive and almost insolent' and refused to give any guarantees about his future conduct.[30] It was, Lloyd later wrote, 'an entirely unsatisfactory interview'.[31] This report produced a marked effect on Chamberlain:

> Whatever doubts remained in my mind were removed by your account

of your . . . interview with Zaghloul. You did and said exactly the right thing, and he behaved – like Zaghloul.[32]

On 1 June Chamberlain told Lloyd that the Cabinet had approved his words to Zaghloul and asked to be informed of the wording of any note of veto sent to him.[33]

Lloyd later confessed to the commander of the British fleet at Malta, Sir Roger Keyes, that he had been 'on delicate ground';[34] but he determined to put his policy through with firmness. His first move was to sow seeds of doubt in Egyptian minds by advising Ziwar to postpone his resignation – giving rise to fears that the British would just ignore the elections. He followed this up by asking Keyes to send the battleship *Resolution* to Alexandria. Lloyd believed that this was the crucial move in breaking Zaghloul's nerve. Then came the resignation of Judge Kershaw, the only British judge at the trial of those accused of Lee Stack's murder, which further weakened Zaghloul's position. Kershaw alleged that the acquittal of two of the accused went clean contrary to the evidence, which served to revive rumours that the Wafd were heavily involved in the whole murder plot.[35]

Zaghloul did not hold out for long; on 3 June he announced that, to protect his declining health, he would not accept the premiership. He was in a much-chastened mood when Lloyd saw him on 5 June, professing his willingness to support the Government of Adly Pasha and his utter unwillingness to hold office again.[36]

Having been hesitant right up to the end, Chamberlain now wrote congratulating Lloyd on his success in

> handling a very difficult and critical situation. The Cabinet was particularly struck by the clearness and force of your presentation of the case both *pro* and *contra* the course you ultimately advised.

He accurately summed up Lloyd's problem thus: 'We have got at each point not only to do the right thing but to do it in such a way that everyone sees it to be the right thing.' Conscious perhaps that his letters to Lloyd were open to more than one interpretation, Chamberlain assured him that there was no thought in London that he had been 'intemperate', and he promised full support for the future.[37]

This came as a relief to Lloyd, who had felt that the Foreign Office was less than whole-heartedly behind him. The British press, on the other hand, had been loud in his praises, the right-wing *Morning Post* declaring on 6 June that: 'It is now apparent that Lord Lloyd has scored a notable diplomatic victory', whilst G. Ward Price told the readers of the *Daily Mail* that Lloyd 'knew one fundamental fact – that the secret of British success in dealing with oriental peoples is not suppleness of wits but strength of character'.[38]

As for the hero of the hour, he was relieved that he had won, but he had no illusions as to the extent of his triumph, telling Keyes on 9 June:

> This is only the first round of the fray which will probably have to be resumed next autumn about November, if not earlier, but we shall then be able to fight on surer ground and on an issue selected by ourselves.[39]

But for the moment, with the eye of the political hurricane traversed, Lloyd was free to depart for his annual leave on 9 July.

# 18

# HIGH COMMISSIONER FOR EGYPT

Lloyd's lines had indeed been cast in stormy waters; once again, as in Bombay, his first months had been fraught with crises which had drawn heavily upon his nervous energy. But Egypt, unlike India, was his 'part of the east'. He wrote in *Egypt since Cromer* of the English traveller's first view of the East:

> The light that never was upon the land or sea of his home strikes now for the first time upon his eyes. The swift and colourful daylight sinks as if by magic to a softly luminous afterglow, and then to the unearthly peace and remoteness of the desert night. An imagination that is awake and receptive may catch from that vision an infection that will last a lifetime.

This was certainly true in his case.

But when he came to Egypt in October 1925 it was not for the first time and so he had eyes for other things. Soon after his arrival he had written to Puss Gaskell that his predominant emotion was 'indignation'

> that we should have thrown away needlessly the respect and affection of the masses here on the bidding of a handful of lawyers and pressmen – that we should have forced upon them with all the weight of our power a form of Government which they did not want, which can never work and which has put them today in the power of autocracy and tyranny – 'For Allah made the English mad, the maddest of all mankind'.[1]

Egypt was part of that East to which he had given his youth and his heart and he hated the idea of its being 'westernized'.

He felt a 'kinship, unanticipated but powerful' with this 'scene so foreign', deriving 'from the Bible training that has so strongly influenced our childhood'. Those scenes from childhood books and imagination were here made real:

> Two women will be grinding together still, and still the ox will be

treading the corn. The locusts still have no king, and still go forth by bands. The traveller may still pass by the vineyard of the slothful, the stone wall whereof is broken down. He may still hear the crackling of the thorns under the pot. . . . We know these sights and sounds: they are the companions of our youth magically restored to us: and by this link they demand, and obtain, from us a powerful, perhaps subconscious, sympathy.[2]

Despite the use of the pronoun 'we', this reads remarkably like a personal confession. Egypt had for him an appeal that spoke to the deepest part of his being.

The fascination of the British with all things Arab is borne witness to by the existence of the phenomenon of the 'Arabist': Harry St John Philby, Glubb 'Pasha' and Lawrence 'of Arabia' are merely the most prominent examples of this type; Lloyd belonged firmly to it. The vast, clean, open spaces appealed to the coenobite in him and he found in the Near East an Eden where his restless spirit could be at peace. But duty allowed little time to indulge this aspect of his character.

The conflict so often noted between his ambition and his wanderlust took on flesh in the contrast between the life dictated by ceremonial and that to which his spirit inclined naturally. The Prince of Wales is said to have remarked that he had never known what regal pomp was before visiting Lloyd in Bombay, and this sort of talk led some to think of him as terribly grand and severe in a Curzonian sort of way; but this was to confuse the mask and the man. On duty he was the representative of the King-Emperor. In diplomatic uniform, with the star of the Grand Cross of the Indian Empire gleaming on his breast athwart the blue riband of that order, he did seem the very embodiment of Imperial Power; and that, of course, is what he was – when on duty. He knew how much importance orientals attached to appearances, and a High Commissioner in a shabby suit would have impressed no one.

But these were the trappings of office, and even as his ambition struggled with his wanderlust, so did the 'ankle-ropes' of office chafe his free spirit. He was, of course, naturally fastidious about his personal appearance. His normal daytime outfit was a well-cut, lightweight grey three-piece suit, an immaculately white shirt, black tie and grey top hat; his lithe, small form could not escape being described as dapper. Always immaculately groomed, he carried with him on journeys a small box containing shoe-cleaning equipment and a clothes-brush; his tidy mind abhorred sloppiness – in any form.

There was, however, one respect in which he could never look the part of the stern proconsul; Blanche noted that:

He would have liked to have an aquiline profile and a hatchet-face; but

the Almighty gave him the round face, high cheek-bones and black hair
of the Welshman and . . . big brown eyes like a bumble-bee's back.[3]

Far from being tall and imposing, he was only half an inch taller than
Blanche at five foot nine, and that was if she did not wear high heels!
With his naturally dark complexion burnt brown by years of exposure
to the hot climes which he loved so well and his jet-black hair, there was
about him an un-English, almost Semitic air.

Such then was the external aspect of the High Commissioner,
playing up to his reputation as the 'Indian tiger' and bringing that
tireless energy to bear on all aspects of business at the Residency – but
what of the man underneath?

That the public career should dominate his biography is only natural
as it was to this that he sacrificed so much, even his love of tramping the
world with the wild wind as his mate. Lloyd the imperial administrator
took precedence over George Lloyd the mystic because of his own
burning desire to put his talents and ambition to the service of a cause
greater than himself. But his intimates saw a different picture beneath
the carapace.

Con Benson, who was so close to him in India, recalled that:

> Off duty he was the easiest man to 'rag', accepted being 'ragged' with an
> ingenuous outward appearance of hating it, which could but lead to
> more 'ragging'. His capacity for laughter and his infectious giggle, were
> something one will always vividly remember, neither did he ever take
> offence if one remonstrated with him over his irritating restlessness, the
> tricks he had, when in conversation, of jumping from one chair to
> another, plucking at his collar, or the ceaseless twiddling of the string of
> his monocle around his finger.
>
> George wasn't difficult to know, but to know him was not necessarily
> to understand him, and that few people did. Those who achieved it
> became *sous le charme* for life.

Those who did fall under the spell were usually male:

> George, with his magnetic charm and absorbing personality, could
> hardly fail to hold the interest of the majority of women with whom he
> came into contact. He definitely preferred the company and mentality of
> his own sex, though to those women whom he knew well, and believed
> had merit, he extended the same loyal support and interest, as he did to
> any of his male friends.[4]

But it was in the company of his ADCs, the 'boys' as he called them, that
he could (as far as was possible for him) relax and forget the cares of the
great world which waited to reclaim him.

By his manner and tone he seemed, to younger men who knew him,
to be inviting comradeship; there was no 'side', no pomposity or

posturing. For all his vast acquaintanceship he was, at heart, a lonely man who, approaching the great world through the medium of his own powerful vision, sought reassurance from others that he could succeed in it; it was to this inner vulnerability that his intimates were drawn.

The absence of women from the inner recesses of his life will no doubt suggest to the suggestible that Lloyd was homosexual and the response to the fact that there is no evidence for this will doubtless be that he was 'repressed'; to this there is no answer other than despair at the late twentieth-century habit of mind which insists upon finding sex everywhere.

One woman had pierced his defences, and Blanche remained essential to him. Although she had her own formal role to play, as she had had in Bombay, her main job was to comfort and support a husband who always drove himself to the limit of his powers; as Con Benson put it:

> His wife provided no dumb puppet show in his life. With her devotion, intelligence, graciousness and loyalty, she was his confidante and inspiration. She did much of the donkey work for him, and because of her unswerving belief in him, she bravely and uncomplainingly met the depression in his life as imperturbably as she coped with his successes.

The most she would allow herself by way of complaint was to admit that he could be 'somewhat exacting', and that his lavishly employed hair-oil marked the furniture.

Blanche delighted to see him back in harness, knowing how much he had detested the House of Commons, and Egypt provided her with advantages which Bombay had not possessed. The climate was 'very delicious', at least 'for most of the eight months that I shall spend here', she told Percy Loraine, soon after their arrival in Cairo,[5] and it was also near enough to allow David, now aged thirteen, to come out for the Christmas vacation.

In later life David would reflect upon how little time the fates allowed him to spend with his father for the first two decades of his life. He had been not quite two when the war had taken his father away and, after only a few years in Bombay, he had had to leave to go to school in England. Blanche, who adored her only child with all the love she would have liked to have been able to spread over his siblings, fretted at his departure, but was assured by her husband, who had been through the system himself, when it seemed that David was unhappy: 'I always expected that he might have rather a bad time to begin with for he used even here to be a bit impatient and "nervy" when thwarted and inclined to make too much of trifles.'[6] But this was no reassurance as she recognized in these traits a reflection of her own personality.

During the latter part of his time in Bombay Lloyd had been regaled by Blanche with news of David's various troubles at school; these he met with the phlegm expected of the British father:

> He will probably always take things unnecessarily hardly. One can do little for him in those ways except just exactly what you are doing for him – talking it out, thus giving his mind relief. . . and furnishing him with a new stock of self-confidence for his next bout of troubles. The troubles must come; they are inevitable and are what will make his character.[7]
>
> I did not somehow think he looked for them or indeed would want them while he had you at home with him. Neither my father nor my mother wrote to me very often when I was at school – my mother 3 or 4 times a half, my father perhaps once – and I suppose that has altered my angle of vision.[8]

Thenceforth he had corresponded regularly with his son, but at this stage and during the Egyptian years David was still closer to his mother than to his remote and ever-busy father.

In 1924 David went to Eton and the ease of communications with Cairo enabled him to spend many vacations with his parents. For Blanche the sorrow of having once more to leave him was mitigated by the knowledge that he would spend Christmas 1925 with her. But the pleasure of having David with her for Christmas was matched by the pain she felt at their parting. His tears made her wretched and he looked so small and vulnerable with those skinny legs which seemed scarcely strong enough to bear even the weight of his body; she felt so sad at the thought of that very lonely little boy on that very large ship somewhere in the middle of the Mediterranean.[9]

Blanche's role was not confined to the sphere of her own, largely ceremonial, duties. Her diaries bear witness to the regularity with which she was consulted by her husband on political matters. She did not aspire to anything like the position of Lady Willingdon and, given the nature of her spouse, that was as well; but she did provide the completely trustworthy and sympathetic audience which he needed.

Egypt offered, as India had, the opportunity for sightseeing whilst her husband toured his domain. Blanche went with him on his trip to the Sudan in late January 1926; the fact that her 'beloved Whelk' (her sister Helen) was with them made it all the more 'heavenly'. She wrote to Sibell Glyn from the ss *Meroe* at Assouan:

> How I wish you could be with me at this moment, for we are doing the thing I always longed to do when I was here, only never achieved – drifting down the Nile in one of those nice little white steamers, going our own pace, and stopping just where we choose. It is quite heavenly – a perfect temperature and the most lovely lights on the river and shore all

the time – an ideal way of doing a journey and a real rest.

This was too leisurely for Lloyd who toured the Sudan by car and spent ten days in Khartoum enquiring into every facet of the administration and having long talks with the Governor, Sir Geoffrey Archer. The result was 'a very nasty septic throat and fever, and he had to take to his bed for some days'.[10] He spent most of late February there, fretting: first at being absent from his desk and then at being denied a trip to the Valley of the Kings to revisit the tomb of Tutankhamun; but most of all at missing a chance to talk with two important visitors – his old friend Edward Wood, who was *en route* to India to become Viceroy, and Ivy Chamberlain, wife of the Foreign Secretary. Blanche recorded that she had never 'seen him more depressed'.[11]

Fortunately Lloyd had been well again for the *dénouement* of the crisis with Zaghloul, and although Blanche worried that he was over-straining himself, by her presence and her willingness to act as the audience for all his difficulties and frustrations, it was she who prevented this. Above all there was, as she had written to Loraine in March, 'the saving grace that everything automatically goes to sleep during the summer, when everybody quite properly expects to have a holiday'.[12] Therein lay one of the main advantages of Egypt: it allowed Lloyd to get home for two or three months a year; this was necessary not only for his health, but also to see how opinion at home was moving.

Lloyd was aware that Chamberlain had not been enthusiastic about the course he had followed in the crisis with Zaghloul; he wrote on 6 June:

> I always have a fear you think me intemperate: I would like to cause you to change this opinion if I could. I believe in the east that if you choose your moment you must be bold and definite, but such an attitude must be consonant with a fair deal for the people you have hit! I won't pretend that the situation is good. It is not. I can only say that I think our shares stand higher now than they did. I hope I am not claiming too much.[13]

Letters could help ease misunderstandings, but there was no substitute for sniffing the air of Whitehall to discover whether there was a more fundamental difference at the root of the matter.

# 19

# GUNBOATS AND DIPLOMACY

Lloyd's fears about the attitude of the Foreign Office did not extend to the man he left in charge at the residency, Nevile Henderson; that this was a grave mistake is apparent from a letter which Henderson sent to Walford Selby of the Egyptian department on 31 July 1926:

> *Entre nous* I do not see eye to eye on many things with Lloyd. What I find hardest is to do good work and loyal service with a man who is set upon a policy which, though it may promise him kudos for a while and the praise of the *Daily Mail* and the Diehards, I regard as contrary to our ultimate advantage. I mean going back if possible on the Milner report and the 1922 declaration; the suspension of the constitution and parliament and the reassumption by ourselves of increased responsibilities here involving more and more interference in Egyptian internal affairs. I may be fainthearted but I do not stand for any of those things, and, at the bottom of his stouter heart, Lloyd does.

He thought that Lloyd's intransigence would wreck any negotiations for an Anglo–Egyptian treaty.[1] Such disloyalty could only help reinforce the view taken by the diplomats that Lloyd was a danger to the policy they wished to pursue in Egypt.

With Lloyd in London, British policy in the summer of 1926 was informed more by the Conservatism of the Cabinet, however, than by the mutterings of the Foreign Office. Lloyd attended a meeting of the Cabinet on 26 July in order to explain the Egyptian situation; he found the atmosphere there congenial. Ministers agreed that Egypt could not join the League of Nations, and asked him to stop the Egyptian Government from raising the matter; they were firmly of the opinion that the contracts of British officials, which expired in 1927, must be renewed and 'the *status quo* maintained till the four points were settled'. When Lloyd pointed out that this would almost certainly 'lead to a considerable "situation"', they seemed

> all to feel that unless we are to be fatally weakened we must now stand pat on what is left of our position. All this [he told Henderson] augurs a

stormy winter I fear, but fundamentally I think they are right. They wish
me further to secure an early reduction of the Egyptian army both for
purposes of safety, and for the purpose of enabling them to make a
corresponding British reduction with the economies that ensue.

These things could only be secured by intervention in Egyptian
politics and at the risk of provoking crises, but Lloyd's colleagues
recognized this and 'concluded by giving me a completely free hand to
do the best I could towards strengthening our position with promises of
backing'. Thinking that Henderson would be cheered by this news,
Lloyd concluded this letter by saying: 'I can't tell you what a difference
having you at the other end means to my peace of mind';[2] had he seen
Selby's post-bag he would have been less sanguine.

The tone of this Cabinet meeting was far removed indeed from that
prevailing inside the Foreign Office. T. E. Lawrence (as he then was
not, having adopted the name of Shaw) wrote in 1934: 'Nobody lets
daylight into the corridors of the FO. Why not? Why should the clerks be
kept in cotton wool? A little fresh air and exercise would clear their
pallid faces.'[3] The passage of half a century opens the window to let in
at least a draught.

Professional pride lay close to the root of the poor relationship
between Lloyd and the 'clerks'. Lloyd was, after all, an amateur,
whereas the diplomats in the Egyptian Department were, as Selby
recalled much later, 'possibly the strongest Egyptian combination that
has ever been at the disposal of any Foreign Secretary with cumulative
Egyptian experience stretching over the years'. Sir Ronald Lindsay,
Mervyn Herbert, Jack Murray and Selby himself were certainly a
formidable team; but experience brought with it some disadvantages.
Selby was the principal negotiator of the 1922 Declaration and had
been, like Murray and Herbert, involved in the subsequent negotiations; they were all, naturally, heavily committed to the idea that a
treaty could be obtained. Then Lloyd came along; as Selby observed
later: 'It was this very powerful combination at the FO which Lloyd had
succeeded in challenging within a year or so of his arrival in Cairo.'[4] In
Cairo itself Lloyd had an unsuspected fifth column; Henderson's views
have already been noted and to his name may be added that of the
Oriental Secretary at the Residency, Lawrence Graffty-Smith, who
admits in his memoirs to sending back material to London which cast
doubt on Lloyd's own reports.[5]

Whilst Lloyd was obtaining the approval of the Cabinet to a policy of
maintaining the *status quo*, the diplomats were coming to somewhat
different conclusions. By the beginning of 1927 they had concluded that
only two of the four 'reserved points' – the safeguarding of imperial

communications and the defence of Egypt – were essential. The diplomats were prepared to countenance the withdrawal of all other British forces from Egypt provided a force could be maintained in the Canal zone. There was some fear that the Egyptians might increase their armed forces and threaten the security of the Canal and to avert this they were prepared to offer the Egyptians military and naval training to make their small forces more efficient.[6]

On the question of the retention of British officials in Egyptian service upon which the Cabinet had pronounced so firmly, the Foreign Office was prepared to give way if the Egyptians would allow the British a veto over any foreign officials being appointed. Writing in 1929 (for a Labour Foreign Secretary), Murray even went so far as to say that the decision to keep the officials on 'was obviously calculated to produce a difficult situation'.[7] So much for government policy.

To men in favour of a policy so far in advance of the declared British position, it was natural to see Lloyd's insistence upon implementing that declared policy as tiresome.

In fact Lloyd's views on the prospect of a treaty were by no means die-hard; he told Henderson on 28 August 1926:

> I have always made it clear to Adly and Sarwat, I think also Saad, that I for one would never recommend HMG to resume negotiations unless there were very evident and public proofs of the existence of those friendly sentiments towards Great Britain which have been so often affirmed in private but so rarely alluded to by the responsible leaders in public. To recommence negotiations with a Government and a press who display nothing but hostility to us in public would be productive in my opinion of nothing but grave harm.[8]

It was this view which informed both his presentation of policy to the Cabinet and his implementation of that policy once he returned to Cairo in October.

Lloyd's feelings at the end of his vacation can be gauged from a letter which he wrote to his old friend Edward Wood (now Lord Irwin) in India on 21 October:

> I am just leaving again for another year's dogfight in Egypt. That problem is so insoluble and of such constant worry and anxiety that I feel often very pessimistic about my capacity to deal with it adequately.[9]

There was some comfort to be gained, however, from the Cabinet's promise of support over the two main problems which confronted him on his return: the size of the Egyptian army and the employment of British officials.

Emilia Lloyd, George's mother

Sampson Samuel Lloyd, George's father

'Georgie', 1883

George and Sam Cockerell at Eton, *c.* 1891

The young attaché: Lloyd at
Constantinople, 1905–6

Drawing of Blanche Lloyd,
1918

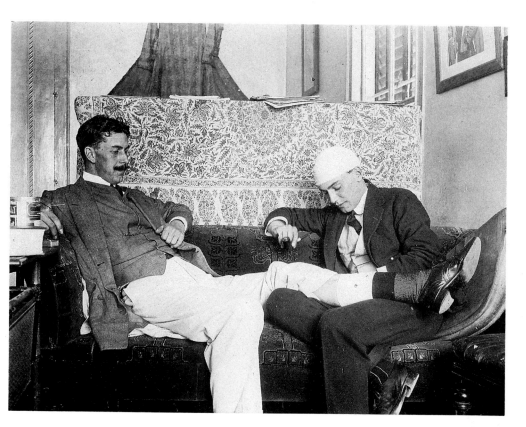

The perils of polo: Lloyd, with bandaged head, examining Percy Loraine's wounded leg, Therapia 1906

The intelligence officer: Lloyd interrogating a Turkish prisoner in Egypt, 1916

'Lloyd of Arabia', 1917

With T. E. Lawrence on a bombing mission, 1917

'Off duty': boating at Bombay, 1920

Inaugurating the Sukkur barrage, 24 October 1923

Staff group, Bombay, 1920: back row, left to right: Capt. Hon. J. Verney, Capt. G. Brook Short, Capt. C. Benson, Mr Grant, Capt. Vansittart, Capt. A. Lascelles; front row, left to right: Mlle Duflot (David's governess), Major Ross-Stewart, Col. Greig, David Lloyd, Blanche Lloyd, George Lloyd, Mr Cowie, Capt. Nethersole, Capt. MacEwan

Mother and child: Blanche and David,
1922

The dapper man about town: George Lloyd,
1930s

The High Commissioner at the unveiling of the war memorial to the Indian dead at Port Said,
1926

Blanche by Glyn Philpot, early 1930s

'Air Ace': George Lloyd winning his wings at
the age of fifty-eight

Lloyd at Portman Square, 1935

Lloyd as Colonial Secretary, 23 July 1940, inspecting the Palestinian Auxiliary Military Pioneer Corps

Lloyd greeting George VI at the Colonial Office, 1940

Lloyd summed up the last issue in a letter to Admiral Keyes on 27 January 1927:

> It is a thoroughly difficult and distasteful task. We were mad enough to agree in '22 that all British officials should leave Egypt in spring '27. If they are allowed to go we may as well put up the shutters here, and as we don't mean to, or at any rate, I don't, we have got to 'persuade' the Egyptian Government to keep them.

But the Egyptians, witnessing Britain's involvement in Shanghai, calculated that the Baldwin Government would not want to take on a fresh crisis;[10] nor were they far wrong, as Lloyd complained to Irwin: 'the situation in China is rendering Austen even more timid than usual as regards Egypt'.[11] However, perseverance prevailed and most of the contracts were renewed; but of backing from London there was not a sign.

This timidity did nothing to improve Lloyd's opinion of the Foreign Office which, for its part, was less than pleased with the way in which he pressed for a more lavish distribution of honours to British officials in order to improve morale. By the end of 1926 he and Willy Tyrrell were writing stiff letters to each other, with the latter resenting bitterly the insinuations (which were quite true) that Chamberlain's letters on the subject were no more than Foreign Office briefs bearing the signature of the Foreign Secretary.[12] Chamberlain wrote to him in late December to say 'you do occasionally hold rather severe language to your Secretary of State and speak to him more imperatively than our other representatives abroad', but Lloyd continued to press his point pertinaciously, thus decreasing the stock of 'goodwill' available to him at the Foreign Office.[13]

Such pertinacity showed a lack of proportion on Lloyd's part which did not pass unnoticed. He was also, in early 1927, expending large amounts of time and energy on defending the Back Bay scheme against Indian charges that its finances were unsound.[14] Sir Samuel Hoare, the Minister for Air, who stopped off in Cairo in March, told him to stop worrying because 'nobody in England takes the least interest in the whole affair'; he told Irwin:

> As you may imagine, the restless George had the same effect upon me as a gale of wind upon an aeroplane. He was brimming over with talk and there seemed to me to be a perpetual atmosphere of potential crisis about the regime. There is no denying, however, the fact that for the moment his position is very strong.[15]

In fact the crisis was not far off. In March, Adly Pasha's Government brought forward a bill which proposed to increase the size of the army and its reserve as well as weakening British influence by restricting the powers of the Inspector-General and abolishing the post of Sirdar; this was a clear challenge.

On 9 March Lloyd sent a long telegram to London arguing that the time had come to stop the rot by making it plain that they would not accept such measures even if the Chamber passed them:

> Are we going to stand by the 1922 Declaration or are we not? We are dealing with a Government which has refused to admit the validity of the Four Reserved Points . . . and if we do not make a stand now I cannot see where we ever shall.[16]

Lloyd thought that they should try to increase the powers and prestige of the Inspector-General and secure the appointment of a British Deputy Inspector; thus ensuring British supervision of the army.

The diplomats were by no means so eager to take a stand. Control of the army was not, in their view, essential. They were not unwilling to face a crisis but would do so only if it was clear to all that British policy was 'so obviously reasonable and constructive' as to 'justify recourse to extreme measures to enforce it if that became necessary'. What the Foreign Office wanted was a 'provisional and temporary working arrangement pending a general settlement of outstanding questions'; to this end it was prepared to offer the Egyptians an important concession by allowing the abolition of the post of Inspector-General.[17]

This was anathema to Lloyd, who warned in his reply on 21 March that the Egyptians were most unlikely to give a straight answer to London's proposals; in the meantime the situation would worsen and the British, faced with riots, would concede everything – including the message that rioting paid dividends.[18]

There usually prevailed in Whitehall a view that Lloyd's reporting of events was biased towards his own conclusions, but in March 1927 Tyrrell happened to be on holiday in Cairo and he confirmed on 28 March everything the High Commissioner had said; he thought Lloyd's policy of insisting upon effective control of the size and control of the Egyptian army should be followed.[19]

Chamberlain, who had clearly hoped for a different answer, put the whole question before the Cabinet in a memorandum on 1 April, in which he argued that 'Lloyd's telegrams convey rather a misleading impression of the historical background and tend to over-estimate the dangers of the present position'.[20] Despite this remarkable document, which was tantamount to expressing no confidence in Lloyd, the Cabinet decided in his favour on 13 April; there were to be no concessions to the Egyptians.[21]

Chamberlain did not accept his defeat graciously; he told Lloyd on 25 April:

> Personally I remained to the last inclined to the course of action which we suggested . . . and a good many of my colleagues shared my view; but I and they felt that, in the face of your strong and reiterated views and of the concurrence of Tyrrell . . . we should not be justified in insisting further upon it.[22]

Selby later commented: 'Our view was rejected in the Cabinet for the reason George Lloyd *said* he had the support of Sir William Tyrrell.'[23] As Tyrrell's telegrams were laid before the Cabinet, this is evidence only of how badly the diplomats took Lloyd's victory; their behaviour in the final act of the crisis suggests how far they were prepared to go to make sure this did not happen again.

Adly Pasha, who was now trapped between fear of 'the Lord' and of Zaghloul, resigned on 19 April and his successor, Sarwat Pasha, decided to push forward with the bill to enlarge and politicize the army. With a deliberate challenge to the British position looming, Lloyd sent Chamberlain on 25 May a copy of the text of the demands which he proposed to present to Sarwat: the main points were an increase in powers of the Inspector-General; the appointment of a British Deputy along with no increase in the size of the Egyptian army.[24]

Although Chamberlain agreed with the terms of the document, he still wanted the way left open for the conclusion of a general, formal agreement on the subject.[25] Lloyd accepted this on the premise that it was 'manifestly entirely contingent on us having previously secured the terms of our note'.[26] Writing to Chamberlain on 29 May, he declared:

> The fact now clearly emerges that Parliamentary Government in its present form is incompatible with the preservation of the reserved points. So long as we allow these to be encroached upon the system functions without serious crises; the moment you have to insist upon a reserved point you arrive at a complete deadlock. A situation where we have to work a declaration which the Egyptians have refused to recognize, still less to accept, is impossible.

The time had come to ask for an unequivocal acceptance of the 1922 Declaration.[27] The British demands were presented to Sarwat on 30 May 1927. The following day Lloyd sent a series of telegrams to London designed to prepare the ground for action if they were rejected, but as he suggested that they should suspend the 1922 Constitution and abandon the idea of a treaty, all he did was to arouse suspicions in the Foreign Office.[28]

The Egyptian reply came on 4 June and was seen by Lloyd as 'evasive, equivocal and quite inadequate'. He had done his best to impress upon Sarwat the dangers of such a response; now it was time for action. His position seemed secure: in July the Cabinet had promised their backing and said they wanted no further erosion of the British position; in April they had supported his view about the importance of the Inspector-General; at the end of May they had authorized Keyes to send two battleships from Malta to Alexandria and Port Said. Lloyd was sure that Sarwat would give in when he saw the British meant business and on 5 June told Chamberlain that they should prepare to implement his emergency plan, asking first for an unequivocal answer to his note of 30 May.[29] The reply stunned him.

His messages went not to Chamberlain, who was away from the Office, but to Tyrrell who went to lunch at Chequers on 6 June where he got Baldwin 'to sanction a telegram to Lloyd interposing an intermediate stage before the delivery of the ultimatum – should the latter become inevitable'.[30]

The Foreign Office reply rejected the idea of taking stern action, characterized Sarwat's reply as 'not wholly unsatisfactory . . . [and as containing] useful admissions which are capable of development', and offered to let the Egyptians abolish the post of Inspector-General.[31] Tyrrell stressed that Baldwin was concerned to be able to show Parliament, if firm action had to be taken, that it was all the fault of the unreasonable Egyptians.[32]

Lloyd told Baldwin on 8 June that this was 'a severe blow' as well as 'a complete reversal' of British policy which could only result in the Egyptians concluding that he did not have the confidence of his own Government and had been trying to bluff them.[33] In an acid telegram to Tyrrell he observed that he had never forgotten the domestic political aspect of the Egyptian problem, but that

> My primary responsibility . . . is to lay before you clearly what result the acceptance of a virtual defeat upon the issue in question would have upon our position in Egypt and the Near East.[34]

Tyrrell responded that there was little difference between their policies; a line which did not convince Lloyd.[35]

Baldwin's views were not necessarily shared by his colleagues. In Churchill's papers there is a letter to Baldwin dated 11 June arguing that the Cabinet should support Lloyd. It is an odd document as it claims that 'I was the last of our colleagues to have seen George Lloyd', when Churchill had not seen him since October.[36] The letter was a copy of one which Hoare sent;[37] Lloyd enjoyed support from both men and from others in the Cabinet. But on this occasion he was able to get his way without help from outside as the delay in any British response allowed the threat of the battleships to work its effect.

On 13 June Sarwat let it be known, unofficially, that he was prepared to accede to the British demands. Lloyd took great pleasure in emphasizing that Zaghloul had only let Sarwat give way because the latter had stated that 'the alternative would be an immediate ultimatum and the dissolution of the Chamber'.[38] Thus the crisis ended and the congratulatory telegrams went out to Cairo from Chamberlain and Baldwin; but the effect on relations between Lloyd and the Foreign Office was traumatic.

The depth of Tyrrell's mistrust of Lloyd, as well as the extent of his dominance over his chief, is demonstrated by the account of the crisis which he gave to Chamberlain on 15 June. He said that throughout the crisis 'Lloyd was in a very nervous condition and apparently quite unable to understand our instructions'. He had, he confessed, 'been apprehensive as to what would happen there owing to George's neurotic condition' and argued that he must be persuaded to take 'a lengthy retreat, during which he must pledge himself never to mention or think of Egypt'.[39] In a further letter on 17 June he wrote:

> It is quite evident to me that when Lloyd arrives next month we shall have to have a heart to heart talk and lay down very clearly for him what the policy of the Government is to be. My impression is that there is a very serious misapprehension on his part as to what we want in Egypt, or rather, as to what we can maintain in Egypt in present conditions, both here and in Cairo.[40]

Lloyd was equally anxious to clear the air. As he wrote in some rough notes prepared for an interview with Baldwin:

> [It is] really important for the future that what happened should be cleared up because it is too dangerous to be risked again. Someone lost their nerve completely at the last moment and the instructions I got were tantamount to 'no confidence'.[41]

He later confided to Blanche that he thought Tyrrell had been the nigger in the woodpile. His visit to Cairo had been a mixed blessing. The Lloyds had been glad to see him as an old friend, but had been shocked to discover that he had a bottle of whisky sent up to his room every day. Tyrrell had already been threatened with dismissal from the service because of his heavy drinking and could not have been too pleased that his hosts had discovered him. Blanche came to believe that it was from this time that Tyrrell put himself in the 'enemy camp',[42] but as we have seen, the view of the Foreign Office on Egypt had long been antagonistic to that taken by Lloyd.

For Lloyd, the time had come for plain speaking. He told Keyes on 19 June:

> Whilst the object . . . of our row has been fully achieved . . . I think the position here an impossible one and I am going to tell the Cabinet at home that the time has come when outstanding questions have got to be steeled – failing which we must go back on the 1922 Declaration. That Declaration was in my judgement a pure fraud on our part. To tell a country she is independent while you keep an army of occupation is not only a contradiction in terms but a fraud.

His logical mind rebelled against the idea of telling a country she was independent whilst 'reserving to yourself all the main attributes of sovereignty':

> We can't clear out of Egypt and we know we don't mean to. The sooner we clear up these ambiguities, fatal to the welfare of Egypt and still more fatal to our prestige in the East the better. That is my considered view after this year.

Because the Foreign Office was 'so feeble and hesitant' he had 'no idea what I shall get the Cabinet to do', but if they did nothing he was 'doubtful how much longer I can honestly associate myself with conditions that must lead to a serious crash'.[43]

It promised to be a stormy summer.

# 20

# SECRET DIPLOMACY

The gulf dividing Lloyd and the Foreign Office derived from two very different habits of mind: where he was concerned with exerting the 'will to power' the diplomats, conscious of Britain's weakness, were looking for a quiet life.

In one of his earliest letters from Cairo Lloyd had told Puss Gaskell: 'I do not wonder that we came a cropper in this country – we deserved it. I shall try all I know to rebuild but it is going to be even harder than I thought.'[1] He had told Churchill in December 1925 that it would be 'hard work to repair big breaches in our position'.[2] This rhetoric and the spirit which underlay it was shared by many in the Conservative Government. He saw his 'riding orders' from the Cabinet thus:

> a) to protect British and foreign interests at all costs, and b) not to interfere in the internal affairs of Egypt!! Each one contradicts the other. . . . But I plod along trying to square the circle between the rival views of Parliament, Palace and foreign interests here, as well as those of the Foreign Office at home. Not an easy task.[3]

He was not the first to labour in Egypt making bricks without straw; but straw was available at home. He had kept in touch with sympathetic colleagues like Churchill, and one of the first things he did when he arrived back in England in July 1927 was to seek out such men.

The first person Lloyd saw was Austen Chamberlain's half-brother, Neville. The two men had a long talk on 15 July with Chamberlain being sympathetically impressed by Lloyd's account of the problems facing him and British officials in Cairo; he agreed that the time had probably come when the Egyptians should be asked to accept, unequivocally, the four reserved points, Lloyd did not trouble to hide his dismay at the timidity of the Foreign Office:

> George said he had discussed the past with Austen but he had not yet

had time to discuss the future. But he was afraid Austen was so much taken up with Europe that he had little time or interest left for Egypt. Consequently he was inclined to leave things to the officials who were weak, particularly in the Egyptian department. . . . George went on to say he wanted to put his views to the Cabinet but was afraid Austen might decline to let him appear before them. Or the Cabinet might be unwilling amid the press of other matters to hear him.

Chamberlain said that:

> The Cabinet could not divest itself of responsibility and that it would resent being deprived of any information which was offered to enable it to come to a proper decision. I myself considered the future of Egypt to be of vital importance to the Empire and was strongly of the opinion that the Cabinet ought not to take any hurried decision.

He advised Lloyd 'not to be too modest but to ask for a special Cabinet for the purpose'.[4]

Chamberlain told his sister Hilda on 16 July:

> I must say that my sympathies are with Lloyd, for it is tragic to hear of the decay of all the good work which we have done there and of broken-hearted officials in despair over the future of the country.

He was, however, aware that there might be 'other considerations which make it difficult to take a firm line and face such risks as may be involved'.[5] When he talked to his brother on 21 July he learned that negotiations were afoot with Sarwat, who was in London, and that the draft of a treaty had already been prepared:

> I fear from what Austen said that he is going to have trouble with George Lloyd. The latter is naturally very sensitive; he feels that in Cairo these proposals will be represented as going over his head and his instinct is therefore against them.

When Neville begged his brother to treat Lloyd 'with trust and sympathy', he received the discouraging response that 'he was exhausting himself in the effort to do so'; he doubted this: 'I know what his manner is when he is being asked to do something he doesn't want to and I am anxious.'[6]

That negotiations should have been opened with Sarwat behind Lloyd's back is an indication of how much he was distrusted by the diplomats. When he was told of them, at the end of July, the official excuse was that the treaty had been sprung on the Foreign Office by Sarwat and that 'life was so hectic here and everything was in a state of flux'.[7] Neither of these explanations was true.

Although Sarwat did indeed initiate the exchange of draft treaties, he did not do so unprompted. When Austen Chamberlain talked to him on

12 July, it was agreed that the way should be prepared for conversations between him and Lloyd 'when they both returned to Egypt';[8] but when Selby and Tyrrell saw the Egyptian the following day, they raised the subject of concluding a treaty whilst he was in London. In the face of what seemed to be a willingness to go behind Lloyd's back, Sarwat was not indisposed to co-operate: 'He did not indicate that he saw any insuperable difficulty in the way of achieving such an agreement as would give HMG their necessary requirements.'[9]

As Tyrrell and Selby had always maintained that a treaty could be had, they went ahead and negotiated. There were good reasons for keeping all this away from Lloyd. Selby, who saw him on 19 July, told Austen Chamberlain that: 'From the whole tenor of Lord Lloyd's argument [it was apparent] that his object was to exercise a fairly wide measure of control over every branch of the administration in Egypt.' It is indicative both of the Foreign Office view of Lloyd and of the self-confidence of the diplomats that Selby should have added that, if the Cabinet decided, as its predecessors since 1882 had, to 'reject anything savouring of an annexationist solution, at least for the present', a treaty was the only way forward.[10]

Any doubts nurtured in Austen Chamberlain's mind by his brother's comments were more than soothed by flattery:

Tyrrell says: 'You put your European policy on the right footing by Locarno; you did the same for China by your December declaration; now you've done the same for Egypt, you're on firm ground in all three.'

Selby laid it on with a trowel:

Do you remember saying some time ago that you had won your niche in the temple of foreign affairs by your work in Europe, and ought to get out before you lost it in China or Egypt? Well, you won't lose it now in Egypt. I can't tell you how delighted I am, for I have been anxious about Egypt.[11]

With this encouragement he took the draft treaty to the Cabinet on 21 July and was given permission to proceed further.

Lloyd was not informed of anything until after 28 July when the Cabinet had already approved of the draft treaty, and even then he was encouraged by Chamberlain to go on holiday; he declined to go,[12] but when he requested a meeting he was put off with the excuse that the Foreign Secretary was on holiday.[13] Lloyd did not go on holiday himself until 20 August. When Zaghloul died he was tempted to return to Cairo but decided not to; he told Henderson on 30 August 1927 that he was glad that I stayed on the spot . . . had I been away things would not have gone to my liking. A.C. implored me to go away and take a holiday and leave him to handle the Sarwat business; I said no and reminded him of how Cromer had been crushed over Denshawai during his absence in Scotland and how his repute [sic] had never got over the mess that was made in the FO at that time. I find the Cabinet in a very good state of mind over Egypt and I think I have still their very solid and practically unanimous support which more than balances other minor difficulties with which I have been confronted; and I remember always Plutarch's description of Pericles who 'especially in his mild and upright demeanour bore the crossgrained humours of his colleagues in office and thus became useful to the country'!![14]

But however 'sound' the Cabinet was, it was the diplomats who were negotiating with Sarwat and they were not anxious to keep Lloyd informed of their progress. Selby, in Geneva with Chamberlain for a meeting of the League of Nations, reported to Tyrrell on 1 September on the conversations which had taken place between Sarwat and the Foreign Secretary:

I presume a copy of my record and Sarwat's observations will have to go to the High Commissioner as well. He will of course oppose vigorously, but I hope he can be persuaded to confine his comments to the Foreign Office. We don't want the Cabinet to go off at a tangent while the Prime Minister and the Chief are away.

Nor was it merely Lloyd and the Cabinet who aroused the suspicion of the mandarins; Lloyd's *aides de camp* came under the diplomatic lash. They were, Selby wrote, 'almost as active as their chief' and had been

ostensibly expressing the views of the High Commissioner to any and sundry who make [sic] like to lend an ear of the personnel of the Department of which he is a member. I give him a present of his views on myself. They are as strong as mine are as regards him.

He complained that it was

all part and parcel of the system to which we are now becoming accustomed. For instance, we learn through the Admiralty that the High Commissioner expects another flare up in the autumn when more battleships will be required than those required at Alexandria the other day for 'the final decision'. Very interesting. I hope he will soon tell us about it as well.[15]

In a letter to Chamberlain on 13 September, Tyrrell complained that Lloyd had 'obtained the loan from Godfrey Locker-Lampson [Under-Secretary at the FO] of his room in the Foreign Office' and had been 'making a perfect nuisance of himself, interfering everywhere with fussy and ill-thought-out suggestions'.[16] His description of a recent conversation with Lloyd deserves prolonged quotation as a perfect illustration of the tone of relations between the diplomats and the High Commissioner:

> He developed to us such grandiose schemes that I confronted him with a statement that his schemes seemed to me to indicate a policy in Egypt that included the control over Egyptian affairs. I told him that that was not the policy which you had described to him in July in my presence and which he had promised faithfully and loyally to carry out. I told him that the policy you had laid down for Egypt necessitated for him the best diplomatic staff we could give him, whereas he was aiming at creating for himself an Indian secretariat at Cairo on the model of his Bombay administration. I told him frankly that I could not reconcile that with the policy which he had accepted from you. I also told him he would be well-advised to confine his dealings about Egypt to dealings with us, and not to seek recruits outside the Office in support of his policy. He was considerably upset I believe by my frank speech, but came to heel for the present very quickly withdrawing his eastern scheme which he described as a purely tentative proposal that I had taken too seriously.

Tyrrell thought that 'one of our root difficulties with George lies in his misconception of his relations with you'. Lloyd had told another diplomat that 'he did not consider himself to be a common-or-garden ambassador', which led Tyrrell to say that before he returned to Cairo it would have to be 'made clear to him that he goes out there, not as your partner, but as your subordinate'. He could not, he warned his chief, 'face another crisis such as we went through last June, which showed clearly that he does not feel bound, in the ultimate resort, to obey instructions from here'. He proposed to 'bring these points to the notice of the PM'

> and urge upon him that, unless he gives you his whole-hearted and determined support in clearing up our relations with George, we may be running the risk of serious trouble in Egypt at a time when Zaghloul's death may give us an opportunity of securing a working agreement with the Egyptians based on a policy of close partnership.

Chamberlain confessed himself 'disappointed' with Lloyd's attitude and begged Tyrrell to 'speak fully and frankly with the PM on the subject' because he felt that a crisis was coming in which 'I shall need and am sure I shall receive, the PM's full support'.[17] Tyrrell replied saying that he was sure they had done the right thing, as

> I feel pretty certain that in consequence of all the wire-pulling George has done we may have to face a crisis, and I have always felt that you must give the PM plenty of time to absorb his subject.[18]

On 1 October he sent Baldwin a memorandum by Selby entitled

'Cromerism in Egypt', which put forward the pure milk of the Foreign Office view whilst subtly denigrating the High Commissioner.[19]

Lloyd's own account of his conversation with Tyrrell in early September has been lost, but it is clear from other letters of this period that Tyrrell had told him that public opinion demanded a settlement of the Egyptian question 'at any price'. This ignored the probability that Sarwat would not be able to sell a treaty which satisfied the British to his fellow-politicians in Cairo. Nevile Henderson, who supported the idea of a treaty and did not want 'things left to the W[inston] C[hurchill] section of the Cabinet', was nevertheless alive to this, telling Lloyd on 15 September 1927 that he shared 'your apprehension lest our treaty proposals should suffer the same fate as the Milner report'.[20] Lloyd saw himself as having to 'steer between those who would wreck all prospects by asking too much' and 'those who for the sake of an agreement would accept any agreement'; it 'was not easy'.[21]

Included amongst the latter group was Henderson himself, who told the Foreign Office in early October, when Sarwat was embarking upon a third re-draft of the treaty, that 'bargaining is a mistake and it should be the most generous treaty compatible with our vital requirements'; it was, he argued, 'worth taking a risk to secure the friendship of this country'.[22]

Despite staying in London to be available for the negotiations, Lloyd was not consulted on the treaty until he was shown a final draft just prior to his departure for Cairo. He resented being asked to give an opinion when he was so far from his papers and felt embarrassed at being asked to address the Cabinet, telling Chamberlain that he could hardly avoid revealing the differences between his position and that of the Foreign Office; but, with the encouragement of the Foreign Secretary[23] and of his half-brother and Leo Amery, he went ahead and did so.[24]

At the Cabinet meeting Sir Laming Worthington-Evans, the Minister of War, showed 'remarkable acumen . . . in picking out the weak points' in the treaty, most notably those dealing with the terms upon which a British military presence would remain in Suez. For this he received congratulations from Churchill but, as Neville Chamberlain noted:

> Others had observed that George Lloyd who was sitting next to him had written these points down on a piece of paper. And that, said S[tanley] B[aldwin], is George Lloyd's idea of loyalty to Austen.[25]

Even for Baldwin it was an asinine remark; it was not Lloyd's duty to act as echo to the Foreign Secretary.

Baldwin thought Worthington-Evans was trying to curry favour with Churchill, but the same could not be said of the other ministers who sympathized with Lloyd's doubts about the treaty – the Home Secretary, Joynson-Hicks, and the Lord President of the Council, Lord Salisbury; still less could it be said of King George v who also shared Lloyd's apprehensions that the treaty weakened Britain's position in Egypt.[26] On 28 October Salisbury warned Chamberlain that Sarwat was after an 'extension of Egyptian independence':

> As you will know, many of us view advances in this direction with misgivings, and I was even bold enough to think we had already gone too far in accepting the theory of the freedom of the Egyptian Government to govern Egypt as badly as they like.

In warning against over-optimistic assumptions about Sarwat's ability to deliver the goods, and in counselling against making too many concessions, Lloyd was doing his duty.

The diplomats did not like this fact and, as they could hardly sack the Cabinet, turned their attention to Lloyd. Chamberlain told his sister Hilda on 22 October that:

> I have big problems confronting me in the near future over Egypt for Lord Lloyd does not heartily accept my policy and my principal advisers would wish me to get rid of him, which would risk a first-class row inside and outside the Cabinet in this country.[27]

Foreign Office policy and Conservative attitudes towards Egypt were not wholly the same thing and Chamberlain knew it; he lacked the courage to risk 'a first-class row' especially when so many senior Tories shared Lloyd's opinions.

Lloyd left England in early November but had got no further than Paris when, on 10 November, he received news of further amendments. As he had already expressed doubts about some of the treaty's clauses,[28] this seemed very like the last straw and he was tempted to resign on the spot; he decided, however, not to do so because he was still not sure exactly what would be in the treaty.[29] When he reached Egypt and consulted his advisers he decided to 'accept it loyally and do my utmost to get it through';[30] but he remained sceptical of Sarwat's ability to sell it to the Wafd, particularly as there was no Zaghloul to give the party cohesion.

Having, in effect, negotiated a treaty behind Lloyd's back, the diplomats were committed to an optimistic view of Sarwat's ability to deliver it and they treated any warnings from Lloyd as signs of obstruction. Nevile Henderson, however, pointed out in early November that, ' "The fear of the Lord is the beginning of wisdom" . . . wholesome apprehension, in fact, of what the High Commissioner might do next.' Trapped between fear of Fuad's absolutism and Lloyd's intentions, the parliamentarians in Egypt were peculiarly anxious for a treaty;[31] but could Sarwat sell them one which recognized Britain's right to station troops in the Canal zone and to control Egyptian foreign policy?

In the event Lloyd's counsels of caution proved justified, but the process of disillusion was slow and painful for the diplomats. In November it was thought that a treaty was in sight, and Chamberlain praised Sarwat for his 'courage, statesmanship and frankness' and asked Lloyd to get him to sign it as soon as he arrived back in Cairo.[32] Instead of signing Sarwat pleaded for more time to persuade his colleagues. By early December Chamberlain was asking Lloyd to tell Sarwat that the British wanted a treaty by 20 December.[33] Lloyd reported that the Pasha 'seemed somewhat surprised that there should be any question of so immediate action on his part'; he wanted, instead, further 'conversations'.[34] Unable to accept the obvious implications of Sarwat's prevarication, Tyrrell fell back on blaming Lloyd.

Tyrrell could not accept that Lloyd's warnings about undue optimism might have been right – indeed he positively refused to believe that Sarwat was prevaricating. He told Chamberlain on 12 December that if Lloyd's telegrams were to be 'taken at face value' then they would

> appear to indicate that Sarwat was going to prove both slippery and unreliable. This you will recollect was the impression of him which Lloyd was very anxious to create when he was over here this summer. Again, I find it difficult to reconcile Sarwat's apparent wish to reopen discussions with Lloyd on a number of points of detail with the very genuine anxiety he displayed a few weeks ago to clear up everything during his negotiations with you and to leave as little as possible for settlement in Cairo.

He thought that Lloyd was trying to sabotage negotiations and suggested that they should send a despatch urging him to go faster.[35] But alas for Tyrrell, Sarwat did prove both 'slippery and unreliable'. From mid January until early March he engaged in a series of manoeuvres designed to secure from the British an interpretation of the treaty which would whittle away the safeguards for imperial interests: he wanted freedom to make commercial treaties without British supervision; to restrict British influence over Egypt's armed forces; and generally to secure an interpretation of the treaty which he could present to the Wafd as a defeat for Britain.

This was the circle that could not be squared. Throughout January

1928 the Foreign Office continued to negotiate, showing all the pliability of a piece of plasticine, much to Lloyd's disgust; but it was impossible to bend far enough to accommodate Sarwat's needs. Blanche noted in her diary in February:

> It becomes more and more abundantly clear that Sarwat has absolutely no good faith in the matter and is trying to shuffle out of all the obligations he entered into with Austen in London – just as George warned he would do the moment he got back here and had to face his extremist colleagues.[36]

Lloyd felt more than half inclined to resign because of the stream of concessions which were being made to Sarwat and he warned Chamberlain on 28 January 1928 that even if Sarwat 'eventually summons up courage and takes the treaty to his Cabinet, I doubt if he will advocate it . . . [he is] more likely to lay it before them saying that it was the best he could get out of us'.[37] And so it proved.

Eventually, losing patience, Chamberlain telegraphed on 4 February telling Lloyd to press Sarwat to sign the treaty.[38] Four days later Lloyd reported that Sarwat had at last shown the treaty to his Cabinet and that the omens were not good.[39] The unedifying farce came to an end when George telegraphed on 4 March that the Egyptian Cabinet had rejected the treaty as 'incompatible with the independence and sovereignty of Egypt' – and that Sarwat had just resigned.[40] Secret diplomacy had received its due reward, but Lloyd could expect no thanks for being proved right.

# 21

# PRELUDE TO A CONSPIRACY

The diplomatic eye discerned Lloyd's hand in the fulfilment of his prophecy concerning the Sarwat treaty; unwilling to believe in their own fallibility, the diplomats preferred to attribute the failure of their project to Lloyd's perfidy. Nor were they slow in discovering fresh evidence for this belief.

During the period when the heady wine of illusion still ran strong in Whitehall, Zaghloul's successor as leader of the Wafd, Nahas Pasha, had introduced into Parliament legislation which Lloyd reported would 'make it impossible for the Executive authority effectively to control the carrying of dangerous weapons and prevent public meetings'.[1] In March 1928, with the concurrence of Chamberlain, Lloyd had warned the Egyptians that firm action would be taken if these bills became law. Lloyd again tried to prepare the Foreign Office for what would have to be done in the event of an Egyptian refusal and suggested that they would have to 'dissolve Parliament and appoint a *Cabinet d'Affaires*'; but until the Egyptians obligingly provided a pretext for this 'it would be best to pursue this unhappy farce of democracy'.[2]

Such counsels, reminiscent of those given by Lloyd in the army crisis of 1927, set ringing the diplomatic alarm bells. On 19 March Chamberlain asked Lloyd to elaborate upon his proposals; as he did so he took care to fire a warning shot across the proconsular bows:

> Let me say in passing but very firmly that I hope you will use no language to anyone to indicate that you expect such a crisis or that the solution to which you look forward is an abrogation of the existing constitution.

Warning lest impulsive action should create a party political question out of Egypt, Chamberlain asked for a detailed account of what Lloyd would do in a crisis. On 27 March, in a 'most urgent telegram', he pressed for an immediate reply to his letter: 'You should explain fully and exactly what you are aiming at and by what means you propose to secure it.'[3] In a long letter dated 28 March he revealed what lay behind such very overt signs of suspicion.

Chamberlain's fears had, it transpired, been aroused by reports from an American journalist (Mr von Wiegand) and an Italian diplomat (Signor Paterno) of conversations with Lloyd during which he was supposed to have expressed pleasure in the failure of the Sarwat treaty because he 'was in favour of force here and in India'; Chamberlain found it 'impossible to believe that both these men have invented the conversations'. It was, he told Lloyd, 'not merely obviously improper' for him to have used such language, it was also 'directly contrary to the discretion which I have particularly begged you to observe'; he demanded from Lloyd a 'clear statement of what he had said'.[4]

This letter reached Lloyd just as Nahas rejected British protests about the Assemblies Bill; he reported this fact to London and awaited instructions. The interval he occupied in responding to the astonishing and discouraging letter. Protesting that he had, in fact, worked as hard for the treaty as anyone, despite his misgivings, he accurately observed to Chamberlain that:

> Your letter shows that you entertain accusations against me of seeking to deprecate your treaty at the very moment when facts in your possession show that I was straining every nerve to secure agreement for it. Such conduct would be worthy only of a knave or a fool. Nevertheless I could only understand from your letter that on the word of a foreign diplomat and a stray American journalist you are prepared to think it possible conduct on my part.

The diplomats placed credence in the reports only because they confirmed their own long-nurtured suspicions; but this could hardly be owned. Lloyd reminded Chamberlain that if the impression had been created that there was a division between the High Commissioner and the Foreign Office over the treaty, that was the fault of those who had not let him sit in on the negotiations; as to the words attributed to him, he haughtily denied them.[5]

Chamberlain's reply, written on 28 April, was as grudging as Lloyd's had been dignified:

> I of course accept your denial, and therefore will not reply to the rest of your letter, though you must let me say that it is largely occupied by just such a criticism of the decisions of the Government and of my own conduct of the negotiations as was implied in the statements of Paterno and von Wiegand.[6]

Proconsular criticisms were to be taken not as signs of an independent spirit based upon first-hand knowledge, but rather as evidence of disloyalty; thus were the affairs of the Empire ordered in the days of its decline.

Meanwhile it had become necessary to confront the Egyptians over the Assemblies Bill. By the end of April even the Foreign Office had to contemplate what to do if the Bill was proceeded with;[7] and the ever-reliable Keyes was asked to despatch warships to Alexandria.[8] On 2 May the British demands were formally rejected by Nahas who took the Wafdist 'high-line' that Britain had no right to meddle with internal Egyptian matters and gave no assurances that the offending measures would be dropped. Lloyd urged that they should press him for a satisfactory reply before proceeding to deliver an ultimatum[9] and was thunderstruck when told that London considered the Egyptian response 'not unacceptable'. Nahas had not, after all, said that the Bill would be introduced in the near future and acquiescence was, the diplomats counselled, 'better calculated than insistence on a more categorical response, to facilitate the formation in due course of a moderate Ministry'. It was thought that further insistence would 'take on far too closely the character of an unlimited offensive towards ill-defined objectives against opposition of an unknown strength'.[10]

Against this last remark Lloyd pencilled a large exclamation mark, but he carried out his orders. Although the Assemblies Bill was not proceeded with, Lloyd was not happy with the attitude evinced by his chiefs; in her diary Blanche recorded:

> The FO as usual retreated at the last moment and the conclusion of the business was therefore about 50% less good than it might have been if they had stuck to their guns at the crucial moment.
> It is futile to think that one can deal with these childish half-baked people by vacillation. I wish Austen was less of an old woman. There it is, you have to work with the people the Almighty sends to you.[11]

Lloyd was not trusted, this much was clear, and yet what had Tyrrell's policy produced? There was no treaty, nor yet that 'moderate Ministry' which had been the *ignis fatuus* of British diplomacy in Egypt for so long; in June 1928 the King sacked Nahas and replaced him with Mahmoud Mahmoud, suspending Parliament as he did so; in the battle between autocracy and oligarchy the former seemed to gain the lead.

But the focus of all groups in Egypt now began to shift to events in London for within the year there would have to be a general election in Britain. Should Baldwin's mandate be renewed it was likely that changes would be made at the Foreign Office and these might encompass Lloyd; should Labour win, then Lloyd's days in Egypt would be numbered; Wafdists, Liberals or Monarchists, Egyptian politicians were agreed that nothing was to be extracted from the British as long as 'the Lord' sat in the Residency. So it was that an uneasy peace settled over Egypt, one reinforced by the fact that Chamberlain was absent from the Foreign Office for the rest of 1928 recovering from a severe illness.

There was fixed between Lloyd and the diplomats a great gulf. The imperial administrator stood aghast at the effects of allowing the Egyptians to run their own affairs; he told Irwin in November 1927:

> The administration is steadily falling to pieces, corruption, nepotism, and intrigue are hurrying back to the resumption of the old sway they exerted in the early days of Cromer and our hands are largely tied by the blundering commitments we entered into in 1922.[12]

This he could not bear and there can be no doubt that he itched to bring his own expertise to the service of the Egyptian fellahin. The diplomats were not concerned with the lot of the peasant but rather with securing imperial interests and they continued, despite all evidence to the contrary, to imagine that there was some way of securing Egyptian acknowledgement of these; Lloyd knew otherwise but was not believed. Where Lloyd still trusted in the imperial spirit, the diplomats predicated their actions upon its demise; this was his chance to prevent the recall of the legions. The following decade was to provide a melancholy commentary upon this endeavour.

The quiet which settled over affairs in Egypt in 1928 allowed Lloyd to enjoy, for once, a trouble-free holiday in England and, upon his return, to face the unprecedented situation of the absence of any crisis. This allowed him to devote more time to aspects of Egypt which lay outside the political sphere.

Like any High Commissioner he had to put up with dinner parties and formal balls, but he did so with some impatience; away from the Residency there were things more to his taste to be found. The desert spaces continued to exercise their attraction, and if he lacked the companionship of a Lawrence or an Aubrey Herbert, this was compensated for by the presence of his own son, David; to him was extended not only Lloyd's customary delight in the company of the young, but also something more. He longed to show his son the scenes amidst which so much of his own life had been passed and he took intense pleasure when David evinced enthusiasm for them; together they would ride off into the wilderness where the bonds of blood, which had perhaps been loosened by circumstance, were reinforced.

One of the chief delights offered by life in Egypt was the High

Commissioner's duck-shoot at Ekiad to which Lloyd invited the most important Egyptian Pashas and European visitors. It was here too that David learned to shoot, watching the fellahin dash out in their boats to collect the bag from the water. There was always considerable competition to get the highest score and the rules were not, as David discovered on one occasion, always strictly observed:

> One Pasha managed to bring a number of dead duck into his butt. I heard a dull booming from a neighbouring butt and found that the Pasha in question had a retainer with a gun with him. When he had about a dozen duck sitting in the water he would kill the lot with one shot.[13]

The quieter tempo of events also allowed Lloyd to spend more time than usual upon his annual visit to the Sudan in January. His usual propensity for discovering work which only he could do was, for once, matched by an opportunity for relaxation, as Blanche's description of their progress down the White Nile shows:

> We left Korti at five this morning and have been steaming along all day quite slowly, looking at every kind of wonderful bird flying about. We have seen various herons, fishing eagles (fine black birds with yellow hooked beaks), darters and cormorants, spin-winged plovers, bee-eaters (copper-gold with a turquoise band above their tails), ruffs, all sorts of ducks and teals, two or three different kinds of dove, and flocks of crested cranes, like the ones we have in the Residency garden. We have also seen countless crocodile, some quite small and some enormous, and a great many hippo – we are already getting quite blasé about them. We stopped at five, and had a little walk along the bank, and then went on again.

But his spirit could bear only a few days of lotus-eating and when they reached the Upper Nile province in early February, Lloyd took to the Residency Rolls in order to explore the region more fully.

After a few days Lloyd and his party rejoined their companions. Blanche recorded that:

> They have covered a great deal of ground . . . George in the Rolls, the others in Fords – with a whole fleet of lorries carrying supplies and machine guns for defence! so they looked like an army coming in.[14]

Lloyd swiftly donned his ankle-ropes, getting down to work on his mail, which went off the same evening by aeroplane to Cairo; even on the further reaches of the Upper Nile, the High Commissioner was in touch with what was happening throughout his domain. It was not, however, until the beginning of March that he returned to Cairo.

In early April his old friend Rudyard Kipling visited the Residency with his wife. Blanche found the great writer

> just the same as ever – only . . . a little thinner and a little older; his

eyebrows still look as if they had been stuck on and might fall off – and work from side to side in moments of excitement.

They discussed Lloyd's future:

> He asked me point-blank what was to come next in his life after this, and whether he ought really to stay on here and finish the job he has begun – or go on to India. I told him that I was perhaps biassed by my knowledge that India has been the goal of all his hopes and dreams ever since he was a boy of eighteen and that he has trained himself for the job for thirty years – but that apart from his personal ambition, and trying to judge as fairly as one could, he did seem to me the best person in sight, with the necessary knowledge *and* the necessary character, to pull India round after two successive Viceroyalties of weak and short-sighted policy – such as Reading's – and I fear Edward's – for all the latter's wonderful nature. He said that Mr Baldwin had said to him when they were talking over who was to go to India before Edward went, and he, Kipling, had suggested George: 'Lloyd can wait' and that he might say this again. I said 'Yes, but can India wait?' and Kipling agreed that India probably couldn't.[15]

Hindsight is necessary to the writing of history and confers, as one of its additional benefits, a sharpening of the sense of irony which the study of the past so stimulates, but in this exchange the irony is unbearable. Not only were the events of the next six months to bring Lloyd's career in Egypt to a spectacular end, but the very characteristics which Blanche regarded as his main qualifications for the viceroyalty were to put him out of the running for it and to set him at odds, for the next decade, with the consensus which was to dominate British politics.

With the approach of the general election in Britain the short interlude of peace came to an end and the differences between Lloyd and the Foreign Office once more came to dominate the foreground of Anglo–Egyptian relations.

# 22

# CONSPIRACY

It should not be supposed that the differences which existed between Lloyd and the diplomats were confined to matters of policy – or that knowledge of them was restricted to the Foreign Office. Leo Amery recalled in his memoirs that the diplomats had 'long disliked Lloyd's exceptional position' and had 'wanted the post to be held by an ordinary member of the Diplomatic Service in the due course of promotion'; Lloyd's 'policy and . . . tactics' served only to aggravate 'their resentment';[1] whilst Lord Vansittart, a diplomat himself, recorded that:

> A set in the Foreign Office had long incited Austen against George Lloyd, our High Commissioner in Egypt. The professionals never wanted an outsider there, and I could never agree with them, having grown used to outsiders of less ability. The Department murmured that he was trying to put the clock back, when he insisted on winding it in his own way. While it nagged at a fault, his energies had already carried him to what it deemed another. He reported by letter rather than despatch, and often to S[tanley] B[aldwin] over Austen's head. The Foreign Office hated the first trait, Austen the second.

'Van' observed that:

> George hated control – a comprehensible and impractical passion – was secretive and suspicious, driven by flagrant love of his country and the Empire, which was bound to strand a dynamist in such an age. His high sense of duty and dignity was thus termed pompous by his staff, even more by the Foreign Office. It had several coins in which to repay him.[2]

The form of 'repayment' had already been worked out before the 1929 election. Pressure from the diplomats, led by Tyrrell's successor, Sir Ronald Lindsay, ensured that had Chamberlain remained at the Foreign Office Lloyd would have been moved elsewhere, probably to supervise the creation of an East African federation of Kenya, Uganda and Tanganyika.[3] The election result was to make superfluous any such gesture of courtesy; but even before the campaign took place, the diplomats were making their dispositions.

In May 1929, Hafiz Afifi, the Egyptian Minister in London, raised the question of whether British residents in Egypt should continue to be exempt from the payment of various local taxes; on the surface a simple enough question, and one to which the Foreign Office was disposed to lend a friendly ear. Lloyd did not agree with the proposal that foreigners should be liable to pay these taxes. In his usual thorough way he sent an exhaustive and well-researched account giving the reasons for his view, and came to the conclusion that the one tax which should not be paid was the stamp tax. The response from London, which took him by surprise, shows the diplomats preparing their ground for Lloyd's removal, for they took the opportunity to restate 'the governing principles of our policy', thus, as he observed, implying that in offering his opinion, Lloyd had 'departed' from them.

That such a matter should have produced the *verbosa et grandis epistola* from Whitehall should have put Lloyd on the alert; it was characteristic of his lack of tactical political sense that he should, instead, have responded to it with a despatch on 7 June in the best proconsular manner. This telegram, which was to be used by the diplomats as evidence of his contumacious spirit, restated his conviction that it was 'a most dangerous course to make further substantial concessions' except as part of a general agreement 'involving Egypt's acceptance of our minimum requirements';[4] Chamberlain's comment was laconic: 'That if he might be permitted a criticism he thought that my policy was fundamentally wrong.'[5]

Lloyd's political antennae were not totally insensitive; he suspected that the diplomats were manoeuvring against him, but thought that he was merely facing another episode like the Sarwat treaty. He was quite correct in suspecting that negotiations for a treaty had already opened between Mahmoud's Government and the Foreign Office; but he did not realize that his days were numbered. His own attention was fixed upon the election results which had produced a Socialist Government. Although perfectly willing to carry on at his post, he did not look forward to serving under Labour; the diplomats were about to relieve him of any anxiety on this score.

Chamberlain's departure from the Foreign Office smoothed the way for Lloyd's removal. The new Foreign Secretary, Arthur Henderson, brought two prejudices with him to Whitehall: animosity against his Prime Minister, MacDonald, whom he could not forgive for having taken his place as Labour's leader;[6] and an inherent distrust of the mandarins of the Foreign Office;[7] he was determined to assert his own control over foreign policy. That one of the first documents across his desk was a plea from the diplomats to remove Lloyd must have come as a welcome surprise; here was an opportunity to assert himself at little cost.[8] Lloyd was an imperialist Tory whose departure from Egypt would be greeted with Labour cheers; such a dramatic start to his period in office would also demonstrate to his party that he was not a man who could be run by his officials; Labour demonology did not incorporate the notion of senior diplomats conspiring against a Conservative politician.

The principal mover in the conspiracy was the Permanent Under-Secretary, Sir Ronald Lindsay. He told Henderson that Chamberlain had 'pursued a liberal policy in Egypt' and that although 'Lloyd had always carried out instructions which were sent to him', it

> was no use pretending that his mind worked on liberal lines and I did not consider that in the spirit he had ever been completely in harmony with the policy . . . [Chamberlain] had laid down.

He made it clear that Lloyd's presence would make it difficult for him to pursue even a line of policy as liberal as that of his predecessor; the implication was clear.

Henderson's response was that of the cautious politician who sensed trouble ahead; he suggested that 'Perhaps if spoken to when he came on leave Lord Lloyd might acquiesce in liberalism of policy in the spirit no less than the letter.' This was not what Lindsay wanted to hear. He argued that 'Lord Lloyd's views were so ingrained in his character that he would not be able to change.' Retailing this conversation to Chamberlain on 17 June, Lindsay stated bluntly: 'I did not hide my own desire to see Lord Lloyd replaced by some other High Commissioner.'[9]

That Lindsay should have felt compelled to tell his Conservative former chief the details of his conversation with his new master is suggestive; for a Labour Foreign Secretary to remove a Conservative political appointee on the ground that he had disagreed with an outgoing Conservative Government would be, to say the least, a novel proceeding; it was imperative that Chamberlain should say and do nothing to defend Lloyd.

Chamberlain, who was quite as cautious as Henderson, quickly replied to Lindsay's letter on 18 June distancing himself from the whole business:

> If I had remained in office I should have been obliged to take a decision, but, as I think you will have seen I was much puzzled and I really

couldn't say on which side of the fence I should have come down. . . .
After thinking over your letter for an hour my inclination at the moment
is to advise Henderson to explain his views and policy plainly to Lloyd
and to ask Lloyd whether he feels he can carry them out with conviction
and with satisfaction to himself. If Lloyd feels his answer must be
negative I presume he would tender his resignation. If his reply is
affirmative I would not, if I were Henderson, make a change now.

Such a move would, he thought, create misunderstandings in Britain
and in Egypt.[10]

Such unwonted caution by the politicians made it essential to wheel
out the big guns to explain exactly why Lloyd had to go at once. Upon a
copy of Lloyd's reply to Chamberlain's restatement of British policy,
Murray of the Foreign Office minuted on 19 June:

Sir A. Chamberlain gave clear expression to the view, consistently held
in the department, that the interventions of His Majesty's Government
into the purely internal affairs of Egypt should be reduced to the
minimum, and this in order that when we do have to intervene our
intervention should be effective.

Lord Lloyd replies that further substantial concessions to Egypt,
however reasonable in themselves, would be most dangerous except as
part of a general settlement involving Egypt's acceptance of our
requirements. What his interpretation of those requirements would be
can easily be surmised from his attitude during the Sarwat negotiations
and, indeed, during his whole tenure of the High Commissionership. We
want to avoid having to intervene, Lord Lloyd is on the look out for an
excuse for intervention. To him non-intervention or failure to insist on
the maintenance of privileges which are difficult to justify and out of
harmony with modern developments, spells concession and concession
disaster, or as he puts it 'ill-advised reliance on an Egyptian sense of
gratitude which has, to say the least, been consistently inconspicuous
since 1922'.

Both despatches are characteristic and furnish a striking example of
the fundamental antithesis between our conception and Lord Lloyd's of
what British policy ought to be.

Although Henderson could hardly have missed the point, Lindsay
thought it as well to underline it, minuting that 'These two documents
show the divergence of view which existed between Lord Lloyd and
those of the late Secretary of State.'[11]

To back this up the diplomats had prepared a long paper for
Henderson setting out in detail the case against Lloyd; it also revealed
the rift which had existed between the imperialist wing of the Cabinet
and Chamberlain.[12] Documents covering twenty-nine pages of
foolscap are surprisingly easily overlooked by busy men, but for this
eventuality a shorter version of it had been produced; Lindsay had also

drafted for Henderson's use two telegrams (drafts A and B) to Lloyd; along with them was an explanatory note:

A, the stronger.
B, the weaker.
*A* would have the effect of forcing Lord Lloyd's resignation on the ground of the despatch he wrote to Sir A. Chamberlain and the divergence of view therein revealed. You are on good ground.
To *B*, it is likely, in my opinion, that he would reply expressing complete readiness to acquiesce in your policy and to render to it the loyal support of a civil servant. This, however, would not prevent him from resigning as soon as your policy was revealed to him, and on the ground of *your* policy; and this action of his would of course do much to rouse Conservative opposition to your policy which otherwise might be inclined to moderate itself.[13]

Henderson was too experienced a politician to miss the point here. If he made Lloyd resign because of his disagreements with the previous Conservative Government, the Conservatives would be plunged into disarray and not only would he get his way over Egypt, he might also secure a parliamentary triumph: it was a plum batting wicket.

Lindsay's draft A allowed Lloyd the choice of voluntary retirement if he felt he could not agree with a policy which 'will certainly be not less liberal than that of my predecessor'; draft B asked if he felt he could agree with the (unspecified) policy of the new Government. Henderson sent the drafts to MacDonald on 29 June, along with the departmental memorandum on Egypt and Lloyd's telegrams to Chamberlain. Of the documents he wrote:

[They] have been drafted on my instructions by the Department who, as you doubtless know, are unanimously of the opinion that Lloyd should be withdrawn from Egypt on the ground that as he was incapable of carrying the policy of the late Government in Egypt still less can he be expected to be a competent mouthpiece with the Egyptians for the policy of which we are likely to approve.[14]

MacDonald, who was much taken by what Lindsay had written about the political advantages to be gained from forcing Lloyd out on the ground of his disagreement with Chamberlain, added to the telegram a sentence designed to provoke this:

I would like to discuss the situation with you on your return because I should not be candid with you were I not to warn you that it is difficult for me in the light of these despatches to feel confident that your ideas can be harmonized with those of either my predecessor or myself.[15]

Lindsay strongly approved of MacDonald's amendments, telling Henderson on 2 July:

I think myself that the Prime Minister's version is a great improvement on both the drafts previously prepared. *But the main point is that Lord Lloyd shall be removed from his post the moment he arrives in England. If he is given any occasion to intervene in the business which is in progress, I feel certain that all prospect of success is lost.*[16]

The 'business in hand' referred to the negotiations which had already been opened with the Egyptians and which made Lloyd's removal a matter of urgency. The MacDonald version of the telegram was sent on 3 July; Henderson candidly admitted to the House on 24 July that it was 'of such a character that I think most people would have accepted it as an invitation to terminate their position'.[17]

Even before he received this Lloyd knew that all was not well. His letters to Henderson had all been met with anodyne responses and he told Blanche on 7 July that *The Times*'s correspondent, Gerald Delaney, 'has been very busy intriguing against me and poisoning Ramsay's mind against me'. This, he thought,

indicates definitely that Selby is in it and they may have got Austen to agree to my eviction. The wording of Arthur Henderson's telegram to me certainly suggests that they have done this.

But he found it 'hard to believe . . . that either Baldwin or Winston, especially not the latter, would concur quite so easily'. He had concluded that 'the sooner I get back the better'. Separated by two thousand miles from Blanche, he poured out his feelings to her on paper:

I am not worrying very badly my dear about all this – whatever happens will probably turn out for the best in the long run. I have a clear conscience that I have worked hard and done all that I could. These are not days when people who are charged with great responsibilities overseas and who are guarding vital interests of the nation have the smallest right, merely in order to please this chief or that, to acquiesce in a policy of surrender. There is far too much of this going on: indeed I am convinced that one of the reasons for the failure of our party to win support in the election was the feeling of the public that we had been too supine and stood up too little abroad for our rights. If I am turned out of office here for refusing to acquiesce in the feeble frittering away of our position here I shall not be ashamed of that and I hope you will feel no cause to be either.

He sounded a less pessimistic note in his postscript:

Of course you must remember that I may be able to talk Ramsay round when I get home. The question has to be considered whether in the circ[umstance]s I sh[oul]d be wise in staying or not. I am very anxious to get out of Egypt without the appearance of a crash.[18]

This letter is extraordinarily characteristic of the man in its firm imperial patriotism, anxious concern for his own career and, alas, in the complete misunderstanding of the political position at home.

Lloyd's England was still that of the pre-war decades; after all, he knew no other, having been abroad for most of the years since 1914. Whilst he had been trying to save the outlying parts of the imperial edifice, the foundations upon which the whole thing rested had begun to shift. In Bombay and Cairo he had put up a magnificent rearguard action for his paternalist conception of Empire; but at home the new democracy inaugurated by the 1918 Reform Act was not interested in such matters. Baldwin, that astute interpreter of England, had been quick to observe the new priorities which would be demanded. As he told the schoolboys of Harrow in 1926: 'Just as at the time of the Renaissance the age devoted itself to intellectual inquiry, so today it is devoting itself and will devote itself to social inquiry.'[19] The democracy wanted employment and better housing, not the burdens of Empire. Both Baldwin and Lloyd harboured romantic notions about the English people; but where one offered a quiet life, the other demanded strenuous effort. The next decade was to show which 'the people' preferred.

Before her husband arrived back in England Blanche asked Bob Vansittart how the land lay:

> He told me that George's diagnosis of the situation is the correct one – that the Foreign Office, headed by Austen, have long been anxious to get rid of him – but that as long as the Conservatives were in power they could not prevail. He added that very often while he was Baldwin's secretary he had been able to do good work by telling him first the true version of events in Egypt, before the FO had been able to get at him. Now that the Socialists are in power with very little experience of foreign affairs, the FO can do what they like with them. Bob's view is that George could probably turn the corner by being firm with Henderson and pointing out that there have been no differences over questions of policy – but if he did and went back for another year in Egypt, the FO would be able to make his position intolerable and it would be doubtful if he could do any good there.[20]

But in one respect, as we have seen, 'Van' was wrong: there was no intention of allowing Lloyd to go back to Egypt; once he arrived in London the conspiracy would envelop him.

# 23

# CRISIS

Lloyd arrived back in London on 18 July 1929. He and Blanche spent a troubled evening at the house they had taken in Curzon Street; talking things over neither of them could understand why the Socialists 'should be taking such a step in such a violent hurry'.[1] The following morning he saw Vansittart, who 'did not disguise from him that he thought the FO were determined to do him down and that the Socialist Government are not prepared to resist them'. Blanche, who met Lord Salisbury at a luncheon party, let him know 'what was in the wind', but he could not believe that even the Socialists would do such a thing. When she got back home she discovered that the trap had been sprung.

Her account of what she was told by her husband deserves prolonged quotation:

> In the afternoon he saw Ronald Lindsay – who came to see him at the Carlton, where he is staying. He came round before dinner to Curzon Street and told me about the interview – which is so amazing that we cannot explain it in any way. RL, who should be a gentleman, who has known us both for years, and who, as far as we know, has no reason whatever to feel any enmity against either of us – allowed himself to be offensive and insulting in the highest degree, treating George *de haut en bas*, telling him that unless he chose to resign he would be fired – that the FO had enough against him to break him! and throughout the interview used the most threatening and objectionable language.

Although taken aback by this, Lloyd had remained calm and 'naturally declined to hand in his resignation to him there and then as he was invited to do'. This drew from Lindsay the ungracious response that 'he must not think he could continue to go round to functions as the High Commissioner!' Lloyd replied that 'he really did know his own job at his time of life'.

The Lloyds were stunned by the turn events had taken and

concluded that the Socialists were negotiating with the Egyptians and wanted to get rid of him, justifying their 'sudden change of policy' by 'insisting that there were differences with the late Cabinet'.[2] The only question now was whether to resign or wait to be dismissed.

In this crisis of his fortunes, Lloyd sought the advice of senior Conservative colleagues and received various counsels. Lord Salisbury thought he should resign 'because it is in the best tradition of British public service', but Edward Irwin was inclined to think that 'he ought to say to Henderson that he didn't understand what all the trouble was about and that he had had the full support of the late Government'. Bob Vansittart was strongly for the Salisbury line as it would allow Lloyd to retain some of the initiative, and he helped him to draft a letter before he went off to see Henderson.[3] He had hoped to see MacDonald first, thinking that he would be less in the grip of the diplomats; but this would not have saved him.

The fatal interview with Henderson was retailed to Blanche immediately afterwards.[4] In marked contrast to his senior civil servant, the Foreign Secretary had been 'very courteous' and had seemed so embarrassed that Lloyd had had to raise the subject of his resignation:

'Ramsay and I are very sorry about this, Lord Lloyd, very sorry indeed.' So George said, 'Sorry about what, Mr Henderson?' 'Well,' he said, 'we both like and respect you a great deal – but the fact is there are certain members of my party who don't like you – they don't like you at all; and there are one or two men in my Cabinet who 'ate you, they want you to go.'

It was not, he replied, news to him that he had few friends on the left of the Labour Party:

'But still . . . Mr Henderson, we seem to have reached the apex of our conversation rather abruptly, and there are one or two things I want to learn from you. You say that the Government want me to go, and your telegram implied that you thought I should disagree with your policy, but how can you know that I should? You have not told me yet what your policy is to be?'

Lloyd asked bluntly whether negotiations were in train with the Egyptians, but secured nothing beyond a hesitant statement that nothing could be said about any diplomatic conversations. When he asked to be told Labour's policy on Egypt, Henderson said that he was not able to tell him anything about that either:

'This makes the situation rather an impossible one,' said G. 'It's meant to,' said Henderson. 'Well,' said G., 'if HM's Government desires my resignation there will be no difficulty on my side about the resignation being forthcoming – but I think I am entitled to ask you, Mr Henderson, after the uncompromising line which you have taken with me, whether, in the event of my deciding against handing in my resignation this morning, you intend to take the course of dismissing me here and now?'

Henderson replied: 'I suppose that's about it.' Upon this George handed him the letter which he and Vansittart had drawn up:

Dear Mr Henderson,

Since my return from Egypt I have been thinking over, in the light of my recent conversation with you, the situation caused by the advent of a new Government in England and the policy which I understand is to be pursued in regard to Egyptian affairs.

I had every hope and desire to continue to serve under the new administration, but I have reluctantly come to the conclusion that my views are not likely to be in sufficient harmony with yours to enable me conscientiously to discharge my duties to His Majesty's Government.

I should be grateful therefore if you would submit my resignation to His Majesty.

Yours sincerely
Lloyd[5]

Henderson 'hummed and hawed and said he didn't think that would do at all, whereupon George said, "Well then give me back my letter and dismiss me upon your own grounds – but I will resign on no other statement than the true one." ' Much to Lloyd's surprise Henderson gave in and accepted it. Lloyd asked if he would read out the letter when he made his statement on the affair in the House; having secured a promise that he would do so, he left.[6]

The time that had to elapse before the news was made public gave to the rest of that day an air of impending doom. When he lunched with Blanche at Sybil Colefax's, Lloyd talked to Noël Coward whom he had last seen at the disastrous premiere of his play *Home Chat* when he had been hissed off the stage. Lloyd said: 'Read your evening papers tomorrow and you will see all about another call taken by someone who is being hissed off the stage.' Dinner was at the Egyptian legation where they attended an official function for Mahmoud Mahmoud. Blanche found it 'a nightmare', sitting there and talking as though nothing had happened – and no one, save for the man sitting directly opposite Blanche, and one or two others, knowing what had happened; she sat across from Lindsay and spent the whole dinner cutting him dead.

When Henderson told the House of Lloyd's 'resignation' on 24 July he did not read out Lloyd's letter, nor did he release it to the press. The reaction from the Tories amused Henderson's Under-Secretary, Hugh Dalton: 'Winston and certain Tory backbenchers howling with fury . . . Winston was half-drunk.'[7] Churchill's intervention was not unprompted. Lloyd had seen him the previous afternoon and had 'appealed to me to do him justice'.[8] He now angrily demanded to know whether the 'resignation' had been 'extorted'. Baldwin sat 'silent and disapproving', but Churchill's pertinacity secured the promise of parliamentary time to discuss the issue.[9] Leaving the House Blanche noticed posters on the news-vendors' stands: 'Lord Lloyd dismissed'; they were now at the centre of a major political storm.

The newspapers on the morning of 25 July were dominated by the 'unexpected' resignation and, on the whole, they took Lloyd's part. *The Times*, which referred back to his disagreements with Chamberlain, forecast with unwonted prescience that the debate, which was due to take place in the Commons on 26 July, 'would not be on Party lines'.

When their Lordships debated the matter that afternoon, the Labour spokesman, Lord Parmoor, suffered 'orgies of abuse'[10] from Lord Birkenhead and cut a most inadequate figure against other senior Conservatives such as Lord Salisbury. But the real test came when the Commons discussed the matter on 26 July.

It may be that Churchill took up Lloyd's case out of a genuine desire to defend a man who had been wronged by the Socialists, but this was not how the matter presented itself to his colleagues on the Conservative front bench; as Neville Chamberlain wrote to his half-brother afterwards:

> All through this short session he has been trying to take the lead away from S[tanley] B[aldwin] and he thought he saw his way to make a real spash in the Adjournment and leave the House the hero of the day.

He told his sister that they had had 'warnings of the most definite character as to the case which the Government could put up' which had been passed on to Churchill and other Conservative MPs;[11] the word had gone round that Lloyd had no case.

Thus it was that Churchill found himself an isolated figure. The tone of the Conservative response was set by that greatest of party managers, Baldwin, who

> began on a very quiet note but entirely forgot to say a single word in praise of Lloyd's work. Worse still, he never made it clear, I suppose in his anxiety to cover Austen, that George had the late Government's confidence.[12]

The reason for his reticence became apparent when Henderson got up. As a counter-attack it was as devastating as it was underhand. He gave the House a detailed account of Lloyd's disagreements with the previous Government, pointing out that it was hardly to be expected that a Labour Government would enjoy better relations with such a man. He made it plain that any attempt to press the issue must result in a full examination of relations between Lloyd and the Conservative administration; it was no wonder that Baldwin kept quiet. The Labour benches cheered 'Uncle' Arthur to the echo; he had the Tories on the run.[13]

When Churchill rose to speak it was 'without a Tory cheer'. He told Lloyd on 28 July that:

> The wind was very bleak in the House of Commons. The Labour Party, backed by a vindictive Foreign Office, feeling sure of themselves and triumphant, and the Liberals sourly impartial. As for the Tories, it appears that the Whips went about all Thursday afternoon damping down the enthusiasm of our friends, telling them that we had no case and that very likely a change would have been made in any case. I felt the current running so strongly that I did not push matters beyond a certain point, and even going so far I encountered censure.[14]

Others were more brutal about Churchill's performance: Dalton noting with delight that he 'got the worst of it in the exchange with Uncle. Even began to lose the House';[15] Neville Chamberlain, who had watched Churchill's efforts to take the leading role without much favour, commented with satisfaction that the debate which was to thrust him to the fore had

> resulted in much discomfiture for Winston and I must say he deserved it ... he insisted in rushing in to his fate and the result was that while S.B.'s speech was greatly applauded as equally dignified and proper, Winston was made to look exceedingly foolish.[16]

His attacks on the Foreign Office merely aroused anger that civil servants should be so impugned and MacDonald had no trouble in dealing with him when he came to wind up the debate. Even Blanche, who was watching from the gallery, thought Winston's speech 'unwise and unhelpful'.[17]

It was 'an overwhelming parliamentary triumph for the Government' and enabled Labour to finish the session on a high note.[18] When Henderson went into the Cabinet afterwards he was greeted by choruses of 'See the conquering hero comes!' MacDonald 'at the head of the table, sat silent'.[19]

In Amery's eyes the debate was 'a bad fiasco',[20] but for Neville Chamberlain and those who had watched with unease Churchill's performance during the session it was one which could be borne as it was at his expense. Few tears were shed for Churchill. Austen Chamberlain, who had been conveniently out of the country, wrote to his half-brother that he had been tempted to send Winston a transcription of a message which Lord Melbourne had once sent to Lord John Russell: 'I hope you did not say anything damned foolish. I thought you were rather teeming with imprudence when I left you yesterday.'[21]

Lloyd, who found his fate caught up in these stronger currents, was the main loser. His record had been publicly traduced and although senior Conservatives such as Salisbury, Joynson-Hicks (now Lord Brentford) and Birkenhead had all said that he had enjoyed the confidence of the previous administration, neither Baldwin nor Austen Chamberlain had done anything to confirm this. The latter wrote feebly:

> Well, I am not sorry, or at least not altogether sorry, to have missed the discussions on Lloyd's recall. I had not decided what I should have done myself, but the office was pressing strongly that Lloyd's appointment should not be renewed.[22]

He told Neville that although Lloyd was

> a first-class man for a crisis or for an administrative job . . . he has not one iota of diplomacy in his composition and I could not help sharing the Foreign Office feeling that in present circumstances he was something of a danger in Egypt and created needless difficulties for us.

Had he remained Foreign Secretary, Chamberlain had thought of moving Lloyd to East Africa where he could put his organizing abilities at the service of the creation of an East African federation;[23] now Lloyd found himself without employment.

The debate over Lloyd's recall reveals an interesting fault-line in the Conservative Party which was to be very significant in August 1931 when the National Government was formed. On his side were those members of the late Cabinet who had supported him since 1925: Leo Amery, Birkenhead, Churchill, Joynson-Hicks and Lord Salisbury. This phalanx was too strong for Baldwin to overcome, and had he won the 1929 election then places would have had to be found for Amery, Churchill and Lloyd at least, and most probably for Salisbury too.[24] Yet these men had been an obstacle to the more liberal policy in imperial affairs favoured by men like Irwin, Austen Chamberlain and Baldwin himself and they would have continued to be so. What the defeat of 1929 did was to give Baldwin a chance to distance himself from them; the Lloyd debate was the first sign of this distancing. The crisis of August 1931 provided a perfect opportunity for ditching them altogether and none of the men mentioned ever obtained office under Baldwin again. The division between Baldwin and the 'die-hards' which was to be such a feature of the early 1930s was already visible.

Deserted by his party's leaders, Lloyd found consolation in the scores of messages of support which poured in on him. Churchill caught their general purport in sombre and sonorous phrases:

> I cannot help thinking about you this Sunday and hoping that you will not let yourself be distressed, and still less discouraged, by the events of last week.
>
> You have done a fine work in Egypt and the place is left in a high state of order and tranquillity. The march of events will vindicate your administration; and your reputation will grow step by step with the melancholy decline in British and Egyptian affairs. . . . There is nothing for it but to await developments, which I am sure will be swift and evil.
>
> Never mind, you have done your best, and if Britain alone among modern States chooses to cast away her rights, her interests and her strength, she must learn by bitter experience.[25]

But although such letters brought balm to his wounded spirit, nothing could heal the grave hurt which had been inflicted on him. He found himself, in his fiftieth year, suddenly torn from his labours and from dreams of becoming Viceroy, rudely treated by his opponents and neglected by the leaders of his own party. Such a turn of events would have wounded a man less sensitive to his reputation than Lloyd; to him it was wormwood and gall. Worse still was the fact that he now had to stand impotent while the Empire was in danger; but worst of all was being out of harness. One of those who wrote saw these things and offered indignation and advice; this was Aircraftsman Shaw (better known as Lawrence of Arabia):

> This disgusts me: first me, then you. G.L. what in God's name is the matter with our blasted governors? Thank the Lord the worst lot are out. Winston I liked, and Philip Sassoon: but if all the rest were drowning across the way in a ditch I wouldn't take the trouble to go over and push 'em under.
>
> It's a magnificent bang, you've come out with: go to the National Portrait Gallery and look at the head of Warren Hastings, and learn how to grow old: but I've been sick at fearing how you would hate the ending of things. *You* haven't an Air Force to fall back on: only the mouldy House of Lords.
>
> Let us meet sometime. I'm not a corpse, quite: but it's horrible being out.[26]

It was.

# 24

## 'BALDWINISM'

Among those who wrote to Lloyd was Sir Henry Page Croft who, in 1917, had invited him to join his new 'National Party'. The failure of that right-wing ginger-group had not dimmed the indefatigable Sir Henry's determination to uphold the banner of true Conservatism and he wrote:

> I am much exercised about the Party – all is not well with us. It is not organization so much as inspiration that we lack. We seem to depend on Widows' Pensions, the authors of which the Widows forgot within a year and derating which I told Baldwin at the time would not win us any support from the masses. . . . We must convince people that we can win or at least strive for a better world, but we had no Empire policy and no industrial policy and we have none now nor are we preparing one.[1]

But although Lloyd agreed with these sentiments, he excused himself from participation in the good fight on the ground that he had been away from England for too long;[2] this was not the sole reason.

Lloyd was not unaware that he had the reputation of being a 'die-hard', nor was he unconscious of the dangers such a label could do to his political career.[3] On the evening of 30 July he had a long conversation with Edward Irwin about India. Already the paths of the two friends were beginning to diverge and Lloyd,

> in the hope of stiffening E's point of view about it all, laid stress upon the fundamental unsuitability of modern western democratic methods of government to any Oriental people – but least of all to the miscellaneous collection of them which constitute our Indian Empire.

Blanche feared that such views gave the impression that he was 'an impossible die-hard' and she persuaded him to write to Irwin to dispel it. He did so, telling Irwin:

> *Of course* I agree that one must face realities, and that we have got to find

a way of satisfying the British public's belief that political freedom, as they conceive it, is the right of every people under the British flag and that the best way of achieving this is the general form of democratic government.

When I talked of going a step backwards, I was not so foolish as to imagine that we could ask any Parliament in this country, under present conditions, to take any step as regards India in contravention of that main tenet: and I am afraid I may have left the impression on you that this was what I desired . . . my tirade was not meant as any expression of practical politics, but only a letting off of steam to you as a friend.

I am afraid it was a sort of reaction against the sloppy international view which I have been brought up against rather closely this last week – and which I fear may be going to ruin our position in Egypt.[4]

Despite this, and Blanche's opinion that for the moment it was best to keep quiet about the shortcomings of democracy because 'the British people, for the time being, believe that the vote is an inestimable benefit which must be bestowed on every individual living under the British flag',[5] Lloyd's attitude towards the effects of democracy upon imperialism remained cool.

A gap thus existed between Lloyd and some of the leaders of his party; that it became a gulf owed everything to the 'sloppy international view' which those leaders decided to take about India. In October 1929 Irwin announced that the ultimate aim of British policy in India was 'Dominion status', thus outflanking the report being prepared by the Simon Commission which since 1927 had been assessing the success or otherwise of the Montagu–Chelmsford reforms. Even before he had left India, Lloyd had become dubious about the prospect of introducing further democracy there, and he had always been doubtful about any scheme to give India a federal constitution. The idea of announcing that India was destined for Dominion status was not one that appealed to him at all; he found that his view was shared by others who had supported him over Egypt; indeed, the two questions were obviously connected. Birkenhead had told the Unionist India Committee in 1928 of

his own opposition at the time to the Montford reforms and how he and Winston had both then, and in the case of granting greater independence to Egypt, done their best to defeat the proposals, stating that all his conviction as to the unworkability of dyarchy in India had been justified.[6]

This opinion was held by many Conservatives, including Lloyd. Yet Baldwin chose to announce that the Conservative Party supported the Irwin declaration.

Lord Salisbury spoke for many Conservatives when he told Baldwin of the 'shock' he felt that this should have been done without any consultation with the 'Business Committee' (i.e. 'Shadow' Cabinet).[7] Churchill warned Irwin in January 1930 that the forces of resistance to Indian nationalism 'are growing very much stronger in this country' and that the Conservative Party 'must certainly constitute the core of national and imperial opposition'.[8] Given his political beliefs, it was inevitable that Lloyd would take a leading part in such an opposition; what could be foreseen neither by Churchill nor by Lloyd was that, by an accident of history, the Conservative Party would become the instrument of 'Irwinism'.

Irwin no doubt spoke the truth when he told Baldwin that amongst those Conservatives who opposed his policy there was a 'considerable element who thought the temptation to have a simultaneous whack at you and at the Labour Government was irresistible';[9] but it was not the whole truth. This was recognized by Sam Hoare in 1931 soon after he became Secretary of State for India when he wrote to the new Viceroy, Lord Willingdon:

> There is a general feeling [in the Conservative Party] that defeatism has corroded the machine of Government. . . . My own view . . . is that the great body of opinion in this country is dead against anything in the nature of a surrender on the lines of the Irish Treaty.[10]

Lloyd's maiden speech in the Lords in December was made in opposition to the treaty which the Labour Government was trying to negotiate with the Egyptians and in it he warned of the consequences for the Empire of any weakening of the imperial will.[11] He did not share the conventional political wisdom encapsulated in Irwin's telling comment to J. C. C. Davidson that:

> The day is past when you can make nations live in vacuums. The day is also past in my humble opinion when Winston's possessive instinct can be applied to Empires and the like. That conception of imperialism is finished, and those who try to revive it are as those who would fly a balloon that won't hold gas. . . . The thing just won't work.[12]

To Lloyd this was no more than a prophecy which would fulfil itself. With their habitual reverence for those whose arguments appear to have been correct, historians have given the palm for long-sightedness to Irwin and those who thought like him. But it may be that their sight extended only to the middle distance. Irwin's whiggish spirit did not perceive what Lloyd's imperial vision foresaw, which was that without her Empire Britain must become a small overpopulated island off the coast of Europe which would soon be impoverished and of little account in world affairs. Lloyd knew that the Empire had been founded by the exercise of will and power; by the exercise of both it might still, he thought, be saved. Whether he was right we shall never know, for the attempt was not made.

In his speeches and newspaper articles in the early 1930s he established himself as one of the fuglemen of the imperial wing of the Conservative Party; but, first on India, then defence and finally on foreign policy, he was to find himself in conflict with what he came to call 'Baldwinism'.

In March 1930 he contributed six major articles to the *Daily Telegraph* in which he argued the economic case for the retention of British rule in India.[13] His case was not merely Anglocentric but enumerated the benefits which imperial rule had conferred upon the Mohammedans and the 'untouchable' castes by alleviating the effects of Brahmin domination and bettering the economic lot of the poor. To those who argued that the moment had come to move from diarchy towards 'Dominion status' he offered a sombre message:

> It is certain . . . that no recent happenings can be held to justify any shifting from the British Government of the onus of judging the 'time and progress' of India's political advance. It would be the height of cowardice and injustice to attempt to shuffle out of that duty at a time when racial antagonisms, doctrines of political violence, and religious animosities are holding the field in India. Whatever the difficulties, it is we who must face them, and we must bear the heavy but honourable burden of deciding what is best to do.[14]

He could not bring himself to believe that handing India over to a Brahmin-dominated Congress Party was in the best interests of the Indian people.

The bewilderment with which he confronted Labour's imperial policy can be captured in the tones of a speech which he addressed to the Ladies Carlton Club in December 1929:

> What has come about that all this should, so suddenly as it seems, have happened to us; what lynch-pin has broken from the wheel of our fortunes; what has become of our old genius to rule and our instinct to understand, better than all others, the needs of our Indian Empire?

He could only think that 'we have lost our sense of perspective' and were seeking 'to do in days what can only be done in decades'.[15]

Propaganda is the natural weapon of all oppositions and it was by this means that Lloyd sought to recall the Conservative Party to Chamberlain's old dream of tariff reform and imperial unity. In the summer of 1930 he became chairman of the Empire Economic Union which he, Amery, Page Croft and Lord Melchett formed to provide links between Business and the Conservative Party and to campaign for Imperial Preference.

On this issue, as on India, Lloyd found himself under the necessity of disagreeing with Baldwin, but the degree of estrangement was not great – yet. In early 1930 there were rumours that Lloyd might become Chairman of the Conservative Party[16] and later that year it was possible for Amery to mention him to Neville Chamberlain as a candidate for Foreign Secretary in a future government. Amery was undoubtedly right to say that 'the business world in the north of England think him a much bigger man than any of the "old gang"', but the suggestion says more for his loyalty to friends than it does for his political judgement.[17] Whilst the Conservatives were in opposition and Lloyd was harassing the Labour Government, the differences between himself and Baldwin were no more than the natural give and take of party politics; only after August 1931 did they become something more fundamental.

For the first time in two decades Lloyd was unharnessed from the mills of Empire. The word leisure had no meaning to him, as his brother-in-law, Tommy Lascelles, had noted in 1919:

> It is a distinct weakness in G. that he is a bad holiday-maker; he doesn't seem to realize the vital importance of *anapausis* [relaxation] to a man who works as he does. . . . He is at all times an exceptionally difficult subject to divert, for talking to him is like hailing a man in a stream of traffic; he has passed on his mental way before you can finish your sentence. It kills people young that sort of thing.[18]

With no official duties he voluntarily harnessed himself to any cause which asked him to serve the Empire. By 1931, in addition to making thirty or forty speeches a year, and his responsibilities as head of the Empire Economic Union, he had also taken on the presidency of the Navy League; this last position he utilized as a platform from which to preach the message of rearmament – a full two years before Churchill took up the same theme.

If the events of 1929 marked a caesura in Lloyd's political career, they initiated an even profounder one in his personal life. Official life had its drawbacks, but it had provided Blanche with a role and a place by his side; now these things were gone. On to her shoulders fell the burden of finding a house at short notice in 1929. Left to herself she would have shunned metropolitan life in favour of the country, but the exigencies of her husband's career dictated a home in the capital. They acquired a lease on 30 Portman Square in 1930, but it was more of a base from which he could sally forth than a home for her. Increasingly she found herself excluded from the busy life her husband imposed upon himself and it was with distress that she witnessed his pain at what had happened and the anguish he felt at what was happening to the Empire; she felt deeply her inability to assuage the furies that tore at him.

She found much consolation for these things in their son David who was coming to the end of his time at Eton and whose future had soon to be mapped out. Aircraftsman Shaw described him to Lloyd in early 1929 thus:

> A nice kid you have produced. He is more ornamental than ever you were, and less truculent. Of course he has a father to fight his battles. Perhaps his mouth will harden after he leaves home: do you think we should all fight our own courses? Since I changed ways, and learned to run and hide, life has been far happier. These days I am very meek and obedient. Indeed the officers begin to like me, here and there. A doormat. . . . I wonder if such shyness as his is one of your secret vices? It makes him very nice. The (apparent) lack of it does not injure your central goodness any the more. It would have been a freak of nature if the child of you two had been nasty.[19]

These observations matched those of David's Eton masters: he was charming and not without academic ability, especially in history, but he seemed immature and easily discouraged. Lloyd, who did indeed think 'we should all fight our own courses', wanted to get to know his son better and so took him on holiday to the Continent in the summer of 1930.

The descriptions which Lloyd sent back to Blanche reveal that he was not altogether pleased with what he found. In Venice David started 'one of his "bolshie" moods' and went into a prolonged sulk when told to brush his coat and hands – 'a hot competition between the two for dirtiness having been going on . . . for two days previously'. Finally, at Como, he flew 'into an ungovernable rage like early days' and locked himself into his bedroom for two hours. Nevertheless Lloyd enjoyed being alone with the son he had had so little time to get to know, even if he was 'far younger at his age than I had any idea of at all'.[20] He decided that David would have to spend a year in Germany before he could go up to Cambridge, and when that fell through he arranged for him to have six months in the Coldstream Guards. Although he disliked the idea, David complied with his father's wishes.[21]

As the only son and the heir to the title, David was the repository of all his father's considerable dynastic hopes; the letter he received on his eighteenth birthday made that quite clear:

> [I hope] you will go from strength to strength in mind and body and fit

yourself to play the great part for your country that someday you must play. I have tried to stand courageously and obstinately for the causes that were in my charge, one of them, Imperial Preference and tariffs after thirty years of struggle (started by my grandfather remember), is please God coming through. That shows it is worth sticking to. India is in *great* peril: some of us are fighting hard for that cause and have risked all our careers for it: if we have faith and play our part truly we shall perhaps save that cause: that's another thing that belies that office, or preferment or honours [are all politicians care for ] – all these you will carry on some day. Inshallah.[22]

If Baldwin's agreement to include tariff reform in the next Conservative manifesto pleased Lloyd, his continuing support for 'Irwinism' in India did not. In October 1930 he sanctioned Conservative participation in the first Round Table conference on India. Lloyd had consumed his own smoke before the report of the Simon Commission was published in the summer of 1930; thereafter he felt free to speak his mind. He made over thirty speeches between July 1930 and March 1931. The first major one was in the normally uncontroversial atmosphere of the annual dinner of the Central Asian Society on 9 July; the report in the *Evening News* furnishes a good picture of the orator at his task:

> When Lord Lloyd is making a fighting speech, he raises himself on tiptoe and, while the fingers of one hand lightly touch the table, takes off his glasses and puts them on again a surprising number of times each minute . . . he was in a real fighting mood as he spoke about India.[23]

In December at the Glasgow Chamber of Commerce he infused an elegiac tone into his message:

> Remember what happened to Rome, a far greater Empire than ours in many ways, as far as consolidation was concerned. Remember what happened when they withdrew the legions. They lost faith in themselves. They not only lost faith in themselves, they lost Gaul and Britain. Had we better not be careful that we don't withdraw our legions.[24]

When the Round Table Conference endorsed the Irwin declaration, Lloyd saw it as a portent of the withdrawing of the legions. In an attempt to get the Congress Party to join the negotiations for an all-India federation, Irwin released Gandhi on 18 January 1931 and entered into a series of talks with him; this was more than Lloyd could stomach. Writing in the *Daily Mail* on 21 January, he described the Round Table Conference and its results as 'nothing less than the surrender of our Indian Empire' and of the Irwin–Gandhi talks he was as scathing as Churchill: 'You have seen the extraordinary spectacle of the Government of India drinking tea with treason and actually negotiating with sedition.'[25] If he stopped short of calling Gandhi a 'half-naked fakir', it was not by much and he told Baldwin in March that:

> Those of us who feel deeply on the Indian question object on strong grounds of principle to what Edward is doing. If Gandhi was not the head of an avowed revolutionary movement . . . then Edward had no right to send him to gaol, still less to keep him there without trial. If, on the other hand, he is the avowed head of revolution in India – not merely the protagonist for self-government under the Crown but for complete independence – then Edward had absolutely no moral or political right to negotiate with him on equal and intimate terms.[26]

The Irwin–Gandhi pact inflamed Conservative opposition to Baldwin's acquiescence in Labour's India policy.

At a meeting of the Unionist India Committee on 9 February Lloyd made (in Amery's words) 'a forcible die-hard speech', which bluntly posed the question of whether the next Conservative Government would move quickly towards granting India Dominion status. Amery, who dined with him, Willingdon and Austen Chamberlain that evening, described Lloyd as being in

> a fearful state of mind about India and [he] cannot conceive of any other point of view as due to anything but cowardice and time-serving. . . . He was quite unreasonable, talking of it being far better to wreck the Conservative Party and let the Socialists rule indefinitely than acquiesce in Baldwin's attitude.[27]

This was the voice of the real 'die-hard'.

Baldwin entered 1931 threatened on the one hand by Lloyd and company on India and on the other by Beaverbrook and his Empire Free Trade campaign fighting for tariff reform. By-elections early in the year brought Baldwin to the brink of resignation. During the East Islington by-election in mid February Beaverbrook (no doubt in an effort to unite Baldwin's opponents) announced that the Conservative leader intended to commit the party to Dominion status for India. This placed Lloyd, who was due to speak for the Conservative candidate, in a difficult position. On 18 February he wrote at once to ask Baldwin if this was true. After a little delay the necessary denial was forthcoming and, to Beaverbrook's annoyance, Lloyd spoke at the meeting, telling his audience that had the report been correct then, 'not only should I not be on this platform tonight, but I should no longer be a member of the Conservative Party'.[28]

Whatever he said in moments of irritation, Lloyd was not anxious to break with the party's official leadership. He wrote to Baldwin on 2

March urging a compromise whereby the party would accept feder-ation as an ultimate objective but move first towards autonomy for the provinces, thus removing the objections felt by those who argued that India was not ready for immediate federation.[29] But Baldwin preferred to follow his usual habit of refusing to be drawn.

On 3 March Lloyd pressed his leader for a statement on India. When he saw Baldwin the following day, he found him in a sombre mood. Lloyd told him that in the light of the Irwin–Gandhi pact he 'must not be surprised if there was a grave split in the party in the next two or three days'; Baldwin replied by asking if he ought to resign.[30] He came under further criticism from Lloyd and Churchill at another meeting of the India Committee on 9 March, when, to the horror of his own supporters, he allowed a statement to be issued announcing that the Conservatives would not be taking part in the second Round Table Conference due to begin in September.

But Baldwin's spiritual home was in the last ditch; his political Micawberism had paid off in the past and did so now. Pushed by the die-hards over India on 9 March, he retrieved any lost ground in a magnificent speech in the House three days later which made it clear that he was committing the party to 'the granting of self-governing institutions with a view to the progressive realization of responsible Government in India as an integral part of the Empire'. Then, a week later, his position was immensely strengthened when Duff Cooper inflicted a drubbing on the Beaverbrook candidate at the St George's by-election on 19 March. Once more fortune had dealt Baldwin a good hand.

# 25

# INTO THE WILDERNESS

Safe for the moment, Baldwin's position depended upon the result of the next election. There were rumours that he would leave Churchill and other right-wing figures out of his next Cabinet,[1] but it was by no means certain that he would be in a strong enough position to do so when the time came. Lloyd and Churchill were secure in the support of a large body of Conservative opinion to whom 'Irwinism' was anathema. Sam Hoare, who became Secretary of State for India in 1931, told the new Viceroy, Lord Willingdon, in September:

> You know as well as I do how very nervous the Conservative opinion – and by this I do not mean Party Conservative opinion – is in England. . . . They are horrified at the suggestion that we are engaged in shuffling out of our difficulties and liquidating a bankrupt state.[2]

Whether even Baldwin could have led a Conservative Government towards home rule for India is doubtful; but once more he proved to be the spoilt child of fortune.

Lloyd's prediction that Socialist economics would lead the country onto the rocks of bankruptcy came true in August 1931; but he was not among those who benefited from the political consequences of financial catastrophe. When Baldwin committed the party to a 'National' Government led by Ramsay MacDonald, Lloyd thought he had 'eliminated' himself 'for the future';[3] but he supported the decision on patriotic grounds.[4] However, far from doing himself any harm, Baldwin was correct when he told Page Croft: 'Politically we are on velvet.'[5]

The Government which had been formed as a temporary measure to deal with the economic crisis lasted for the rest of the decade. Having failed in its declared aim of keeping Britain on the gold standard, the administration called an election in October at which it won a landslide victory over the discredited socialists; its Commons majority was more than 500 seats and it contained 473 Conservatives. Not only was the new Government in an impregnable parliamentary situation, but Baldwin was free to dispense with the services of men like Churchill and Lloyd. When the new Government announced that it would continue the second Round Table Conference and that it accepted the goal of Dominion status for India, Conservatives like Lloyd found themselves in a very difficult situation.

Between 1929 and 1931 Lloyd had been opposing a Labour Government's India policy and fighting a leader who had been weakened by defeat; henceforth he was battling against a policy put forward by an all-party government with an immense majority. Baldwin no longer had trouble from senior Conservatives on the right of the party because he left most of them out. One of the few such figures in the Government, the Minister of War, Lord Hailsham, had doubts about the India Bill, but he kept them to himself.

When Lloyd led the opposition to the Government's India policy in the Lords on 5 December 1931, he thought it wise to stress that he was no die-hard. Disclaiming any hostility either towards the Government or home rule for India, he adopted the moderate posture of asking whether it was 'mere reaction or . . . prudence and statesmanship to be sure of solid foundations before we attempt to build so great a house?' He criticized the resolutions of the second Round Table Conference, saying that they were so vague that they could mean anything, as MacDonald had unconsciously revealed when he had asked Churchill to withdraw his amendments in the Commons on the ground that they were all met by the government measure:

> I think your Lordships will agree that any form of words which so comfortably comprehends the views of the Prime Minister and Mr Winston Churchill must have been eviscerated beyond all meaning.

He acutely probed the weak point in the Government's case by referring to all the safeguards which any India Bill would incorporate; from his Egyptian experience he knew that either 'responsibility must become a shadow, or . . . if full responsibility is attained, the safeguards are worthless'.[6]

It was a good performance and with a supporting speech full of moderation by that respected elder statesman, the Marquess of Salisbury, brought his amendment 58 votes to the Government's 106. As Hoare warned Willingdon, it had 'shown the need for caution'.[7] The Government decided, after prolonged discussion, that the best way forward was to introduce a single comprehensive bill which would deal with both the federal and the provincial aspects of the problem, but they did not produce a White Paper to embody their proposals until March 1933.

Lloyd saw the new policy towards India as merely one symptom of the 'pernicious anaemia' which was afflicting the Empire. The exhaustion of war had helped foster a decade of illusion in which people had come to believe that organizations like the League of Nations and treaties outlawing war had inaugurated a golden age of peace. Lloyd had no time for such cant, as he made clear in a broadcast in December 1931:

> I am afraid it is very clear to-day that, despite the elaborate machinery devised by the League of Nations for the pacific settlement of inter-national disputes . . . there is as yet *no sign that a real peace mentality has begun to establish itself* . . . every nation except ourselves is still arming to the maximum of its capacity.

He reminded his audience that if prophets of peace had always been popular, they had also usually been wrong in their predictions.[8] He regarded talk of further disarmament as folly and was ever mindful of the dictum of the great Francis Bacon that:

> When a war-like state grows soft and effeminate they may be sure of a war. For commonly such states are grown rich in the time of their degeneracy: and so the prey inviteth, and their decay in valour encourageth a war.[9]

Such views were unpopular in the early 1930s and tended to confirm the impression created in the public mind by the debate over India that Lloyd was a hopeless reactionary.

Nor were such impressions altogether incorrect, as an article he wrote for *The Graphic* in late April 1932 showed. Asking whether the British Empire was fated to follow the path of ancient Rome, he wrote:

> In trying to answer that question we had better face the facts and frankly admit that the policy of the Imperial Conference of 1926, as recently embodied in the Statute of Westminster, has weakened to the point of absolute renunciation the Constitutional framework of the Empire, that post-war policy, as evidenced in our repeated and hardly foiled attempts to abandon great duties in Egypt, in the feeble and loosely worded Declaration of Dominion Status for India, or in the almost unconditional surrender of treaty rights in China, has needlessly destroyed much of our own authority and prestige in the East: and that in the domain of home affairs the policies pursued have led to nothing more than the ruin of our agriculture, to something like the destruction of our basic

industries and to the collapse of currency while those who had the temerity to protest and point out a more prudent path have been written off as mere realists or liquidated like Kulaks!

He was, however, unable to believe that 'decay has indeed set in, and that our day of world leadership is done'. But the 'signs of revival'[10] which he thought he could discern were, in reality, no more than the phantasms of his own mystical faith in the destiny of the English people. Nor is mystical too strong a word.

> I am so sure of the miracle that was our deliverance in war that I can't help feeling that after our people have suffered enough for all their post-war ignominy and unworthiness that somehow God will pull them through again, for I think we are more like to be his special people than any other.[11]

This confidence in Providence was reinforced by a mysterious occurrence in June 1932 when he went to unveil a war memorial at St Bees school in Cumberland and a bomb was discovered under the platform upon which he was speaking. For some weeks afterwards he was equipped with police protection and the incident prompted a letter from Aircraftsman Shaw:

> Dear G.L.
> This is, you know, immensely distinguished. Most Kings and Presidents . . . but very few private persons. . . . Off-hand I can remember only Rathenau. It is magnificent, and I congratulate you heartily.
> Of course it was only a miss, for which those of us who like you are personally grateful: – and misses do not live in history like hits . . . what a scoop: O most fortunate of politicians, what a scoop![12]

Quite who planted the bomb and why was never discovered.

Lloyd's political views won him a reputation as a would-be dictator, but although there was much of the autocrat in his make-up, he preferred, in Western politics, to rely in good Tory democrat style on the good sense of the 'people', and it was to the ordinary Conservative that he turned for support against Baldwin; nor did he do so in vain, as the Conservative Party Conference at Blackpool in October 1932 demonstrated.

Lloyd's appearance at the rostrum on 6 October produced 'an ovation so prolonged and enthusiastic as clearly to indicate that he and his convictions had the support of the great majority'.[13] In Churchill's absence he led the opposition, once more stressing that it was the untimely haste and not the idea behind the bill which he deplored; he also attacked the proposals produced by the committee which had been considering the franchise question and had recommended increasing the size of the Indian electorate from six and a half to thirty million.[14] The *Morning Post* described the outcome:

> The discipline of the Conservative Party secured a paper victory for the Government's India policy. . . . But not before the delegates had plainly shown by their demeanour that the Party in the country is nearing the limit of its patience.

Hoare had clearly taken in the same message for, as he confessed to Willingdon, the narrowness of their victory over Lloyd's resolution opposing the India Bill had been an unpleasant shock:

> There was no doubt about it that the sentiment of the meeting was on one side. George Lloyd, who is a much better platform speaker than he is a Parliamentary speaker, had a surprisingly good reception and I thought when he sat down most people would have said he would carry Winston's resolution with a big majority.[15]

He drew from it the lesson that he had to take care to conciliate those Conservatives 'who are genuinely anxious about the constitutional changes'.

Lloyd was not easily reassured and he wrote to Hoare on 4 December.

> It is easy enough to argue that progress is less dangerous than inaction. That is, in any case, a matter merely of conjecture. But so far as I know no one of any importance has ever urged inaction as an alternative to your plans of progress. I . . . have . . . only urged that you should move forward very slowly . . . such a counsel is not that of an 'obscurantist' or a 'diehard', it is really only a counsel of wisdom and statesmanship in so great an affair as this.[16]

With the India Bill due to come before Parliament in early 1933 Churchill warned that 'Irwinism' had rotted the soul of the party and that with the Whips on 'they will vote for any measure however disastrous'.[17]

He was right to anticipate a fight. At the same time as he was lamenting the state of the party's soul, Hoare was telling Baldwin:

> As to the future, my course is set, neither Winston nor George Lloyd will deflect it. Will they sink the ship? I don't think so, for although my guns may be light – yours are very formidable.[18]

He anticipated, he told Willingdon on 10 February 1933, an 'extensive attack from the extreme right wing' once Parliament reassembled,[19] and the week before the Bill was debated in Parliament he warned that whilst they were doing all they could to secure a government majority, 'there is no gainsaying the fact that the Conservative Party as a whole is very jumpy'.[20]

If the early 1930s saw Lloyd establish for himself a reputation as a die-hard on India and an enemy of the League of Nations, they also saw, by the same token, his exclusion from official life. Private life offered few compensations for his extrusion from the Councils of State.

Finance, which had been such a worry before the Great War, once more became a consuming anxiety. The failure of the board of Lloyds Bank to offer him back his seat was not only an affront to his pride, it was a heavy financial blow. Egypt, like Bombay, had made heavy demands on his private purse, and the sudden ending of his official salary along with the urgent need to find a house in London came as an extra burden upon a financial structure which had been under strain for some time; his other principal sources of income – dividends from Stewart and Lloyds and his other investments – had been cut into first by socialist taxation and then by the economic crisis of 1931. Characteristically, he set about restoring the family's finances. The underwritership which he had acquired at Lloyd's of London in the early 1920s provided a solid base from which to start, and he was able to add to this in late 1929 a directorship in the International *Wagons Lit* Company, followed in 1932 by a seat on the board of the Chartered Company of Rhodesia and Southern Africa. Neither of these last two were sinecures, and both companies benefited from his business experience and energy; and for him there was the additional advantage that both offered opportunities to indulge his wanderlust.

That he should have added to these labours those entailed by authorship is indicative of how hard Lloyd worked. In 1931 he began work on the first volume of *Egypt since Cromer*. Even with help from Colin Forbes Adam, it took up most of what would have been, for anyone else, his spare time. The book was published in early 1933 but, characteristically, the author was abroad at the time, on Chartered Company business in Southern Africa. He was delighted with the favourable reception accorded him by the critics, but suspected that some were keeping their powder dry for the second volume.

Lloyd's enjoyment of his African trip was spoilt by a recurrence of the intestinal trouble which had bothered him from time to time ever since his earliest travels; but there were compensations even to this:

> You will be [he told David] very envious when you see the slenderness of my figure on my return. I haven't eaten anything since December 2nd and since January 1st I have been on the charming diet of a glass of water and the yolk of an egg in it six times a day! Not very invigorating but I am

glad to say it has not stopped my doing anything at all. . . . Not too bad on the diet for an aged one please admit!

By 6 February he was down to nine stone twelve pounds which was, he told David, 'something like a figure which I consider suitable for my age'.[21]

Lloyd was back in England by early March 1933 when the Government White Paper on India was published. Despite Hoare's fears, the debate in the Commons was a tame affair; Churchill left the attack to Page Croft who presented few problems. Outside the Commons it was a different story. At a meeting of the National Union of Conservative Associations in late February Hoare's policy was approved only by the narrow margin of 189 to 165 votes. He warned Willingdon on 1 March that there was 'the making of a first-class crisis here and a break away of three-quarters of the Conservative Party'.[22]

The India Bill as published was no more than the terms of reference for the Joint Select Committee (JSC) of Parliament which the Government had decided to set up to counter claims from Churchill that the normal constitutional channels were being circumvented. Hoare told the Cabinet on 10 March that his proposals involved the federation of 'very incongruous units' and safeguards which would be too much for Congress and too little for Lloyd and company; he acknowledged that it was 'complicated and liable to attack', but took refuge in the curious argument that it was better than nothing, particularly when the Indians had been led to expect so much.[23]

A purely Conservative Government would have found great difficulty proceeding with such a measure, as Hoare tacitly acknowledged when he told Willingdon on 10 March that

> Winston is out to make the maximum of trouble. He is determined to smash the National Government and believes that India is a good battering ram as he has a large section of the Conservative Party behind him.[24]

His offer of places on the Joint Select Committee were rejected by Lloyd and Churchill. Lloyd 'did not feel that we had been over-well treated' and thought that 'the representation offered to critics of the Government was grotesquely insufficient';[25] they would have had only nine places as opposed to twenty-five for government supporters. On 7 April Lloyd wrote formally to Lord Hailsham declining the offer.[26] Lloyd's letter could have occasioned no surprise when, only the day before, he had (despite a bad attack of influenza) made what the *Morning Post* called 'the most virile anti-abdicationist attack upon the Government that has been made in either House since the debates on the India

White Paper began', in which he called for the Government to return to the lines laid down by the Simon report; of that there was neither sign nor hope.

On 20 April Lloyd suggested to Churchill that all opponents of the India Bill should combine to form an India Defence League.[27] This drew from Baldwin the charge that they were trying to split the Conservative Party. Lloyd delivered a forthright response on 2 May:

> If by his statement Mr Baldwin suggests that I am disloyal to Conservative principles, may I invite him to indicate to me what Conservative cause I have ever abandoned since I entered public life. Some of us, indeed, have suffered not a little in our attempts to conserve what 'Conservative' leaders have sometimes been ready to abandon.

Summoning up an infinity of scorn for the concerns of the party manager, Lloyd concluded:

> When the future of India is at stake, does Mr Baldwin really expect that we should subordinate the future of the Empire to considerations of Party harmony?[28]

That Lloyd's single-mindedness was not shared by all Conservatives was demonstrated at the meeting of the Council of the National Union of Conservative and Unionist Associations at Friends' Meeting House in Euston Road on 28 June, when the India Defence League confronted Baldwin before an audience of some 1,200 Conservatives. Lloyd moved a resolution expressing 'grave anxiety' at the proposals to transfer authority and responsibility from the central to provincial governments.[29] Baldwin spoke first and merited Hoare's comment that he did 'very well and had a remarkable reception';[30] he certainly delivered a most skilful speech. Steering away from the inconvenient detail of the proposals under the cover that they were under 'quasi-judicial' consideration, he pleaded with his listeners to keep India out of the arena of party strife; gently rebuking his opponents, he appealed to them to be reasonable.

It was not easy for Lloyd to follow such an emollient performance. Amery thought he was 'ill and very husky' when he came to move the resolution but that he put his points 'clearly and with sincerity, if not very effectively'.[31] His speech was along familiar lines and was supported by one from Page Croft which Amery characterized as 'flapdoodle really, but sincere and eloquent'. The aged Lord Carson, the great champion of Ulster, made an emotional contribution on Lloyd's side, but Churchill's speech, which was subject to constant interruption, failed to move his audience. Hoare was disappointed that the Government won only by 838 to 356 votes and the liberal press shared the view expressed in the *Manchester Guardian* headline: 'Mr Baldwin wins the first round. But the victory inconclusive. Surprisingly large majority for the Diehards.'[32]

In fact this was the high-water mark for the India Defence League. At a purely Conservative meeting Baldwin had carried the day; the fight now had to go to Westminster, where the odds were heavily weighted in his favour. Moreover, the battle now became one against the official policy of the Conservative Party. Lloyd foresaw the consequences of carrying on under such conditions, but as he said on 28 June:

> I, who have come out of public life and as far as I am concerned crashed my career for my belief – not [for] the first time – beg you to believe that it is with deep sincerity that we feel these questions about India.[33]

No one doubted his sincerity; it was his judgement and sense of proportion which were called into question and which exiled him from power.

# 26

# WILDERNESS POLITICS

On 19 June 1933 the *Daily Express* published a profile of Lloyd:

> Panther-like Lord Lloyd, who returns by air from the South of France today after spending only a week-end there, is regarded by some of his admirers as a possible future dictator. He would possibly make an excellent dictator – for say three years. . . . He is an almost fanatical patriot. He is the hot-gospeller of the British Empire . . . has snappy black eyes and a dominating manner. He has, accordingly, devoted slaves and apprehensive enemies. . . . Certainly he has more enemies than friends . . . he is 53 years old. He is still lithe and youthful. He loathes the League of Nations, professional politicians. . . . He admires Lady Houston. His career is certainly not at an end.[1]

It was not only journalists who thought that Lloyd's career might take him along the road being followed by Oswald Mosley. In October 1932 he had received a long telegram from an admirer urging him to run a campaign based on 'good old-fashioned Conservative policy', promising to bear all its expenses. This had been followed by a letter which concluded: 'You are the right man to be Prime Minister', and promised £100,000 towards this end.[2] These curious communications came from Lady Houston.

'Poppy' Radmell had been born into a poor cockney family but had risen in the world by the exercise of character and feminine charms. After a number of wealthy and aristocratic husbands, she settled for the enormously rich shipping magnate, Sir Robert Houston – the 'Robber Baron'. Upon his death in 1926 she was left with a fortune of £6 million and her own paranoia about Communism; she proceeded to soothe the latter by copious employment of the former. Baldwin and MacDonald were, to her eyes, traitors. Lloyd, on the other hand, was the masterful figure who would thwart their designs and ensure the triumph of 'good Conservative principles'.[3]

Intrigued, Lloyd did not, however, hasten to her call. In October

188

1933 she sent her secretary to Portman Square with a cheque; according to Mr Wentworth Day, Lloyd

> took the cheque, looked at me hard. I understood why plotters quailed before those eyes. 'An extraordinary old lady,' he said. 'Of course I can't accept this money if I have to give any undertaking that I or anyone else is going to form a new Party. That's impossible. As to overthrowing the Government – it may well overthrow itself. But we can use this money to fight the India Bill.'[4]

He accepted £5,000 as a contribution towards his India campaign, but only on condition that she did not interfere in what he said or did.

News of what was afoot began to circulate as rumour in the press with the *Sunday Despatch* commenting on 1 November that he was going to 'launch a back-to-Conservatism campaign', with the *Mail* adding that he would find 'abundant support'. The *Daily Herald* noted that:

> Lord Lloyd comes into the open tomorrow as an avowed opponent of the 'National Government'. Together with Lord Carson, the idol of true-blue Toryism, Lord Lloyd intends to make a bold bid for the leadership of the growing number of Tories who are sick and tired of the alliance with the Simonites and MacDonaldites.[5]

Lloyd was not, in fact, trying to form a new party, but the impression that he was gained ground; his failure to do so contributed in large measure to the frustration of his real objective. The much-heralded speech was given at the *English Review* lunch club's dinner at the Savoy on 21 November 1933. The *Review*'s editor, Douglas Jerrold, was a great admirer of Lloyd's, seeing him as 'the only man in the party who could rely on the support of the die-hards and who could command a following among the young men'.[6] He planned the occasion as the climax to a campaign of several months during which he had argued the virtues of the corporate state in the columns of his journal; lest anyone should miss the significance of the event, it was presided over by that idol of true-blue toryism, Lord Carson.

Alas for Jerrold: Lloyd's speech was a failure. Amery thought it had been 'over-prepared',[7] but the chief reason for its lack of success was that it was not the clarion call to action which most of the audience expected. Lloyd began by attributing the formation of the National Government to the will of the people during the 1931 crisis and went on to argue that MacDonaldism was now frustrating the popular desire for radical action to halt the drift towards disaster. With unemployment at two million and rising, he asked:

> Are we prepared to acquiesce in this terrible state of affairs? Are we content to wait expectantly for the return of Victorian conditions of

international trade? I for one am not. I cannot sit by silent and see the manhood of our people destroyed by a policy of reliefs and doles, which robs them of hope and opportunity.

He wanted a concerted programme of action – paternal toryism in action rather than the Victorian liberal nostrums peddled by MacDonald and Baldwin: he called for schemes of youth training; industrial and agricultural protection; revival of basic industries, especially coal; and he made a strong plea for rearmament. He warned that attempts abroad to 'achieve political unity without unity of purpose' had been but the 'prelude to dictatorships'; he did not want this in Britain:

> I have seen it suggested that it is my intention to form a new party or a new section of an old party. You who have listened to me with such forbearance tonight will realize that I have no such intention. It is not new parties that we need but principles and the pluck to pursue them. . . .
> I could not any longer look on in silence while all that we value is being frittered away. I intend therefore to do my best to warn the people up and down the country that, if we continue as at present, we may expect, overseas, the progressive decline of our position and the steady disruption of our Empire; and at home revolutionary experiments in our methods of government.[8]

Conscious that he had not given his listeners what they had expected, Lloyd was 'very depressed' after his speech. Beaverbrook told Amery that Lloyd was 'muddle-headed' and doubted whether he would get very far;[9] but if the latter was true, it was not for want of effort. During the next six months Lloyd made twenty-one speeches, most of them either on India or 'National Policy'. With Churchill he was the driving force in the India Defence League and he used Lady Houston's money to set up an office to co-ordinate propaganda, ably assisted by a young ex-diplomat, Duncan Sandys, and a young Conservative MP, Patrick Donner.

Trying to capture the Conservative Party offered to the IDL its only chance of success; although the campaign failed, it did give the leadership some anxious moments. Hoare told Willingdon in May 1934 that:

> The Conservatives are getting into the same mood into which they got at the end of the L[loyd] G[eorge] coalition and the Government of India Bill will not only drive some of them into open opposition, but, however necessary it may be, is regarded by some of them as an unpopular nuisance. Unless independent leaders like Eddie [Derby] and Austen [Chamberlain] back us neither the Government nor the Bill will survive.[10]

Hoare wrote as one who had just become the object of a bitter attack on his personal integrity by Churchill.

In April 1934 Churchill pressed for the Committee of Privileges of the House of Commons to investigate charges that Hoare and Lord Derby had improperly influenced the Lancashire Chamber of Commerce in the evidence which they had given to the Joint Select Committee in November. There was more to the charge than some contemporaries and historians have believed,[11] but the manner in which Churchill conducted his campaign laid him open to Amery's damaging charge that his policy could be summed up as: 'If I can trip up Sam, the Government's bust.' Derby told Lloyd in June that: 'While Winston is out to break the Government that is far from being your wish.'[12]

Inevitably such impressions did harm to the IDL. Most Conservatives took the line set out by one of the uncommitted members of the JSC, Eddie Cadogan, in a letter to Salisbury in March 1934, namely that it was vital not to split the party and let the Socialists in.[13] If Salisbury's reply expressed the high ideals which he and Lloyd embraced, it also showed why they failed to capture the party:

> This Indian question is not only an important question, it is one of the capital issues of our generation and to think that it may be decided not upon the grounds of the welfare of the Indian people or of the Empire, or upon what is workable as a Constitution, but upon wholly extraneous matters, however important in themselves, connected with the triumph of socialism in this country, will only add to the condemnation into which democracy is falling in all parts of the world.[14]

It was magnificent but it was not party politics.

For that self-styled Boadicea, Lady Houston, the IDL campaign was altogether too slow and sedate. In her impatience she made the mistake of telling Lloyd that he was 'afraid' of the party machine. The morning afterwards her secretary, Wentworth Day, received a telephone call from him: 'I've had an impossible telegram. I want your advice. Come and have a kipper.' Over breakfast he was told by Lloyd that Lady Houston must understand 'that I won't be dictated to'; he was, he said, finished with her. No doubt Day's account is a little exaggerated – the claim that Lloyd wrote out a cheque for the £8,000 he had already spent is certainly not true, as he had spent just less than £2,000 – but the connection with Lady Houston certainly came to an end in June 1934.[15] Lloyd wrote to her on 25 June:

> I do not deny that I was disappointed with the immediate result and I realise that if a better speaker than I had been available swifter progress might have been achieved. None the less, I do feel that a great deal was actually accomplished at rather a critical moment in influencing

opinion. The present anxiety of the Government shows that this is the case and I believe that when the crucial struggle over India comes on in the autumn, we shall find that we have gained more ground than we knew.[16]

Although India occupied the forefront of Lloyd's political vision, the middle distance was increasingly held by defence policy. The need for rearmament was a staple part of his speeches on 'National Policy' and had formed part of his plans since 1931. In October 1934 he brought it before the Conservative Party annual conference which was held in Bristol. On 4 October he moved a resolution that: 'This Conference desires to record its grave anxiety as regard to the inadequacy of the provision made for Imperial Defence.' Together with an amendment from Neville Chamberlain that, 'heavy as are the burdens it prefers the security and safety of our native land above all benefits', the resolution was approved.[17] In this cause, too, he found himself at Churchill's side; but over the next two years it was to become apparent that many of those in the IDL would not accompany their two leaders down this new path.

The Government introduced a bill based around the JSC report in the autumn session. With safeguards for defence and for other British interests and the avowed support of the Conservative Party machine, the India Bill was sure of a fair wind. On 4 December 1934 at a meeting of the Conservative National Union Council, Salisbury moved an amendment designed to substitute provincial self-government for federation, but with Baldwin and Austen Chamberlain in opposition it was decisively defeated by 1,102 votes to 390. At the end of the report stage in the Commons on 12 December an anti-government amendment was defeated by 410 to 127 votes – with five members of the IDL voting with the majority and another six abstaining. Events in the Lords were equally depressing for the IDL. Salisbury and Lloyd made powerful speeches against the Bill but their amendment was lost by 239 to 62 votes.[18] The question of what road to take next divided the ranks of the IDL.

At the end of January, without warning his father, Randolph Churchill stood as an Independent candidate at the Wavertree by-election. This action, which exhibited in equal degree the courage which warmed the hearts of his friends and the lack of judgement which made his enemies rejoice, posed a dilemma for the IDL. Many of the members did not wish to support a candidate who was fighting the official Conservative, and although Churchill eventually received an endorsement from the IDL, the business strained its unity. Lloyd flung himself into the conflict on Churchill's side, telling the electors that he was proud to fight for one who was making 'a bold and brave stand for those principles of the Conservative Party for which the . . . party stood when it was a party and not a coalition'.[19] He was in favour of fighting every by-election as it arose, but the majority of the IDL executive refused to follow him. This was, he told Lord Wolmer, 'the turning point in our campaign' and an acceptance of certain defeat.[20] It was no use. Randolph's success in splitting the Conservative vote and letting the Socialist in was too much for most Tories.

On 11 February 1935 the India Bill was given its second reading by 404 to 133 votes, and during the committee stage which lasted from 19 February through until May, although Churchill assailed it vigorously, it was noticeable that even some of his supporters were becoming alarmed by the violence of his language. After he was defeated by 283 to 89 votes on 26 February, Salisbury told Wolmer that Winston had 'entirely lost Parliamentary touch' and that, unless he changed his methods, 'I doubt whether we will do anything in the House of Commons'; he had, he wrote, refused to chair a meeting for Churchill at the Albert Hall:

> I am afraid I am not prepared to identify myself with Winston and the kind of speech which he will wish to make on that occasion . . . my impression is that the Bill is becoming more and more discredited and I really believe that if Winston were to have a long spell of influenza a great deal more might be done. But if it comes to be believed that our object is to break up the party, the House of Commons may stick its toes in and vote black is white to save the Government – *and* the House of Lords may do the same.[21]

The activities of the IDL continued to cause the Government concern, but the Third Reading of the Bill in June resulted in a vote in its favour of 386 to 122 (84 Conservatives being amongst the minority). Lloyd wrote to Churchill on 12 June congratulating him on his final speech and concluding: 'What we should have done in this controversy without your leadership I can't begin to conceive.'[22] It was a generous and deserved tribute; but for both men the course of the struggle had taken them far out into the political wilderness. Aircraftsman Shaw had told Lloyd in September 1934 that 'what has harmed you politically has been your break with Austen and Baldwin. To be sacked by the Labour Government was glorious: to have been at odds with the Tory chiefs is less assuring';[23] he was quite correct.

Lloyd had played little part in the final stages of the campaign. In April 1935 he travelled to North Africa and took a small bungalow on the edge of the Tunisian desert where he could 'feel at home again' and sit in shirt-sleeves in the hot sun and talk once more 'the good strong desert Arabic'. The letter which he wrote to David on 9 April is an eloquent testimony of his state of mind as he saw the defeat of his hopes:

> I try hard to forget about India, but my heart sinks as the days go on and I see the strands chafing and parting one by one and chain by chain in Parliament.
>
> What could never be wrung from us by the sword is being given up by words. A strange way for an Empire to fall – say rather dissolve. I am not many miles here from Carthage and look out over the same scenes as they did when they – dissolved. I wouldn't mind so much if there were some sudden collapse – some dramatic tragic firm end of so great a body of achievement, if on *flammantia moenia mundi* – on the flaming ramparts of the world – there should be sounded our Last Post – but to disintegrate, decay and die by our own doing – as history will note – is unutterably sad I think – to say nothing of the pestilence, famine and misery that must be left by the ebbing tide! *Che peccato.*[24]

That the Dover Beach of Lloyd's imperial vision should have been near the ruins of the Empire of Carthage was fitting. His world now contained neither certitude nor hope nor help for pain.

# 27

## AT BAY

The site of ancient Carthage was a suitable place in which to indulge despair, but Lloyd was made of too resilient a stuff to yield to it permanently. Writing to Blanche in April 1934 he had commented that: 'In spite of much to discourage one – not least the sense of one's own shortcomings – I feel that life is fine and so immensely worth living to the very full'; he had then provided himself with a text which he could now use to restore his own sense of perspective:

> There must be moments of course when one sees ignoble people in power, losing chance after chance and bringing our greatness very low that one feels depressed, but the wheel turns – surely a fresh opportunity of service may yet come. Besides it's all service isn't it – the more so if it is seasoned with a spice of sacrifice for what one believes in.[1]

Aware that he had probably sacrificed his political career, something which he could not hold of no account, he took consolation from the reflection that, as he told James Lees-Milne in a valedictory letter: 'I hope you will have gone away able to feel that all politicians aren't *all* crooks!'[2]

The relationship which had developed between private secretary and employer emphasizes one of Lloyd's most attractive characteristics as he entered middle age – his helpfulness to the young. Lees-Milne came to Lloyd after an indifferent career at Oxford and with no great idea of what to do next with his life, and found in him both a friend and an inspiration – as well as a demanding employer. He would arrive at 30 Portman Square before nine o'clock to sort out Lloyd's papers and arrange his schedule for the day, a job done against the clock as he strained his ears to sounds coming from the dining-room beyond the library where he could hear Lloyd talking with whoever was sharing a kipper with him that morning: 'It might be Sir Roger Keyes, Noël Coward, or (self-invited) T. E. Lawrence.' Only at breakfast did Lloyd allow himself to relax in easy conversation with a friend – even if some of the friends would have disputed the adjective; before rising, he would have read all the morning papers and be fully prepared to discuss the issues of the day.

But for Lees-Milne, delightful and stimulating as these breakfasts were when he experienced them himself, they were

> nothing like so rewarding as those occasions far into the night when business was finally set aside. He would then thrust that compact, tight little body which never properly belonged to him, however adorned and cared for, but was treated as a convenient machine like his expensive two-seater, and driven to the last ounce of his inner energy, into the corner of a deep sofa, and talk and talk of his soul's problems and aspirations until the small hours. Over a large tumbler of whisky and soda, which was the only alcohol this ascetic man allowed himself, the endearing character of George Lloyd was revealed and the anagogical labours of his tortured psyche were partially disclosed.[3]

One of the main topics of discussion was religion. In the spring of 1934 Lees-Milne became a Roman Catholic. This 'reversion' fascinated Lloyd. His own churchmanship put him firmly on the Anglo-Catholic wing of the Church of England. He told Blanche in January 1937 that 'what keeps me from going over to Rome is nothing less or more than Cranmer's litany and his wondrous English'. He did not 'Pope', but Rome exercised a continuing appeal and he questioned Lees-Milne about his reasons for 'reverting'. He never followed suit, but by 1940 he was, as he confessed to Ronald Storrs, 'so close' that 'if Blanche died tomorrow, the day after he'd go over to Rome'.[4] David, who followed his father in churchmanship, was also, in later life, tempted to convert but, despite 'new' prayer books and a theology dominated by the Third World rather than the next world, never did so and it was left to his daughter, Davina, to take the step which her father and grandfather had contemplated.

Like Compton Mackenzie, Lees-Milne learnt from Lloyd that imperialism could touch a man's soul as deeply as religion. But in Lloyd's lamentations for the fate of the Empire there was also something deeply personal. Since adolescence he had devoted his life and energies to the Empire, in it he had invested his youth; now, like that youth, it seemed to be passing away. Lloyd was not to be numbered among those who heeded not the passing years; youth to him meant energy, opportunity and travel whilst old age signified the absence of these things. In battling for the Empire he was trying to preserve the best part of his own youth, and the fight itself availed something in this respect, for, as he told Blanche in April 1934:

You see I don't want to feel that I am older – in spirit – than I must be or unable to compete a little still in the life struggle. It's only when that weakness assails one and conquers one that one is really ageing. The looking-glass forbids one to harbour any illusions about one's body but there is no mirror, thank God, to the spirit.[5]

Perhaps it was partly for this reason that he preferred the company of the young, for, as Lees-Milne and others discovered, there was no better companion and support than George Lloyd; and if he fostered their careers, he gained from them a talisman against middle age. Leo Amery's son, Julian, remembered half a century on that the Empire 'really excited him' and that he was 'very good at conveying that excitement to youth'.[6] He would not patronize the young, expecting them to hold their own in conversation, but he had the gift of convincing them that he was genuinely interested in their opinions. On first sight, however, he could appear rather formidable, and one of David's friends took a long time to recover from an initial *faux pas*; having been trying to hold his own in conversation the young man remarked: 'Is it not odd that very clever men tend to marry rather plain women?' – to which he received the devastating reply: 'Are you suggesting that I am a fool or that my wife is plain?'[7]

The young man whose fate he watched over most anxiously was, of course, his son David. After Eton David had been summoned into 'the presence' where the following scene was acted out:

'I suppose that now you've finished Eton you think I'm going to increase your allowance?'
  'Yes, papa.'
  'Well I'm not, you have your £300 a year, if you want more you'll have to earn it.'[8]

Conscious of his own premature introduction to the responsibilities of the adult world, Lloyd refused to compensate at David's expense by over-protecting him. David did his stint in the Coldstream Guards and then went up to Cambridge where, having thoroughly enjoyed himself for two and a half years, he settled down with a crammer for six months and emerged with a second-class degree in history to add to the many friendships he had made.

After Cambridge the question of a career loomed large. Lloyd used his business contacts to try to get David a place in the City and, to the end that he should be equipped for the world of finance, sent him to a firm of accountants to learn bookkeeping. Relations between father and son were close and affectionate, but it was not until 1935–6 that they blossomed into an intimacy which became the great comfort of Lloyd's life.

In November 1935 he offered to pay for David to go on a round-the-world trip on two conditions: that he never left the Empire and that he travelled alone. The results of this trip were to be entirely beneficial for both men. The efflorescence of their relationship came at a crucial time for Lloyd and helped fill the vacuum in his personal life created by the effects of events since 1929 on his marriage.

The bond which had been forged by the impetus of first love, strengthened by the fortunes of war and nourished by the roles available to Blanche as wife of the Governor and High Commissioner, wasted in the 1930s. Politics and travel took him away from her and his chronic restlessness became an affliction to a middle-aged lady who longed for a home in the country where she could put down roots. Lloyd recognized something of all this; he knew she did not love the London life he lived, nor did she want to tramp the wide world: so he cast round for the means to satisfy his country girl.[9]

The effect of the Great War and of the 1931 slump upon Lloyd's finances has already been touched upon. His various directorships and investments brought in about £3,000 a year, but his life-style was an expensive one: the travelling, entertaining, the house in Portman Square, the Rolls and his yawl, the *Samphire*, all meant that he lived up to his income. He decided to sell the latter to provide the wherewithal to buy Blanche a home in the country. In June they bought, for just under £4,000, ninety acres of land and the old Vicarage at Offley, near Hitchin, which they called Clouds Hill in memory of T. E. Lawrence (who had just died and whose cottage was thus named).[10]

Clouds Hill provided Blanche with the 'nest' she had always craved. She sought to make out of it a home to which her restless husband could retire when the time came. But he was far from thinking of such an event – as his new hobby demonstrated. Having given up sailing, he took to flying, thus consummating an interest which went back to the days before the war when he had flown with Sam. He took lessons at Heston, a short drive from Clouds Hill. Flying provided him with a fresh challenge and the company of adventurous young men, and was, in short, a tonic for his spirits – which was more than could be said for the Government's foreign policy.

Lloyd had approved of the so-called Stresa Front, the Anglo–French–Italian declaration of April 1935 which implicitly condemned Hitler for his repudiation of the Versailles treaty and warned him against trying to annex Austria. But almost at once the agreement was put in jeopardy by Mussolini's ambitions in Abyssinia. Although Italy did not finally declare war until October, her aggressive policy towards Abyssinia led to calls for sanctions to be imposed. Lloyd, who saw Italy as a useful ally against the real threat posed by Nazi Germany, was disturbed by such talk. He telephoned Neville Chamberlain on 22 August and asked to talk to him about the situation.

Lloyd and the editor of the *Observer*, J. L. Garvin, visited Chamberlain that evening. Lloyd stressed that 'policy came after power' and that, given the weakness in Britain's defence forces (which he had now pointed out at three party conferences) it would be folly to take any action against Mussolini at the behest of the League. Chamberlain's reply revealed that the Government had no intention of doing any such thing. He told them that he was relying on France to ensure that 'the Left and Middle Wing of public opinion in this country' would be unable to accuse the Government of evading their obligations to the League; he was confident that the French would refuse to implement sanctions and he would use this as Britain's reason for not acting alone. Lloyd's reactions to this were, as he told Blanche, mixed:

> It was a relief, of course, to hear that all [the] Government's professions and threats about sanctions meant nothing, and I refrained from commenting as bitterly as I might have done on the manifest dishonesty of the whole policy.

He was, however, positively disgusted by Chamberlain's reply to his suggestion that they could not afford to wait another few months before announcing a programme of naval rearmament: 'You seem to have forgotten, George, that there is to be a general election.'[11]

What Chamberlain said came to pass, but it almost brought the Government to grief. The general election came in November. Lloyd campaigned in support of the Government, but more out of fear of the Socialists than anything else, confessing to David that he was 'conscious that I am asking people to vote for men who have themselves brought this crisis upon us'.[12]

The new Government was little to Lloyd's taste, with Baldwin becoming Prime Minister and Hoare going to the Foreign Office; indeed, he regretted the size of its majority. But almost at once it got itself into grave difficulties. Speaking at a meeting of the League, Hoare gave the impression that the Government was behind a policy of sanctions, yet, during a meeting in Paris with his French counterpart, Pierre Laval, in December, he came to an arrangement which would have allowed Italy to annex large parts of Abyssinia. There was a great outcry from British public opinion and it was made clear to Hoare that he had better resign. Lloyd read his resignation speech whilst on a tour of the Near East and wrote to Blanche in disgust: 'How *can* Baldwin survive such treachery and abandonment of one of his own colleagues – Have we been wrong about B? I should say not!!'[13]

Lloyd spent Christmas in Kenya where he managed to rendezvous with David. There he managed to have long talks with him about the future and to relax. But he no longer felt, as he had twenty-five years before, that Kenya was another Eden:

> I have come to the conclusion that it is rather an unhappy country. It is so beautiful, its climate so perfect and its riches so varied that its people should be prosperous and contented and yet they are all at sixes and sevens, quarrelling, bankrupt and some of them showing a bad example to the natives. It is really rather sad but I am thankful that I never took Ewart's advice or took any real stake in the country.[14]

With David departing for India Lloyd left for Cairo.

He had been asked by the British Council to look at British schools there, but he hated the prospect of revisiting Egypt: 'It will renew all the pain I had there.'[15] In fact, with the sole exception of the King, everyone gave him a cordial welcome and the visit allowed him to lay at least one of the ghosts that haunted him.

From Cairo he went to Jerusalem, again on British Council business. There he met the ex-Khedive, Abbas Himli, who, unlike his successor, affected great pleasure at meeting him. Lloyd's greatest pleasure in the meeting came with Himli's remark: 'I think Mussolini he surely go bum.'[16]

Lloyd continued his inspection of British schools in Cyprus and then Athens. Whilst he was there he heard the news that George v was dying. He immediately left for home, stopping off only in Rome where he had a brief interview with Mussolini, and in Paris, where he heard the news of the King's death; with the latter came a summons to attend a meeting of the Privy Council at 4 o'clock the same day. He described what happened next to David:

> I caught the midday plane, arrived Croydon 2.55 pm, fled through the customs barriers, reached 30 Portman at 3.35 pm, leapt into my uniform and paraded at St James as 3.55 pm. Not too bad going.[17]

He felt sorry for the new King, Edward viii, who faced 'a European crisis of unprecedented proportions' with an army, navy and air force 'entirely insufficient in size, personnel and equipment'.[18]

Lloyd's tour had stirred up his old wanderlust and he confessed to David that:

> Somehow since my return I feel more and more restless – travelling, especially at such a swift pace, goes to my head like wine and I shall [need] a little time to settle down again! But I feel that in a few years' time I shall, if I am still alive, be in a bath-chair in Brighton probably and that I must make the most of this wide wide and wonderful world – *douce viventi.*[19]

Returning from the tropics to a London winter was enough in itself to depress him, but there was more to it than that; he felt out of joint with the times.

The financial strain of taking Clouds Hill had, he thought, been 'worth it' just for the 'boundless enjoyment' which it had given to Blanche who was 'like a child with a new toy'.[20] But he had been conscious for some time of how much more she seemed to enjoy herself in his absence: 'I am afraid I rather cloud the sun these days don't I?'[21] It was against this backcloth that the development in his relationship with David was so important.

Through David's letters Lloyd relived his old journeyings: 'It is an indescribable pleasure to me to feel how much better you will understand all the sights, sounds and smells that have been part and parcel of my life.'[22] He wrote in April 1936 to say that he hoped their paths would cross in the Near East because:

> I long to show you Gallipoli and Constantinople and all my old haunts there though all the beauty has now gone under reformed Turkey. Still there will be the 'reckless blue sea and sky' and you to talk to.[23]

He thought that:

> If you have anything of me in you, which Allah forbid, I tremble to think how restless it will make you, 'and the poplar breezes will blow in your head' . . . for many a long year to come: and you will never forget the scent of the garlands – frangipan and jasmine [sic] and all and all. . . . Lord! how I have loved it all; nearly *thirty years of it* David in different parts of God's wonderful Asia. It's often hot and dirty and beastly, but it gets you all the same. That's why I want you to taste it. I love bits of Africa, but Asia is my ticket and has always been.
>
> You see your letter has set me a-fire in happiness and pleasure that you are going to love it in some measure as I do.[24]

He not only told David about his anxieties about the international situation, but confided in him more personal feelings, telling him on 17 March:

> I miss you very much, and perhaps on account of your absence am feeling rather old and often find myself contained by a spiritual – though not at all by a physical – loneliness. Your mother is entirely possessed and preoccupied by domesticity or horticultural details in respect of Clouds Hill. For the rest I hate more and more this woman-run world of today. Women's ideals hold the political field so completely today – they infect the churches and wreck dinner tables. The things I care about, the sea, the air, the East and the Empire mean nothing to them – so I feel lonely. But perhaps it is my liver, and anyway you'll be back again in a few months, Inshallah, and you always understand. Besides, no doubt

this year or next we shall see the sun again and that will make a difference.[25]

Alas! neither the international situation nor the weather improved much before Lloyd set out to meet his son at Constantinople in May 1936.

On 13 March, as Lloyd was delivering a speech in Paris advocating an Anglo–French alliance to counter the threat from Hitler,[26] the Nazis marched into the Rhineland in defiance of the Locarno and Versailles treaties. Lloyd prophesied, correctly, that 'there will be no war at present – Germany is not ready and no one else wants war'. At least the Government now decided to speed up the pace of rearmament, but:

> They have left it so terribly late that whatever they do now the next three years are bound to be ones of great anxiety if not actual peril. Some of us, as you know, have long ago foreseen and constantly warned the Government, but were not heeded – were indeed abused and mocked for our warnings![27]

He dismissed Hitler's promises that he had no further territorial ambitions but knew that thanks to 'Baldwin's slack leadership' pro-German feeling had been allowed to grow; with that, and the League, it remained difficult to get anything done:

> At present in this country public opinion is hesitating, the politicians are vacillating and Baldwin is mute: it is believed that he is already jealous of the publicity which Eden is getting and waiting his chance – by lying back – to debunk him as he debunked Sam and others – myself included in that long list.[28]

In the Lords, and privately in talks with French politicians and with the Italian Ambassador in London, Dino Grandi, Lloyd called for a reassertion of the Stresa Front and an end to sanctions against Italy.[29] For this he received the thanks of Mussolini and Grandi, but his frustration at his lack of power grew strong at such times. He told Blanche in May: 'I sometimes wish I were Foreign Secretary. I think I could do something more than these minnows can.'[30]

A cold, wet and windy English spring did nothing for either his spirits or temper; he told David in mid April: 'Everything here is too politically damnable and the weather is foul as well. . . . You are fortunate to be away from it all.'[31] It was with the hope of escape from the malaise which afflicted him that he set off on his beloved Orient Express in late May bound for Constantinople.

# 28

# THE ROAD BACK

The 'wonderful rest and peace of the journey from Calais to Constantinople' was a tonic for low spirits. Lloyd knew 'every inch of the road' and there were so many memories connected with it that he was 'never half weary of it'; journey's end brought meetings between past and present.

There was the presence of David, morose and irritable as he was after so much travelling; but Lloyd tried to enthuse him with his own love of the city. There too was his old friend from pre-war Constantinople, Sir Percy Loraine, now installed as Ambassador where O'Conor had once held sway. Everywhere the memories haunted him. An interview with Ataturk at what had been the Sultan's palace brought back 'a host of Hamidian memories' and Lloyd thought how 'desolate and bleak' the vast rooms were 'without the sword clatter, the colour and romance of those peculiar days'. But not all was loss. Entering Hagia Sophia, he told Blanche:

> Only those of us who knew Aga Sophia in Abdul Hamid's days and had sensed the fierce fanaticism, of which its retention and guardianship was then the expression, could realise what it meant to me to see it no longer a mosque, its carpets gone (we used to talk in the war of how, when we reached Constantinople and had forced the Straits, we 'would straighten the carpets in S. Sophia'), the infidel permitted to walk freely over its floors in shodden feet and the great shrine given over as a public monument!

Neither grey skies nor David's moods could avail against memory, though both served to reinforce its message:

> Nothing can destroy the deep love I have for this place for the sake of the Aubrey days as well as for our honeymoon days. I realise now how much I learnt here, how much I planned. Thirty years ago and I have accomplished so little of what I set out to do.[1]

Such thoughts intensified the sombre mood which had afflicted him since the failure over India and he felt 'the sense of one's own power' coupled with a 'terrible sense of frustration'; but it was, he supposed, 'my own fault: if I had the necessary qualities adequate to the situation I should be able to break through the Baldwin darkness and free the country from it – that is my failure.'[2] Only that ever-present help in trouble, work, provided an opiate.

As in the previous year, Lloyd's trip was connected with the educational work of the British Council. The Maltese community in Turkey had been badly affected by Turkish discrimination against them in employment and Lloyd found it inconceivable that the Imperial Government, which was 'finding homes and work for German Jews in Palestine', should not help its own subjects. He wanted the Treasury to fund the schooling of the young Maltese who could then be of use to the Empire.[3]

The moodiness of David and his evident dislike of Constantinople acted as irritants upon his father, who described to Blanche how he managed to keep his temper:

> I think so much of you always and of all your goodness to me and patience with my tempers and moods and I want you to understand – one can write these things, I think, more easily than one can say them – how grateful I always am for all you are and do for me. I look out of this window on to the water below over to Sultan Achmet just as I used to do when I was 24 and grinding away in the little hotel next door to the Embassy at Turkish – and sometimes when one looks back one wonders if one is really the same person.

He seldom revealed so much of himself in writing and, perhaps conscious of this, he hastily concluded: 'I must stop these reflections and get busy for the conference downstairs.'[4]

He left Constantinople on 31 May bound for Belgrade and thence to Italy. Everywhere the same message met him: the minister in Belgrade told him: 'our prestige, lately so high here, has fallen to zero over the sanctions business – the same is I know true in Bulgaria and in Greece'.[5] In Italy he found that 'even the Italians look down on us'.[6] One Anglophile senator spoke sadly to him about 'the lack of leadership in England':

> All Europe, said he, and of course all Italy, talked of little else today except of the change that had come over England – he understood that the people had not changed, only the politicians, but even so it must be bad for her prestige he thought. Always the same story – shall we never be done with Baldwinism? Good Lord deliver us. It should form a special item in the Church's Litany.[7]

Lloyd saw everywhere the signs of growing German influence and, with her speedy rearmament, he feared that the day of nemesis would not be long in coming. He felt, he told Blanche, 'terribly frustrated today – knowing so well what needs to be done but incapable of breaking through this *devilish* Baldwinism'.[8]

In September, on his way home, he went with Churchill to see the Maginot Line, taking some comfort from that, but, like Churchill, he regarded his own Government's defence policy with something akin to despair.[9] The problem for both men was that although they could see clearly what needed to be done, neither was in a position to do anything other than warn, which was, given the circumstances, a position of overpowering frustration.

Lloyd had been called before the Defence Select Committee in late July 1936 in his capacity as President of the Navy League. Then he had warned of the dangers to Britain's food supply in time of war posed by the decline of the merchant marine;[10] and both he and Churchill were part of a parliamentary deputation which called on Baldwin on 23 November to discuss the state of Britain's defences.[11]

Only a few days earlier Lloyd had made a speech in which he smote Baldwin hip and thigh for his statement in the House on 12 November in which, 'with an appalling frankness', he had explained that he had not rearmed earlier for electoral reasons. Lloyd thought this not only a confession of Baldwin's unfitness for the office he held but also a 'libel' on the British people:

> I am not one of those who believe that the people of this country cannot stand being told the truth. . . . It is his duty to educate the people – not to complain that they are reluctant to follow him.[12]

This deputation, like an earlier one in June, put searching questions to the Government; nothing in the replies given by ministers gave Lloyd any grounds for hope. But then Lloyd was already convinced that little could be expected from Baldwin. In March 1936 he had appointed a lawyer, Sir Thomas Inskip, as Minister in charge of Co-ordination of Defence, which prompted Lloyd to pass on to David the apt comment of Professor Lindemann, that it was 'the most cynical thing that has been done since Caligula appointed his horse a consul'.[13]

Late 1936 witnessed a drawing together by Lloyd of the various strands of his critique of 'Baldwinism'. On 19 November he harshly criticized the Government's defence policy (or lack of it) in the Lords. This was followed up six days later with a condemnation of the treaty which had finally been negotiated with Egypt.[14] Everywhere he looked the legions were being withdrawn, despite the fact that the world was full of nations who followed

> The good old rule . . . the simple plan,
> That they should take, who have the power,
> And they should keep who can.[15]

Only the British, blinded by pacifism and pusillanimous politicians, refused to believe that this was so.

Blanche saw in the events of 1936 the prelude to another German war and found 1937 a 'frightening year to be starting on'. She had 'the breathless feeling of a race against Fate. Please God we may survive this year and next without disaster.'[16] Living under the shadow of the Valley of Death over the next two years was to shake her nerves to breaking-point, but in the short term she immersed herself in the refurbishment of Clouds Hill, sharing Lloyd's delight when they managed to purchase neighbouring land which guaranteed their privacy.

Lloyd spent the early part of the New Year in Rome seeking quiet and rest. For much of the last six months of the year he had been suffering badly from intestinal trouble. His doctor, Manson-Bahr, listed his problems:

> The present complaints are: – flatulency, discomfort, diarrhoea alternating with constipation, pain, especially over the gall-bladder area which sometimes comes on at night. . . . Often feels 'livery', complains of pain in the back, especially when he is overtired. Thin and spare he naturally overworks himself and is always under considerable strain. Has low blood pressure and has not lost weight.

He diagnosed duodenitis aggravated by 'stress and strain'.[17] To add to Lloyd's problems an injection which he had just after Christmas punctured a vein and touched a nerve. He wrote on 10 January: 'I am being very genial and lazy and if only my arm would stop aching I should be able to forget my body which is what one always wants to do.'[18]

But it was not easy for one with so many friends in so many places to obtain solitude when necessary. Even when he refused an invitation from the British Ambassador, Sir Eric Drummond, to stay at the Embassy, Lloyd still found himself drawn into political conversations which culminated in an interview with Mussolini on 15 January.[19] But the general decline in British prestige had had its effect in that quarter and by March he was writing that:

> Musso is becoming more and more querulous and bitter – most recently as a result of some prelate's criticisms in England. What a pity it all is. Musso is becoming tiresome and impudent and someone will have to read him a lesson. I am not really sure if the Bolsheviks in Spain may not prove to be the most convenient flail!![20]

The political world still seemed bent on excluding Lloyd from any position of power, but one field of activity had opened up in 1936 which offered him some scope for influence; it was one which expanded in 1937. In June 1935 the British Council had been set up to project a positive image of Britain and her culture to the rest of the world. It was, in part, an attempt to combat the dictatorships and their extensive use of propaganda. Lloyd had been a founder member of its board and had served as Chairman of its Near East Committee ever since. It had been in this capacity that he had toured the area in 1936 and was to do so again in the spring of 1937. The problem of anti-British propaganda spread by Italy in the aftermath of Abyssinia, compounded by the traditional British lack of concern for cultural activities and the decline in imperial prestige in the Near East, made it an area of particular concern to the Council. Lloyd's anxiety to develop educational facilities for imperial subjects in the region fitted into an overall objective of raising the profile of British activities in the region.[21]

What Lloyd saw during his spring tour, which took him to Palestine, Egypt, Cyprus and Malta, did nothing to inspire him with confidence that it would be easy to make any headway in the task of cultural propaganda. In Palestine Jewish terror gangs vied with Arab ones, and Britain's inability to keep order or decide on a policy was dealing a mortal blow to her prestige.[22] Cyprus was better, but the 'horrible defeatism' of Cairo was infinitely depressing,[23] for there

> the *dégringolade* has set in very markedly: the Residency is grubby, the servants ill-dressed, the drive unkempt. But the garden is lovely. The streets are filthy and there is an unhappy feeling in the air – a sort of *fin de saison in excelsis* atmosphere. We all seem from Cromer onwards to have fought or struggled and made our little sacrifices in vain.[24]

He was, he told Blanche,

> very worried about the whole Italian situation. We are now reaping the fruits of the Eden–Baldwin policy in full. The one thing that has impressed me most in this tour is the enormous weight and bitterness of Italian propaganda wherever I have been. There seems no limit to their expenditure. Here at Port Said as elsewhere they are building still bigger and bigger schools and we are of course doing nothing.[25]

In June 1937 the Chairman of the British Council, Lord Eustace Percy, decided to resign and he recommended Lloyd as his successor. This idea was, predictably, less than popular in some quarters of Whitehall. The Foreign Office, which was anxious to take the Council under its wing totally, thought that the former Ambassador to Germany, Horace Rumbold, or the Lord Privy Seal, Lord De La Warr, would do for the post; under either Foreign Office control would have been total. Rex Leeper, the diplomat most concerned with the Council, was anxious to save it from those who wanted its activities to be mainly commercial. But although the idea of De La Warr seemed to go ahead smoothly enough, Percy's choice prevailed.

The reason for this is unclear. As Chairman of one of the Council's committees, an administrator of talent and a man with long experience of the Near East, Lloyd was an obvious choice – particularly now the Baldwin era had come to an end; perhaps this was the deciding factor. In May Baldwin went to the Lords amidst plaudits of unparalleled warmth and unanimity; his successor was Neville Chamberlain. Lloyd's relations with him had always been better than those with Baldwin. Both had started life as Birmingham businessmen and both were keen tariff reformers. At the time of the Ottawa agreements on tariffs in 1932 Lloyd had written a letter of congratulation to Chamberlain who had replied warmly:

> I am very grateful to you for a letter which was both affectionate and generous. . . . Like Hamlet I have been haunted by my Father's Ghost. Now the Ghost can rest in peace.
>
> Feeling like that I cannot help turning to the stalwarts who fought the battle in its first splendid rush and then, when delay and disappointment came and some who had been friends sneaked off, carried on the fight even after the leader had become stricken. I am thankful for the help that you and a few others gave all through. I am sure it was that which sustained his own courage . . . when the history of the whole movement comes to be written your part will be found not the least among those that brought it to the final victory.[26]

Certainly Lloyd enjoyed Chamberlain's support once he had become Chairman of the Council, so it may be that the change in regime helped his chances; but according to Leeper, it was 'only with considerable difficulty that I got the PM's approval in time to talk to Lloyd',[27] so perhaps it did not.

Leeper's main fear was that Lloyd would start hiring and firing staff according to his own prejudices and he was anxious to impress upon him at their meeting on 7 July that he would be in the same position as a minister vis-à-vis his department. To Leeper's surprise Lloyd agreed; he was not, as the diplomat was to discover, quite as unreasonable as Whitehall legend painted him. What Lloyd did insist on was a three-year appointment, 'loyalty and hard work'. He also got from Chamberlain an assurance that he regarded the British Council as a permanent body which was an essential part of Britain's national defence – as well as a promise of more funding.[28] Thus it was that he became, in July 1937, the third Chairman of the British Council; at last a field of action had opened up before him.

# 29

# THE BRITISH COUNCIL

Lloyd has rightly been hailed by historians of the British Council as its second founder and as the man who expanded its sphere of operations and ensured its survival. But it cannot be said that he entered into his new kingdom with much optimism. He wrote to Colin Forbes Adam on 10 August 1937:

> I have taken over the British Council without much elation, partly because it is a very heavy addition to my present work and partly because I am not at all sure how well I shall succeed in doing it. I have barely so far put my nose into the office. . . . I am disquieted by one feature and that is that since the Treasury have been giving us more financial support, they appear to have imposed on Eustace Percy a good deal of Treasury control, and I need not tell you what that means![1]

On 29 August he wrote:

> The dissolution of what we fought to save and consolidate in 1914–18 goes rapidly on. . . . The tragedies of the war were great enough, but the tragedies of the peace which has followed it have been to me infinitely more great and more terrible. I try hard to convince myself that my views and my analysis is unreal: each time I check up the facts – irrespective of my fancies – I find that it is not those who think as I do who are bemused and living in an unreal world but the politicians. Every time I come back home after being on the continent I feel that people in England are living in a world of their own, utterly divorced from the stern doings and preparations across the Channel, in love with their own prosperity, and confident of their own superiority however they are successfully challenged. There is a terrible time coming. I am certain of it, and as yet we have done little to deserve salvation from it.[2]

At the Council he was able to seek salvation by Works – but that was still to leave a wide margin for Faith.

From the start Lloyd's works fell into two categories: the political, in which he saw himself and was seen by others as head of a fifth arm of national defence policy; and the administrative, in which he fought hard to acquire the money and the prestige which would allow the Council to fulfil this exalted role. His appointment was a victory for those diplomats who, like Rex Leeper, wanted the Council to undertake propaganda work for Britain, but the new Chairman's wide range of friendships enabled him to play a personal diplomatic role. One of Chamberlain's first diplomatic objectives was to improve relations with Italy; in this task Lloyd was of considerable use.

After a speech in May 1936 in which Lloyd had defended Italy against those who wanted sanctions, Count Grandi had written to him to convey the 'personal appreciation' of 'the Duce himself'. This reputation as a friend of Italy enabled Lloyd to play what he called 'a discreet and not entirely useless hand in the Italian *rapprochement*.'[3] He encouraged Chamberlain to follow up Grandi's overture in July seeking better relations and received in return from the Ambassador another letter of thanks:

> As I said, I am hopeful now. But I must tell you that if – as I am confident
> – our difficulties will soon be at an end, the merit will first of all be due to
> those faithful friends of my country who, in the critical moment, have
> helped so much and so successfully. Amongst these, my dear Lloyd, you
> are one of the first and foremost, and you know how grateful I am and
> shall always be to you.[4]

Lloyd could 'not make up my mind about Young Italy'. Sometimes he thought it 'very fine', but at others he could not bring himself to 'believe that Mussolini has managed to put any real stuffing in them'. It was, however, necessary to avoid a Berlin–Rome–Spain axis: 'We sowed shame and we must expect to reap humiliation, but even that is better than defeat.' He remained bitter against those who 'with open eyes chanced their arms and willingly pledged the safety of the whole Empire in order to win elections and retain their own power!'[5]

As Chairman of the British Council, Lloyd sought to use propaganda as a weapon whilst the Chamberlain Government stepped up conventional rearmament. Control of the eastern Mediterranean was vital to imperial communications and although the Council could do nothing to supply the ships needed for military dominance in the region, it could try to combat Italian propaganda and increase British prestige. For this money was necessary.

From both Chamberlain and the Foreign Secretary, Anthony Eden, Lloyd secured valuable help in his battles with the Treasury. Chamberlain, who wrote in December that 'I regard the prosecution and development of the Council's activities as of urgent national importance',[6] gave permission for Lloyd to approach private individuals and businesses for funds. An appeal brought in £50,000 from one donor, probably Lord Nuffield. Eden's view of the Council's task was the same as Lloyd's:

> In the fierce war of ideas to which we are inevitably, if defensively, committed, we have to face, with very slender resources, expenditure by foreign countries on a vastly larger scale. . . . If we fail to tackle the situation on a scale commensurate with its urgency, not only shall we find that all our peoples will suffer grave hurt, but serious and perhaps irretrievable damage will be done to our position.[7]

He told the Chancellor, Sir John Simon, on 23 December, that 'Good cultural propaganda cannot remedy the damage done by a bad foreign policy, but . . . even the best of diplomatic policies may fail if it neglects the task of interpretation and persuasion.'[8] Lloyd wanted to double his grant to £110,000 for 1938–9 which would allow him to increase propaganda work abroad, particularly through educational activities and especially in the eastern Mediterranean.[9] The Treasury was alarmed at the cost, but Lloyd managed to persuade Sir John Simon, the Chancellor, that £130,000 would be a more appropriate figure.[10] At last the dynamo was harnessed to the service of the state.

Lloyd's position was an ambiguous one. He refused to accept any salary and regarded himself (and was regarded by others) as a semi-independent agent; yet, at the same time, he was head of a quasi-official body. This ambiguity had its advantages.

In December 1937, when the Foreign Office was casting round for ways of improving relations with Germany and Italy, Leeper suggested that Lloyd might go to see Mussolini in his capacity as Chairman of the British Council; this met with the approval of the Assistant Under-Secretary, Orme Sargent, who thought that 'Mussolini might unbosom himself to Lord Lloyd, who is an old friend, to an extent which might prove very useful to us in eliminating the present situation.'[11] Eden agreed to the project and Leeper wrote to Lloyd on 20 December saying that he had had 'many pricks of conscience' about asking him to do the job:

> But I only put it to you as I did as I am convinced that if this job is to be done, you are literally the only person to do it. I also think this is the most urgent and important job that needs doing at present.

Leeper's qualms were due to the fact that Lloyd was about to go off on a tour of Rhodesia for the Chartered Company:

> For some time past I have felt uneasy at your being away for so long as my heart is so very much in what we are trying to do together and I do

think we are beginning to get a move on. Without your drive and your unselfish enthusiasm we should not have got where we are and the British Council simply cannot get on without you. But you already know what I think.[12]

In the event the plan fell through because the dictator demanded that Lloyd should bring a special message from the Prime Minister with him. Chamberlain wanted to improve relations with Italy – but not at that price. This was the first, but not the last, time that Lloyd proved to have his diplomatic uses.

Lloyd spent the early months of 1938 in southern Africa and then in the eastern Mediterranean on Council business. Whilst he was away Chamberlain's efforts to improve Anglo–Italian relations led to Eden's resignation. His replacement was Lloyd's old friend, Lord Irwin, now Viscount Halifax. Lloyd told Blanche that 'the FO are perturbed and uneasy by Edward's appointment'; his only fear was that Leeper might be moved.[13] Lloyd's host at the time, Sir Miles Lampson, the Ambassador to Egypt, disapproved of Chamberlain's action, thinking that the Germans would see in it only weakness, but Lloyd took a brutally realistic view: 'You can't play power politics without power – and that is what Eden wanted to do.'[14]

He wrote this last comment on 12 March after hearing of the German entry into Austria. With France between governments and Britain negotiating with Italy, and powerless in any event to intervene, 'Again Hitler has selected his moment.' Lloyd could only hope that it would 'show all the pro-Germans at home just where they are'. It would, at any rate, provide Mussolini with an unwelcome neighbour – which might help Anglo–Italian relations.[15]

Amid such stirring events, Lloyd's job of ensuring that British schools were built in Egypt and that professors of English Literature were appointed in Greece was indeed small beer; his own view of it was expressed in a letter to Blanche:

> All dull jobs but necessary and overdue. As Government will not use me for the biggest things I must be content to do the work that's nearest. It will bear good fruit some day I fancy.[16]

But he saw no harm in the circumstances in trying to make the 'work that's nearest' into something bigger.

Perhaps the greatest asset which Lloyd possessed for the ambiguous role which he played was his wide acquaintanceship among the crowned heads, dictators and prime ministers of Europe; if it was not quite true that he could walk into any chancellery in Europe and ask for an interview with the man at the top, it was not far from it. During his spring tour he had stopped off in Athens where he had discussed with his old friend King George II of Greece the founding of a British-style public school at Spetasi. Such a school would, he and the King agreed, be useful for the Greeks and would help British influence; but there was more to his conversation than that. Lloyd cherished the idea of a 'Balkan *Entente*', that is a league of friendly Balkan states which would act as a barrier to German expansion southwards. Once he returned to England he took up the issue with Chamberlain, telling the King in May:

> I have had a long talk with the Prime Minister about the whole tobacco question. . . . I think [he] . . . does realise the enormous importance of building up the Balkan *Entente*: I have told him that if we really can meet the needs of Turkey, Greece and Roumania, and possibly Bulgaria as well later, we shall have built a solid barricade against the *Drang nach ost* which has already reached and nearly overwhelmed Czechoslovakia and Hungary.

Lloyd suggested to Chamberlain and the Foreign Office that if they were to purchase Turkish and Greek tobacco rather than rely entirely upon America, the economic support which they would be giving those countries would pay diplomatic dividends. King George followed all his 'good work and endeavours' to 'get your country to build up the Balkan *Entente* and Greece in particular'.[17] Lloyd was to pursue this policy for the next two years but, as it transpired, with only mixed success. It might be argued that the 'solid barricade' which he sought to erect was, in reality, nothing more than a collection of weak and frightened countries – but there was nothing else on offer.

Lloyd approved of the general direction of Chamberlain's foreign policy. When an agreement was reached with Italy in May, he wrote to Blanche that, apart from the clauses dealing with the Red Sea Islands, it was 'all right and I think Neville has scored and I am glad of that'.[18] Lloyd was prepared to trust 'Musso' 'rather further than most Italians' – although 'that was not saying a heap' and he had doubts as to how he would react under great pressure from Hitler.[19] He told Halifax in May:

> Mussolini is a real Italian peasant, and as such is extremely vindictive; and I am sure that only the duress of circumstances will make him forgive us over Abyssinia, and that in spite of the Anschluss and the Brenner his relations with Germany are likely to be much more durable than some people think. That does not mean that you were not right to make the Italian agreement; but it does mean the mood, I think, of a very watchful attitude.[20]

His views were, as ever, far-sighted and he warned one correspondent in May that: 'The real danger is coming at the end of next year or the beginning of 1940, and unless we can re-arm a good deal faster than we are doing now, the calamity may happen then.'[21]

With Chamberlain as Prime Minister and Halifax as Foreign Secretary, Lloyd was now closer to the inner circle of power than he had been at any time since 1929. Chamberlain's friendly intentions had been shown by the way in which he had backed Lloyd's appeal for more finance for the British Council and he gave a more personal demonstration of goodwill in April 1938 when he was sympathetic to his desire for a seat on the board of the Suez Canal Company. Though he was not able to give him the seat, he left him 'convinced of Neville's friendliness' and hopeful of 'other chances'.[22] Lloyd wrote to Princess Bibesco, daughter of H. H. Asquith, on 24 June 1938:

> I think things are a little easier. Neville Chamberlain is doing marvels and the whole atmosphere has changed for the better since Baldwin went, but you know how I feel about that.[23]

Although the warm friendship which had produced *The Great Opportunity* had congealed into coldness under the impact of events in India, the presence of his old colleague at the Foreign Office was, from Lloyd's point of view, a good thing. There remained a religious affinity and the prerogatives left by a long friendship and he could, and did, write letters of a personal nature to Halifax. Thus it was that, under the shadow of the menace of Hitler, something of their old friendship, sundered by India, revived.

On 10 August Lloyd wrote to Halifax: 'I do not want to be an alarmist, but I am increasingly anxious about the situation in regard to Czechoslovakia'; he enclosed information from a German friend which confirmed the view he had formed from other sources that the Nazis had taken the decision to attack Czechoslovakia.[24] This information, although almost certainly incorrect, fitted with what the Foreign Office had heard from other sources and presaged the onset of the crisis which was to end at Munich.

Not only was that crisis to cast its shadow over Lloyd's relations with Chamberlain, it was also to throw a blight upon his personal life which, by mid 1938, had assumed an aspect more pleasing than at any time since his return to England. Renovation and refurbishment at Clouds Hill was producing a pleasant country house and giving Blanche a fresh interest in life; and if David continued to give his parents the sort of worries which young men do, by announcing an incurable aversion to stockbroking, Lloyd had been able to get him a job with the British Council and had helped him to buy a small flat in London which would give him more independence.[25] With wife and son settled, for the moment, and a congenial job to do which gave him plenty of travel and a chance to serve the Empire, Lloyd's spirits were higher than they had been for years.

Although in his fifty-ninth year, Lloyd looked younger, and there were few signs in the mirror of his real age. By the time he was fifty-nine on 19 September he had managed a feat which enabled him to contemplate even this great age with some equanimity. In 1937 he had been made honorary commodore of the City of London No. 600 squadron and had been offered his 'wings'; he refused to take something he had not earned and set about learning how to fly military aircraft in order to win them. This feat was accomplished in August and Blanche rightly looked upon it as 'one of his greatest achievements'.[26] He had matched himself with younger men and won, which was pleasure enough, but there was more to his flying than that; he rediscovered, in the trackless spaces of the air, the calm and the beauty which his early wanderings in the desert had brought.

Now came the shadow of Munich to put an end to these joys.

# 30

# FROM MUNICH TO PRAGUE

Hitler's designs upon the Sudetenland area of Czechoslovakia created a diplomatic crisis in which there was no role for the Chairman of the British Council, but in his private capacity Lloyd could talk to most of those on the British and French side who were intimately concerned in the crisis.

Of the gravity of events Lloyd had no doubt. He told Blanche that even if war was avoided,

> We shall all have to live in a state of perpetual tension for another 20 months and one wonders if one's public or private nerves are going to stand it without an unrehearsed or intended explosion.[1]

His anxieties had already led him to renew his contacts with Churchill which had lapsed since the heady days of the IDL. He had written to him thus on 17 July:

> I am rather unhappy at never seeing you nowadays. I have made two or three suggestions to see you but as you did not respond I did not like to press them. It is only that after our years of close collaboration I hate being divorced from your mind, policy and plans. If there is any reason I wish you would tell me; if not do let us meet one day. I am more and more anxious about the situation but don't see what can be done. The Eastern Area, in which I am particularly interested just now, is improving, but this end alarms me greatly.[2]

Churchill had responded with an immediate telegram asking to meet him;[3] now, as the crisis deepened, the two men came once more into co-operation.

Lloyd dined and slept at Chartwell on 30 August before going on to London on 31 August where he saw Lloyd George and the French Ambassador, André Corbin. The former was 'convinced we ought to fight' but 'equally convinced this Government would never fight anyone on any issue'; the latter was merely filled with gloom.[4] Lloyd sought relief down in Dorset with his squadron.

There at least he could escape from the tension of impotence into the release of action. He made his first attempt at bombing and found it 'great fun, but not easy' – climbing to 5,000 feet, then nose-diving at the target until, at 2,000 feet, the bombs were released.[5] Knowing that he could still compete in the life struggle and that he was, at fifty-eight, able to conquer his years and fears, refreshed his spirits in a way few other things could.

Back in London on 7 September, he found Corbin 'depressed and anxious'; he asked Lloyd to 'help in any way I could as I had so often done before'; it was an appeal which brought back memories of Cambon's pleas in 1914. But when Lloyd talked with Churchill and Vansittart that evening none of them saw 'what any outside person could do unless [the] Government sought their aid'.[6] On 16 September Roger Cambon of the French Embassy told Lloyd that Corbin had been 'terribly discouraged' by a conversation he had had with Halifax; Lloyd asked to see Halifax.

The two men had a meeting on the morning of 12 September; afterwards Lloyd wrote Halifax a letter which burned with Anglo-Catholic fervour:

> I have thought carefully about what you very confidentially said to me about a Four-Power Conference. My reply to you was that the situation, I was convinced, had gone far beyond any question of conferences and that only action now could avail. I am still of that opinion.

He thought that even the hint that Britain was thinking of such a course would be fatal to the position of the Czech President, Beneš, and a 'complete triumph for German policy because it would show that neither England nor France were prepared to stand up' to them. It was, he begged, essential not to be 'blinded by the speciousness of German racial claims in Czechoslovakia'. If Germany was allowed to annex the Sudetenland not only would Czechoslovakia be at her mercy, but all the smaller European states would draw the conclusion that there was no way of standing up to Hitler and 'you will have opened a path for Germany to the Black Sea':

> May I add this – please forgive me for doing so but it may help. War is truly terrible, but to consider it the worst issue, to be avoided at all costs, is utterly unchristian and wrong. There are worse issues even than war – a still worse issue would be if we were found morally too feeble to stand up and too cowardly to sacrifice ourselves for what is Right over what is manifestly evil and Wrong. It would be worse than war to be unwilling to be the champions of weak peoples or that we should, through a shrinking

from suffering, fail in a task surely set us by Providence. This is the moment to play the man, to face clear-eyed what is coming, confident that we are capable of drinking the cup and that we shall not be left without the power to do so.[7]

To such a pitch were Lloyd's nerves screwed.

On 16 September Lloyd dashed over to Paris to 'find out for myself what the state of feeling was'. As the tension mounted and the possibility of war drew closer, he became anxious lest the Government shirk its duties out of fear. During his visit he saw all the leading French politicians. Reynaud, the Minister of Justice, he found 'steady and resolute'; the Foreign Minister, Georges Bonnet, was, however, 'preparing to sell the pass'; whilst one of his predecessors, Flandin, 'was even worse'. The Premier, Edouard Daladier – *Le taureau avec cornes de limace* (the bull with slug's horns) – was 'fairly steady', but worried by the effects of Britain's lack of support upon Bonnet. Although, on the whole, optimistic, Lloyd came away concerned at what he had seen and anxious to get Halifax and Chamberlain to stiffen the French backbone.[8] Leeper, whom he saw on 18 September, told him that the Government had 'made up their minds to throw the Czechs over'. Lloyd telephoned Churchill, asking him to try to see Daladier who had just arrived in England and 'exhort him to stand firm'. He dined with Churchill the following evening, but they were powerless to influence events.[9]

Under the threat of another war Blanche's nerves began to collapse; her husband's mind turned towards thoughts of mortality. On the evening of 27 September they had a sombre conversation in which, foreseeing his death in the coming war, Lloyd spoke of where he wanted to be buried:

> He said that though this kingdom and Empire of ours meant everything to him – though the bitterness of seeing it all even temporarily eclipsed, if that had to come, would break his heart, and there could be no fun in life again – yet that he was enough of a historian to know that such things had happened and did happen – but that he was deeply conscious of another kingdom which matters more, and more eternally – and which nothing could shake – and for which we should really be fighting.

When his time came he would, he thought, like to be buried in the churchyard at St Ippolyts near Clouds Hill.[10]

The events of the next few days which culminated in the Munich settlement drove thoughts of death from Lloyd's mind and replaced them with ones of national dishonour. Although Chamberlain returned claiming to have won peace 'with honour', the fact was that the Germans entered the Sudetenland on 1 October and the Czechs were, in Blanche's words, 'thrown to the wolves', 'and all because we are not ready. It is an unbelievable tragedy, perhaps the greatest in our history – and I have never seen George in such despair.'[11] To Duff Cooper, who resigned from the Admiralty because he could not stomach what had been done, Lloyd wrote:

> I can well appreciate how poignantly you will feel this divorce from the direction of almost the greatest office of state: all the more are those grateful to you for making this stand against what I believe to be a disastrous foreign policy.[12]

All Lloyd's instincts and sense of honour went against sacrificing one's friends for one's own benefit, and when he spoke in the Lords on 4 October he did so in grief and in anger.

He recognized that the state of Britain's armaments had lain behind the surrender and said that 'he had never disliked differing from a Government as much as he did today', but that 'justice was greater than peace'.[13] Amery thought the speech 'rose to considerable heights of real eloquence'.[14] In a letter to the *Daily Telegraph* Lloyd wrote that it was 'impossible to speak without shame and difficult to speak without indignation, of what we have done to the Czech people'; Disraeli had credited Britain with two great assets, her Fleet and her good name: 'Today we must console ourselves that we still have our Fleet.' He warned that, at best, the democracies had purchased only a respite.[15]

For Lloyd there was no respite. He set off on 6 October for Bucharest on an official visit to King Carol of Romania. This time the Orient Express brought him no pleasure. From a Vienna festooned with swastikas he wrote to Blanche:

> There is sun all over these rich Central European plains – but none in my heart as I travel through them. But with so fine a people as ours and with resources so infinite and a cause so fine there *must* be recovery somewhere.[16]

The King whom Lloyd saw on 11 October was a very different man from the young prince whom he had last seen in Bombay almost two decades before. Lloyd promised to try to secure for him the diplomatic backing of the British Government; but in the immediate aftermath of Munich this carried little weight. Afterwards Lloyd went to visit the schools of English and other British Council works in Romania, before returning to England.[17]

The trip convinced Lloyd that Munich had all but destroyed Britain's prestige in the Balkans. Writing to Percy Loraine on 20 October he commented:

I think that the situation is going to move at a terrific pace and that the next crisis is likely to come not in the next two or three years but in the next two or three months, or perhaps even earlier.

He did not think that the Germans intended to 'wait until our situation is both stronger and easier'.[18]

Once back in London Lloyd tried to make good his promise to King Carol. He tried to persuade the Government to purchase 600,000 tons of Romanian wheat as a way of combating German economic influence, but the Permanent Under-Secretary, Alec Cadogan, told him that 'there is no chance of immediate, striking, decisive action'. It was in vain that Lloyd urged Cadogan to 'exert the imagination to grip the fast fleeting skirts of remaining opportunity in the Balkans'.[19] Halifax's warning, that they must be careful not to encourage the Danubian states to pursue a 'policy which will call down the wrath of Berlin on them', remained in force – as the 'strategic situation' dictated, for it was 'impossible for us to come to their rescue'.[20]

Although he had disapproved of Munich, Lloyd had not wanted to create a breach between himself and Chamberlain and had written on 6 October to say,

how very deeply I have felt differing from you over this crisis. I never particularly minded differing with S.B., for our ways of thought and outlook were entirely different. But with you it has always been different. I have always looked forward to your being PM, admired your courage . . . and felt for the first time for years entirely happy about Conservative leadership. . . . I hope it will not affect our personal relations.[21]

Chamberlain replied on 20 October saying that 'my personal feelings towards you are entirely unaffected' but pointing out that,

the policy I am pursuing is a dual one and that conciliation is a part of it fully as essential as rearmament. I fear that this may bring us into conflict again perhaps, but I can only repeat that I shall respect your sincerity just as much as I know you will mine.[22]

The two men continued to work together, but the earlier bloom was gone and Lloyd increasingly felt that what was needed was 'an alternative National Government'.[23]

Lloyd's plans to help the Romanians did not come entirely to nothing. Although the Foreign Office was chary of leading them on, it was recognized that some British attempt to stop total German economic domination of the Danube basin should be made. Halifax told Chamberlain that buying Romanian wheat would have 'a symbolic value disproportionate to its intrinsic worth'.[24] Britain purchased 200,000 tons of wheat; but Lloyd saw this as only the first step towards the creation of a 'Balkan Entente'.

It might be argued that in attempting to do this Lloyd was stepping outside his brief as Chairman of the British Council. Certainly the Germans did not believe that his role was as innocent as the British Government claimed; in the Romanian business, for example, they were convinced that his mission had been connected with their own efforts to secure a stranglehold on the Romanian economy; nor were they far wrong.[25] The fact was that a man with Lloyd's range of contacts and strength of character was unlikely to confine himself to purely 'cultural' activities – especially given his wide definition of that word. The Government was clearly not unhappy with this situation. Lloyd reported all his important conversations to the Foreign Office, and if the words did not always convey the inflection in his voice or the forcefulness with which he argued the British case, that was too bad. As an unofficial ambassador with the entrée to chancelleries from Paris to Ankara, he was a useful sounding-board whose words could, should it prove convenient, be denied.

To those who persist in seeing in Chamberlain's policy only the element of conciliation or appeasement, such a role might seem incongruous, but then the employment of such a man would itself have been incongruous had the Prime Minister's policy not also contained an element of steel.

Between Munich and March 1939 information reached the Government from many sources suggesting that the Germans were indeed intent on a new *Drang nach Osten* (Drive to the East). Some of this information came from Lloyd who acted as conduit for intelligence material gathered in Berlin by the newspaper correspondent Ian Colvin.[26] In late January 1939 such sources changed their tune and began talking of an imminent drive westwards by the German armies. This 'war scare', whilst not materializing into anything in the way of German activity, did stimulate Chamberlain into activity which included staff talks with the French, the doubling of the Territorial Army and the introduction of conscription.[27] Some months before the German invasion of the rump of Czechoslovakia the Chamberlain Government was well aware of the danger from Germany. Lloyd was impressed by its reaction and foresaw that they were 'moving rapidly towards another "show-down" with the Dictators'.[28]

The small British effort over Romanian wheat had done little to counter the weight of the German economic mission which had arrived in Bucharest at the end of October. By March 1939 the full extent of the German demands was known and on 16 March the Romanian Foreign Minister, Grigoire Gafencu, asked the British and French Ambassadors whether their governments 'envisage indicating clearly in the form most suitable to them their wish to preserve the possibility of "having a say" in this part of Europe'.[29] If they did not then Romania would 'have no other choice but to bow to Germany'.

In any Romanian initiative to seek support from the British, Lloyd was an obvious intermediary; close to the Government but not of it, and a man who had already signalled his interest in helping Romania resist Germany, it was no wonder that the Romanian Ambassador in London, Viorel Tilea, should have sought him out.

Tilea was an Anglophile, opposed the negotiations with Germany, thought little of Gafencu and had already approached the Foreign Office on 16 March warning that he had news from secret sources that the Germans intended to move against his country in the near future. When he received Gafencu's telegram he pressed insistently for an immediate British pledge of support.[30] Early on the morning of 17 March Tilea received a mysterious telephone call from Paris which said that the Germans had presented the Romanian Government with an ultimatum. He used this information at the Foreign Office that afternoon when he asked for a loan and the creation of a Balkan League. He was, however, disavowed by his own Government. The identity of the mysterious telephone caller seems to be cleared up in a letter which Lloyd wrote to Halifax on 20 March after seeing Tilea:

> [He] . . . is anxious that you should be reassured that whatever news you get from Rex Hoare [the British Minister] or anyone else, the German economic ultimatum was in fact given. He was told so on the telephone by Titarescu [*sic*] and Bonnet had confirmed the information. Now that publicity has been given the Germans will no doubt tone down their tune to one of 'normal negotiations'.[31]

Although a recent article has claimed that Tatarescu, the Romanian minister in Paris, was not the mysterious telephone caller, Lloyd's letter seems to suggest that he was – even if he later thought it advisable not to say so.[32]

Tilea's initiative came only the day after German troops had entered Prague, thus creating fresh fears of general war, and it helped focus British attention upon Romania as the place at which the *Drang nach Osten* might be halted. The idea of a Balkan Entente, which Lloyd had been pressing for so long, now came to the forefront of Foreign Office thinking, with Cadogan recording that: 'If we want to stem the German expansion, I believe we must try to build a dam *now*.'[33] In the building of that dam Lloyd was to play an important part.

On 20 March Lloyd wrote to Halifax:

> Tilea is very anxious that you should realise the delicacy of the internal situation in Roumania, but cannot tell you officially. I think that Gafencu is not a strong man and has all along been in favour of concessions to Germany, whilst the King will stand very steady, especially if he gets encouragement from here, but I know that Tilea is right about the pro-German influences that play upon the King from industrialists and other business people in Roumania.[34]

Lloyd also pressed him to get the Government to purchase large quantities of Turkish and Greek tobacco:

> Further conversations with those best qualified to judge, convince me more than ever that if we can put through this tripartite business in respect of Turkey, Greece and Bulgaria, we can consolidate a wall of support in the Balkans that the Germans will find hard to break. Those who hold this view are confident that it would be decisive in bringing Bulgaria on our side. It is the essential and necessary cement for the stones of the Balkan block.[35]

The weak point in all this was that the idea of functioning as an alliance against Germany 'was not one any of the states cast by the British as members of the block found attractive'.[36] Nevertheless, the British Government persisted in this policy which culminated in the guarantees given to Poland at the end of March and Romania in April.

Writing to David on 13 April, Lloyd commented that: 'I think I can say I was responsible for getting the Roumanian guarantee given by the PM today';[37] if this was an exaggeration, it was only a small one. At 9 a.m. Tilea had telephoned to tell him that on the previous day the French had decided to give guarantees to Romania and Greece but that Britain had declined to follow suit unless the Poles did the same. Lloyd and Tilea took the view that the Polish leader, Colonel Beck, was spinning out negotiations with Romania 'with the object . . . of doing a deal with Germany at a propitious moment'. When Lloyd went to put this view to Halifax he found him already engaged and talked to Cadogan instead. He was told that Britain had been leaving the Balkan states to their own negotiations in the hope that the Turks would put pressure on the Romanians to yield up territories to Bulgaria which would allow the Bulgarians to enter an *entente*. This seemed fair enough, but, as Lloyd urged:

> If our secret information was correct, viz. that the German military movements on Poland were a blind and the next immediate onslaught would be on the Roumanian oilfield, we simply had not time left to us for complicated diplomatic action like that which he instituted in respect of Poland. Would he at any rate let Edward know how urgent I thought the matter was.

Lloyd then went on to the French Embassy to see Corbin whom he found talking to Daladier on the telephone. Daladier was refusing to delay the announcement of the French guarantee to Romania, and Lloyd told Corbin that if he was 'stiff' with the Foreign Office, the British would probably agree to follow suit. He was delighted when he heard that this had been the case: 'I think that was a satisfactory morning's work.'[38]

# 31

## INTO THE VALLEY
## OF THE SHADOW

The strain of the post-Munich period proved too much for Blanche; she had one breakdown in November and another in January 1939. Lloyd told Duff Cooper on 11 January that, 'She never got over Munich.'[1] A holiday in Bermuda did something to restore her health and Lloyd wrote on 5 May:

> You are so infinitely too good to me in spite of all the worry I cause you and the racket I have led you and I sometimes feel that all you are going through now is only too much my fault. But it's no use worrying in retrospect and I am only too thankful to see you getting steadily and definitely better.[2]

But her nerves remained in a poor state until they broke down again in February 1941 under the impact of the greatest catastrophe of all.

There were bright streaks on the horizon which he used to try to lighten her gloom. The death of Sir Edmund Davis in February 1939 brought Lloyd a seat on the Rhodesia Railway Trust Board and the chairmanship of the Wankie Colliery Company, which gave them an extra £3,750 a year and meant a postponement of tentative plans to sell Portman Square.[3] Even more satisfying was the fact that David was performing his duties at the British Council impeccably – somewhat to his father's surprise.[4]

On the British Council front too, affairs seemed to be prospering. On 22 February Lloyd had led a deputation to Halifax protesting against proposals to cut the Council's grant by £54,000. It was true that even this reduced figure was £80,000 more than the previous year's grant, but that was beside the point, and Lloyd emphasized that any reduction would mean abandoning projects such as a new British Institute in Bucharest and a series of documentary films which would be shown throughout Europe:

I should like to remind HMG of one factor. Throughout the Middle East
the Germans are steadily pushing forward their economic drive. That is
well known. What is not so easy to realise is that this economic drive is
accompanied by a violently active cultural drive, an important feature of
which is the provision of facilities for bringing students in large numbers
to Germany, not only for their academic, but also for their technical and
political education. If we were now not only [not to] press ahead but
actually to recede from works we have undertaken of bringing these
students to England – to study *our* methods, *our* economics and *our* ideals
– then we must not be surprised if in six or seven years' time we wake up
to find the whole of this area Nazified nationally, spiritually, economic-
ally and militarily.[5]

What was true of the Middle East was true elsewhere and this passage
sums up Lloyd's attitude to the work of the British Council. There was
no cut.

In May he went on a prolonged tour of the Middle East and noted
with satisfaction the progress of the various activities sponsored by the
Council there.

In Cairo he had a long talk with the Italian politician, Italo Balbo,
who told him that war between their two countries was 'unthinkable
and impossible'. Lloyd replied that he had once thought this but now
wondered 'whether the search for new adventure was . . . outstripping
the Duce's judgement'; this prescient comment was matched by
Balbo's that 'there was only one country about whom one could say in
advance with certainty that she would be ruined, and that was Italy'.[6]

When war did come in September, no place was found for Lloyd in
Chamberlain's Government although Churchill and Eden were taken
in as sops to the anti-appeasers. Churchill did not forget his old
comrade and wrote to Chamberlain on 29 September suggesting the
appointment of an additional Civil Lord of the Admiralty to be in
charge of the Fleet Air Arm; he thought the post should go to Lloyd:

He has considerable standing both in the country and the Air Force. His
record of public service is known to you, and I am sure you would not feel
that past political differences about India ought to be a barrier at a time
like this.

He thought that Duff Cooper might take Lloyd's place at the British
Council.[7] This no doubt looked like an attempt to bring some of his
friends into influential positions and was consequently turned down by
Chamberlain.[8]

Lloyd's feelings at this juncture were expressed in a letter to David on
7 September: 'It is a grief to me to be impotent at a moment like this',
especially when, with the exceptions of Churchill and Eden, the

Government was 'formed exclusively of those who by their blindness and wilfulness for personal power have led us into this calamity'.[9] Sam Hoare offered him a post co-ordinating overseas propaganda at the new Ministry of Information (MOI),[10] but after consultation with Churchill, Halifax and Maurice Hankey, the former Cabinet Secretary, Lloyd turned it down.[11] He told David that he thought that the Council would give him enough to do for the time being, but within a few days it was apparent that war had opened in Whitehall between the Council and the new Ministry of Information.

In February it had been agreed that in the event of war the British Council would be incorporated into the Ministry of Information. Lloyd asked Halifax in June whether the MOI was going to be set up; it was, with the lawyer, Lord Macmillan, as the minister.[12] At that stage, expecting another post, Lloyd had let things lie, but once it became apparent that this would not be forthcoming, he went into action. He saw Halifax on 7 September and expressed his fears about the 'diminished role' being offered to the Council, pointing out the wide scope available to it in neutral countries. Halifax was sympathetic, telling Macmillan:

> George Lloyd has been instrumental during the last four or five years in building it up from practically nothing to a real instrument of great value to the country and it would be a thousand pities to throw it all away.[13]

Macmillan agreed to see Lloyd, but the latter was not reassured. He told David on 10 September: 'The MOI is doing all it can to kill the Council but I shall hope to save it by my exertions. They will have their work cut out, so long as I am here.'[14]

On 4 October, accompanied by his old antagonist Willy (now Lord) Tyrrell (who was President of the British Council), Lloyd went to see Halifax to press for the Council to be transferred back to the control of the Foreign Office. He argued that it was 'most undesirable for the post-war work of the British Council that it should have any connection with a purely political wartime machine such as the Ministry of Information' and that until 'the Ministry was re-organized, which might take many months, its chaotic condition made work under it practically impossible'.[15] Halifax 'was entirely disposed to agree', but did not want to raise the principle with Macmillan who was already suffering under the criticism which was to destroy him and his two successors. But it proved easy to secure Lloyd's objective without having to raise the question of principle.

This victory was some solace for the things which made him unhappy: the conduct of the war and his lack of power. Hearing that the

Government had decided to bombard Berlin with pamphlets, he wrote to David on 10 September:

> Pamphlets *with* bombs may do good but without are futile. Military defeat and/or economic defeat will destroy German morale. It is sheer illusion to suppose anything else will do it. The pamphlet policy is the continuation of the old appeasement policy of Munich.

As for his own fate, he did 'not yet know. I wish I did but must not be too impatient.'[16]

Upon the outbreak of war David had been thankful for his father's insistence on some time in the reserve of the Coldstreams, for it had enabled him to join Lloyd's old regiment, the Warwickshire Yeomanry. His father collected the mail from his flat and did not like what he found. In July David had asked his father for £150 to clear his debts. Lloyd investigated his finances and told him: 'You suffer from improvidence rather than actual extravagance.' It had later become necessary to provide him with more money; now it transpired that there were outstanding bills for over £150: 'it has been', he wrote to David on 10 September, 'a worry and a disillusionment to find that you still apparently owe money all round'. What really disturbed him was the fact that David had not told the truth: 'In wartime anything might happen to me or to you at any time, and for the honour of our name I cannot allow these bills to remain unpaid.'[17] So the bills were paid – despite the parlous state of Lloyd's own finances.

In May 1939 Lloyd had asked Vansittart whether he could be paid a salary of £3,000 a year for the work he did as Chairman of the Council; increasing taxation and declining income meant that unless this was done he would have to take on the post he had been offered as Chairman of the Wankie Colliery Company. His wishes were met; but even so he was sacrificing £750 a year.[18]

By staying on at the British Council, even with a salary, Lloyd was making a financial sacrifice he could ill afford and it was necessary to cast round for ways of retrenchment. In September Portman Square was let to the Japanese Embassy: 'To have the house off our hands is', he told David, 'providential in view of the budget which will knock us all sideways.'[19] For the moment he was without a London base and it was from the Bath Club that he wrote to his son on 19 September: 'I am spending the evening of my sixtieth birthday alone in this not very entertaining atmosphere but at least it gives me a moment to write a line to you.'[20] He managed to take Churchill's flat at Morpeth Mansions in October but did not spend much time there, embarking almost at once on a 'difficult but interesting mission' to south-eastern Europe.[21]

As Chairman of the British Council Lloyd could travel to neutral countries, collect information and impressions, and convey the message that Britain was going to win the war; with his wide range of contacts and his own indomitable will and reputation, few men could have been more fitted for such a job.

The first of these missions came in mid October when he set off for Spain. Lloyd's ostensible task was to persuade General Franco to allow the British Council to start work in Spain, but when the two men met on 23 October this was easily dealt with and the main thrust of the conversation turned on the war. Franco probed Lloyd as to Britain's intentions and state of morale, telling him that he thought the French would not put up much of a show when it came to fighting. Lloyd denied this and impressed upon him how united and determined the Empire was in the struggle. He also expressed surprise that the General should allow himself to be friendly with Hitler whose regime was now allied with the Communism from which Franco had saved Spain. Lloyd concluded that Spain would stay out of the war. On his return he was able to suggest to the Foreign Office that if only they could improve their cultural and journalistic presence in Spain and concentrate on the fact that the Allied cause was 'a crusade for the salvation of civilization against paganism . . . the anti-Communist field is ours for the taking'.[22] The Spanish trip was followed by one to the Balkans.

This tour originated in conversations between Tilea and the Foreign Office, but was not universally popular with British embassies in the area: Palairet in Athens and Campbell in Belgrade were particularly reluctant,[23] whilst Rex Hoare in Bucharest wrote anxiously to Sir Orme Sargent:

> Supposing the Lloyd visit . . . does come off, I hope that it will be possible to make it clear to him that we, His Majesties Ministers in the Balkans, are all wonderful fellows and that his mission is not to give us a 'jerk' (to use a word which used to be dear to his heart) but mainly to bring personal impressions of the situation in England, a fairly authorised forecast of what we expect to achieve in the next months and in general his personal impressions of the situation based on his wide contacts.[24]

In Sargent's absence William Strang replied:

> You may rest assured that we shall make it plain to Lloyd before he goes that we consider all His Majesty's Ministers in the Balkans to be quite first class and in no need of any sort of ginger. We shall explain that we are sending him out in order to bring back personal impressions and in order, in particular, to give one or two eminent persons in the Balkans,

more particularly King Carol, a first hand account of the determination of this country to put an end to a state of affairs in Europe during the last few years from which we have all suffered.[25]

Lloyd's personal contacts were to be used to reinforce efforts to 'steady' the Romanians and to create a Balkan bloc.[26]

Lloyd arrived in Bucharest on 13 November. He found Gafencu anxious about Russia and fearful that any Balkan *entente* would founder on the territorial ambitions of Hungary, Bulgaria and Greece.[27] Carol's main concern was to emphasize the Russian menace and he took advantage of their friendship to tell Lloyd 'what he could not say to a Minister or Ambassador', which was that he was 'a thousand per cent for the Allies', but that he must save his powder for the Bolsheviks. The King promised to reconsider his policy of supplying the Germans with wheat and oil. Lloyd explained that the British were unable to expand their guarantee to cover danger from Russia unless the Turks joined in; he also gave it as his own opinion that this was not an impossibility.[28]

Lloyd's business in Romania was not solely concerned with public diplomacy. He spoke with two British agents, Captain Despard and Mr Emery, about ways of blocking the Danube and sabotaging the oilfields in the event of a German attack on Romania and promised to see Churchill about the matter upon his return to London.[29] He told Sargent on 16 November: 'They are in an *awful* fluster here over the Russians and you trip over Germans every yard you walk.'[30]

The next stage of the journey took him to Sophia where King Boris seemed more anxious to find out what Carol had said and to complain about Bulgaria's various wrongs than anything else. Again Lloyd noted the fear of Stalin – 'C'est Pierre le Grand – en rouge', was Boris's verdict – and this seemed to rule out any hope of a Balkan *entente*. Whatever the Foreign Office thought about the King's 'treachery and perfidy', Lloyd did not think he was out 'either for co-operation with Germany or for adventures in respect of their neighbours'.[31]

From thence he travelled by bug-ridden *wagon-lit* to Belgrade where he saw the Regent, Prince Paul, on 24 November. Paul warned Lloyd that he should not believe anything which the untrustworthy Boris had said. Lloyd reminded Paul that he was no newcomer to Balkan politics and argued that, given the constraints upon Boris and the example of what had happened in the First World War when the Bulgarians had come in on the German side, it was time to mend fences; but he did not think he had convinced him.[32]

Lloyd arrived back in England in early December. His verdict on the tour was mixed. He told David in a letter on 6 December that he felt his visit had been 'almost important',[33] but had told Blanche on 20 November that:

> I am not content with what I have been able to achieve in Bucharest but I did my best ... Carol ... was extremely *avenant* and cordial, but France's attitude to Italy on the one hand and Italy's attitude to Turkey on the other is making any hope of a Balkan bloc pretty hopeless. Add to this great Russian pressure on the people here and you see the mess.[34]

He told Halifax in a letter of the same date that Carol's idea of a neutral bloc was a good alternative to an *entente*:

> It gives, as Carol said, such a good *couloir* for Italy to sit in on her way from the Axis to the Allied room. She could tell Germany she was helping her by trying to keep the Balkans neutral and her supply channels open; she could tell us she was helping forward our plans; she could tell her own people she was creating a position of Italian primacy in the Balkans, and she could, in fact, fortify herself against Germany by entrenching herself still further in the neutral position.[35]

If this attractive prospect was frustrated, that was but proof of Lloyd's comment that: 'Balkan policy in war-time – [is a] pure game of chess with players cheating all the time.'[36]

Among the pile of mail awaiting Lloyd upon his return was a long letter from David which apologized for his various misdeeds and expressed his deep gratitude to his father. Lloyd was touched to the heart:

> It almost made me cry even at my advanced age when tears are beyond me. To me you've always been perfect as a son and what is so much more, as a companion and a friend. I too have been – I can say it to you – very often lonely and your comings and goings have been the one light in my life. If I haven't let you know it has been because I have always been afraid of being one of those inquisitive and prehensile parents from whom its progeny fled at first sight.

He told him that if he had ever appeared 'stingy' it 'has never really been so', it had been rather his anxiety 'to leave you comfortable and to get you to believe the inevitable tightness of the future which I had long foreseen as one of Baldwin's most certain achievements':

> You have always been just grand to me and that's all about it – and as you say, we *have* had fun haven't we, and please God will yet have much more. I can't *admit* that Hitler should mess up all our lives; and I have a powerful faith that there are plenty of years in store for you yet.

Thanking David for being so understanding about his having helped one of his young friends to find the right job in the services, Lloyd wrote:

You know how I am; and how easily I give my heart to youth who are kind to me, who are vivid and cheerful and brave and beautiful – and I knew it must be so with him. . . . But I have an entirely different feeling about you and always have had. . . . I have under God, a most confident assurance that the war is going to mean not only life but a great avenue to success – I think all is coming your way – and of that I want to speak when we meet.

These are great days and great moments. We are hazarding more today than ever in our long and fateful history. But I am quietly confident of the issue.[37]

Amidst the swirling fogs of war that flame which had flared between father and son once before, now once more burnt bright. The Christmas season, with its thoughts of peace and family, put Lloyd into an unaccustomed revelatory mood when he wrote to David on 28 December:

You must forgive me if I growl, but I am just so unhappy without you I can't say. So long as one has what one wants close beside one, one never wants it so terribly as when it is far away and that is what has happened to me. Perhaps I didn't realize that nothing counts *at all* in my life except you – I b----y well do now and it's pretty unpleasant. I had better stop lest I get soppy or silly – and anyway it's life and that's all about it – but if you had spent the last two or three days – so alone as I never could have believed I could have felt alone – perhaps you could have understood – anyway that's that and it's off the chest. *Verb Sap.*[38]

The absence of his beloved son; the bitterly grim white winter; the coming to pass of his prophecies: all these were enough to induce a mood of maudlin melancholy at year's ending, but above and beyond these was something else – the longing for action. At the end of December he went to see some Yeomanry troops off to Palestine in his capacity as Honorary Colonel-in-Chief and he had

longed to be going with you all instead of creeping back to the women and the children. Somehow or other I am *determined* to have a more eventful war than seems decreed for me at present. Just how I don't know, but some way *Inshallah* – and you know I am no mean wire-puller for that sort of thing.[39]

To be cut off from the possibility of real action whilst the Empire he loved, the son he adored and the Christian civilization he served all passed through the Valley of the Shadow of Death was an ordeal almost beyond the bearing.

# 32

# PRIVATE WARS

Lloyd's mood set as hard as the winter ice and even when there was little news to give he would write to David, 'if only to pretend to myself for a few moments that I am not living solely in women's company – which is my main destiny these days'.[1] On 24 January 1940 he catalogued his laments:

> I am struggling along – left behind with the women, children and the dogs – attacked daily by Max in his papers – engaged in a mortal fight with the Ministry of Information, under the new and baleful influence of Sir John Reith – to preserve all your post-war jobs for you. I daresay I shall lose – though it is my duty to fight on, defeat will bring its blessings, for then I shall come out and join with Weygand and be with you all please God.[2]

With David he could let his feelings show in a way which had not been possible since the death of Sam Cockerell, but both Max Beaverbrook and Sir John Reith would have been surprised to know that Lord Lloyd was downhearted – he certainly gave neither of them any sign of it.

Beaverbrook's *Daily Express* had been running a campaign against the British Council since July 1939. Lloyd had written to a sympathetic MP, Beverley Baxter, in August of that year to thank him for trying to intercede with Beaverbrook: 'I cannot help liking Max, but I have never been able to understand what he is after, least of all in this particular regard.'[3] Field Marshal Goering reached for his revolver when he heard the word 'culture'; Lord Beaverbrook, who was smaller and slimmer, had much the same reaction except, living in a democracy, he was obliged to reach for his newspaper. The *Evening Standard* and the *Express* enjoyed themselves and gave their readers much harmless mirth by poking fun at 'highbrow' activities, such as teaching silly foreigners English (a pretty worthless activity if it enabled them to read the *Express*, it must be admitted) and showing them Shakespeare plays.[4]

At the beginning of 1940 these attacks became dangerous to the Council because they could be linked with attempts by the new Minister of Information, Sir John Reith, to assert his control over cultural propaganda. Lloyd told David on 21 January: 'Max B. is being a nuisance to the British Council. He and Reith are combined to destroy me. It will be a fine little fight with heavy odds against me but I'm not beat yet.'[5] Nor was he.

With Beaverbrook the velvet glove of persuasion was all that could be used. Lloyd wrote to him on 31 January asking him to come to lunch so that he could 'try to explain to you what the British Council are really doing'. He was, he wrote, sure that 'you would change your views'; if Beaverbrook still thought the Council's work 'superfluous' after a chat that was fair enough: 'But I believe it is doing far finer work for the country than perhaps you realise.'[6] A meeting duly took place and, for a while, the criticism was muted.

With Reith, however, the iron fist was scarcely concealed beneath the threadbare glove of official courtesies. Lloyd and Reith met on 31 January to discuss the sphere of operations of their respective institutions and on 6 February he wrote to say that he was awaiting Reith's views and trusted him to 'see that no decisions are taken in respect of the matters we discussed until you have placed me in possession of your views'.[7] The following day he received Reith's representations.

Reith relied on the fact that it was impossible to say 'where cultural activity ends and begins' to persuade Lloyd that he should concentrate on 'specifically cultural activities'. This would leave everything else to the Ministry of Information including lectures, visual propaganda, grants, the press and broadcasting; Reith suggested that it would help to avoid any problems if he was to serve on the Council's Executive and Finance Committees.[8]

Lloyd's reply has been well characterized by Lady Donaldson as 'a long letter in which the logic is so irreproachable and the willingness to compromise so small that it is both a landmark in the history of the British Empire and a curiosity in the art of letter writing'.[9] It was, in fact, almost completely unyielding. Lloyd did agree to let a representative of the Ministry of Information sit on his Executive Committee (but not the more important Finance Committee) and conceded that the Council had nothing to do with broadcasting, but that was the limit. Using the carefully selected analogy of the BBC, Lloyd told Reith that 'the political effect of propaganda increases in proportion to its detachment from political propaganda' and that like the BBC and *The Times*, it was important that the British Council was not perceived to be under official direction. He asserted the Council's right to control its own lectures and the distribution of books abroad. In short, he refused to give Reith any real concessions.[10]

The Ministry of Information was disappointed, but Lloyd got his way. Even had the matter been taken to Halifax it is doubtful whether the outcome would have been different for, as Lady Donaldson records, when the Treasury tried to enlist Halifax's help in persuading Lloyd to accept a cut in the Council's grant, he merely sighed and said: 'What's the use? He'll only say to me what he has already said to you.'[11] The episode well warrants Bernard Levin's words that:

> Lloyd was a man of such implacable determination to get his own way that he reduced the representatives of the Treasury itself to demoralised wrecks willing to give him money to shut up and leave them alone; some of his letters and memoranda display a ruthlessness which would have made Stalin blench, and some of the equivalent documents from those with whom he was dealing could easily be mistaken for the suicide-notes of a blackmail victim.[12]

Thus was the Council saved.

Lloyd's war was not limited to Whitehall and Fleet Street. At the end of 1939 he stepped into the forefront of the propaganda effort in his own right with the publication of an official statement of why Britain was at war, entitled *The British Case*.

In November 1938 Lloyd had delivered the Walker Trust lecture at the University of St Andrews on the theme of 'Leadership in Democracy'. His main theme was what he took to be the lesson of the Baldwin era, namely that 'leadership . . . is not the art of becoming and remaining a leader, but the art of leading'.[13] He reproached democratic leaders for

> the neglect of the first principle of leadership, which is to set before a people clearly the end which they should seek, and to show how these ends are shaped and determined by the requirements of Christian morality. We are still, I believe, a Christian people, and, if we are, no policy not rooted in the principles of Christianity can energize our wills and hearts to effective action.[14]

In the retreat from the 'task of building up a Christian civilization in Africa and Asia' and in the 'facile and foolish assumption that any other civilization is likely to be just as good', he saw the consequences of this lack of leadership. Then, he had said that: 'For lack of courage and candour we have been brought to the edge of catastrophe. We can be saved only by leadership. In saving ourselves we can surely save the world';[15] now he sought to give that lead in *The British Case*.

In September 1939 after the Nazi–Soviet pact Lloyd had written to Count Grandi that 'what the Nazis have lost in ideology, we have a thousand times gained, for the war is now a clear issue of Christianity against that which opposes it'.[16] In *The British Case* he expanded on this theme. Once more his name and Edward Wood's appeared on the title page of the same book, as the Foreign Secretary gave it the Government's imprimatur. Lloyd's argument was straightforward and powerful: the modern nation state guaranteed the 'survival of individual liberty' which was 'one of the rocks upon which our Christian civilization is founded':

> Ours is the first free civilization, and it became free because Christ asserted not the dignity of some men, but of all, and the capacity and duty of all to win salvation. Man redeemed by Christ could never again be enslaved to man.[17]

Thus it was that Hitler's actions in Poland were 'a gesture of insolent defiance to the Christian tradition of Europe'; it was for this civilization that Britain and France were fighting.[18]

Echoes of this theme resounded in Churchill's great speeches during the summer and it was picked up elsewhere;[19] by the time it was no longer true, that is after June 1941, Lloyd was beyond protesting. To him the war was and remained a crusade for Christian civilization and its chief instrument, the British Empire.

Lloyd told his son on 24 January 1940 that:

> *The British Case* is having an *immense* sale: it has been translated into Spanish, Italian, Yugoslav, Bulgarian and Roumanian and a special American edition appears tomorrow. It has yesterday been adopted as a text-book in the UK. I enclose a circular for the clergy and other irreconcilables: pacifists, pietists, plutocrats, priests, pansies and pessimists.[20]

As though such tasks were not enough of a contribution to the war effort, he took on the presidency of the Anglo–Turkish relief fund in January and also pressed for the construction of a mosque in London which would help Britain's cause in the Islamic world. But all this bustle and expenditure of energy exacted its price, just as it served as a barrier against a fundamental unhappiness.

In mid January, urged on by Blanche's worries about his continual ill-health, he had consulted a heart specialist who had pronounced that his 'cardiogram could not be beaten by any youth of twenty' and added:

> 'From what I know of you Lord Lloyd I know you wouldn't take a rest if I

told you to, but I am glad to tell you that you do not really need a rest – at any rate not until the war is over. Perhaps a little slow-down then might be advisable.' This cruel man then deprived me of five good guineas, wished me a good night – which it wasn't – it was bloody, bad [*sic*] me urbanely to 'mind the step in the dark' and closes the door on me in the street. So much for the sympathy one gets from one's fellow kind. That all comes from taking the advice of women.[21]

In his biography of Eden, Robert Rhodes James provided us with some examples of medical incompetence affecting political careers; this consultation may be added to the list.

The freezing winter lowered Lloyd's spirits and the fight against Reith and the Treasury was carried on with a depleted staff and constant ill-health:

> But by double doses of phensic and constant Turkish baths I have managed to get to the Office and do my daily dozen hours so far without one day's break. . . . I don't really see how I could go to bed in present conditions. I got one Saturday off last week and went flying and was pleased to find that my hand was not out and could still pilot a Blenheim.[22]

In late February he went for a flight over enemy territory – an extraordinary way for an overworked man of sixty to spend his few leisure hours. But on his way back to London from Manston there was an alarming occurrence:

> My arm suddenly swelled violently from wrist to shoulder and I could scarcely drive the car back. I think I scraped it getting out of a machine though I didn't notice it at the time – anyway it got poisoned.

The doctor warned him that he might lose the arm if the poison spread.[23] It later transpired that vibrations in the bomber might have started the poison spreading, and for weeks after he had to keep the arm in a sling and stay indoors.[24] He would have done well to have heeded the warning; instead he relied on 'phensic plus Turkish baths and a modicum of obstinacy' to pull him through.[25]

To these strains were added those imposed by financial problems; the fears expressed in 1939 had come to pass. Lloyd told David at the beginning of January 1940 that after examining their financial position, 'I don't see how we are going to make both ends meet':

> It isn't an easy job I have – to look after your mother – to run Clouds Hill, plus the flat, the Council, the Navy League, six hospitals in wartime – the Squadron – direct six large City companies and do odd jobs of many a kind . . . we are getting right up to the limit and I can't stand much more.[26]

A demand from the Inland Revenue for taxes which amounted to 'slightly more than my total income for the year' created understandable gloom. He wrote to David from Clouds Hill on 21 January:

> I went out a walk by myself this afternoon in the snow through the wood – across Cuckoo Park this afternoon and schemed and planned how I could contrive to manage so that you could live here and have enough money to do so. I think so much of that always.[27]

He decided that it would be necessary to close down Clouds Hill 'and just exist in the flat in the hopes of conserving some money so that eventually you will be able to keep Clouds Hill to live in quietly'.[28] Lloyd was glad to make such sacrifices for the son whose absence he never ceased to lament. But it was seldom that he let himself go in the way he had in late December and he turned away the threat of tears in typical fashion: 'Oh David I miss you quite a bit and London's grim without you – But I've always your bills to pay so why be downhearted.'[29] There were times when David's tardiness in answering his letters caused him to complain – but even then he would confess that the 'growls' were 'to disguise my loneliness and my bleak sense of frustration in being unable to play a part in this great and mortal issue'.[30]

Ronald Storrs, who visited Clouds Hill in early April, recorded in his diary that Lloyd was

> more restless than ever, and it is now no longer a question of whether one will get through a conversation, a topic, even sentences are in doubt because of telegrams, calls and springing asides for every conceivable object.

It was only after dinner that he would slow down and then he treated Storrs to a disquisition on the political situation:

> Amusing talk on Baldwin, who he continues to think an odious hypocrite responsible for most of our troubles. Halifax good company. Neville too shy to be communicative, rather likes K. Wood who is to arbitrate between G. and Reith on the question of the British Council. Interesting on luncheon with Beaver from whom G. gathered that G. nearly got Information himself. Tyrrell now 73 but is brilliant, has appealed to G. to forget the past in the interests of this war and to down the early peace group, apparently run by H. Wilson, Simon, Hoare and Beaverbrook, all of whom would make terms tomorrow if only Hitler could be got out – even with Göring, and believes that so would NC though he will not speak of it now because of his loathing for Hitler. For all George's extremism I do agree with him there.[31]

By the time Storrs rose on Monday morning his host had already departed for London.

On top of all the other causes for dissatisfaction came the biting anguish of exile from power at this moment of supreme trial. A slight government reshuffle in April was characterized by him as nothing more than 'a sort of musical chairs of the old stuff'; it was, he prophesied, 'the beginning of the downfall of the Government'.[32]

The horizon was not altogether without streaks of pink, even if they were so few and far between that they hardly seemed to herald the dawn. The prospect of a British Council tour of the Middle East, carrying as it did the promise of seeing not only his favourite part of the world again, but also David (who was in Palestine), cheered him up, as did a trip over to Paris at Easter when he saw the French Colonial Minister, Georges Mandel, whose fighting spirit had reminded him of Clemenceau. And then came an offer of employment.

On 19 April Lloyd went to see Halifax at the latter's request and was offered the post of Ambassador to Spain. The French had recently sent Marshal Pétain as Special Ambassador to Franco and it was thought that the British ought to follow suit. Lloyd turned the post down:

> If Spain was imminently likely to be coming into the war, and I had that specialist knowledge of Spain which, as Ambassador, I could use better than anyone else to keep her out of it, I would gladly have accepted . . . to go right out of the conflict would be very painful to me and I know I should eat my heart out on the San Sebastian beaches in the summer, especially if the bombs were raining down in this country.[33]

The outbreak of the Norway campaign put back Lloyd's travelling plans. Despite the ebb and flow of battle which turned against the British, he told David not to worry:

> We are going to win this war, please God, in spite of our leaders – Sir Horace Quisling, Sir Samuel Hacha or Sir John Seyss-Inquahardt [sic]. We shall win it because of the splendour of our people at home and overseas. I cry with Kipling 'The people, Lord, the people are good enough for me.'

It was only a grim satisfaction to him that Reith finally surrendered his claims over the Council at this time: 'I want to fight the Germans not our own departments.'[34]

The failure of the campaign brought debates in both Houses of Parliament. Lloyd feared that the 'subservience' of the Conservative Party would leave Chamberlain to wreak fresh havoc, but the course of the debate in the Commons prompted him to tell David, even before it had ended, that Chamberlain would fall and that a 'real National Government' under Churchill would replace him; he was right.[35]

Churchill became Prime Minister on 10 May and immediately

began the process of Cabinet making. In his first draft list he had Lloyd's name against the office of Colonial Secretary;[36] and it was this office which Lloyd accepted on 11 May. 'At last', he wrote, 'the real war has begun.'[37]

# 33

# TRIUMPH

One of Lloyd's first actions was to write to the new Prime Minister:

> I feel I have never thanked you properly for what you have done for me over this Office but I do want you to know how touched I was at what you said the other day and for your 'long memory'! I won't say any more so long as you understand.
> Yours,
> George L.[1]

Storrs recorded that Blanche was 'enchanted' and that 'it is indeed a wonderful return for George after these many years in the wilderness';[2] indeed it was.

To sit in the office which had once been occupied by Joseph Chamberlain was fulfilment enough for even Lloyd's ambition. He told David on 19 May that he had been

> so sorry to leave the Council that I arranged with Edward Halifax that its chairmanship should revert to me at the end of the war if I desired to reoccupy it – but I was glad to be offered a great office of State at a moment of supreme crisis in which I gained an opportunity of playing a definite part in the conduct of the war instead of the long-range work of the Council. It has been a job taking over in the critical hours we are now passing through and I only hope I shall last the course.

The hours were indeed critical, with the British Expeditionary Force (BEF) and the French army giving way beneath the hammer-blows of the Nazi onslaught; yet as Lloyd noted:

> The public is taking this terrific issue entirely calmly: there is of course a sort of hush all over everything – and a look of strain on everyone's faces: gaiety has gone – money there is none – but even so there is quiet and a steady calmness of confidence – for we know if not the worst, we know we are getting through the worst at last.[3]

It soon became apparent that there was worse in store as the Germans steadily advanced:

> These days are almost agonising in their breathless tension and grave anxiety. If ever we had our backs to the wall we have now, and the greatest issue in all history hangs in the balance these next three or four days. If we fail then we are bare to invasion for which we are making preparations day and night. . . . This is the result of ten years of Baldwinism and of Geneva. But in spite of all we shall fight on and as there is a God in Heaven there is in my heart if not peace, a certain tranquillity and serenity which keeps me going.

The Dutch Colonial Minister had told him that some of his countrymen had committed suicide rather than fall into the hands of the Nazis:

> They were right. I don't suppose I shall stand much chance if the Nazis invade. I hope I am on their black list: and should feel dishonoured if I were not! Meanwhile the issue is in God's hands and I am sure that the delivery and victory will come.[4]

Never had simple Faith been more needed.

Lloyd described his life in a letter to David on 22 May:

> I am hard at work clearing up the military situation in the Colonies – Palestine, East and West Africa, West Indies and so on. If only I had had this job a year ago I could have done *so* much, but as it is all I can do is only my best. One works from daylight to dusk without respite of any sort day in and day out, Saturdays and Sundays alike – the only change from day to day being a plus or minus one in a constant factor of anxiety and heavy responsibility. If only I could see you for a few hours it would be Heaven but that, my dear, must just wait for a little mustn't it till duty is done. (Rather smacks of Lady B. Powell in its smugness! but I can't rewrite – too tired.) I think of you more than you can guess and all the time. I like to comfort myself with a pride that we have been chosen out of all time and all the world to confront this hateful evil – and in God's good way and time we shall if we would be valiant 'gainst all disaster.[5]

Soon there was only Providence left in which hope could be reasonably reposed. On 18 May the Germans opened a fifty-mile gap in the French line and by 24 May French units and what was left of the BEF were trapped at Dunkirk; experts pronounced that the 'greatest military disaster' in British history was at hand. On 26 May the evacuation from the beaches began and Britain held its breath. Lloyd wrote on 27 May:

> All the news this morning is *very* bad. . . . But so long as we have command of the sea we cannot, under Providence, be beaten and we shall go on – alone if necessary – till we win. The Germans are suffering terribly and their morale in spite of their successes is bad. But my God

243

hanging is too good for the Nevilles and Baldwins of the past. Even to you I can't write of what I have learnt since taking office. But it's up to each of us to show we can take it and that we aren't depressed and are up on our feet for the next round – and as many as the Hun can stand.[6]

As the evacuations from the beaches proceeded the threat of invasion loomed. On 30 May Lloyd wrote:

We are busy preparing for invasion here, which is, I think, immediately impending. Times are grim but hearts are high. If Italy comes in as I expect, very shortly, you may get a bit busier in Palestine.[7]

By the end of the week it was clear that 'a terrible disaster' had been 'almost turned into triumph by the glorious performance of all three arms working in conjunction. The RAF have been superb, clawing down out of the sky five to one German machines.' Already, though, the death toll among the young men he knew was terrible, and Lloyd told David that his friends would be killed 'just as mine were killed off in the last war. That is what we can never forgive the Hun for': 'But we shall pull out all yet please God. The BEF withdrawal and its manner have heartened us all up – God, St George and St Michael all getting very busy on our side I feel sure.'[8]

Churchill, well aware that 'wars are not won by evacuations', nevertheless rallied the nation, his speeches now touching the soul of the British people as they prepared for the greatest ordeal in their history. On 5 June the Germans launched their attack on what remained of the French army; for the Allies the time of trial had come.

Throughout the crisis Lloyd kept David informed. On 9 June he wrote, not without prescience, that:

We are in the middle of what may prove to be the decisive battle of the war – at least if we hold the Germans in this battle I don't think she can win the war: if the French crack then we may have to go on alone and I think we can still win, though we shall have a bad time in these islands. At last however the country is taking it seriously and we are beginning to look like an armed camp. . . . The peaceful countryside looks more like the Balkans than I thought possible. There is going to be very short shrift for some of our elder statesmen I fancy: a returning army has a lot to say and the evacuated BEF are anxious to know the names of the politicians who sent them to fight in France without tanks and with negligible equipment.[9]

On 7 June Halifax suggested to Lloyd that he might go over to Paris to confer with his opposite number Mandel, a suggestion backed by Corbin 'on the grounds of your personal acquaintance with Weygand'.[10] On 10 June he set off for Paris.

The journey was an eventful one. None of the aerodromes near Paris could be used because of German bombing and when he did get there it was to be told by the British Ambassador that he was about to evacuate the Embassy. Lloyd saw Reynaud and Mandel who were 'solid and firm', but the new French Commander-in-Chief, Weygand, 'had completely crumpled up and was just a wizened old man entirely broken'.[11] It was, he later told David, 'a pathetic sight, and I hope I never see him again'.[12] Lloyd went to Orleans to meet his aeroplane but when he got there found that the place was deserted. Meeting 'two exhausted British Tommies', Lloyd managed to find them and himself lodgings for the night at a French farmhouse. It was 'with much difficulty and one forced landing in a field' that he made it back to England the following day.

The experience had not been one to breed hope, but he adjured David to keep 'a firm upper lip':

> The work and anxiety here is almost overwhelming – up half the night and all day – one cannot look far ahead or conjecture even when we shall next meet. Our bombing ordeal and invasion must now begin very soon and you may be sure we shall render good account of ourselves. God willing they will not be able to land parties large enough to be formidable.[13]

It was some relief to him to find one Frenchman whose firmness matched his own. The Under-Secretary for War in the Reynaud Government, Brigadier-General Charles de Gaulle, asked for permission to broadcast on 18 June and Lloyd was among those who backed his request. The day after what was to become an historic speech and, after Churchill's own 'Finest Hour' oration, Lloyd again set off for France, this time at the request of the Cabinet. His mission had a twofold purpose: to try to persuade the presidents of the two Chambers and President Lebrun to depart for Africa 'so that a constitutional government could be kept in being even after France was overrun'; he also 'had to use my fullest exertions to prevent them from handing over the fleet'.

The flight was even more hazardous than his last one. From the Sunderland flying-boat he could see

> Brest burning in the distance and also – a dramatic sight – a British cargo boat on fire. At Bissarousse, where we landed on the lake, Colyer the air attaché was there to meet us and we drove forty miles into Bordeaux.

All evening and all night 'till about one in the morning' Lloyd 'toiled',

> with old Lebrun first, the President, who was tearful as usual and quite

futile, then with Pétain who is a vain *ramolli* and dangerously ga-ga. . . . Council of Ministers after Council of Ministers was held, but eventually I got agreement as to the move to Africa and also most definite undertakings as regards the fleet. At one in the morning they told me that formal ratification would take place at a meeting of Ministers at 9 a.m. I then, weary but triumphant, went up the street to my hotel to rejoin the Ambassador when the Huns started an air raid, and for two and a quarter hours they pounded us. The newspapers said they dropped 150 bombs. I do not think it was as many as that, but quite enough.

The Germans little realized, he thought, 'how much it would have strengthened France if they had succeeded in bombing both old Brown [Lebrun] and Pétain!':

While the raid was going on the Ambassador and I sat drafting telegrams for the first three-quarters of an hour, but when severe crumps shook the house close by I told him that my sense of composition was failing and we went and sat well away from the window in a passage. After an hour it got worse, and the Manager of the hotel insisted we should go down to the cellar, but the proximity of a crowd of semi-clad Frenchmen plus a dog that kept snapping at my bare legs seemed to me worse than death, and I went back to my passage till about four in the morning, when the Huns disappeared.

Lloyd went to the Council of Ministers at 9.30 a.m. where the decisions of the previous night were ratified and he was told that the Government was leaving for Africa that afternoon. Lloyd then returned to England where he told Halifax and Churchill of his achievement. But the following morning came the news that 'old Brown and Pétain had ratted again'.[14] Campbell telegraphed from Bordeaux with a message from Herriot, President of the Chamber of Deputies, asking that Lloyd should destroy a letter which he had given to him, but he told Halifax:

This letter signed by the Presidents of the Two Chambers is important and as they gave it to me personally I am not going to destroy it. The pencilled signature is Herriot's who wrote in Jeanneny's name in his presence. Would you return it?[15]

According to David Lloyd, his father also brought back a document signed by Admiral Darlan guaranteeing the safety of the French fleet; he refused to give up the paper, telling David that he had put it in a safe place: but when David returned to England no trace could be found of it.

On 21 June the French Government, headed by the aged Marshal Pétain, surrendered to the Germans. Britain stood alone. Hitler is said to have told General Jodl: 'The British have lost the war, but they don't know it. One must give them time and they will come round.' But the dictator had made the first of the series of misjudgements which were to bring the Thousand Year Reich to a premature end: the British were by no means ready to surrender.

The decks were being cleared for action. As Colonial Secretary, Lloyd was involved in the evacuation of thousands of British children. He did not see this as a panic measure: 'We can't fight here cluttered up with women and children. If we could get the women away it would be better still.'[16] At Offley the lane down to Clouds Hill was guarded by a block-house – not that Lloyd had much time for going down there. When he did get away at the end of June, he was summoned back to London within the hour. But even that small taste of nature was enough to point up the contrast between the world of nature and the world of evil man:

> The almost ethereal beauty of this Month of May [*sic*] almost mocks one. Day after day of cloudless sunshine – the spring sparkle in the air, the cuckoo calling, the May smell heavy in the air, the woods blue with blue-bells; the hedges shrill green, the grass tall and lush, the village church bells pealing, the beeches so cool, so tall and gracious; the big sycamore at the end of the terrace with its red trunk flushed with the sunlight – and all, and all and you not here and the gnawing anxiety that lies like lead on your tummy when you awake every day – every day.[17]

It was all too much for Blanche whose nerves again began to give way. The fact that financial necessity was going to force them to let Clouds Hill for the winter did not help her; but there was no aid that Lloyd could bring her. In mid July he wrote to David:

> You see if nations – or people – forget and forsake God, He will bring them back to Him by easy methods if they avail, if not by suffering and hardship. There is indeed no other explanation of the sacrament of suffering. But everyone who walks that road does in fact learn that strangely enough it does lead us to Him. We may forsake Him when things get better for we are clay and clay is frail and forgetful but it still remains that the *via Dolorosa* led to Calvary and Calvary to Christ. That is to me . . . an immense consolation, and I pray it may be so for you.[18]

This was an attitude which could have led to a quietist acceptance of what Fate had to bring, but in Lloyd it provided the foundation from which to fight back against Evil in the name of Good.

The great onrush and relentless pressure of events had dominated the first month of Churchill's administration, but there had already been the first mutterings of dissatisfaction from junior ministers. On 17 June Amery, Harold Macmillan, Bob Boothby and Lloyd discussed what 'practical changes' were needed 'in our system of government'. After typing out a memorandum for Churchill, Amery went round to see Lloyd at the Colonial Office, who advised him against doing anything that night. At Cabinet the following day Churchill made it plain that he would brook no criticism and he told Amery afterwards that Chamberlain had told him that 'it was all an intrigue by George Lloyd and myself to get the Cabinet changed'; Amery 'protested, pointing out that Lloyd at any rate had not discussed these matters with others'.[19] There were no changes and, for the moment at least, Churchill was beyond criticism.

Along with the high drama, summer brought also an echo of an old crisis as it fell to Lloyd to play a part in the Windsor saga. At the end of June Churchill floated the suggestion that the Duke of Windsor should be despatched to govern the Bahamas.[20] As Lloyd told Storrs on 14 July, the idea had come not from Churchill but from the King in order 'to keep him at all costs out of England': 'George never thought that it would come to him to submit to His Majesty a proposal for appointing his late sovereign to work under himself in a relatively small Governorship.'[21] Not everyone welcomed this novel way of disposing of the problem caused by the Windsors. Queen Elizabeth, who felt very strongly that the Duchess was absolutely unfitted to the role of Governor's wife, urged upon Lloyd reasons both moral and practical why the appointment should not be made, whilst Lloyd himself, as he told David, 'very much disliked the Bahamas appointment'.[22] But he gave in to pressure 'from above' and thought it was 'a better alternative than having them both home'.

The Duke wrote a charming letter on 12 July, telling Lloyd that 'I am glad that, by good fortune, my immediate political chief should happen to be an old friend'. He went on to say that although the role of 'governor of a small British colony is . . . a novel one', the fact that 'Winston considers it [one] . . . in which I can serve the Empire' made him take up his 'duties with enthusiasm'. In spite of such sentiments, Lloyd thought that trouble lay ahead; in this he was correct.

The Duke's desire to travel to his post via New York was unacceptable to the Foreign Office. Lloyd saw no reason for vetoing the idea, but, like Churchill, accepted a ruling from on high that the Duke should go straight to the Bahamas.[23] Lloyd was also inclined to agree to the Duke's request to take with him two man-servants of military age, but this time it was Churchill who put a spoke in the wheel. Lloyd reported to Churchill that the King's line was that his brother 'should do what he is told';[24] which is what happened.

But even when he was safely out of the way, the Duke still caused problems. At the end of September the British Ambassador in Washington, Lord Lothian, suggested that he might ask Roosevelt about the possibility of a visit from the Duke. Lloyd, having just 'got the Duke, as I thought, clamped down securely in the Bahamas', scotched Lothian's idea.[25]

If troublesome, the Windsors were amongst the least of Lloyd's problems as Colonial Secretary. The circumstances in which he had reached his office precluded the chance of being able to implement any far-reaching reforms – survival would be achievement enough; but he was not wanting in ideas for more positive action. The collapse of France caused enormous problems for Britain, particularly as regards the future of the French North and West African Colonies, but as Lloyd told David on 16 July:

> Our relations with the French West African Colonies are going pretty well, but I am not so happy about Morocco, where Noguès went wrong from the start. He was always a political soldier and I never had much hope of him. If only General Catroux, who used to be Governor of Marrakesh, had been in Noguès' place, all would have been well. Catroux is now Governor of Indo-China and is busy making faces at the Pétain Government at long range: he will not be easily dispossessed provided the Army of Indo-China and the Navy stand by. Jibouti is standing out well so far. New Caledonia and Madagascar and the island of Réunion and all the smaller overseas possessions are solid with us to a man.[26]

He provided de Gaulle with help to enable him to rally the Cameroons in late August[27] and looked round for other areas where he could take the offensive.

In early August Lloyd had a long conversation with his former chief in Egypt, Sir Reginald Wingate, and together they drew up a conspectus of the situation. Egypt and the Sudan were clearly threatened with invasion from both Libya and Abyssinia once the rainy season was over; Jibouti and Port Sudan should have their defences strengthened and steps should be taken to rally the loyalty of the Sudanese tribes. Wingate wanted the whole civil and military effort in the Middle East co-ordinated and thought that Lloyd should do it. With French prestige having collapsed it was essential for the British to take action against the Italians to ensure that they did not succeed to the French predominance in the region.[28]

Given this concern with offensive action, it was natural that Lloyd should have been in on the small group of ministers which discussed the setting up of the Special Operations Executive (SOE) at the beginning of July. It was a sign of the altered aspect of the times that he should have supported the Socialist Hugh Dalton in proposing a campaign of 'ungentlemanly warfare' and, when Halifax demurred, should have turned on him and said: 'You should never be consulted because you would never consent to anything; you will never make a gangster.'[29]

Although Lloyd had formally given up the British Council, he kept more than a watching brief over its affairs, and when it seemed at the end of July as though the new Minister of Information, Duff Cooper, was going to renew Reith's efforts to absorb it into the Ministry of Information, Lloyd wrote to Halifax:

> With your help we warded off the attack from his predecessor, and I hope shall have no difficulty doing it in this case. I gather it is Max Beaverbrook behind him. I have already successfully mobilized Attlee, [Henry] Snell and [Arthur] Greenwood and I know Archie [Sinclair] will stand behind us.[30]

In this particular branch of ungentlemanly warfare he was again successful.

It was upon such matters that his mind was abstracted from the ever-present danger of invasion and the bombing of London. But even when the bombing got worse he refused to leave the office; he had not come to a position of power at a time of trial to be deterred by anything; in that spirit lay the seeds of triumph.

# 34

# TRAGEDY

When his Government had been formed Churchill had said it was 'the most broad-based that Britain has ever known. It extends from Lord Lloyd of Dolobran to Ellen Wilkinson';[1] Miss Wilkinson no doubt brought her left-wing views to her office at the Ministry of Pensions and Lloyd certainly brought his imperialist faith to the Colonial Office.

As Secretary of State for India, Amery quickly found that Lloyd had abated nothing of his old opinions on India. On 22 July he 'weighed in with a Cabinet paper . . . reasserting in effect the view that any and every form of self-government for India is a mistake'.[2] Lloyd kept a wary eye on Amery and did not hesitate to invoke Churchill's aid when necessary, even, in December, going so far as to advocate an 'attack' without 'any reservations' on the Congress Party.[3]

On India Lloyd could count on Churchill's support; the same was not true on the Palestine question. Right from the start he had anticipated trouble, telling David on 19 May: 'I find myself in a Government which is almost entirely pro-Zionist and anti-Arab, so I may have a good many difficulties ahead of me';[4] he had. Although he was 'pro-Arab', as, given his past experience he was bound to be, Lloyd was not anti-Jewish. He supported Chaim Weizmann's request to Churchill to be allowed to mobilize more Jewish soldiers for inclusion in Jewish units in the British army. However, the Zionists were not satisfied, seeking as they did the creation of a Jewish Division. The leading Zionist and eminent historian, Lewis Namier, saw Lloyd on 7 January 1941 to discuss the matter; they reached no conclusion and their conversation broadened out to wider matters. Namier recorded:

At one point he started his usual song about all the Cabinet being Zionists. Winston from time to time says to him – here he imitated Winston's voice – 'What are you doing to my Jews?' The Prime Minister was a Zionist, his own Private Secretary was a Zionist: here I interrupted 'and poor you are sandwiched between them; but you know it is the stuff in the middle which determines the taste and flavour of the sandwich'.[5]

Namier referred to the fact that it was only now, at the moment of supreme crisis, that Lloyd, Amery and Churchill, 'Kipling Imperialists', had been 'called in to bring back to us the creed of an older generation'; Lloyd said he was 'not ashamed' of such a description.

Despite, or perhaps because of, the firmness of his views, the Zionists admired him. Namier wrote that:

> Had it fallen to him to write his own text on a new page he would not have tried by subterfuges to evade commitments and obligations, but would by an act and effort of true statesmanship have endeavoured to realise the national aspirations of Jews and Arabs.[6]

Many years later David Lloyd received an unexpected invitation from David Ben-Gurion to have tea with him at Claridge's. When he arrived his host said:

> 'I expect you wonder why I asked to see you.' I replied that I did and he said: 'Well you may well be surprised since [your father] had the reputation of being an Arabist and indeed it was a curious confrontation. There he was an aristocrat whilst I was a peasant. There he was a Tory whilst I was a Socialist. Yet we became great friends and I came to the conclusion that he was the only British politician who really understood the Palestine problem. And because of my friendship with him, I wanted to meet his son.'[7]

But Lloyd's most pressing interest was in the development of the Colonies: 'that strange agglomeration of willing peoples that we misname the British Empire'. At a meeting of Colonial Service cadets at the Colonial Office on 25 June he exhorted his listeners not to think that being sent out to the Colonies was some sort of 'second-line' service; their work would be vital to the continuation of the Empire and:

> When all is said and done, you are going out to a grand life. I can speak with some experience, having been nearly thirty years overseas and I have regretted not a day of those years. Think of the opportunity. In what other task can you have so much power so early? You can at twenty-five be the father of your people – you can drive the road, bridge the river and water the desert: you can be the arm of justice and the hand of mercy to millions. You can, in fact, serve England. You can indeed, in this vital moment, serve something that is greater than England itself. You can serve and secure the cause of Christian civilisation.[8]

Lloyd enthusiastically pushed through the Colonial Development and Welfare Act of 1940 which had been originated by his predecessor,

Malcolm MacDonald; his one regret was that, because he had only just come into office, he had accepted the figure of £5 million a year from the Treasury to be spent on development; he would have liked much more.[9]

Given his views on the Empire Lloyd did not look with favour upon the proposals emanating from Churchill and the Foreign Office at the end of the year to hand over leases on some of the British Caribbean Colonies in return for fifty American destroyers. Churchill, of course, saw this as a way of involving the Americans in Britain's struggle; whilst not blind to this, Lloyd thought that Churchill was far too generous towards the Americans – as indeed he was. He prepared a paper for the Cabinet in December which annoyed the diplomats greatly:

> I think this paper is ill-conceived and petulant . . . the real trouble is that
> . . . Lord Lloyd puts the whole basis of our relations with the United
> States in the West Indies on the wrong basis. It is clear that to him any
> form of co-operation with the US in this area is anathema, for he fears
> that it will inevitably lead to a derogation, if not the entire relinquishing
> by us of British sovereignty.[10]

He was, once more, prescient. Lloyd took the view that the Americans would respect the British more if they stood up for their rights, and he was preparing to take the matter up in Cabinet when other things intervened.

At the beginning of September, on orders from Churchill, all senior Cabinet Ministers went away for a week's rest; this Lloyd badly needed. He went up to Clouds Hill. The break did him good and he began to regret that he had allowed Blanche to talk him into letting the house for the winter, partly because he thought it would have been better for her, in her highly nervous state, to remain in the country, and partly because, as he told David:

> I shall terribly miss the peace of this place for to get away into
> comparative quiet for a few hours *is* very refreshing but I don't suppose
> in these days I would get away much.[11]

Back in London in mid September things were becoming grim and he was indeed to miss the haven of Clouds Hill. Ceaseless air raids day and night made the Morpeth Mansions flat unsafe to spend the night in and so:

> I am [he told David] sleeping on a bed in my office and when the third
> warning comes meaning 'planes immediately overhead' I go out into the
> passage which is fairly safe except for a direct hit, or, if it goes on very

long, to the underground shelter. But I don't go there if I can help it for it's so crowded.[12]

Although he did not often go to the shelter himself, he ensured that his staff had a good canteen and a radio there, and he took care to see that they all managed to get either the morning or the afternoon off; he, of course, worked all day.

On 21 September Lloyd returned from dinner to work late to find that an incendiary bomb had hit the roof above his room. He managed to put out the fire 'but the smell was horrible'.[13] Neither this, nor the bombing, nor the advent of his sixty-second birthday on 19 September, prevented him from working a sixteen-hour day. He described his days thus:

> Every morning I get up, in my underground room in the co at 6.30 am., dress, walk down Whitehall into Victoria Street to the flat; shave, bath and breakfast there and drive back to the Office here at 9 am. Cabinet most mornings from 11.30 till lunch. Although I am not a member of the War Cabinet, co affairs touch so many issues that I am called in most days. There is generally a lull in the noise of the *blitzkrieg* about 6 pm till 9 so one goes out to dine – generally at the Club – and returns to the Office about 8.30 pm. – work, bed about 11.30 – *da capo*.[14]

There were particularly heavy raids in early and mid October; he reported to David on 9 October:

> The Huns have been pretty fresh lately. My room at the H. of Lords is completely wrecked and . . . the flat is uninhabitable. Bond Street is in rather a mess and the Council's film section in Savile Row is in ruins. But there's lots more houses and we are all feeling fine. One goes out to the Club to dine in a tin hat with all London's guns blazing away – quite makes you feel at the front. Indeed in the Admiralty if anyone applies to go to sea he gets a white feather given him![15]

On 14 October, as he was getting into the car to go to dinner, 'shrapnel and H[igh] E[xplosives] rained down', and he 'beat a hasty retreat indoors'. Immediately afterwards four bombs came down which 'shook us up a good deal' and the windows in the private secretary's room were all broken:

> One of my private secretaries got pitched onto the floor and under his writing table – the room and passages are full of soot and mess. My room shook a good deal but no damage. I gather the bombs fell one in the Treasury just twenty yards from us, another on Whitehall by the FO steps. Since then someone says the Carlton Club and Travellers have both been hit. It is quiet again so I thought I would write you this line from 'somewhere near the front'! The Hun is shooting better than he did and these misty nights favour him. We really spend a large proportion of

the twenty-four hours under fire these days.[16]

The following night, 15 October, Lloyd had a very narrow escape. He went round to the BBC to broadcast on the Colonies and, as the blitz got really bad after 7.30 p.m., arrived early to have a glass of sherry with the Chairman in his room on the third floor. Lloyd asked if he thought the room was safe. He said it was, and they had just got to the floor below when 'we got a direct hit which wrecked the room we had just left'. As it was a delayed action fuse Lloyd tried to get people out of the building. He went to the floor below to shepherd some secretaries out and was standing by the lift when the bomb exploded:

> The ceiling above us came in but I was standing by the wall and only got immersed in plaster dust and debris and was none the worse . . . the top storey then started burning gaily but someone rushed up and snatched me off to do my broadcast in a reserve room in the basement. I loosed it off looking more like a dustman than a respectable sexagenarian!

He arrived back at the Colonial Office to find the big glass windows of his room smashed by bomb damage and he sat 'in a coat waiting till the plaster board can be got to keep the cold out', writing to David.[17]

Somehow he kept on working and kept his spirit; to those who have never suffered such an ordeal his courage and that of the British people is a matter for wonder and humble admiration. To his sister Milly, who had written to wish him a happy birthday, he replied:

> Yes, life is brisk and noisy here – most of my windows are blown out and I have had one or two very narrow shaves. But who hasn't these days for we are all in the front line.

As for the unwelcome birthday, he commented:

> How old we are all getting, but yet we are very young I think for our ages. At sixty Granny was a really old, and not very active old lady – whilst you and I fly, drive motors and live like the youngsters. We have all that to be very thankful for.[18]

But there was a price to be paid for living 'like the youngsters'.

On 22 November Lloyd told David that he had had 'a bad go of ptomaine poisoning from eating some tinned food, which has attacked all my joints so that I have been much crippled'. The fact that he had had the trouble for a month should have caused him to reflect more than he did upon the diagnoses of his various doctors; as it was he just complained that none of them 'seems to know anything about it except how to take constant and exaggerated fees'.[19]

The illness refused to go away, but Lloyd worked on. He looked forward to early January when Clouds Hill would again be available so that:

At any rate once a fortnight or so I shall, if the going is good, get a Sunday down there in the country. I shall be all the more glad of it as I have had rather an uphill two months – grilling work, plenty of anxiety, and this poisoning in my knees and wrists as well to cope with. If I could get a week's rest I think I should cure up. The doctors do not think there is much chance unless I do, and until certain questions get a good deal straighter than they are at present there is no chance of my taking that week off.[20]

Lloyd was much exercised over the Cabinet reshuffle which was in the offing. The previous one had been in November after Chamberlain's death. He had told David then: 'I still want to go to India but fear I never shall – Yet it might be.'[21] He did not go, but when the Ambassador in Washington, Lord Lothian, died in December, there was talk that Lloyd might succeed him.[22] However, Churchill sent Halifax; this created a vacancy as leader of the House of Lords.

On 3 January 1941 Lloyd saw Churchill and was told that he proposed to appoint Lord Cranborne to the post; in his 'anxiety to fall in with any arrangement you wished', Lloyd did not realize 'until afterwards the full implications as regards myself':

I cannot conceal from myself that it must be damaging to my position in the eyes of the public that someone so much younger than I, who has only a comparatively slender record of public service, who has never sat for a single day in the House and who, if a Privy Councillor at all, is only one of very recent standing – should be preferred to one who has sat in the House for 17 years, been a Privy Councillor for still longer and who has held two periods of high office overseas. It is not even as though it could be said that I had not taken a prominent part in the affairs of the House. On foreign affairs, on defence questions, on shipping and not least in the India debates I have been a regular speaker and upheld the point of view that was yours in the last few years. All these circumstances make what I should imagine must be an unprecedented appointment very marked in my regard.

As I told you yesterday the leadership of the Lords offers no intrinsic attraction to me at all, and above everything I am keenly desirous not to cause you any difficulty or embarrassment when you are already carrying so big a load. At the same time my public reputation must matter to me for it effects my usefulness to the State.

Would it be possible for you to say you had offered me the leadership and that I had asked to be relieved of it on one score or another? That would help very much.

Whatever you decide to say I know I can count on you both as my leader and as a personal friend, whose fortunes I have followed in times both grim and gay, to frame the announcement of Cranborne's appointment in a manner that takes account of the difficulties I have described.[23]

Churchill thought the matter over and consulted Cranborne's father, Lord Salisbury, who advised him to appoint Lloyd. On 5 January 1941 Churchill formally asked Lloyd to take the job on. Thus it was that on 7 January he became leader of the House of Lords.[24]

This was the crowning point of his career and it seemed that, at last, he was coming into his own.

Plenty of work awaited the new leader of the House of Lords, and it might be that he would find his enhanced political position an advantage when it came to opposing the iniquitous American demands for additional territory in the British Caribbean Colonies. Lloyd had brought the whole question to the Cabinet just after Christmas adducing good reasons for supposing that the Americans were bent upon supplanting the British in the area. He told one diplomat that the Americans were 'gangsters and there is only one way to deal with gangsters'.[25] Eden, the new Foreign Secretary, whilst sympathetic to this point of view, thought that there could be no going back on the agreement and Lloyd had been isolated when the Cabinet had discussed the matter on 30 December. However, it had been agreed that the formal terms of the leases would have to be decided by a conference held in London – so that offered further scope for opposition.

But before this could be done it was necessary to throw off the illness which had been bothering him for so many months. He went down to Clouds Hill on 12 January for a rest and had to take to his bed 'with a germ', but he hoped 'only for a day or two'.[26]

There he could give some thought to David's problems. The closeness of their relationship has already been amply demonstrated, but it must not be supposed that it was a case of the father suffocating the son with affection; the process worked both ways. David told him in a long letter written at the end of August 1940:

> I have always told you everything since my earliest days, because I always felt that in you I had a most wonderful friend and adviser and that however wrong or foolish I had been your attitude would always be one of helpfulness and understanding and not one of continual reproof and lack of sympathy. This relationship between us has always been the most grand strength and I felt I must tell you.

What David had to tell his father was that, whilst in Jerusalem, he had fallen in love with a married woman and wanted to marry her. In his letter he opened his heart:

> I have somehow felt . . . that you would always rather that I told you what was on my mind than that I should conceal things from you. Anyway if I have done wrong I know you will tell me.[27]

Those who saw in Lloyd only the stern proconsul would have been surprised by his reply. Because of the timing of the diplomatic bags, he had only fifteen minutes in which to pen a speedy answer:

> *Don't* worry about my worrying as to your love affair. I'm not a bit worried and quite understand. I thought you wrote so calmly and sensibly that I think it *may* be the real thing. Also you may be *quite* sure I will keep it to myself and not even tell your mother. . . . I think of you so much all the time and want you to marry and be happy so much that I will not worry at all and am telegraphing to tell you so.[28]

In a later letter he amplified these sentiments:

> I am unhappy to know what mental stress you have been going through and still more unhappy that I can do so little to help you. . . . I am not going to pretend that I think it ideal . . . moreover one can never be sure that happiness does lie at the end of such a road. But one thing you *can* know for certain and that is that I shall always see you through to the best of my ability in every difficult passage of your life. One can't always travel though dark tunnels with those one loves, but one can always be at the mouth waiting for them as they emerge, and that is where you shall find me so long as you need me.[29]

From Clouds Hill in January he wrote again to reassure David of his love and support. Whatever he did he would be there to help; but if man proposes then only God disposes.

Letters of congratulation upon his new appointment came in. To his old ally Page Croft he replied on 13 January:

> I do not look forward to my new duties. I am afraid I may have to defend policies which I have had no hand in shaping and with which I do not agree. However it may turn out all right in practice; there is nothing to do but wait and see.
>
> I am laid low by some bug which the doctors are trying to rid me of by various methods. I am afraid I shall be here some days still.[30]

On 14 January, with no improvement in his condition, he told Churchill that it was unlikely that he would be back 'before the end of the week' and would not be able to undertake his duties as leader of the Lords at the opening of the session.[31] Four days later Lloyd's private secretary reported that he was 'still in bed with a temperature':

> The doctors are not quite sure what he has got. They think it is something very like German measles though it is not quite following the normal course of that disease. (In any case Lord Lloyd is rather ashamed of having such a childish disease and does not want the fact published!)
>
> I am afraid he is not likely to be back at work for some while yet, certainly not next week and quite possibly not for part of the week after.

He is very unhappy at being laid up like this. He is, as he himself says, a bad 'rester'.[32]

Lloyd replied to those who sent him sympathetic messages, telling General de Gaulle on 15 January that he hoped to see him soon.[33] To Churchill he wrote on 20 January:

I am so sorry to have fallen out of the battle, but I hope it is not for more than about a week longer. The chill I had developed into a very severe attack of German measles! which is a most unpleasant malady when one has reached maturer age.

I am not signing this so as not to risk infection, but am merely telephoning it from the country.[34]

The doctors continued to hope for the best. Dr Manson-Bahr was 'very reassuring' on 28 January, telling Churchill's secretary that Lloyd had had 'nothing but an extremely severe attack of German measles' and should be back at his desk within two weeks; he added that Lloyd had kept up with the office work.[35] Lloyd telephoned the same day to say that he was 'afraid he may have to be away for another ten days'.[36] Nowhere was there any hint of alarm and both he and his doctors looked forward to his complete recovery.

They were all tragically wrong. What had been taken for measles was, in fact, a rare form of leukaemia. On 31 January the news was telephoned through to Churchill that Lloyd had 'Hodgkin's disease' which 'affects the blood and is extremely serious'; the prognosis was bad and 'it is not impossible that he may live only for a few days'.[37] At last the doctors had it more or less right.

In fact they were still by no means sure precisely what Lloyd was suffering from, but they told Blanche that it was a blood disorder which was destroying his white blood cells and that he was going to die; this news was kept from Lloyd himself. He was taken to Manson-Bahr's clinic in Harley Street where the eminent specialist Dr Janet Vaughan was called in, but there was nothing to be done save fight vainly against the end.[38]

On Tuesday 4 February it was decided to give him injections of morphia every four hours to kill the tremendous pain he was suffering. At 5 p.m. Lloyd sent for Manson-Bahr and,

He made the request to me as a friend that he should not be allowed to suffer agonies and he should have, if necessary, further injections to send him to sleep, but no more blood transfusions which caused him great distress.

By 9.30 that night he had had three-quarters of a gramme of morphia which was not, Manson-Bahr later explained to Blanche, enough to 'put him to sleep'.[39] At 11.45 p.m. on 4 February George Lloyd died. Tommy Lascelles wrote to David on 7 February:

> Your father died quite peacefully, and with a triumphant smile on his face. I am convinced that no human skill could have appreciably prolonged his life; indeed it looks to me as if his death-warrant had been signed (though neither he nor anybody else realised it) some months ago ... it appears that the complex machinery by which a man renews his bloodstream had become worn out, either through the destructive influence of the various oriental microbes wh[ich] he had picked up, or because of his dynamic habit of life. He would never admit, as you know, that he was middle-aged; and say what one will, it is a hard physical fact that middle-age is not the same as youth. When this last sharp illness attacked him he simply had not the blood-strength to repel it, and nothing, not even the transfusions, could give him the necessary reinforcements. He died, paradoxically for one so essentially strong, from sheer weakness.[40]

That restless body was still at last and that great soul had embarked upon its final journey.

They laid him to rest, as he had wanted, in the small churchyard at St Ippolyts. Rest was not a word which the many obituarists employed in any of the acres of print which mourned his loss to the Empire and the war effort. As Ronald Storrs observed: 'We could think of dear George as everything except cold and still.'[41]

# EPILOGUE

Lloyd died before the battle was won, but his Faith told him that victory would come. The timing of his death, like the fate of the causes which his life had championed, has diminished his posthumous fame and today the name of Lord Lloyd is not one which evokes a ready response. But it is arguable that his vision was longer-sighted than many of those whom historians have chosen to honour with their attention.

The Empire to which he devoted his career is at one with those of Nineveh and Tyre, and, as he feared, his country has become a small, impoverished island off the coast of Europe, her mission and her faith all but gone; as he foretold, the independence of India was not reached without bloodshed on a massive scale; and where independence has replaced Empire it is not usually the case that prosperity and peace have been the lot of the peoples of Britain's old colonies. Lloyd's tragedy was that whilst none of his dreams came to pass, all his nightmares did.

David carried forward his standard. Not the least of the tragedies of Lloyd's early death at the age of sixty-two was that he did not see David's happiness in the marriage which he made the following year to Lady Jean Ogilvie. Blanche, who had been totally devastated by his death, took fresh comfort in this event and in the grandchildren which it was to bring her and she lived on till a great old age, dying in 1969. David, after his wartime exploits, returned and began to make his career in banking until a telephone call from Churchill in 1951 brought him into politics. He served as Under-Secretary at the Home Office and then at the Colonial Office – which last brought back memories. After January 1957 he returned to banking where he enjoyed a successful and prosperous career.

The memory of his father remained always green, and at Clouds Hill even now the traces of Lloyd are everywhere. After the war Blanche persuaded Colin Forbes Adam to write a biography of his old friend and master. Published in 1948, it was an excellent portrait, especially considering the circumstances under which it was written, so close to the events it was describing. Later she and David sought another biographer who could, perhaps, try to place Lloyd in his proper historical perspective. But when David talked about his father after dinner with the brandy glasses charged and his inevitable cigar smoking, it was not easy to keep in mind that this was the *second* Lord Lloyd of Dolobran who was talking.

That David should have died before this book was completed was the one sadness attending its composition.

Even before the first Baron Lloyd of Dolobran died it was plain that the world he had grown up in and tried to preserve was changing irrevocably. He had diagnosed many of the things that were rotting the bases of British power, but had lacked the means to reverse the process; perhaps it was always irreversible. But the attempt was a noble one.

The newspapers all proclaimed that Lloyd's early death was a tragedy and so it was, for the Empire and his family. But perhaps Tommy Lascelles was not so far wide of the mark when he wrote to David:

> Maybe he is *felix opportunitate mortis suae* [fortunate in the timing of his death]. He was, as Winston said in the H. of C. yesterday, at the apex of his career; on the crest of a wave which had triumphantly vindicated him; and it is hard to believe that, whatever the next phase of history may bring, it will hold much that would have brought him happiness.

# NOTES

The following abbreviations are used in the notes:

L = George Lloyd
AC = Austen Chamberlain
SPC = Sam Cockerell
PL = Percy Loraine
BL = Blanche Lloyd
Puss = Lady Constance Milnes-Gaskell
Whelk = Helen Maclagen (Blanche's sister)
EM = Edwin Montagu
NH = Nevile Henderson
WT = Sir William Tyrrell
WSC = Winston Churchill
GLLD = Lloyd Papers at Churchill College file number

## 1: DOLOBRAN AND BIRMINGHAM

1 Leo Amery Diary, February 1941. I am most grateful to the Rt Hon. Julian Amery MP for allowing me to consult his father's papers.
2 This section is based upon: *The Welsh Dictionary of National Biography*; S. Lloyd, *The Lloyds of Birmingham* (Birmingham, 1908); and H. Lloyd, *The Quaker Lloyds in the Industrial Revolution* (London, 1975).
3 The passages on Lloyd's early life are based on four sources: C. Forbes Adam, *The Life of Lord Lloyd* (London, 1948); notes made by Thomas Lloyd for Blanche Lloyd in the 1940s; and conversations with the late Lord Lloyd and with Mr Charles Janson.

## 2: THE LURE OF THE EAST

1 GLLD 22/20, Speech to the Royal Empire Society, 21 February 1940.
2 GLLD 5/11, L[loyd] to David Lloyd, *c.* 1935.
3 Compton Mackenzie, *Gallipoli Memories* (London, 1929), p. 50.
4 Tom Lloyd's notes.

5  Birmingham University Library, Austen Chamberlain MSS AC 18/1/13, L to A[usten] C[hamberlain], 16 September 1918.
6  Lloyd MSS, L to Miss Gertrude Bell, undated.
7  Lloyd MSS, L to Puss Gaskell, February 1918.
8  R. Graves and B. H. Liddell Hart, *T. E. Lawrence to his Biographers* (London, 1963 edn), part II, p. 88.
9  Lloyd MSS, L to Miss Bell, 21 May 1906.
10  Mackenzie, *op. cit.*, p. 330.
11  GLLD 8/1, S. P. C[ockerell] to L, 21 November 1905.
12  *Ibid.*, SPC to L, 3 December 1905.
13  L to Miss Bell, 21 January 1906.
14  GLLD 8/2, SPC to L, 7 April 1906.

3: EASTERN EXPERT
1  L to Miss Bell, 21 May 1906.
2  SPC to L, 3 December 1905.
3  L to Miss Bell, 2 July 1905.
4  *Ibid.*
5  GLLD 16/48, O'Conor to Grey, 17 July 1906.
6  GLLD 7/6, Despatch 507, 24 July 1906.
7  *Ibid.*, Confidential Print 39619, Narclay to Grey, 17 November 1906.
8  GLLD 8/2, SPC to L, 4 August 1905.
9  GLLD 7/12, O'Conor to Grey, 25 August 1905.
10  GLLD 7/1, Wilson-Fox to L, 5 January 1907; GLLD 7/12, Board of Trade (telegram) to L, 18 January 1907.
11  GLLD 5/11, L to David Lloyd, *c.* 1935.
12  GLLD 7/1, P[ercy] L[oraine] to L, 27 February 1907.
13  GLLD 8/3, SPC to L, 28 January 1907.
14  GLLD 7/1, L to Mr Ridley, 26 February 1907.
15  GLLD 7/5 dairy.
16  *Ibid.*
17  Lloyd MSS, L to Gwen, 23 August 1907.
18  GLLD 7/2, PL to L, 20 July 1907.
19  GLLD 8/3, SPC to L, 20 July 1908.
20  GLLD 16/48, L to Grey, July 1908.
21  GLLD 7/3, Chirol to L, 26 August 1908.
22  GLLD 23/1, *National Review*, November 1908.
23  GLLD 7/3, L to Wintour, 13 October 1908.
24  *Ibid.*, Miss Bell to L, 29 September 1908.
25  GLLD 23/1, *Daily Mail*, October 1908.
26  GLLD 7/2, PL to L, 24 September 1908.
27  GLLD 7/10, Report on Trade Conditions.

4: POLITICS AND LOVE
1  GLLD 7/3, L to Mr Docker, 15 December 1908.
2  GLLD 7/4, Fitzmaurice to L, 26 June 1909.
3  GLLD 23/2, ms. note 12 September 1909.
4  GLLD 21/1, ms. note 1909.

5 GLLD 16/56, *Pall Mall Gazette* election extra, 1910.

6 GLLD 7/4, Fitzmaurice to L, 17 December 1909.

7 GLLD 16/35, Parliamentary Questions, 1910.

8 GLLD 1/24, L to Leo Maxse, 20 June 1910.

9 GLLD 1/24, Long to L, 20 December 1910.

10 GLLD 8/4, L to SPC, 4 May 1911.

11 Conversation with the late Lord Lloyd, 20 September 1984.

12 The letters between George and Blanche Lloyd had not been deposited at Churchill College when I worked on them. They will eventually form section GLLD 4. I have given no file number in referring to this correspondence, but I have always given the date of the letter.

13 Annoyingly, George's letters for this period are usually dated only by the day of the week, but comparison with Blanche's properly dated letters has usually allowed me to date his letters to within a day or so.

14 Blanche Lloyd MSS.

## 5: TOWARDS THE STORM

1 Birmingham University Library, Austen Chamberlain MSS AC 9/5/57.

2 GLLD 8/6, L to SPC, 4 August 1914.

3 GLLD 17/36, L to Ian Colvin, 18 May 1914.

4 AC 14/2/7, L to AC, 31 July 1914.

5 GLLD 17/36, L to Ian Colvin.

6 Amery diary, 1 August 1914.

7 GLLD 17/36, L to Colvin.

8 Amery diary, 1 August.

9 K. Wilson, *The Policy of the Entente* (Cambridge, 1985), pp. 135–42.

## 6: WAR

1 GLLD 8/6, L to SPC, 4 August 1914.

2 *Ibid.*, SPC to L, 20 August.

3 GLLD 9/14, War Office telegram to L, 24 September.

4 GLLD 8/6, L to SPC, 12 October.

5 *Ibid.*, 3 November.

6 GLLD 9/14, War Office telegram to L, 12 November.

7 GLLD 8/6, L TO SPC, 22 December.

8 Forbes Adam, *Lloyd*, p. 64.

9 GLLD 8/6, SPC to Blanche Lloyd, 15 January 1915.

10 Forbes Adam, *op. cit.*, p. 65.

11 *Ibid.*, p. 67.

12 GLLD 9/4, Diary 1915.

13 GLLD 8/4, SPC to L, 11 September 1911.

14 GLLD 9/4.

## 7: GALLIPOLI

1 Mackenzie, *op. cit.*, p. 51.

2 Forbes Adam, *op. cit.*, p. 73.

3 GLLD 9/1, Lawrence to L, 29 June 1915.

4 Mackenzie, *op. cit.*, p. 54.

5 Documents concerning the genesis and execution of L's mission to Russia are to be found in GLLD 9/1 and all quotations should be assumed to come from that file unless indication to the contrary is given.

6 Lloyd MSS, Letter to Blanche, 8 January 1916.

7 GLLD 9/8 for the papers on this episode.

8: AMBITION AND FRUSTRATION

1 GLLD 9/2, Puss to L, 22 February 1916.

2 *Loc. cit.*, L. S. Amery to L, 26 February 1916.

3 *Ibid.*, P. Ashworth to L, 27 February.

4 *Ibid.*, J. Deakin to L, 11 March.

5 GLLD 9/13, L to Amery, 31 March 1916.

6 GLLD 9/2, Herbert to L, 22 March 1916.

7 *Ibid.*, Herbert to L, undated.

8 GLLD 9/13, L to Chamberlayne, 7 April 1916.

9 D. Garnett (ed.), *The Letters of T. E. Lawrence* (London, 1938), p. 204.

10 Lady Bell (ed.), *The Letters of Gertrude Bell* (London, 1930 edn), p. 307.

11 GLLD 9/13, L to Chirol, 28 June 1916.

12 GLLD 9/8 for the report and papers on it.

13 GLLD 9/13, L to Amery, 24 April 1916.

14 GLLD 9/8, L to Deedes Bey, 25 May 1916.

15 Blanche's diary, 9 September 1916 [henceforth BLD].

16 BLD, 20 September.

17 BLD, 21 September.

18 GLLD 9/13, L to Birdwood, 8 October.

19 *Ibid.*, L to Bell, 15 October.

20 Lloyd MSS, L to Milly Pilkington, 17 November 1916.

9: LAWRENCE AND THE ARAB BUREAU

1 Elie Kedourie, *In the Anglo–Arab Labyrinth* (Cambridge, 1976).

2 Books on Lawrence are legion; the two I have found most readable and most helpful are: John Mack, *A Prince of our Disorder* (London, 1976); and Desmond Stewart, *T. E. Lawrence* (London, 1977): the former is better on Lawrence's early life, but Stewart's knowledge of Arabic and Arabia make him the better guide for the period to which Lawrence owes his fame.

3 Lloyd MSS, L to Puss, 18 December 1916.

4 GLLD 9/8, L to General Bell, 15 November 1916.

5 *Ibid.*, Telegram from the Sirdar to Grey, 16 November 1916.

6 *Ibid.*, L to Deedes Bey, 19 November 1916.

7 *Ibid.*, L to General Bell, 22 November.

8 *Ibid.*, L to General Clayton, 25 November.

9 L to General Bell, 2 December.

10 Sir Ronald Storrs, *Orientations* (London, 1943 definitive edn), p. 183.

11 GLLD 9/8, L's record of conversations with the Sherif.

12 *Ibid.*, Sirdar to A. J. Balfour, 14 December; L to General Bell, 22 December; L to Wingate, 22 December; L to General Bell, 27 December.

13 Lloyd MSS, L to Puss, 18 December 1916.

14 Birmingham University Library, Austen Chamberlain MSS, AC 12/139, L to AC, 11 January 1917.

15  Lloyd MSS, L to Blanche, 17 January 1917.
16  GLLD 9/3, Birdwood to L, 15 January 1917.
17  BLD, 3 January 1917; L to BL, 17 January 1917.
18  BLD, 14 March 1917; GLLD 9/9 for papers on the Ottoman Bank (5 March) for Balfour and also for L to Wingate, 28 February; L to Bell, 28 February.
19  GLLD 9/9, Memo by L, undated.
20  *Ibid.*, L memo, 17 May 1917.
21  Lloyd MSS, L to Puss, 6 May 1917.
22  GLLD 9/13, L to Brigadier French, 3 Sepember 1917.
23  *Ibid.*, L to French, 12 June and 3 September, and to Blanche, 12 June.
24  GLLD 9/4, Chamberlain to Steel-Maitland, 9 March 1917.
25  Lloyd MSS, Letters from Blanche, May and June *passim*; GLLD 9/3, Amery to L, 25 June, 22 October; Chamberlain to L, 1 August, and to Blanche, 15 September; Herbert to L, 11 July.
26  GLLD 9/3, Page Croft to L, 31 August 1917.
27  Lloyd MSS, L to Puss, 31 May 1917.
28  *Ibid.*, L to Puss, 25 July 1917.
29  *Ibid.*, L to Puss, undated but *c.* August 1917.
30  GLLD 9/13, L to Wingate, 17 August 1917.
31  Lloyd MSS, L to Puss, undated but *c.* August 1917.
32  *Ibid.*, L to Blanche, 13 September; Lloyd MSS, L to Puss, 4 October 1917; Austen Chamberlain MSS, AC 18/1/1, L to AC, 6 September 1917.
33  GLLD 9/13, Copy of letter L to Clayton, 30 September.
34  *Ibid.*, L to Clayton, 20 October.
35  GLLD 9/11, Diary of journey with Lawrence to El Jaffer.
36  GLLD 9/10, Undated ms. note by L.

10: THE ROAD TO INDIA

 1  Lloyd MSS, Blanche to L, 27 July 1917.
 2  *Ibid.*, L to Puss, 4 October 1917.
 3  *Ibid.*, L to BL, 22 June 1916.
 4  GLLD 9/3, Mr Deakin to L, 2 November.
 5  *Ibid.*, BL to L, 19 December.
 6  *Ibid.*, L to Clayton, 20 December; L to BL, 21 December.
 7  BLD, 31 December 1917; Lloyd MSS, BL to L, 20 December.
 8  Lloyd MSS, L to Puss, 5 January 1918.
 9  GLLD 9/13, L to Chamberlain, 8 February 1918.
10  GLLD 9/10 MEC, 4th minutes 18 February 1918; L to Balfour, 16 April 1918.
11  Lloyd MSS, L to Puss, undated but February 1918.
12  BLD, 27 April 1918, recording events since February.
13  *Ibid.*; also GLLD 9/13, L to Long, undated, 2 April, 26 April, 4 May, and Sir George Fiddes, 3 and 4 April; GLLD 9/3, Walter Long to L, 12 March, 4 April, 3 May 1918.
14  BLD, 27 April 1918.
15  BLD, 2 May 1918.
16  BLD, May and June 1918.
17  GLLD 9/3, Montagu to L, 21 September 1917.

18  BLD, 2 July 1918 (p. 146).

19  The Earl of Halifax, *Fullness of Days* (London, 1957), p. 67; Lord Birkenhead, *The Life of Lord Halifax* (London, 1965), p. 95.

20  'A Gentleman with a Duster' (Harold Begbie), *The Conservative Mind* (London, 1924), p. 47.

21  Birkenhead, *op. cit.*, p. 123.

22  BLD, 2 July 1918 (p. 152).

23  *Ibid.*, pp. 152–3.

24  Birkenhead, *op. cit.*, pp. 123–4.

25  India Office Record Library (IORL) Montagu Papers, MSS EUR D.523/2 fo. 101, Montagu to Chelmsford, 7 August 1918.

26  Lloyd MSS, L to Montagu (henceforth EM), 21 August 1918.

27  *Loc. cit.*, L to BL, 22 August.

28  GLLD 10/2, Letters from Cambon, 13 November; Wolmer, 1 October; Frederick Lascelles, September 1918.

29  *Loc. cit.*, AC to L, 14 September; Chamberlain MSS AC 18/1/3, L to AC, 16 September.

30  GLLD 10/2, Letters from Garvin, 1 and 3 October; Dawson, 30 September; Beaverbrook, undated; Tom Lloyd, undated and unsigned.

11: THE GREAT OPPORTUNITY

1  IORL Montagu Papers, MSS, MSS EUR D.523/2 fo. 101, Montagu to Chelmsford, 7 August 1918.

2  *Ibid.*, fo. 107, Montagu to Chelmsford, 5 September 1918. Lord Ronaldshay, later the Earl of Zetland, was Governor of Bengal 1917–22 and Secretary of State for India 1935–40 and played a part in shaping the India Act of 1935.

3  *Ibid.*, L to EM, 1 December 1918.

4  BLD, 7 December 1918 (pp. 248–9).

5  BLD, 9 December (pp. 254–5).

6  GLLD 2/1, *Advocate India*, 17 December 1918.

7  BLD, 16 December (pp. 263–4).

8  Lloyd MSS, BL to Whelk, 29 January 1919.

9  IORL MSS EUR D.523/24 fo. 1, L to EM, 21 November 1918.

10  *Ibid.*, fos 8–9, L to EM, 26 December 1918.

11  *Ibid.*, fo. 8.

12  *Ibid.*, fos 13–15, L to EM, 10 January 1919.

13  *Ibid.*, fo. 17, L to EM, 25 January.

14  BL to Whelk, 29 January.

15  MSS EUR D.523/24 fo. 21, L to EM, 12 February 1919.

16  BLD, 6 January 1919.

17  MSS EUR D.523/24 fos 30–1, L to EM, 26 February 1919.

18  GLLD 10/19, L to Lord Birkenhead, 9 March 1924; Forbes Adam, *op. cit.*, pp. 125–9.

19  Forbes Adam, *op. cit.*, p. 129.

20  MSS EUR D.523/8 fo. 103, Chelmsford to Montagu, 9 April.

21  *Ibid.*

22  R. Kumar (ed.), *Essays on Gandhian Politics* (Oxford, 1971), is the best account of

the unrest; see in particular Chapter VII (James Masselos on 'Bombay') and Chapter X (D. A. Low on 'The First Non-Cooperation Movement'): I am most grateful to Professor Tony Low of Cambridge for drawing this collection to my attention.

23 BL to Whelk, 30 May 1919.
24 *Ibid.*, 16 April 1919.
25 *Ibid.*, undated fragment *c.* April 1919.
26 MSS EUR D.523/8 fos 117–18, Chelmsford to EM, 30 April.
27 *Ibid.*, D.523/27 fo. 18, EM to L, 1 May 1919.
28 *Ibid.*, D.523/24 fo. 65, L to EM, 23 May 1919.

12: BOMBAY LIFE
 1 AC 18/1/5, AC to L, 18 June 1919.
 2 MSS EUR D.523/24 fo. 17, L to EM, 25 January 1919.
 3 MSS EUR D.523/26 fo. 70, L to EM, 31 May 1919.
 4 Lloyd MSS, L to BL, 26 August 1918.
 5 MSS EUR D.523/22 fo. 31, EM to L, 25 June 1919.
 6 MSS EUR D.523/24 fos 94–5, L to EM, 18 July 1919.
 7 MSS EUR D.523/22 fo. 390, EM to L, 27 August 1919.
 8 MSS EUR D.523/24 fos 120–1, L to EM, 21 September 1919.
 9 Ormsby-Gore was heir to Lord Harlech, Wood to Lord Halifax.
10 AC 18/1/6, L to AC, 11 JULY 1919.
11 MSS EUR D.523/24 fo. 113, L to EM, 5 September 1919.
12 Lloyd MSS, Blanche to Whelk, 3 February 1919.
13 MSS EUR D.523/24 fo. 128, L to EM, 7 October 1919.
14 MSS EUR D.523/25 fo. 23, L to EM, 20 March 1920.
15 BLD, 16 December 1918 (p. 270).
16 Forbes Adam, *op. cit.*, p. 115.
17 BLD, 6 January 1920.
18 Lloyd MSS, L to BL, 24 August 1918.
19 Forbes Adam, *op. cit.*, p. 217.
20 Lloyd MSS, Blanche to Sibell Long, 5 January 1919.
21 *Ibid.*, BL to Whelk, 1 May 1919.
22 BLD, 31 December 1918. Portofino, the Herbert villa in Italy, was where they had first met.
23 BLD, 31 October 1918 (pp. 211–12).
24 Lloyd MSS, Reminiscence by Con Benson, *c.* 1941.
25 BL to Whelk, 18 September 1919.
26 BLD, 6 October 1919 (p. 188).
27 MSS EUR D.523/24 fo. 105, L to EM, 17 August 1919.
28 BL to Whelk, 10 October 1919.
29 BLD, 13 December 1919.

13: TAKING THE STRAIN
 1 BL to Whelk, 30 January 1920.
 2 *Ibid.*, 9 April 1920.
 3 BLD, 31 March 1920.
 4 MSS EUR D.523/22 fo. 9, EM to L, 14 April 1920.
 5 MSS EUR D.523/3 fo. 49, Montagu to Chelmsford, 22 April 1920.

6  Lloyd MSS, BL to Freda Nixon, 17 June 1920.
7  BLD, 7 June 1920 (p. 107).
8  *Ibid.*, 31 July (p. 139).
9  AC 18/1/8, L to AC, 13 June 1920.
10  MSS EUR D.523/5 fo. 23, L to EM, 26 March 1920.
11  *Ibid.*, fo. 34, L to EM, 30 April 1920.
12  AC 18/1/8, L to AC, 13 June 1920.
13  MSS EUR D.523/25 fos 76–80, L to EM, 13 August 1920.
14  Lloyd MSS, L to Sibell Long, 20 August 1920.
15  MSS EUR D.523/25 fo. 108, L to EM, 15 October 1920.
16  AC 18/1/15, L to AC, 15 October 1920.
17  K. Jeffrey (ed.), *The Military Correspondence of Field Marshal Sir Henry Wilson 1918–1922* (London, 1985), p. 211.
18  MSS EUR D.523/25 fo. 84, L to EM, 27 August 1920.
19  A. W. Lawrence (ed.), *Letters to T. E. Lawrence* (London, 1961), pp. 124–5, L to TEL, 26 August 1920.
20  GLLD 10/15, L to Willingdon, 25 August 1920.
21  AC 18/1/15, L to AC, 15 October 1920.
22  MSS EUR D.523/25 fo. 13, L to EM, 5 November 1920.
23  MSS EUR D.523/26 fos 1–2, L to EM, 1 January 1921.
24  BLD, 9 January 1921.
25  MSS EUR D.523/26 fo. 4, L to EM, 15 January 1921.
26  MSS EUR D.523/23 fo. 5, EM to L, 9 February 1921.
27  MSS EUR D.523/26 fo. 16, L to EM, 4 March 1921.
28  Forbes Adam, *op. cit.*, p. 148.

14: DEALING WITH GANDHI
1  BLD, 2 April 1921.
2  MSS EUR D.523/14 fo. 2, Reading to Montagu, 13 April 1921.
3  MSS EUR D.523/26 fo. 39, L to EM, 19 May 1921.
4  IORL Reading Papers MSS EUR F.118/95, L to EM, 15 July 1921.
5  MSS EUR D.523/14 fo. 38, Reading to Montagu, 28 July 1921.
6  MSS EUR D.523/23 fos 65–9, EM to L, 17 August 1921.
7  Lloyd MSS, L to Puss, 5 September 1921.
8  MSS EUR D.523/26 fos 78–80, L to EM, 23 September 1921.
9  *Ibid.*, fo. 93, L to EM, 5 November 1921.
10  MSS EUR F.118/48 fo. 26, L to Reading, 26 October 1921.
11  AC 18/1/27, L to Chamberlain, 24 March 1922.
12  MSS EUR D.523/14 fo. 108, Reading to Montagu, 5 January 1922.
13  MSS EUR D.523/26 fo. 117, L to EM, 13 January 1922.
14  *Ibid.*, fo. 122, L to EM, 20 January 1922.
15  *Ibid.*, fos 127–31, L to EM, 17 February 1922.
16  IORL Reading Papers MSS EUR E.238/4, Montagu to Reading, 23 February 1922.
17  AC 18/1/27, L to Chamberlain, 24 March 1922.
18  *Ibid.*
19  MSS EUR D.523/26 fos 132–5, L to EM, 3 March 1922.

20 *Ibid.*, fo. 85, L to EM, 14 October 1921.
21 MSS EUR F.118/48 fo. 22, L to Reading, 5 October 1921.
22 MSS EUR D.523/23 fo. 80, EM to L, 10 November 1921.
23 S. D. Waley, *Edwin Montagu* (London, 1964), pp. 271–2.
24 MSS EUR D.523/26 fo. 137, L to EM, 11 March 1922.
25 AC 18/1/33, L to Chamberlain, 11 August 1922.
26 MSS EUR D.523/14 fo. 124, Reading to Montagu, 2 March 1922.
27 BLD, 14 January 1922 (p. 13).
28 MSS EUR E.238/5 fo. 7, Reading to Peel, 20 April 1922.
29 AC 18/1/30, L to AC, 9 June 1922.

15: ENDINGS AND BEGINNINGS
 1 L to BL, 1 September and 22 September 1922.
 2 Lloyd MSS, L to Puss, 29 April 1921.
 3 *Ibid.*, 5 August 1921.
 4 L to Puss, 21 March 1921.
 5 *Ibid.*, 22 July 1923.
 6 *Ibid.*, 16 September.
 7 L to BL, Empire Day 1923.
 8 L to Puss, 22 July 1923.
 9 L to BL, 20 October 1923.
10 *Ibid.*, 22 October 1923.
11 GLLD 2/3 for the press comments.
12 GLLD 10/21, L to Leslie Wilson, 29 June 1923.
13 MSS EUR E.238/6 fo. 188, Reading to Peel, 23 August 1923.
14 MSS EUR E.238/6 fo. 144, Peel to Reading, 26 September 1923.
15 *Ibid.*, 26 September 1923.
16 *Ibid.*, fo. 212, Reading to Peel, 18 October 1923.
17 *Ibid.*, fo. 152, Peel to Reading, 3 October 1923.
18 Lloyd MSS, L to BL, 7 January 1923 [*sic* for 1924].
19 Cambridge University Library, Baldwin MSS vol. 35 fo. 115, L to Baldwin, 17 November 1923.
20 L to Puss, 17 November 1923.
21 *Ibid.*, 23 November 1923.
22 BLD, 12 December 1923.
23 L to Puss, 25 December 1925.
24 *Idib.*, 6 January 1924.
25 AC 18/1/38, L to AC, 16 March 1925.
26 Leo Amery MSS, Diary, 31 May 1924.
27 *Ibid.*, 16 April 1924.
28 Lord Beaverbrook, *Men and Power* (London, 1956), p. xv.

16: EASTBOURNE, AMBITION AND INTRIGUE
 1 L to Puss, 17 September 1924.
 2 AC/1/38, L to AC, 16 March 1925.
 3 BLD, 28 December 1924; *Eastbourne Gazette*, 15 October 1924.
 4 BLD, 28 December 1924.
 5 *Sussex County Herald* (Eastbourne edition), 1 November 1924.

6   L to Puss, 9 November 1924.

7   BLD, 1 January 1925.

8   GLLD 13/1 for the correspondence on Kenya.

9   *Ibid.*; BLD, 12 March 1925; Amery diary, 28 February, 17 March.

10  GLLD 13/1; Amery diary, 12 March 1925.

11  AC 18/1/38, L to AC, 16 March 1925.

12  BLD, 12 March 1925.

13  AC 18/1/38, L to AC, 16 March 1925.

14  Amery diary, 28 February 1925.

15  BLD, 14 March 1925.

16  John Campbell, *F. E. Smith* (London, 1983), pp. 744–5.

17  BLD, 14 March 1925.

18  *Ibid.*, 21 March 1925.

19  *Ibid.*

20  AC 18/1/39, AC to L, 19 March 1925.

21  BLD, 31 March 1925.

22  GLLD 13/1, Baldwin to L, 23 March 1925.

23  Lord Lloyd, *Egypt since Cromer*, vols I and II (London, 1933 and 1934 *passim*); Lord Wavell, *Allenby in Egypt* (London, 1943), pp. 101–30; and for a decidedly anti-Lloyd and more recent study, L. al Sayyid-Marsot, *Egypt's Liberal Experiment* (California, 1977).

24  BLD, 31 March 1925.

25  GLLD 13/1, L's record of talk with Chamberlain on 6 April.

26  *Ibid.*, L's record dated 13 May 1925; BLD, May 1925.

27  Public Record Office, London, Foreign Office Miscellaneous MSS FO 794/14 fos 55–6, L to AC, 30 May.

28  BLD, May 1925.

17: FIRST ROUND WITH ZAGHLOUL

1   PRO Henderson MSS FO 800/264, Henderson minute, 23 September 1925.

2   GLLD 13/4, N[evile] H[enderson] to L[loyd], 19 June 1925.

3   *Ibid.*, and letters from NH, 5 July, 15, 22 August, 6, 12, 26 September.

4   GLLD 14/8, Report on Egypt 1925–6, pp. 3–4.

5   GLLD 13/4, Letters from NH, 25, 17 July.

6   GLLD 13/2, Percy Loraine to L, 18 May 1925.

7   Royal Archives, Windsor, W. Geo. V. 1431.63. Lord Stamfordham to Lord Esher, 11 November 1925. I am most grateful to Mr James Lees-Milne for this reference.

8   BLD, 25 October 1925.

9   *Ibid.*

10  GLLD 13/16, L to Sir Lionel Earle, 24 October 1925.

11  GLLD 13/4, L to A[usten] C[hamberlain], 25 October 1925.

12  GLLD 13/4, L to AC, 28 November 1925.

13  GLLD 14/8, Report on Egypt 1925–6, pp. 8–9.

14  PRO MacDonald MSS 30/69/1435 fo. 591.

15  GLLD 13/5, Sir W[illiam] T[yrrell] to L, 6 January 1926.

16  GLLD 14/8, Report on Egypt, pp. 11–12.

17  BLD, 14 January 1926.

18  GLLD 13/4, L to AC, 14 February 1926.
19  PRO Henderson MSS FO 800/265, fo. 20.
20  GLLD 13/5 WT to L, 10 March 1926; AC 53/553, WT to AC, 11 March.
21  IORL MSS EUR F.118/100, Birkenhead to Reading, 21 June 1925.
22  GLLD 13/4, L to AC, 23 April and 2 May; 12/15 tel. 216/20 May.
23  GLLD 13/3, AC to L, 1, 21 April, 11 May for letters urging caution, and GLLD 12/3 tel. 160, AC to L, 20 May.
24  PRO Chamberlain MSS FO 800/259 fo. 455, WSC to AC, 21 May.
25  AC 53/17, Amery to AC, 21 May.
26  FO 800/259 fo. 454, AC to WSC, 21 May.
27  GLLD 12/15 tel. 247, L to AC, 29 May; GLLD 13/4 L to AC, 29 May.
28  GLLD 12/3 tels 178, 179, AC to L, 29 May.
29  al Sayyid-Marsot, *op. cit.*, pp. 92–3.
30  GLLD 12/15 tels 249 and 250 to FO, 31 May.
31  Lloyd, *Egypt since Cromer*, II, p. 165.
32  GLLD 13/3, AC to L, 11 June.
33  GLLD 12/3 tels 183 (31 May) and 185 (1 June) to L.
34  Lloyd MSS, L to Keyes, 9 June.
35  GLLD 14/8, Report on Egypt, p. 17.
36  GLLD 13/15 tel. 278, L to AC, 5 June.
37  GLLD 13/3, AC to L, 11 June.
38  GLLD 2/7 for press reports of the crisis.
39  Lloyd MSS, L to Keyes, 9 June.

18: HIGH COMMISSIONER FOR EGYPT
1  Lloyd MSS, L to Puss, 15 November 1925.
2  Lloyd, *Egypt since Cromer*, II, p. 2.
3  Lloyd MSS, Notes on L by Blanche written after his death.
4  *Loc. cit.*, Notes on L by Con Benson.
5  Lloyd MSS, BL to Percy Loraine, 9 November 1925.
6  *Loc. cit.*, L to BL, 8 August 1922.
7  *Ibid.*, 12 September 1922.
8  *Ibid.*, 29 September 1922.
9  BLD, January 1926.
10  Lloyd MSS, BL to Sibell Glyn (formerly Long), 3 February 1926.
11  *Loc. cit.*, BL to Loraine, 16 March 1926.
12  *Ibid.*
13  AC 52/436 ,L to AC, 6 June 1926.

19: GUNBOATS AND DIPLOMACY
1  PRO Henderson MSS FO 800/265 fo. 64.
2  *Ibid.*, L to NH, 2 August 1926.
3  GLLD 1/22, T. E. Shaw [Lawrence] to L, 30 September 1934.
4  Memorandum by Sir Walford Selby, 20 October 1948. I am very grateful to Mr Ralph Selby for letting me see his father's papers.
5  L. Graffty-Smith, *Bright Levant* (London, 1970), p. 105.
6  GLLD 17/10, J591/219/16, FO memo, 21 February 1927.
7  PRO Foreign Office general correspondence, FO 371/13843 J 1747/5/16, Memo

by Murray, 13 June 1929, p. 5.

8  FO 800/265 fos 98–9, L to Henderson, 28 August 1926.

9  IORL Irwin Papers MSS EUR C.152/17 no. 128, L to Irwin, 21 October 1926.

10  Lloyd MSS, L to Keyes, 27 January 1927.

11  MSS EUR C.152/17 no. 171, L to Irwin, 10 January 1927.

12  For this episode see Tyrrell's letters at GLLD 13/5.

13  GLLD 13/3, AC to L, 28 December 1926; GLLD 13/4, L to AC, 1 and 9 January 1927, and AC 18/1/42, Tyrrell minute, 18 January 1927.

14  MSS EUR C.152/17 nos 36, 37, 55, 90, 111, L to Irwin 1925–6 for the background, and nos 125 (21 October 1926, 135 (9 November), 171 (10 January 1927), 180b (7 February) chart the progress of this obsession.

15  MSS EUR C.152/17, Hoare to Irwin, 2 March 1927.

16  GLLD 14/18 tel. 74, L to Foreign Office, 9 March 1927.

17  *Ibid.*, tel. 67, Foreign Office to L, 11 March; see also Murray's account at FO 371/13843 J 1747/5/16, pp. 8–9.

18  GLLD 14/18 tel. 88, L to Foreign Office, 21 March.

19  *Ibid.*, tel. 83, Foreign Office to L, 25 March, and GLLD 13/4, L to AC, 28 March.

20  GLLD 14/18, J841/184/16, AC memo, 1 April.

21  *Ibid.*, tel. 101, Foreign Office to L, 13 April.

22  GLLD 13/3, AC to L, 25 April.

23  Selby MSS Memo by Sir Walford Selby, 11 July 1949.

24  GLLD 14/18 tel. 208, L to Foreign Office, 25 May.

25  *Ibid.*, tels 134 and 135, Foreign Office to L, 27 May.

26  *Ibid.*, L's marginal note on Foreign Office tel. 156 of 27 May.

27  GLLD 13/4, L to AC, 29 May.

28  GLLD 14/18 tels 221–5, L to Foreign Office, 31 May.

29  *Ibid.*, tels 242, 243, L to Foreign Office, 4 June.

30  AC 54/475, WT to AC, 7 June.

31  GLLD 14/18 tel. 174, WT to L, 6 June.

32  *Ibid.*, unnumbered tel., WT to L, 6 June.

33  *Ibid.*, tel. 250, L to Baldwin, 8 June.

34  *Ibid.*, unnumbered tel., L to WT, 7 June.

35  *Ibid.*, J 1514/8/16, Sir J. Murray to L, 9 June.

36  Churchill College, Chartwell Papers CHAR 2/152 fo. 98, WSC to Baldwin, 11 June 1927.

37  Baldwin MSS vol. 115 fo. 227, Hoare to Baldwin, 11 June 1927.

38  GLLD 14/18 tel. 268, L to Foreign Office, 14 June.

39  AC 54/476, WT to AC, 15 June.

40  AC 54/478, WT to AC, 17 June.

41  GLLD 14/18, L's notes.

42  BLD, April 1927; notes prepared for me by David Lloyd.

43  Lloyd MSS, L to Keyes, 19 June 1927.

20: SECRET DIPLOMACY

1  L to Puss, 15 November 1925.

2  CHAR 2/142 fo. 111, L to Churchill, 5 December 1925.

3  MSS EUR C.152/17, L to Irwin, 22 November 1927.

4 Birmingham University Library, Neville Chamberlain MSS NC 2/22 diary entry, 15 July 1927.
5 *Ibid.*, NC 18/1/582, N. Chamberlain to Hilda Chamberlain, 16 July 1927.
6 *Ibid.*, NC 2/22 dairy entry, 21 July 1927.
7 FO 800/265 fo. 125 foll., Murray to Henderson, 3 August.
8 GLLD 14/19, Austen's report, 13 July 1927.
9 *Ibid.*, Selby's report, 13 July.
10 FO 800/261 fo. 125–8, Selby to AC, 20 July 1927.
11 AC 5/1/426, Austen to Hilda Chamberlain, 1 August 1927.
12 FO 800/261 fo. 176, L to AC, 4 August 1927.
13 GLLD 14/19, L to AC, 10 August; AC to L, 11 August.
14 FO 800/265 fos 248–9, L to NH, 30 August 1927.
15 FO 800/261 fos 225–8, Selby to WT, 1 September 1927.
16 FO 794/14 fo. 37, WT to AC, 13 September.
17 AC 54/480, AC to WT, 15 September.
18 AC 54/481, WT to AC, 17 September.
19 Baldwin MSS vol. 112, WT to Baldwin, 1 October 1927.
20 GLLD 13/15, NH to L, 15 September 1927.
21 FO 800/266 fos 23–4, L to NH, 29 September 1927.
22 GLLD 13/15, Henderson to L and Murray, 8 October.
23 Lloyd, *Egypt since Cromer*, II, p. 234.
24 Amery diary, 16 July 1927.
25 NC 2/22 diary entry, 4 December 1927.
26 AC 54/443, Salisbury to Chamberlain, 28 October; 54/203, Lord Stamfordham to Chamberlain, 2 November.
27 AC 5/1/435, Austen to Hilda Chamberlain, 22 October 1927.
28 AC 54/358, L to AC, 10 November; Baldwin MSS vol. 115 fo. 229, L to Baldwin, 10 November 1927.
29 Lloyd, *Egypt since Cromer*, II, p. 234.
30 GLLD 13/7, undated draft letter to Sir Robert Vansittart.
31 FO 800/266 fos 63–6, Henderson to Murray, 14 November.
32 GLLD 12/8 tel. 283, Foreign Office to L, 14 November.
33 *Ibid.*, tel 308, Foreign Office to L, 7 December 1927.
34 GLLD 12/20 tels 409–11, L to Foreign Office, 10 December; GLLD 13/4, L to AC, 11 December.
35 FO 800/261 fos 655–8, WT to AC, 12 December.
36 BDL, 18 February 1928.
37 GLLD 13/4, L to AC, 28 January 1928.
38 GLLD 12/8 tel. 53, Foreign Office to L, 4 February 1928.
39 GLLD 12/20 tel. 89, L to Foreign Office, 8 February.
40 GLLD 13/4, L to AC, 4 March 1928.

21: PRELUDE TO A CONSPIRACY
1 Lloyd, *Egypt since Cromer*, II, p. 257.
2 GLLD 13/4, L to AC, 11 March 1928.
3 GLLD 13/3, AC to L, 19 March; GLLD 12/9, AC to L, 27 March.
4 GLLD 13/3, AC to L, 28 March.
5 GLLD 13/4, L to AC, 8 April.

6 GLLD 13/3, AC to L, 28 April.
7 GLLD 12/9 tel. 191, Foreign Office to L, 28 April 1928.
8 GLLD 12/21 tel. 253, L to Foreign Office, 29 April.
9 *Ibid.*, tel. 259, L to Foreign Office, 2 May.
10 GLLD 12/9 tels 199 and 202, Foreign Office to L, 2 May.
11 BLD, May 1928.
12 MSS EUR C.152/17, L to Irwin, 22 November 1927.
13 Notes made by David Lloyd for me in 1984.
14 BLD, February 1929.
15 BLD, April 1929.

22: CONSPIRACY
1 L. S. Amery, *My Political Life*, vol. II (London, 1953), p. 306.
2 Lord Vansittart, *The Mist Procession* (London, 1958), p. 372.
3 Neville Chamberlain MSS NC 1/27/28, AC to NC, 9 August 1929.
4 GLLD 12/21 tel. 141 from Foreign Office; 12/24 tel. 173 to Foreign Office, 6 May.
5 NC 1/27/28.
6 D. Carlton, *MacDonald versus Henderson* (London, 1970), pp. 15–18 and *passim*.
7 *Ibid.*, pp. 21–2.
8 PRO FO 794/14 fo. 11, draft statement by Henderson for his speech in the Commons. This file, which has not, to my knowledge, been used before by historians, contains invaluable material on this episode, filling in gaps in the FO 371 material; the question of why it is in this very obscure classification instead of being in the FO 371 section has no obvious answer.
9 AC 55/315, Lindsay to AC, 17 June.
10 AC 55/314, AC to Lindsay, 18 June.
11 PRO FO 371/13843 J 1694/5/16, Murray and Lindsay's minutes, 19 June 1929.
12 FO 371/13843 FO memorandum, 13 June, drawn up by Murray.
13 FO 794/14 fos 25–8, Minute by Lindsay with attached telegrams flagged A and B.
14 *Ibid.*, fo. 23, Henderson to MacDonald, 29 June 1929.
15 *Ibid.*, MacDonald's handwritten comments on draft A, fo. 27, and on draft B fo. 28. His comment on Lindsay's minute at fo. 25 shows that he had picked up the political implications.
16 FO 794/14 fo. 32, Lindsay minute, 2 July.
17 House of Commons Hansard, 5th series, vol. 230, col. 1301.
18 Lloyd MSS, L to BL, 7 July 1929.
19 Stanley Baldwin, *Our Inheritance* (London, 1938 edn), p. 14.
20 BLD, 11 July 1929.

23: CRISIS
1 BLD, 18 July 1929.
2 *Ibid.*, 19 July.
3 *Ibid.*, 23 July.
4 *Ibid.*
5 FO 794/14 fos 15–16.
6 BLD, 23 July, pp. 183–7.
7 British Library of Political and Economic Science, Dalton MSS diary vol. 10, fo. 163, 24 July 1929.

8 Martin Gilbert, *Winston S. Churchill*, vol. v (London, 1976), p. 337.
9 House of Commons Hansard, 5th series, vol. 230, cols 1301–2.
10 Dalton diary vol. 10 fo. 165, 25 July.
11 NC 18/1/663, Neville to Ida Chamberlain, 28 July 1929.
12 Amery diary, 26 July.
13 Dalton diary vol. 10 fo. 165, 26 July 1929.
14 Lloyd MSS, Churchill to L, 28 July 1929.
15 Dalton diary *loc. cit.*
16 NC 18/1/663, Neville to Ida Chamberlain, 28 July 1929.
17 BLD, 26 July, p. 198.
18 Dalton diary, 26 July.
19 *Ibid.*, vol. 10 fo. 171, 1 August 1929.
20 Amery diary, 26 July.
21 NC 1/27/98, Austen to Neville Chamberlain, 9 August 1929.
22 AC 5/1/479, Austen to Ida Chamberlain, 1 August 1929.
23 NC 1/27/98, Austen to Neville Chamberlain, 9 August 1929.
24 Gilbert, *op. cit.*, pp. 321–3; David Dilks, *Neville Chamberlain*, vol. 1 (Cambridge, 1984), pp. 558–60, 567–8, 579–80.
25 Lloyd MSS, Churchill to L, 28 July. The other letters are at GLLD 13/19.
26 GLLD 1/22, Shaw to L, 29 July 1929.

24: 'BALDWINISM'
1 GLLD 13/19, Page Croft to L, 1 August 1929.
2 Churchill College, Page Croft MSS CRFT 1/15 fo. 37, L to Page Croft, 3 August 1929.
3 BLD, 30 July 1929 (pp. 204–5).
4 MSS EUR C.152/28 fo. 8, L to Irwin, 31 July (copy in Lloyd MSS).
5 BLD, 30 July (p. 203).
6 MSS EUR C.152/18, G. R. Lane-Fox to Irwin, 17 May 1928.
7 Baldwin MSS vol. 103 fo. 63, Salisbury to Baldwin, 23 October 1929.
8 M. Gilbert, *Winston S. Churchill*, vol. v, companion volume 2, (London, 1981), p. 128.
9 Baldwin MSS *loc. cit.* fo. 79, Irwin to Baldwin, 26 November 1929.
10 IORL Hoare Papers MSS EUR E.240/1 fo. 3, Hoare to Willingdon, 2 September 1931.
11 House of Lords Hansard, vol. 75, cols 1129–43.
12 Gilbert, *op. cit.*, p. 312.
13 GLLD 17/26 for the articles.
14 *Ibid.*, *Daily Telegraph*, 15 March 1930.
15 GLLD 22/10, Speech, 5 December 1930.
16 GLLD 2/8, *Daily Mail* and *Daily Telegraph*, 29 May 1930, and *Sunday Times*, 1 June.
17 Amery diary, 9 November 1930.
18 Duff Hart-Davis (ed.), *End of an Era* (London, 1986), p. 285.
19 GLLD 1/22, T. E. Shaw to L, 22 January 1929. I found this letter in a copy of one of L's lectures; it was not printed in Garnett's edition of Lawrence's letters.
20 Lloyd MSS, L to BL, 19 August 1930.
21 GLLD 5/1, L to David, 13 March 1931.

22 *Loc. cit.*, L to David, 28 September 1930.
23 GLLD 2/8.
24 *Loc. cit.*, *The Scotsman*, 11 December 1930.
25 *Loc. cit.*, Speech in Edinburgh, 11 February 1931.
26 GLLD 19/5, L to Baldwin, 5 March 1931.
27 Amery diary, 9 February 1931.
28 GLLD 2/8, *Daily Telegraph*, 19 February 1931; GLLD 19/5, Baldwin to L, 18 February; L to Baldwin, 18 February (also in Baldwin MSS vol. 104).
29 GLLD 19/5, L to Baldwin, 2 March 1931.
30 GLLD 19/5, L's memo of conversation.

25: INTO THE WILDERNESS
1 CHAR 2/177 fo. 1, Beaverbrook to Churchill, 19 January 1931.
2 IORL MSS EUR E.240/1 fo. 3, Hoare to Willingdon, 2 September 1931.
3 Amery diary, 26 August 1931.
4 Baldwin MSS vol. 44 fo. 88, L to Baldwin, 5 September 1931.
5 CRFT 1/3 fo. 16, Baldwin to Page Croft, 26 August 1931.
6 House of Lords Hansard, 5 December 1931, cols 313–22.
7 MSS EUR E.240/1 fo. 90, Hoare to Willingdon, 10 December 1931.
8 GLLD 17/33, 'War or Peace?', 14 December 1931.
9 *Loc. cit.*, L's note from Bacon's *Of the vicissitudes of things*.
10 GLLD 23/4, *Graphic* article, May 1932 (but pub. 28 April).
11 Lloyd MSS undated letter *c.* 1932, Gl to BL.
12 GLLD 1/22, T. E. Shaw to L, 23 June 1932.
13 GLLD 2/9, *Morning Post*, 7 October 1932.
14 GLLD 22/12, Speech, 6 October 1932.
15 Gilbert, *Churchill*, vol. v, companion vol. 2, p. 481.
16 GLLD 11/1, L to Hoare, 4 December 1932.
17 CHAR 2/192 fo. 2, Churchill to Lord Sydenham, 7 January 1933.
18 Baldwin MSS vol. 106 fo. 4, Hoare to Baldwin, 9 January 1933.
19 MSS EUR E.240/3, fo. 601, Hoare to Willingdon, 10 February 1933.
20 *Loc. cit.*, fos 607–8, Hoare to Willingdon, 17 February 1933.
21 GLLD 5/2, L to David, 25 January, 6 February 1933.
22 MSS EUR E.240/3, Hoare to Willingdon, 1 March.
23 PRO Cabinet Minutes, Cab. 23/75 meeting on 10 March 1933.
24 MSS EUR E.240/3, Hoare to Willingdon, 10 March.
25 Salisbury MSS S(4)198/43, L to Salisbury, *c.* 1 April 1933.
26 GLLD 11/1, L to Hailsham, 7 April 1933.
27 GLLD 11/1, Press report of L's statement.
28 CHAR 2/197 fo. 28, Telephone message for Churchill, 20 April.
29 GLLD 17/17, *The Times*, 29 June 1933.
30 MSS EUR E. 240/3, Hoare to Willingdon, 30 June 1933.
31 Amery diary, 28 June 1933.
32 GLLD 2/9, *Manchester Guardian*, 29 June 1933.
33 GLLD 17/7, *The Times*, 29 June 1933.

26: WILDERNESS POLITICS
1 GLLD 2/9, *Daily Express*, 19 June 1933.

2  GLLD 19/2, Lady Houston, October 1933.

3  J. Wentworth Day, *Lady Houston* (London, 1958).

4  *Ibid.*, p. 178.

5  GLLD 2/9, *Daily Herald*, 20 November.

6  R. Griffiths, *Fellow Travellers of the Right* (London, 1983), p. 48.

7  Amery diary, 21 November 1933.

8  GLLD 22/13 for the text.

9  Amery diary, 21 November 1933.

10  MSS EUR E.240/4 fo. 1068, Hoare to Willingdon, 22 May 1934.

11  Gilbert, *Churchill*, vol. v, Chapter 28.

12  GLLD 19/5 Derby to L, 18 June 1934.

13  Salisbury MSS S.(4)205/141, Cadogan to Salisbury, 12 March.

14  *Ibid.*, S.(4)205/147, Salisbury to Cadogan, 15 March.

15  Wentworth Day, *op. cit.*, pp. 184–5.

16  GLLD 19/2, L to Lady Houston, 25 June 1934.

17  GLLD 17/43 for the reports.

18  GLLD 11/2 for the text.

19  GLLD 2/9, *Evening Standard*, 29 January 1935.

20  GLLD 11/1, L to Wolmer, 19 February 1935.

21  Salisbury MSS S.(4)208/30–32, S to Wolmer, 28 February 1935.

22  CHAR 2/240B, L to Churchill, 12 June 1935.

23  GLLD 1/22, Shaw to L, 30 September 1934.

24  GLLD 5/4, L to David, 9 April 1935.

27: AT BAY

1  Lloyd MSS, L to Blanche, 12 April 1934.

2  Lees-Milne MSS, L to Lees-Milne, undated but *c.* May 1935.

3  James Lees-Milne, *Another Self* (London, 1970), p. 100.

4  Pembroke College, Cambridge, Storrs Diary VI/3, 7 April 1940.

5  Lloyd MSS, L to BL, 10 April 1934.

6  Conversation with Julian Amery, 30 April 1986.

7  David Lloyd's notes, 1984.

8  Conversation with David Lloyd, 20 September 1984.

9  This and the next two paragraphs are based upon numerous conversations with David Lloyd.

10  GLLD 1/30 for the details.

11  Lloyd MSS, L to BL, 23 August 1935.

12  GLLD 5/4, L to David, 12 November 1935.

13  Lloyd MSS, L to BL, 21 November 1935.

14  *Ibid.*, 2 January 1936.

15  *Ibid.*, 9 January 1936.

16  *Ibid.*, 17 January 1936.

17  GLLD 5/5, L to David, 27 January 1936.

18  *Ibid.*, 3 February 1936.

19  *Ibid.*, 27 January 1936.

20  *Ibid.*, 3 March 1936.

21  Lloyd MSS, L to BL, 4 April 1935.

22  GLLD 5/5, L to David, 27 February 1936.

23  *Loc. cit.*, L to David, 10 April 1936.

24  GLLD 5/11, undated letter L to David, *c.* February 1936.

25  GLLD 5/5, L to David, 17 March 1936.

26  GLLD 2/10, *L'Excelsior*, 13 March.

27  GLLD 5/5, L to David, 17 March 1936.

28  *Ibid.*, 25 March 1936.

29  GLLD 22/16, Speech in the Lords, 14 May; Lloyd MSS, L to BL, 19 April 1936.

30  L to BL, 24 May 1936, with enclosure from Grandi.

31  GLLD 5/5, L to David, 17 April 1936.


28: THE ROAD BACK

 1  Lloyd MSS , L to BL, 28 May 1936.

 2  *Ibid.*, 29 May.

 3  *Ibid.*

 4  *Ibid.*

 5  *Ibid.*, 2 June 1936.

 6  L to BL, 24 August 1936.

 7  L to BL, 27 August 1936.

 8  L to BL, 28 August 1936.

 9  L to BL, 16 September 1936.

10  GLLD 17/50 for details of evidence, 29 July 1936.

11  M. Gilbert, *Churchill*, vol. v, companion volume 3, pp. 425–36.

12  GLD 2/10, *Morning Post*, 20 November 1936.

13  GLLD 5/5, L to David, 25 March 1936

14  GLLD 22/16, Speech, 25 November 1936

15  *Loc. cit.*, Speech, 8 July 1936.

16  BLD, 1 January 1937.

17  Lloyd MSS, Résumé of Lloyd's case, 15 December 1936.

18  L to BL, 10 January 1937.

19  L to BL, Letters January 1937.

20  L to BL, 24 March 1937.

21  P. M. Taylor, *The Projection of Britain* (Cambridge, 1981), pp. 169–71.

22  L to BL, 22, 24 March 1937.

23  L to BL, 31 March 1937.

24  L to BL, 5 April 1937.

25  L to BL, 3 April 1937.

26  Lloyd MSS, Neville Chamberlain to L, 7 February 1937.

27  PRO British Council files BW 82/5, Leeper to Bridges, 8 July.

28  Taylor, *op. cit.*, pp. 167–8; Frances Donaldson, *The British Council* (London, 1984), pp. 52–4; British Council files BW 82/5 for papers on Lloyd's appointment. I should like to record my thanks to my research student, Miss Louise Ramsden-Atherton, for discussing with me the circumstances of Lloyd's appointment.


29: THE BRITISH COUNCIL

 1  GLLD 19/6, L to Forbes Adam, 10 August 1937.

 2  *Ibid.*, 29 August 1937.

 3  Lloyd MSS, Grandi to L, 23 May 1936.

4  GLLD 17/49, Grandi to L, 4 August 1937.
5  GLLD 19/6, L to Forbes Adam, 29 August 1937.
6  Taylor, *op. cit.*, p. 168.
7  PRO Treasury files T 161/907, L to Eden, 22 December.
8  *Ibid.*, Eden to Simon, 23 December.
9  *Ibid.*, L to Eden, 22 December.
10  *Ibid.*, Simon note, 12 January 1937.
11  PRO FO 371/21626 C 95, Leeper to Vansittart, 6 December; Orme Sargent minute, 7 December 1937; FO 371/21165 R 8571 minutes by Sargent, Cadogan and Eden, 16–18 December.
12  GLLD 19/6, Leeper to L, 20 December 1937.
13  Lloyd MSS, L to BL, 10 March 1938.
14  L to BL, 12 March 1938.
15  *Ibid.*
16  L to BL, 14 March 1938.
17  L to George II, 4 May 1938; George II to L, 13 July 1938.  *VI, perhaps*
18  L to BL, 17 May 1938.
19  GLLD 19/7, L to Geoffrey Byron, 25 May 1938.
20  GLLD 19/6, L to Halifax, 30 May 1938.
21  GLLD 19/7, L to Byron, 25 May 1938.
22  Lloyd MSS, L to BL, 15 April 1938.
23  GLLD 19/7, L to Princess Bibesco, 24 June 1938.
24  FO 371/21730 C 8189, L to Halifax, 10 August 1938.
25  BLD, 2 May 1938.
26  BLD, 26 August 1938.

30: FROM MUNICH TO PRAGUE
1  L to BL, 29 August 1938.
2  CHAR 2/330 fo. 124, L to Churchill, 17 July 1938.
3  *Loc. cit.*, fo. 126, Churchill to L, 18 July 1938.
4  L to BL, 31 August 1938.
5  *Ibid.*, 5 September 1938.
6  *Ibid.*, 9 September.
7  *Ibid.*, 12 September; L to Halifax, 12 September.
8  GLLD 19/6, Crisis visit to Paris – diary.
9  BLD, 19 September 1938.
10  BLD, 27 September 1938.
11  BLD, 30 September 1938.
12  J. Charmley, *Duff Cooper*, (London, 1986), pp. 127.
13  GLLD 22/18, Speech, 4 October.
14  Leo Amery diary, 5 October 1938.
15  *Daily Telegraph*, 6 October 1938.
16  L to BL, 7 October 1938.
17  L to BL, 11 October 1938.
18  GLLD 19/8, L to Percy Loraine, 20 October 1938.
19  GLLD 19/7, Cadogan to L, 15 October; L to Cadogan, 25 October; David Dilks (ed.), *The Diaries of Sir Alexander Cadogan* (London, 1970), p. 121 (17 October).
20  GLLD 19/7, Halifax to L, 19 October 1938.

21 K. Feiling, *Neville Chamberlain* (London, 1946), p. 384.
22 GLLD 19/7, Chamberlain to L, 20 October 1938.
23 GLLD 19/7, L to the Duchess of Atholl, 28 October 1938
24 FO 371/22459 R 8196, Halifax to Chamberlain, 13 October 1939.
25 These arguments are explored further in Miss Ramsden-Atherton's thesis.
26 Colvin's letters are in GLLD 19/9. See also his book, *Vansittart in Office* (London, 1965), pp. 278–305 *passim*.
27 D. C. Watt, 'Misinformation, Misconception, Mistrust', in *High and Low Politics in Modern Britain* (Oxford, 1983), pp. 214–54.
28 GLLD 19/9, L to S. P. Powell, 2 February 1939.
29 Quoted in Dov B. Lungu, 'The European Crisis of March–April 1939: The Romanian Dimension', *The International History Review*, August 1985, pp. 390–414.
30 *Ibid.*, pp. 392–3.
31 GLLD 19/9, L to Halifax, 20 March 1939.
32 Lungu, *op. cit.*, p. 393 fn. 9.
33 Dilks, *op. cit.*, p. 163, 26 March 1939.
34 GLLD 19/9, L to Halifax, 20 March 1939.
35 GLLD 25/5, L to Halifax, 20 March 1939.
36 Watt, *op. cit.*, p. 246.
37 GLLD 5/8, L to David, 13 April 1939.
38 GLLD 19/11, L to BL, 13 April 1939.

### 31: INTO THE VALLEY OF THE SHADOW

1 Churchill College, Duff Cooper Papers, Duff to Diana Cooper, 11 January 1939.
2 L to BL, 5 May 1939.
3 L to BL, 22 February 1939.
4 L to BL, 10 March 1939.
5 GLLD 22/19, Minute of discussion, 22 February 1939.
6 L to BL, 16 May 1939.
7 Chamberlain MSS NC 7/9/59, Churchill to Chamberlain, 29 September 1939.
8 NC 7/9/60, Chamberlain to Churchill, 30 September.
9 GLLD 5/8, L to David, 7 September.
10 GLLD 19/12, L to Hoare, 25, 26 August, 5 September; BW 82/7, Hoare to L, 26, 31 August.
11 GLLD 5/8, L to David, 7 September.
12 PRO Halifax MSS FO 800/322 H/XXX/4, L to Halifax, 13 June; H/XXX/5, Halifax to L, 16 June.
13 FO 800/322 H/XXX/6, Halifax to Macmillan, 7 September 1939.
14 GLLD 5/8, L to David, 10 September 1939.
15 GLLD 19/14, Memo of conversation with Halifax, 4 October.
16 GLLD 5/8, L to David, 10 September 1939.
17 *Ibid.*, 3 July 1939.
18 Lloyd MSS, Correspondence, May–June 1939.
19 GLLD 5/8, L to David, 10 September 1939.
20 *Ibid.*, 19 September.
21 *Ibid.*, 13 October.
22 GLLD 20/6, Report on visit to Spain, 19–23 October.

23  FO 371/24900, Palairet to Halifax, 11 October; 23759, Campbell to Halifax, 11 October.
24  PRO Sir Orme Sargent MSS FO 800/278 RO/39/5, Hoare to Sargent, 11 October.
25  *Loc. cit.*, RO/39/6, Strang to Hoare, 27 October.
26  BW 82/13, Notes for Lord Lloyd, 7 November 1939.
27  GLLD 20/4, Diary of Balkan tour, 15 November.
28  *Ibid.*, 17 November.
29  *Ibid.*, 15 November and the fuller account in GLLD 20/6.
30  FO 800/278 RO/39/6, L to Sargent, 16 November.
31  GLLD 20/6, Balkan diary, 21 November.
32  *Ibid.*, 24 November.
33  GLLD 5/8, L to David, 6 December.
34  L to BL, 20 November.
35  GLLD 20/6, L to Halifax, 20 November.
36  L to BL, 20 November.
37  GLLD 5/8, L to David, 6 December.
38  *Ibid.*, 28 December.
39  *Ibid.*, 30 December 1939.

32: PRIVATE WARS
 1  GLLD 5/9, L to David, 7 January 1940.
 2  *Ibid.*, 24 January.
 3  BW 2/161, L to Baxter, 11 August 1939.
 4  BW 2/161 has many examples of these criticisms.
 5  GLLD 5/9, L to David, 21 January.
 6  GLLD 19/16, L to Beaverbrook, 31 January.
 7  GLLD 19/17, L to Reith, 6 February.
 8  BW 69/5, Reith to L, 6 February.
 9  Donaldson, *op. cit.*, p. 73.
10  BW 69/5, L to Reith, 16 February.
11  Donaldson, *op. cit.*, p. 75.
12  Review of Donaldson in the *Observer*.
13  Lloyd, *Leadership in Democracy* (Oxford, 1939), p. 4.
14  *Ibid.*, p. 16.
15  *Ibid.*, p. 21.
16  GLLD 19/12, L to Grandi, 27 September 1939.
17  Lloyd, *The British Case* (London, 1939), p. 14.
18  *Ibid.*, p. 48.
19  K. Robbins, 'Britain, 1940' and 'Christian Civilization', in D. Beales and G. Best (eds), *History, Society and the Churches* (Cambridge, 1985), pp. 279–99.
20  GLLD 5/9, L to David, 24 January.
21  *Ibid.*, 14 January.
22  *Ibid.*, 15 January.
23  *Ibid.*, 24 February.
24  *Ibid.*, 2 March.
25  *Ibid.*, 1 April.
26  *Ibid.*, 1 January 1940.

27 *Ibid.*, 21 January.
28 *Ibid.*, 24 January.
29 *Ibid.*, 3 January.
30 *Ibid.*, 24 January.
31 Storrs diary VI/3, 6 April 1940.
32 GLLD 5/9, L to David, 7 April.
33 PRO FO 794/14 ff. 2–4, L to Halifax, 20 April.
34 GLLD 5/9, L to David, 28 April.
35 *Ibid.*, 2, 7 May.
36 CHAR 20/11 fo. 31, draft list of ministers.
37 GLLD 5/9, L to David, 10 May 1940.

33: TRIUMPH
 1 CHAR 20/11 f. 74, L to Churchill, 15 May 1940.
 2 Storrs diary VI/3, 13 May 1940.
 3 GLLD 5/9, L to David, 19 May.
 4 *Ibid.*, 22 May.
 5 *Ibid.*
 6 *Ibid.*, 27 May.
 7 *Ibid.*, 30 May.
 8 *Ibid.*, 3 June.
 9 *Ibid.*, 9 June.
10 FO 800/312 H/XIV445, Halifax to L, 7 June.
11 GLLD 5/9, L to David, 17 June.
12 *Ibid.*, 22 June.
13 *Ibid.*, 17 June.
14 *Ibid.*, 22 June.
15 GLLD 17/59 tel. 487 from Campbell, 20 June, and L's minute.
16 GLLD 5/9, L to David, 22 June.
17 *Ibid.*, 26 June.
18 *Ibid.*, 16 July.
19 Amery diary, 17, 18 June 1940.
20 M. Bloch, *The Duke of Windsor's War* (London, 1982), p. 97.
21 Storrs diary VI/3, 14 July 1940.
22 GLLD 5/9, L to David, 16 July.
23 CHAR 20/9 fo. 63, L to Churchill, 16 July.
24 *Ibid.*, fo. 85, Message from L to Churchill, 20 July.
25 *Ibid.*, fo. 191, L to Halifax, 28 September 1940.
26 GLLD 5/9, L to David, 16 July 1940.
27 GLLD 21/5, L to de Gaulle, 28 August 1940.
28 GLLD 21/6, Wingate note, 5 and 12 August, and L's notes.
29 B. Pimlott (ed.), *The Second World War Dairies of Hugh Dalton 1940–45* (London, 1986), p. 52 (1 July 1940).
30 FO 800/322 fo. 101, L to Halifax, 25 July 1940.

34: TRAGEDY
 1 Dalton diary, p. 13 (18 May).
 2 Amery diary, 22 July 1940.

3   Churchill College, Grigg MSS PJGG 8/4/19, L to Grigg, 8 December 1940.
4   GLLD 5/9, L to David, 19 May 1940.
5   N. Rose, *Lewis Namier and Zionism* (Oxford, 1980), p. 108.
6   *Ibid.*, p. 109.
7   David Lloyd's notes for me.
8   GLLD 19/6, Speech, 25 June 1940.
9   D. J. Morgan, *The Origins of British Aid Policy 1924–1945* (London, 1980), pp. 90–1.
10  FO 371/24262 A 5203, D. Scott minute, 18 December 1940.
11  GLLD 5/9, L to David, 9 and 15 September.
12  *Ibid.*, 15 September.
13  *Ibid.*, 22 September.
14  *Ibid.*, 4 October.
15  *Ibid.*, 10 October.
16  *Ibid.*, 14 October.
17  *Ibid.*, 16 October.
18  Lloyd MSS, L to Milly Pilkington, 16 October 1940.
19  GLLD 5/9, L to David, 22 November.
20  *Ibid.*, 15 December.
21  *Ibid.*, 30 September.
22  Dilks, *op. cit.*, p. 341 (18 December 1940).
23  GLLD 21/5, L to Churchill, 4 January 1941.
24  *Ibid.*, Churchill to L, 5 January 1941.
25  D. Reynolds, *The Creation of the Anglo-American Alliance 1941–45* (London, 1981), p. 170.
26  GLLD 5/9, L to David, 12 January 1941.
27  *Ibid.*, David to L, 26 August 1940.
28  *Ibid.*, L to David, 9 October 1940.
29  *Ibid.*, 22 November.
30  CRFT 1/15 fo. 42, L to Page Croft, 13 January 1941.
31  PRO Prime Minister's Papers, PREM. 4/7/11 fo. 930, Colville to WSC, 14 January 1941.
32  *Ibid.*, fo. 928, Eastwood to Eric Seal, 18 January 1941.
33  GLLD 20/6, L to de Gaulle, 15 January 1941.
34  GLLD 20/5, L to Churchill, 20 January 1941.
35  PREM. 4/7/11 fo. 924, Eastwood to Seal, 28 January 1941.
36  *Ibid.*, fo. 922, Bevin to Churchill, 28 January 1941.
37  *Ibid.*, fo. 918, Note for Churchill, 31 January 1941.
38  Lloyd MSS, Janet Vaughan to BL, 8 June 1941.
39  *Ibid.*, Manson-Bahr to BL, 13 October 1941.
40  *Ibid.*, Tommy Lascelles to David, 7 February 1941.
41  Storrs diary VI/4, 5 February 1941.

# Sources

PRIMARY SOURCES

## Manuscript collections

*Birmingham University Library*
Papers of:
  Austen Chamberlain
  Neville Chamberlain

*Bodleian Library*
Papers of:
  Lord Altrincham (Edward Grigg)
  Lord Selborne

*British Library of Political and Economic Science, London*
Papers of:
  Hugh Dalton

*Cambridge University Library*
Papers of:
  Lord Baldwin
  Lord Templewood (Samuel Hoare)

*Churchill College, Cambridge*
Papers of:
  Winston Churchill (Chartwell MSS)
  Sir Alexander Cadogan
  C. Bonham-Carter
  Duff Cooper
  Lord Croft
  Lord Esher
  P. J. Grigg
  Sir Hughe Knatchbull-Hugessen
  Lord Lloyd
  Sir Eric Phipps

  Sir Malcolm Robertson
  Sir Louis Spears
  Lord Vansittart

*India Office Record Library*
Paper of:
  Lord Birkenhead
  Lord Halifax
  Sir Samuel Hoare
  Sir George Lloyd
  Edwin Montagu
  Lord Willingdon

*Pembroke College, Cambridge*
  Diary of Sir Ronald Storrs

*Public Record Office, Kew*
Foreign Office General Correspondence FO 371
Private papers FO 800 series:
  Sir Austen Chamberlain
  Lord Halifax
  Arthur Henderson
  Sir Nevile Henderson
  Sir Orme Sargent
Treasury files
British Council files BW 2 series
Ramsay MacDonald (PRO 30)
Sir Percy Loraine (FO 1011)
Neville Chamberlain (PREM 1)
Winston Churchill (PREM 3 and PREM 4)
Anthony Eden (FO 954)

## Private Collections

Leo Amery Diaries (Courtesy of the Rt Hon. Julian Amery MP)

GL's correspondence with James Lees-Milne (courtesy of Mr Lees-Milne)

Papers of the Fourth Marquess of Salisbury (Hatfield House, by courtesy of the Sixth Marquess of Salisbury)

Walford Selby Papers (courtesy of Mr Ralph Selby)

The following sections of the Lloyd papers which were lent to me by Lord and Lady Lloyd are now at Churchill College:

GL's correspondence with Blanche, 1911–40

Blanche's correspondence with GL, 1911–40

GL's correspondence with David, 1925–41

David's correspondence with GL, 1925–41

David's correspondence with Blanche, 1918–69

Blanche's correspondence with David, 1918–69

GL's diaries, various dates up to 1915

Blanche's diaries, 1908–60s

Lascelles family correspondence:

Sir Alan Lascelles to Blanche, 1908–68

Frederick Lascelles to Blanche, 1890s–1928

Blanche's letters to her sister Helen, 1908–42

Blanche and GL's letters to Sir Percy Loraine, 1906–29

GL's letters to Lady Constance Milnes Gaskell, 1915–29

### SECONDARY SOURCES

C. Forbes Adam, *The Life of Lord Lloyd* (London, 1948)
Lady Bell (ed.), *The Letters of Gertrude Bell* (London, 1930)
Lord Birkenhead, *The Life of Lord Halifax* (London, 1965)
M. Bloch, *The Duke of Windsor's War* (London, 1982)
Elizabeth Burgoyne, *Gertrude Bell from her personal papers 1914–26* (London, 1961)
John Campbell, *F. E. Smith* (London, 1983)
J. Charmley, *Duff Cooper* (London, 1986)
J. Colville, *The Fringes of Power* (London, 1985)
M. Cowling, *The Impact of Hitler* (London, 1975)
J. Wentworth Day, *Lady Houston* (London, 1958)
D. Dilkes (ed.), *The Diaries of Sir Alexander Cadogan 1938–1945* (London, 1970)
Frances Donaldson, *The British Council* (London, 1984)
M. FitzHerbert, *The Man who was Grrenmantle* (London, 1983)
D. Garnett (ed.), *The Letters of T. E. Lawrence* (London, 1938)
M. Gilbert, *Winston S. Churchill*, vol. v (London, 1976)
M. Gilbert, *Winston S. Churchill*, vol. v, companion volume 2 (London, 1981)
M. Gilbert, *Winston S. Churchill*, vol. v, companion volume 3 (London, 1982)
M. Gilbert, *Winston S. Churchill*, vol. vi (London, 1983)
R. Graves and B. H. Liddell Hart, *T. E. Lawrence to his Biographers* (London, 1963)
R. Griffiths, *Fellow Travellers of the Right* (London, 1983)
Duff Hart-Davis (ed.), *End of an Era: diaries and letters of Sir Alan Lascelles* (London, 1986)
J. Harvey (ed.), *The Diplomatic Diaries of Oliver Harvey* (London, 1970)

K. Jeffrey (ed.), *The Military Correspondence of Field Marshal Sir Henry Wilson 1918–22* (London, 1985)

Elie Kedourie, *In the Anglo-Arab Labyrinth* (Cambridge, 1976)

R. Kumar (ed.), *Essays on Gandhian Politics* (Oxford, 1971)

A. W. Lawrence (ed.), *Letters to T. E. Lawrence* (London, 1961)

James Lees-Milne, *Another Self* (London, 1970)

Lord Lloyd, *Egypt since Cromer*, vol. I (London, 1933)

Lord Lloyd, *Egypt since Cromer*, vol. II (London, 1934)

Lord Lloyd, *The British Case* (London, 1939)

Lord Lloyd, *Leadership in Democracy* (Oxford, 1939)

Humphrey Lloyd, *The Quaker Lloyds in the Industrial Revolution* (London, 1975)

Samuel Lloyd, *The Lloyds of Birmingham* (Birmingham, 1908)

George Lloyd and Edward Wood, *The Great Opportunity* (London, 1919)

D. B. Lungu, 'The European crisis of March–April 1939: the Romanian Dimension', in *International History Review*, August 1985

J. E. Mack, *A Prince of our Disorder: the life of T. E. Lawrence* (London, 1976)

L. al Sayyid-Marsot, *Egypt's Liberal Experiment* (California, 1977)

B. Pimlott (ed.), *The Second World War Diaries of Hugh Dalton 1940–45* (London, 1986)

H. Rumbold, *Watershed in India* (London, 1979)

Desmond Stewart, *T. E. Lawrence* (London, 1977)

Sir Ronald Storrs, *Orientations* (London, 1943)

P. M. Taylor, *The Projection of Britain* (Cambridge, 1981)

S. D. Waley, *Edwin Montagu* (London, 1964)

D. C. Watt, 'Misinformation, Misconception, Mistrust', in M. Bentley and J. Stevenson (eds), *High and Low Politics in Modern Britain* (Oxford, 1983)

Lord Wavell, *Allenby in Egypt* (London, 1943)

K. Young, *The Diaries of Sir Robert Bruce Lockhart*, vol. 2 (London, 1980)

# INDEX